SAYRE P. SCHATZ

NIGERIAN CAPITALISM

UNIVERSITY OF CALIFORNIA PRESS

BERKELEY • LOS ANGELES • LONDON

University of California Press
Berkeley and Los Angeles, California
University of California Press, Ltd.
London, England
Copyright © 1977 by
The Regents of the University of California
ISBN 978-0-520-30297-6 (pbk. : alk. paper).
Library of Congress Catalog Card Number: 74-16718

NIGERIAN CAPITALISM

For Letta, Judy, and Ben

CONTENTS

PREFACE

Nigeria at this writing is one of Africa's most optimistic countries. Buoyed up by a great surge in oil revenues, it has high hopes of entering a new era of rapid economic development. The *Third National Development Plan 1975-80* calls for annual public investment (at constant prices) at almost nine times the rate achieved during the preceding plan period.

The strategy underlying the Plan is a familiar one in Nigeria. It is a continuation in an ebullient form of the basic economic development orientation that has shaped Nigerian development policy since 1949, an orientation we call nurture-capitalism. This is an approach in which private enterprise is expected to provide the development thrust in the directly productive sector of the economy, in which it is considered necessary for government to strengthen development by nurturing the capitalist sector generally, in which at the same time government nationalistically favors indigenous enterprise in particular, and in which continuing conflict between the general and the nationalistic nurturant elements inevitably results.

Though the foreign investors are the major source of dynamism in Nigeria's private sector, the role of indigenous private enterprise, already important, is sure to expand. Such an expansion will be brought about by the nationalistic element of nurture-capitalism with its programs to assist indigenous enterprise in particular, by the powerful antagonism toward dependence upon foreign corporations which partially underlies that nationalistic element, and by the increasing power and affluence of the Nigerian capitalist class buttressed by the new oil prosperity.

It is therefore important to analyze the experience of the indigenous private sector and of government measures to assist that sector. The major portion of this book undertakes that task. The study first examines the development of Nigerian nurture-capitalism from 1949 to the launching of and early experience with the Third Plan, 1975-80, with emphasis on the post-Civil War 1970s and on the impact of the new oil affluence (Part I). We then turn to an intensive study (in Part II) of indigenous business and (in Part III) of business-assistance measures in the period up to the Civil War. In the final Part, we discuss broader issues of African development strategy and propose some conclusions regarding pragmatic capitalism, pragmatic socialism, and thoroughgoing socialism and their relation to a partial orientation that we call pragmatic developmentism.

The book is intended not only for economists but also for others interested in Africa. I have attended carefully to the writing with this in mind. I cherish the hope also that policy-makers in Africa will find it clear and significant.

It is the product of long study. I first became seriously interested in Nigeria in 1958, devoted the 1959-60 academic year fully to the study of Nigerian economic development (in the United States) with the aid of a Ford Foundation grant, spent the four years 1961 to 1965 engaged in research in Nigeria at the Nigerian Institute of Social and Economic Research, returned again in 1968, worked in Nigeria for a year and a half in 1974-75 as an economic advisor to the Nigerian government, and worked more or less continually on the Nigerian economy in the intervening years. In all, the book represents about seventeen years of research and reflection.

My major research sources were government documents and papers, internal as well as published, other published materials and unpublished studies, extensive interviews with Nigerian businessmen in all sections of the country and observation of their business operations, a considerable number of interviews with foreign businessmen, unrestricted access during the years 1962-65 to all the files of the Federal Ministry of Commerce and Industries, and innumerable interviews with federal, regional, and state government officials, often accompanied by access to relevant materials.

I have also carried out a great deal of research on Nigeria that the book does not incorporate in any direct way: on the development of economic policy in Nigeria from World War II on; on planning and plan implementation beginning with the antecedents of the Colonial Development and Welfare Program of 1946; on the operation of the various investment-incentive measures such as the Pioneer Industries, Import Duties Relief, accelerated depreciation, and other programs; on the multifaceted assistance provided to several indigenous firms that were accorded special governmental attention; on a variety of programs to promote rural and handicraft industries; on a broad range of efforts to provide technical, commercial, bookkeeping, and other advice and assistance to indigenous firms in endeavors to improve their operating effectiveness; on systematic government efforts to promote and assist trade associations, joint ventures among Nigerians, and cooperatives; on programs to discuss and publicize profitable business opportunities; on the operations of foreign-run agencies providing investment capital and advice, such as the Investment Company of Nigeria, Northern Development (Nigeria) Limited, the Colonial Development Corporation, and the Commonwealth Development Finance Corporation; and on many other development programs and efforts. The resultant research materials, unincorporated here because the scope and length of this volume had to be limited in some way and moreover because these materials may be used in subsequent work, probably exceed in volume all those I have made direct use of. The unincorporated materials have, however, helped to provide the foundation for the judgments and appraisals embodied in the book.

A note about usage should be made here. Nigeria's monetary unit was the Nigerian pound until January 1, 1973, when the country adopted the naira, at the rate of two naira (₦2) to one pound. Following the convenient Nigerian practice, in any time series extending into both currency periods, one of the units (usually the naira) is used consistently for the entire series.

Since I have worked on the topic for so long, some of the ideas and materials have already been published. Chapters 4 and 12 are based upon my books, *Development Bank Lending in Nigeria: The Federal Loans Board* (Ibadan and London: Oxford University Press, 1964) and *Economics, Politics and Administration in Government Lending: The Regional Loans Boards of Nigeria* (Ibadan and London: Oxford University Press, 1970), and my article, "The Capital Shortage Illusion," *Oxford Economic Papers* 17:2 (July 1965): 309-316. Chapter 6, Chapter 11, and part of the section entitled "The Economic Problem" in Chapter 13 are largely drawn from my articles, "Development in an Adverse Economic Environment" in Sayre P. Schatz, ed., *South of the Sahara: Development in African Economies* (Philadelphia: Temple University Press, 1972), "Aiding Nigerian Business: the Yaba Industrial Estate," *Nigerian Journal of Economic and Social Studies* 6:4 (July 1964): 199-217, and "The High Cost of Aiding Business in Developing Economies: Nigeria's Loans Programmes," *Oxford Economic Papers* 20:3 (November 1968): 427-434 respectively. However, most of the material has never before appeared. Here all of the materials are integrated in a single coherent exposition.

A list of those who have assisted in various ways in this study would be virtually endless. Nigerian businessmen, businessmen of various other nationalities, officials of the various governments of Nigeria, representatives of foreign governments, and others who granted me interviews number literally in the hundreds. The helpfulness of most, despite busy schedules, was far greater than one could have expected, and my gratitude is great. In addition I have benefited from the comments, suggestions and criticisms of numerous academic colleagues: Ojetunji Aboyade, S. Adebisi Adu, Eme Awa, J. Lee Auspitz, Nicholas Balabkins, Ranjit S. Bhambri, William M.L. Bispham, Rudolph H. Blythe, Jr., Samuel Bowles, Charles V. Brown, John Dydo, S.I. Edokpayi, E.U.

Essien-Udom, Kalu Ezera, S.H. Frankel, Reginald H. Green, John R. Harris, Gerald K. Helleiner, W. Lynn Holmes, Joop Koopman, Jay R. Mandle, Robert Melson, Frederic Menz, Chandler Morse, E. Wayne Nafziger, J. Randolph Norsworthy, James O'Connell, Bernard Okun, Obasanmi Olakanpo, Dupe Olatunbosun, Ola Oni, Oladipo Onipede, H.M.A. Onitiri, Ehigie D. Osifo, Idrian Resnick, Ann Seidman, Richard L. Sklar, O. Sonubi, O. Teriba, Warren O. Williams, Janusz Zielinski. Some of these colleagues will undoubtedly feel that I have stubbornly adhered to questionable judgments, so I must take full responsibility for the views expressed.

I also want to acknowledge with appreciation two one-year research fellowships from the Ford Foundation, a Summer Research Award from Temple University, and an African Research Grant from the Social Science Research Council. The Nigerian Institute of Social and Economic Research, whose director is H.M.A. Onitiri, was an invaluable home base in Nigeria and a major source of assistance and stimulation for four years.

PART I

Development Orientations in Nigeria

Chapter 1

EARLY NURTURE-CAPITALISM:

1949-1966

The Nigerian economy has entered the final quarter of the twentieth century ebulliently. The buoyancy sprang directly from an enormous increase in the rate of oil revenues that occurred over a seven-month period beginning in November 1973, an increase that climaxed something of an oil boom over the preceding four years.

The country has abundant economic promise. It is a large nation with a variety of natural resources and climatic conditions: it stretches from the tropical rain forest in the south to the edge of the Sahara in the north. It has had an assortment of major exports; palm products, cocoa, peanuts, cotton, rubber, and tin were prominent for many years, although they have diminished sharply in importance. Since the first petroleum exports in the 1950s, oil has become steadily more important, eclipsing all other exports. The people are vigorous, industrious, economically responsive. The population has a superabundance of the entrepreneurial attributes: willingness to work hard for economic gain, to take risks, to persevere and persist, to undertake new occupations and new ways of doing things.

However, despite great optimism at the end of Nigeria's Civil War[1] the performance of the economy had been disappointing,[2] and so the 1974 surge in oil revenues provided a vital stimulus. Even before the great leap, the average price[3] that Nigeria received for her oil had been increasing at

---

[1]The Civil War began in May 1967, after a period of rapid disintegration starting in 1966, and ended in January 1970.

[2]Discussed in Chapter 2.

[3]Oil prices are multifaceted and variable, and the concept of an average price is an elusive one, so figures for average price can only be approximate.

Average price involves, among other things, averaging (a) the amount per barrel (including production costs, taxes and royalties) paid by the oil companies on their *own* share of their production and (b) the (higher) price at which the Government of Nigeria sells *its* share of oil-company production, mainly to the oil companies. This share has been, for the most part, 55 percent since April 1974 when the Nigerian Government acquired 55 percent equity, although production-sharing contracts varying from 65 percent to 70 percent were signed with some of the newer oil companies. Federal Republic of Nigeria, *Third National Development Plan 1975-80* (hereinafter referred to as *Third Plan*), Vol. 1 (Lagos: Federal Ministry of Economic Development, 1975), pp. 42, 13. Page numbers in the "Special Launching Edition" of the *Plan*, referred to here, all are two higher in the subsequent edition, e.g., page 15 becomes 17, etc.

TABLE 1

Nigerian Government Net Oil Revenues (Monthly)

($100 million)	
September 1973	1.6
October 1973	2.2
November 1973	3.2
December 1973	3.3
January 1973	5.7
May 1974 (peak)	7.7

SOURCE: *Petroleum Intelligence Weekly*, New York, various issues.

a not-insubstantial rate. It was $2.46 per barrel during 1971, $2.70 per barrel during 1972 (this increase being primarily attributable to devaluation of the dollar), and had reached $3.00 per barrel in October 1973. Then came the dramatic increases. The average price rose to $5.60 per barrel in November 1973, $9.80 in January 1974, and in April 1974 it reached a more-than-year-long plateau at $11.20.[4] Thus price nearly quadrupled (to 373 percent) in six months.

Oil production rose at the same time, reaching 2 million barrels per day in 1973 and 2.34 million in mid-1974. Government revenues increased most dramatically, as shown in Table 1. Net oil revenues earned by the Nigerian Government[5] almost quintupled (to 481 percent) in a nine-month period. These revenues increased not only because of the rise in prices but also because of the growth of production and an enlargement of the Nigerian Government ownership share of the oil production companies from roughly 35 percent to 55 percent.

The new oil wealth was responsible for an exuberant application of an economic development orientation which, not surprisingly, was a continuation of the approach Nigeria had followed in the past.[6] This orientation (i.e., basic outlook on and way of addressing the job of development) we call nurture-capitalism.

[4]The posted price, essentially a fiction used as a device for arriving at taxes and royalties, went from $4.13 per barrel in October 1973 to $8.40 in November 1973 and to $14.69 on January 1, 1974, at which level it remained throughout 1974 and into 1975. (It was reduced to $12.05 in March 1975.)

The source of the oil data is *Petroleum Intelligence Weekly* (New York), various issues.

[5]Shown here are what may be called oil revenues earned, i.e., production for the month times net revenue per barrel (after production costs) earned by the Nigerian Government that month. The revenues are not actually received until approximately two months later on the average.

[6]Production declined severely after October 1974, falling from the mid-1974 peak of 2.3 million barrels per day to 1.6 million barrels per day in April 1975. Oil revenues also declined from the May 1974 peak of $770 million to approximately $400 million in May 1975. However, these decreases were viewed as temporary and did not impair the new oil-based optimism upon which the development orientation embodied in the 1975-80 plan was based.

Economic Development Orientation

Nurture-Capitalism

Nurture-capitalism is a development orientation characteristic of Nigeria and of many other developing countries in Africa and elsewhere. It comprises four major policy elements. The first is capitalism. Economic activity in the directly productive sector of the economy is primarily the function of private enterprise while government provides a framework of law and policy. Although there may be some public investment in directly productive enterprises, governmental investment is concentrated mainly on the infrastructure, the foundation on which directly productive activities are based. Universal and nationalistic nurturant approaches constitute the second and third elements of policy. It is felt that, to transform the technologically simple, subsistence-oriented colonial economy into a modern economy, the government must make strenuous efforts to promote private enterprise. Government attempts this through the creation of a congenial economic climate and through a constellation of programs and policies designed to assist and nurture private business universally, whether foreign or indigenously owned.

However, given the relative capabilities, resources, and circumstances of foreign-owned and local businesses, development on this basis is thoroughly dominated by foreign firms. In the intensely nationalistic atmosphere characteristic of the decolonization and post-colonial periods, such dependence upon international investors is anathema. Thus there emerges the third policy strand, a nationalistic nurturant element—a set of policies and programs intended to promote indigenous business enterprise in particular.

The universal and the nationalistic nurturant elements inevitably conflict. Indigenous business is promoted by business-assistance programs designed exclusively or primarily for nationals. It is also promoted by indigenization, that is, government measures that encroach directly upon spheres and prerogatives that had been open to foreign business. These are measures that exclude foreign-owned companies from certain fields of economic activity, that evict them from others in which they were already engaged, or that require transfer of partial or full ownership to indigenous interests in still other fields. These means of favoring local business, particularly indigenization policies, clearly disfavor foreign firms. Consequently there is an inherent ingredient of conflict between universal and nationalistic nurturing. This conflict, with its varied and changing manifestations, constitutes the fourth element of nurture-capitalism.

Despite the conflict, accommodation occurs on most issues. The foreign firms accept the inevitable. They accede to the principle of differential advantages for indigenous business and also to the much more intrusive principle of indigenization. So long as the foreign companies feel moderately secure about the rights and spheres of activity that do obtain for them, they continue to operate and even to thrive. On its side, government tends to cooperate by providing a certain degree of assurance and stability regarding foreign business prerogatives, considering this necessary for national economic development. In this, government is encouraged by important members of the indigenous business community who stand to gain by association with the foreign firms, particularly in the climate of nationalism. The accommodation is nevertheless accompanied by a persisting, ever-shifting zone of tension and uncertainty. The disquiet is engendered primarily by a continuing extension of the scope of indigenization. The zone of tension centers on the changing boundaries between the indigenous and foreign business spheres, as rights, limits, stipulations, and rules of the game are altered. Uneasiness and strain also arise where rights and game rules are unclear.

Development of Nigerian
Nurture-Capitalism: 1949-1966

In order better to understand Nigeria's nurture-capitalism orientation and to appraise its economic prospects in the final quarter-century, we turn back in the rest of this chapter and in the succeeding one to the development and modulation of that approach. The particular character of nurture-capitalism has changed in different phases of Nigerian development depending on the relative strengths of nationalism and universality in business nurturance, the level of government investment in directly productive activities, the degree of emphasis on welfare, and other factors. The changes in Nigerian nurture-capitalism cannot be simply characterized, for stated and actual orientations usually differed. Moreover, the divergences between ostensible and actual approaches have tended to widen and can be expected to persist.

The economic orientation of the British colonial government in Nigeria changed in 1949. In the early post-World War II years, the orientation had been one of improving but nevertheless essentially maintaining the existing colonial economy; this continued the prewar approach except that there was heightened emphasis on raising efficiency and increasing output. The new approach after 1949 involved the dual goals of promoting some measure of modern development of the economy and increasing the degree of Nigerian participation in the modern sectors, both to be sought largely by government nurture of private enterprise. The newly announced aims of the Department of Commerce and Industry were "to develop secondary industries on the widest possible scale by methods that will ensure the maximum participation by Nigerians themselves in industrial enterprise" and "to provide all possible opportunities for Nigerian businessmen to take an increasing share in the trade of the country. . . . The emphasis throughout is to develop industry and trade in such a way that Nigerians themselves will play an increasingly important part in the commercial life of the country. That is the main objective, and it is the general wish that it should be pursued with vigour and with the utmost possible speed."[7]

The major elements of Nigeria's economic development orientation—reliance on private enterprise, intention to nurture private business, nationalism—are limned in the foregoing statements. The strength, even the fierceness, of the nationalistic desire for enhanced Nigerian ownership and control of private enterprise of all kinds and sizes required attention to Nigerianization of business, but there was considerable emphasis in this period, some formal and some informal, on generating the desired development through Commonwealth and especially British investment and enterprise, and also on producing goods that would alleviate Sterling Area balance-of-payments problems. Thus we can call the orientation colonial nurture-capitalism. This approach was moderated by a Labour Government-initiated welfare-economy leaning. We can therefore characterize the economic course of the early 1950s as *colonialist nurture-capitalism with a welfare tendency.*

As Nigerians took over increasing power in the mid-1950s,[8] this economic orientation was modified in two important respects. First, intensifying nationalism sharply heightened the emphasis on Nigerian participation, Nigerian benefits, and Nigerian control in the development of the modern economy.

Second, as the Nigerians, who were assuming control of the country, soberly recognized that indigenous business was not yet able to provide the initiative, leadership, or managerial and technological expertise needed to generate substantial modern-sector economic development, government assumed an increasingly active role in the directly productive sector of the economy. In the mid-1950s, public corporations undertook a growing number of directly productive enterprises that were intended to be run as profitable ventures. This was seen as a way of promoting national (as opposed to foreign-dominated) development of the large-scale modern activities which few if any indigenous businessmen were capable of undertaking. To some degree, this turn to public enterprise also reflected a socialist ideology almost universally espoused by those in authority though usually rejected in fact—as for example when Premier

[7]Nigeria, Federation, *Annual Report of the Commerce and Industries Department, 1949-50* (Kaduna: Government Printer, 1951), pp. 4-5. E. O. Akeredolu-Ale (incorrectly, in my view) places the initiation of "serious" efforts to promote domestic industrialization in 1957: "Values, Motivations and History in the Development of Private Indigenous Entrepreneurship: Lessons from Nigeria's Experience, 1946-1966," *Nigerian Journal of Economic and Social Studies* XIII:2 (July 1971): 210.

[8]Increasing degrees of self-government were embodied in successive constitutions in 1951, 1954, and 1957; by the latter year, Nigerian control over the government apparatus was substantial. Formal independence was achieved on October 1, 1960.

Okpara of the Eastern Region explained that his party's "Pragmatic Socialism" was a system in which everyone had the right to start his own business.[9] However, the public corporations were close counterparts of private enterprise, intended to operate according to the same criteria and to promote economic development in the same way as private firms.

With these modifications in the mid-1950s, the country moved to a chosen economic development orientation of *nationalist nurture-capitalism with state-capitalist and welfare tendencies.*[10]

A divergence between the stated and actual development orientations soon emerged, however, and grew wider. Disillusionment with the indigenous capitalists, mentioned above, was followed by disappointment with the poor performance of the public corporations engaged in directly productive activities. For reasons having to do with political abuse of the corporations, their rather narrow profitability orientation, and Nigeria's limited managerial capacity, virtually none of the undertakings were profitable and few could be called successful by any economic standard.[11] The consequence was a somewhat reluctant, unacknowledged shift in the actual economic orientation: the country placed increasing reliance upon foreign-owned enterprises for the development of the modern economy. While the foreign firms were constrained to a limited degree by government pressures to Nigerianize middle- and upper-level staffs, to make minority holdings available at attractive prices to government or potential Nigerian stockholders, and by other government measures, this shift to reliance on foreign investment in the modern sector amounted to a de facto change from nationalist to internationalist or economically dependent nurture-capitalism.[12]

This shift evoked a mixed reaction. Many among the political class and its allies and retainers who made lucrative arrangements for themselves[13] and many workers who were fortunate enough to get prized jobs with

[9]"On the ideological plane, everyone was fashionably one kind of socialist or another; but in practice everybody accepted the ethical basis of capitalism." Ojetunji Aboyade, "The Economy of Nigeria," in Peter Robson and D.A. Lury (eds.), *The Economy of Africa* (Evanston: Northwestern University Press, 1969), pp. 191-192.

[10]C.R. Frank, Jr., describes Nigeria's pattern of industrialization as one involving "emphasis on private enterprise combined with the use of national development corporations and other quasi-governmental bodies," and also as one in which "private enterprise is encouraged but the role of national development corporations is conspicuous." Charles R. Frank, Jr., "Public and Private Enterprise in Africa," in Gustav Ranis (ed.), *Government and Economic Development* (New Haven: Yale University Press, 1971), pp. 96, 90.

[11]The economic performance of the public development bodies will be discussed in the final chapter.

[12]Economic dependence may be defined as the absence of "national control over or at least co-determination of basic decisions affecting national levels and patterns of output, consumption, investment and international trade . . .": Reginald H. Green, "The Role of the State as an Agent of Economic and Social Development in the Least Developed Countries," *Journal of Development Planning* 6 (1974): 6.

[13]"In fact, the political and economic power structure was such that a handful of Nigerian middle class in collusion with powerful foreign interests increasingly gained control of the government apparatus largely for the promotion of their joint interests." Aboyade, p. 191.

TABLE 2
Economic Development Orientations in Nigeria after World War II

Period	Stated Orientation	Actual Orientation
to 1949	Maintenance of the existing colonial economy, with heightened emphasis on increasing efficiency and output	
1949 to mid-1950s	Colonialist nurture-capitalism with a welfare tendency	
mid-1950s to Civil War	Nationalist nurture-capitalist with state-capitalist and welfare tendencies	Dependent (or internationalist) nurture-capitalism
1970-74	Guided internationalist nurture-capitalism with a welfare tendency	Dependent (or internationalist) nurture-capitalism
1975—	Nationalist nurture-capitalism with state-capitalist, welfare and accelerated-development tendencies	Nurture-capitalism[a]

[a]Expected by the author.

foreign companies were content. The prevalent feeling, however, was one of frustration and resentment at dependence upon foreign investors.

The gap between the stated economic orientation, which remained essentially the same, and the actual approach continued to widen in the late 1950s and the 1960s. There were de facto retreats on two further aspects of the declared orientation. The loss of confidence in public enterprises widened and deepened. The capital sunk into the public development corporations was largely lost or frozen, and financial stringency set in. As a result, reliance on government to implement new development in the directly productive sectors of the economy went on receding, though existing public enterprises continued to function. This diminution of the governmental role as directly productive investor amounted to relinquishment of the mixed-economy facet of the development orientation.[14]

The welfare-economy aspect of the orientation was also retrenched. In the increasing competition for the ever-scarcer capital resources, the

[14]"To the extent that one can talk at all of a definite development strategy in Nigeria for the decade before Independence, it can be characterized as diffused and weak public intervention." The period was one of "increasing reliance on private enterprise and private initiative without a clear and coherent leadership from the public sector." Aboyade, pp. 151, 191. Aboyade also states that the public sector had the resources and opportunity to play a much more decisive role, but failed to do so for various reasons, not the least of which was the fact that "there was no coherent underlying philosophy to guide the pace and character of development through public intervention." Aboyade, p. 191.

welfare-economy leaning was inexorably relegated to a lower order of priority and largely neglected, although measures that enhanced the welfare of those with political power or influence continued.

After the mid-1950s, then, the nationally based approach to development gave way to dependence on international enterprise for modern-sector development[15] (indigenous enterprise was still favored for all activities it was believed capable of carrying out); the reliance on publicly owned, directly productive enterprises for further development decreased sharply, so that the mixed-economy orientation withered away; and the welfare leaning was largely dropped. Thus, the actual development orientation from the late 1950s to the Civil War can simply be called internationalist or dependent nurture-capitalism. The changing orientations are recapitulated in Table 2, which also anticipates Chapter 2. It can be seen that actual economic development orientations have varied little since the mid-1950s or even from 1949. Variability occurred primarily in the more insubstantial intended orientations.

Performance

Appraisals of Nigeria's pre-Civil War economic performance under the nurture-capitalism orientation differ.

On the one hand, most economists working in Nigeria during the period, Nigerian and foreign, disapproved. The general opinion was that the economy was functioning badly. Economists in close touch with the day-to-day realities of Nigeria (who were often disdainful of what they regarded as rather fanciful official statistics)[16] were critical of the nature of economic policy,[17] of increasing unemployment, of income maldistribution;[18] they were dubious about the growth of the economy,[19] and about overall economic performance.[20]

[15]According to Wallerstein: "No doubt the most significant difference of economic policy between 'revolutionary' and 'moderate' states [in Africa] has been in terms of the indigenous commercial bourgeoisie." Immanuel Wallerstein, "Left and Right in Africa," *Journal of Modern African Studies* 9:1 (May 1971), p. 9.

[16]"We should not delude ourselves by using questionable statistics and reporting substantial progress in the national economy when little has in fact changed." F.L. Osunsade, "When Is Progress Not Progress," *Nigerian Opinion* 1:5 (May 1965): 7.

[17]"Developmental policies have only been superficially relevant to the real problems of the people . . . ." Ojetunji Aboyade, "The Relations Between Central and Local Institutions in the Development Process," *Nigerian Opinion* IV:2, 3 (February and March 1968): 294. Aboyade also wrote of economic policies which were neither "coherent" nor "positive" nor "consistent" and which helped create the strains that led to the 1966 coup and the Civil War. Aboyade, "Economy," pp. 191-192.

[18]Pius Okigbo (Economic Adviser to the Federal Government) spoke of the growing "immiseration of the poor" in Nigeria, "Presidential Address," *Nigerian Journal of Economic and Social Studies* VII:1 (March 1965): 8.

[19]"Successive Progress Reports and Comments on the country's national plan have indicated that performance has significantly fallen short of expectation . . . ." "Progressing the Present Plan," *Nigerian Opinion* II:2 (February 1966): 23 (unsigned).

[20]A foreign economic observer wrote a sympathetically received article that began:

On the other hand, some appraisals of the Nigerian economy in the period up to the Civil War were commendatory. In its review of the period, the Second National Plan characterized pre-Civil War economic achievement as more than satisfactory despite some spottiness and deficiencies. The growth rate was considered good: "the achieved rate of growth of gross domestic product was generally better than anticipated" (p. 44). The advance in manufacturing was deemed laudable: "Progress in the manufacturing sector (including crafts) of the economy has been remarkable over the last ten years [1958-67]" (p. 137). Although government investment (and consumption) fell short of what was planned, the performance of the private sector was considered impressive, with private gross capital formation growing at the rate of 14.4 percent per annum from 1962-63 to 1965-66. There was also, according to the Second Plan, salutary structural change. On the eve of the Civil War, the economy was "already showing signs of structural changes associated with the early stages of a growing and dynamic economy . . . the prime movers for generating general development were already shifting to a combination of intensive industrial activities, expansion of food production for domestic consumption and a gradually streamlined set of public policies" (p. 17; also see p. 137). Investment in plant, machinery, and equipment, considered "a very crucial element" in investment, grew from 27 percent of private sector gross capital formation in 1962-63 to 34.6 percent in 1965-66 (p. 276). Some problems were recognized. The growth of GDP was slowing down by 1965. "By the middle of the 1960s, the national economy seemed to have lost some of the impetus for its impressive growth in the preceding decade" (p. 20). Indigenous private participation in modern-sector investment was extremely low (pp. 143-144). Unemployment was high (p. 64). Balance-of-payments reserves had been depleted (p. 69). And despite some improvement the nation had a "defective economic structure" (p. 37). Nevertheless, the official appraisal was favorable, a view shared by some capable independent economists as well.[21]

A favorable appraisal is implicit in the official statistics. Table 3 shows official estimates of gross domestic product at current and at constant (1962-63) prices. The average annual rate of increase from 1958-59 to 1965-66[22] was 7.6 percent in current prices and 6.1 in constant prices. This

---

"Nigeria, sometime showplace of Western Welfare Capitalism . . . is a sick country with a sick economy." Reginald H. Green, "Economic Policy of the Political Class," *Nigerian Opinion* 1:12 (December 1965): 6.

[21] The most prominent is W. Arthur Lewis, *Reflections on Nigeria's Economic Growth* (Paris: Office for Economic Cooperation and Development, 1967).

[22] In appraising the nurture-capitalism orientation up to the Civil War, we use 1965-66 as the terminal year; it would be unduly prejudicial to include 1966-67, for economic achievement in that year was substantially impeded by the intensifying series of disturbances that led up to the Civil War.

TABLE 3

Gross Domestic Product
Nigeria, 1958-59 to 1965-66

Years	GDP at current factor cost			GDP at constant (1962-63) factor cost		
	N£ million	Index (1962-63=100)	Annual percentage increase	N£ million	Index (1962-63=100)	Annual percentage increase
1958-59	924.3	70.3	—	1023.9	77.8	—
1959-60	982.2	74.7	6.3	1102.7	83.8	7.7
1960-61	1122.3	85.3	14.3	1250.2	95.0	13.4
1961-62	1186.7	90.2	5.7	1256.0	95.5	0.5
1962-63	1315.4	100.0	10.8	1315.4	100.0	4.7
1963-64	1403.2	106.7	6.7	1425.7	108.4	8.4
1964-65	1457.0	110.8	3.8	1463.4	111.3	2.6
1965-66	1540.3	117.1	5.7	1543.0	117.3	5.4

SOURCES: *Gross Domestic Product of Nigeria 1958/59 - 1966/67* (Lagos: Federal Office of Statistics, August 1968).

Annual Abstract of Statistics, Nigeria, 1969 (Lagos: Federal Office of Statistics, 1970).

Economic Indicators, September 1974, Vol. 10, No. 9 (Lagos: Federal Office of Statistics, 1974).

NOTE: Different official sources present slightly different figures. The basic source used here is the one cited first.

is a substantial rate of growth. It exceeds considerably the growth rates calculated by Hagen and Hawrylyshyn for less developed economies as a whole, which show growth for all less developed economies of 4.4 percent per annum from 1955 to 1960 and 4.7 percent from 1960 to 1965, an average growth rate of 4.55 percent per annum for the decade. [23]

The critical views of Nigerian economic performance discussed in the opening paragraph of this section and the sanguine appraisal in the Second Plan and implicit in the official statistics are in sharp contrast. We therefore attempt as careful and objective an assessment as possible of the country's economic growth by subjecting official figures for GDP to critical examination and by making certain adjustments.[24] Other criteria for appraising economic performance, such as income distribution and employment and unemployment, are neglected here. It should be explicitly mentioned, however, that Nigeria's record with respect to these criteria is generally considered inferior to its record of GDP growth.[25] A broader appraisal would thus result in lower marks for the Nigerian economy than the growth-centered appraisal presented here.

The reader should realize, in any case, that no matter how carefully and judiciously one works with a statistics, definitive statements about economic growth are impossible. The underlying data are simply too unreliable. National product statistics are generally poor, especially for less developed economies,[26] but Nigeria's have been particularly weak.

[23]Everett E. Hagen and Oli Hawrylyshyn, "Analysis of World Income and Growth, 1955-65," *Economic Development and Cultural Change* 18:1, part 2 (October 1969): 47. These authors estimated Nigeria's GDP growth rate, including petroleum, at 3.0 percent for 1955-60 and 5.1 percent for 1960-65, or 4.05 percent for the decade (p. 52). This falls short of our estimate with petroleum excluded. These figures show Nigeria's economic performance during the decade before the Civil War as less satisfactory than our figures indicate, but Hagen and Hawrylyshyn's estimates cannot be accepted as accurate. For example, there is general agreement that Nigeria's growth slowed down in the first half of the 1960s, and the official GDP estimates and all other estimates with which this writer is familiar show this, but Hagen and Hawrylyshyn estimated a substantial acceleration from 3.0 percent in 1955-60 to 5.1 percent in 1960-65.

[24]Of course, we must recognize that "while in some circumstances the actual rate of growth of GNP may be an important indicator of economic performance, it is not necessarily so." Andrew Kamarck, "Appraisal of Country Economic Performance," in Sayre P. Schatz (ed.), *South of the Sahara: Development in African Economies* (Philadelphia: Temple University Press, 1972), p. 267.

[25]See, e.g., Edwin R. Dean, *Plan Implementation in Nigeria, 1962-66* (Ibadan: Oxford University Press, 1972), p. 213: "A major disappointment in the economy's performance concerns the high level and probable growth in urban unemployment."

[26]Despite a large-scale, well-financed, decade-long effort to collect comparable statistical materials from a group of developing economies (centering on in-country studies of a year or more in duration in which "bugs" in official estimates were to be worked out), the Director of the Economic Growth Center of Yale University felt unable to compare various macroeconomic ratios because "GNP measures in the LDC's are quite unreliable. The 'noise' from this source might obscure any actual existing relationship." Lloyd J. Reynolds, "Public Sector Saving and Capital Formation," in Ranis (ed.), *Government and Economic Development*, p. 551. See also P. T. Bauer and B. S. Yamey, *The Economics of Underdeveloped Countries* (Chicago: University of Chicago Press, Cambridge Economic Handbooks, 1957), pp. 21-22.

Helleiner correctly wrote in 1966: "The estimates for Nigeria are surely at the low end of the international reliability spectrum."[27] There have been improvements since the mid-1960s, and subsequent national product estimates have been carried out more carefully but they still have been based upon weak underlying data.[28]

The first adjustment concerns petroleum. The increase in oil production in the pre-Civil War period tells us nothing about the effectiveness of Nigerian development policy or of the economy of the 1960s. From that point of view, the petroleum boom was a fortuitous windfall. As Dean points out, "oil production statistics reflect only very indirectly the performance of the Nigerian economy: oil was produced by foreign companies, which relied mainly on imported capital equipment, materials and technicians; and the plan, and general economic policies, did not influence oil production strongly."[29] Thus our first adjustment is to subtract oil production from GDP.[30] This is a minor adjustment in any case, for oil extraction constituted less than 4 percent of GDP in 1965-66.

There is a supplementary reason for this subtraction. An exceptionally high proportion of the proceeds from oil exports in this period accrued not to Nigerians or the Nigerian economy, but to foreigners. Thus, a large part of the value of the petroleum output entered into gross *domestic* product but not gross *national* product, i.e., it did not constitute income of or value produced by the Nigerian national economy.[31]

[27]Helleiner continues: "Close to half of the gross domestic product during the 1950s was made up of domestic food production about which very nearly nothing is known. Indeed the procedures necessarily employed to obtain estimates for this major component are so bizarre that it is worth recounting them in greater detail . . . one can have practically no confidence in the final absolute figures or annual changes therein . . . Estimates for several other less important sectors are, unfortunately, obtained equally impressionistically. Some of these estimates may be even worse . . . When one is told that some of the post-1957 Nigerian national income data are even rougher . . . one feels a sense of horror as to what *now* underlies the aggregates . . . One must conclude that the Nigerian national accounts are not very useful for gauging the level of aggregate economic activity or estimating growth rates thereof." Gerald K. Helleiner, *Peasant Agriculture, Government and Economic Growth in Nigeria* (Homewood, Illinois: Richard D. Irwin, 1966), pp. 392-394.

[28]See, e.g., Dean, *Plan Implementation.* After carefully appraising the work on the national accounts for the years 1958-59 to 1966-67, Dean states: "the study which led to the published estimates of GDP, though carefully carried out, necessarily relied on extremely weak statistics" (p. 204). His own observations on the relationship between GDP and capital formation also "should be regarded as guesses, in view of the weaknesses in the statistics on domestic product and capital formation, in the nineteen-fifties as well as the nineteen-sixties" (p. 217).

[29]Dean, p. 204.

[30]With oil production subtracted, the GDP figures nevertheless still reflect the stimulation the oil industry provided to the rest of the economy. For example, investment in petroleum exploration increased rapidly during the 1960s and accounted for more than half of foreign investment in Nigeria. Kathleen Langley, "Financing Development in Nigeria: An Appraisal," in Schatz (ed.), *South of the Sahara,* p. 229.

[31]GDP differs from GNP by including the income of (and thus the value-added attributed to) foreign manpower and other foreign and foreign-owned inputs in the domestic production

TABLE 4

Gross Domestic Product Excluding Production of Oil
(at current factor cost)
Nigeria, 1958-59 to 1967-68

	GDP without oil		
Year	N£ million	Annual percen- tage growth	Oil extraction (N£ million)
1958-59	923.7	—	0.6
1959-60	981.3	6.2	0.9
1960-61	1118.8	14.0	3.5
1961-62	1176.1	5.1	10.6
1962-63	1299.6	10.5	15.8
1963-64	1386.7	6.7	16.5
1964-65	1429.4	3.1	27.6
1965-66	1480.8	3.6	59.5

SOURCE: *Annual Abstract of Statistics, Nigeria, 1969.*

Table 4 presents GDP with oil production excluded. GDP without oil shows an average growth rate of 7.0 percent per annum. However, this is at current prices, which leads to the other adjustment—for the increase in the price level—that we must make in official GDP statistics.

Three alternative price-level indexes are shown in Table 5. The official deflator or price index was implicit in the conversion of current-price GDP to constant-price GDP in Table 3, and was calculated by dividing the former by the latter. It is widely accepted that this understates the price-level increase. As Dean said in assessing official GDP statistics: "There is special reason to doubt the reliability of the deflation process in view of the variety of the methods used, and in view of the fact that the deflator increased more slowly, between 1961-62 and 1965-66, than either . . . [Dean's own] 'National consumer price index' or the import price index." The official deflator increased 6 percent between 1961-62 and 1965-66, while Dean's national consumer price index increased 10 percent from calendar year 1961 to fiscal 1965-66, and the import price index increased 12 percent between calendar years 1961 and 1965.[32] An element of surprise and skepticism even creeps into some official discus-

process. The oil export figures in GDP, incidentally, are based on the oil companies' announced export prices, which bear little relationship to the actual market prices. Kathleen Langley, "The External Resource Factor in Nigerian Economic Development," *Nigerian Journal of Economic and Social Studies* X:2 (July 1968): 159-162.

[32] Dean, pp. 204, 225.

TABLE 5

Price Level Indices

1958-59 to 1968-69

Year	Official deflator	Dean consumer price index	Official consumer price index
1958-59	90.2	96	96.0
1959-60	89.1	100	99.6
1960-61	89.7	102	101.3
1961-62	94.4	108	107.8
1962-63	100.0	118	111.8
1963-64	98.4	112	108.7
1964-65	99.5	114	111.0
1965-66	99.8	117	116.0
1966-67	101.3	130	128.8
1967-68	106.9	118	119.8
1968-69	*	121	121.8

SOURCES: Official deflator calculated on basis of data in Nigeria, Federation, *Gross Domestic Product of Nigeria: 1958/59-1966/67* (Lagos: Federal Office of Statistics, 1968). See note below.

The Dean Consumer Price Index is based upon consumer price indexes "for the lower income group in Nigeria" calculated by the Federal Office of Statistics and published in several places, including the *Digest of Statistics, Economic Indicators* and the Central Bank's *Annual Report and Statement of Accounts.* For the years 1961-62 to 1966-67 Dean used the indexes for four major cities—Lagos, Ibadan, Enugu and Kaduna—and assigned them weights of 0.06, 0.25, 0.29, and 0.40, respectively (Edwin R. Dean, *Plan Implementation in Nigeria, 1962-66* [Ibadan: Oxford University Press, 1972], pp. 80-81, 225). This writer calculated the index numbers for 1958-59 to 1960-61 following Dean's procedures, i.e., using Federal Office of Statistics data for the same four cities and using the same weights. Data were not available for the first quarter of 1961 although they were available for the year 1961 as a whole. The index number for 1960-61 was therefore estimated by adding one fourth of the increment between 1960 and 1961 to the index number for 1960.

The official consumer price index is calculated from the monthly "All-Cities Consumer Price Index for the lower income groups in Nigeria" for nine cities (Lagos, Ibadan, Kaduna, Zaria, Ilorin, Benin, Kano, Sapele, Warri): Central Bank of Nigeria, *Economic and Financial Review* 8:1 (June 1970): 18-27. Index numbers from 1958-59 and 1959-60 were calculated by the author in precisely the same way they were calculated for the Dean consumer price for those two years. (See note just above on the sources.)

*The official deflator for 1968-69—and somewhat different sets of figures for GDP and the official deflator—can be calculated from various sources, such as *Economic Indicators,* published monthly by the Federal Office of Statistics and Central Bank of Nigeria, *Annual Report and Statement of Accounts,* various years. However, there are various mistakes, adjustments and other unaccountable discrepancies. Such problems are common; Dean confirmed this in a careful study of selected official Nigerian publications. Dean, pp. 268-269. Thus, *Economic Indicators,* September 1974; yields virtually the same figure for the official deflator for 1967-68 as that used here (107.0 rather than 106.9) but previous years differ by varying, generally small, amounts.

sions of the price level. "Surprisingly, the price level appeared to have fallen by about 1.7 percent in 1963-64"; "The analysis of price level changes in Nigerian national accounts is compounded by a number of problems. . . . the basic data themselves are not too strong on reliability and consistency."[33]

Edwin Dean dealt with the inadequacy of the official deflator by constructing a national consumer price index (Table 5, column 3). It is presented for informational and comparative purposes only and we will make no further use of it, for it is necessary to consider the Dean index superseded by a later and more broadly based consumer price index calculated by the Federal Office of Statistics. This is the official "All Cities Consumer Price Index for the lower income group in Nigeria," which we will call the Official Consumer Price Index (Table 5, column 4). This index was first calculated in 1970, perhaps in implicit recognition of the criticisms of the official deflator.

We consider the Official Consumer Price Index the best available one for making price-level adjustments, but it is an imperfect instrument for this purpose and probably understates the rise in the price level. In the light of the frequent public complaints about rising food prices during the first half of the 1960s, one is particularly skeptical about the index of food prices (which is by far the largest component in the overall Official Consumer Price Index, with a weight of 45.5 percent). For the entire 1960-68 period covered by the Official Consumer Price Index study, foods showed "a relatively low rate of price increase" of 1.8 percent per annum.[34] The food price index declined in 1963 and again in 1964 and was still considerably below the 1962 level in 1965 (118.0 down to 110.5). Dean also expressed skepticism about official data on consumer prices. Commenting specifically on the recorded fall in consumer prices from 1966-67 to 1967-68 and 1968-69, he stated flatly that prices "did not fall as much as the 'National Index' [i.e., the Dean index] indicates."[35] The Dean index, incidentally, shows a slightly higher rate of price increase than the Official Consumer Price Index. As an indicator of the national price level the Official Consumer Price Index is too narrow: it slights the great bulk of the population, which is rural, for it is based on urban workers; and it ignores prices other than consumer prices. Finally, the underlying surveys in the various cities were inadequately financed and staffed. Thus, there are legitimate reasons for dubiety about the Official Consumer Price Index, but we must use it nevertheless, for there is nothing better.

[33]Two other, more technical, problems are then mentioned. Federal Republic of Nigeria, *Second National Development Plan 1970-74* (hereinafter referred to as *Second Plan*) (Lagos: Federal Ministry of Information, 1970), pp. 44, 45.
[34]Central Bank of Nigeria, *Economic and Financial Review* 8:1 (June 1970): 19.
[35]Dean, p. 81.

Table 6
Gross Domestic Product at Constant Prices

Years	GDP excluding oil extraction, at constant prices (official deflator: 1962-63=100)		GDP excluding oil extraction, at constant prices (official consumer price index: 1960=100)		GDP including oil extraction, at constant prices (official consumer price index: 1960=100)	
	N £ 000,000	Annual percentage increase	N £ 000,000	Annual percentage increase	N £ 000,000	Annual percentage increase
1958-59	1024.1	—	962.2	—	962.8	—
1959-60	1101.3	7.5	985.2	2.4	986.1	2.4
1960-61	1247.3	13.3	1104.4	12.1	1107.9	12.4
1961-62	1245.7	– 0.1	1091.0	– 1.2	1100.8	– 0.6
1962-63	1299.6	4.3	1162.4	6.5	1176.6	6.9
1963-64	1409.2	8.6	1275.7	9.7	1290.9	8.9
1964-65	1436.6	1.9	1287.7	0.9	1312.6	1.7
1965-66	1484.8	3.4	1275.9	– 0.9	1327.8	1.2
Average	—	5.6	—	4.2	—	4.7

SOURCE: Preceding tables.

We are now ready to adjust our data for changes in the price level. Two alternative sets of figures are presented in Table 6. GDP not including oil extraction is deflated both by the official deflator (columns 1-2) and by our preferred measure, the Official Consumer Price Index (columns 3-4). According to the official deflator, constant-price GDP excluding oil extraction increased at an average annual rate of 5.6 percent between 1958-59 and 1965-66. According to the Official Consumer Price Index, which we deem more accurate though still understated, constant-price GDP excluding oil extraction increased during that period at an average annual rate of 4.2 percent.

Table 6 also shows GDP including oil extraction deflated by the Official Consumer Price Index (columns 5-6). The average annual rate of increase from 1958-59 to 1965-66 was 4.7 percent.

Moving from aggregate to per capita growth, we find that Nigerian population figures are subject to considerable doubt. There is a penumbra of uncertainty around the national censuses of 1952-53, 1962, and 1963. Simply comparing the official censuses of 1952-53 and 1963 yields an annual population growth rate of well over 5 percent. We will call this the high official estimate. It is generally agreed, however, that fear of taxes and other problems led to undercounting in the earlier census while political competition caused overcounting in the latter, so that the high official estimate is exaggerated. A second official estimate, which we will label the low official estimate, is provided by the Federal Office of Statistics. Implicitly accepting criticisms of the official censuses, but carefully skirting the political controversy surrounding them, the Office of Statistics, without discussion, assumed an annual population growth rate of 2.5 percent during the 1960s (up to the outbreak of the Civil War in 1967).

Another estimate, falling between the two official figures, was made by Chukuka Okonjo and the Centre for Population Studies, University of Ibadan, of which he was the director. Okonjo estimated an 11.7 percent undercount in the 1952-53 census. He also estimated that the 1962 population was approximately 11.4 million below the official 1963 count of 55.7 million, which means that in his judgment there was an overcount of approximately 22 percent in the 1963 census. With these adjustments, he arrives at an estimate of average annual population growth of 2.8 percent between 1952-53 and 1962.[36] We assume that each of these three population growth estimates can be projected to cover the 1958-59 to 1965-66 period we are considering.

We now have three population growth rates and four GDP growth rates (with and without oil and deflated by the official deflator or the Official Consumer Price Index). There are, consequently, twelve different possi-

[36]Chukuka Okonjo, "A Preliminary Medium Estimate of the 1962 Mid-Year Population of Nigeria," in John C. Caldwell and Chukuka Okonjo (eds.), *The Population of Tropical Africa* (New York: Columbia University Press, 1968), Tables 8 and 9 and p. 96.

ble estimates of the change in GDP per capita, extending over a considerable range. The lowest per capita growth figure (for GDP excluding oil,
deflated by the Official Consumer Price Index, and using the high official
population growth estimate) is a *negative* annual growth rate of more than
one percent. The highest per capita growth figure (for GDP including oil,
deflated by the official deflator, and using the low official population
growth rate) is 3.5 percent per annum. In our judgment, the best growth
estimate for the purpose of appraising the effectiveness of Nigerian development policy and the performance of the economy is that based on
GDP excluding oil extraction, deflated by the Official Consumer Price
Index, and using Okonjo's population growth rate. This yields an annual
growth rate of GDP per capita of 1.4 percent. Inclusion of oil would boost
this to 1.9 percent.

Our brief survey indicates that Nigeria's growth rate under pre-Civil
War nurture-capitalism was merely average. The aggregate growth rate
according to the estimate we deem most accurate (4.2 percent excluding
oil extraction and 4.7 percent including it) does not compare favorably
with the growth of the less developed economies as a group. We have
seen that Hagen and Hawrylyshyn estimated the average annual growth
for the group at 4.4 percent between 1955 and 1960 and 4.7 percent between 1960 and 1965, or 4.55 percent for the decade. With oil extraction
excluded, Nigeria's growth was slightly below the developing-economy
average, while with oil included it was an equally slight amount above the
average.

Furthermore, if a criterion of self-sustaining economic growth is that
GDP should rise more rapidly than exports, so that the economy's development is increasingly generated from within and becomes decreas-
ingly dependent upon uncertain export markets, the Nigerian showing is
certainly disappointing. While GDP increased at a 4.2 or 4.7 percent
annual rate depending on whether oil production is included, exports
showed a 10.2 percent annual increase during the same period.[37]

Like aggregate growth, per capita growth in Nigeria also was mediocre
when compared with that of the less developed economies as a group.
Hagen and Hawrylyshyn found that the annual rate of growth in per
capita GDP for all developing economies was 1.8 percent from 1955 to
1960 and 2.0 percent from 1960 to 1965, or 1.9 percent for the decade.[38]

[37]Sayre P. Schatz, Rudolph H. Blythe, Jr., and Warren O. Williams, "A Look at the
Balance Sheet," *Africa Report* (January 1970): 21.

[38]Hagen and Hawrylyshyn, pp. 47-48. These authors have assumed inexplicably low
population growth rates for Nigeria of 2.3 percent per annum during the 1955-60 quinquennium and 2.0 percent per annum during the 1960-65 quinquennium. Consequently they arrive
at annual growth rates in per capita GDP of 0.7 percent and 3.1 percent during these two
quinquennia, or 1.9 percent for the ten-year period (p. 52). Footnote 23 has pointed out that
their aggregate growth figures for Nigeria are highly dubious; the per capita figures cannot be
taken seriously at all.

This exceeds Nigeria's per capita growth rate of 1.4 percent when oil extraction is excluded and equals Nigeria's 1.9 percent rate when oil is included. The Nigerian increase in real output per capita falls far short of the dictum of the Economic Commission for Africa "that real product per head in the developing African countries should grow by at least 3 percent per annum if they are to come close to satisfying the aspirations of their peoples."[39]

If the pre-Civil War Nigerian economy is to be judged more broadly, on the basis of such other criteria as income distribution and unemployment, the record is even less satisfactory.

Our discussion of the development of Nigerian nurture-capitalism bypasses the special circumstances of the Civil War economy and the troubled year preceding the war and continues in the next chapter with an examination of the post-Civil War years.

[39]"Planning Newsletter of the Economic Commission for Africa: Report of the Third Session of the Conference of African Planners, Addis Ababa, May 1970," in Colin Legum (ed.), *Africa Contemporary Record: Annual Survey and Documents, 1970-71* (London: Rex Collings, 1971), p. C-257. The Economic Commission for Africa estimated that African gross domestic product per capita had increased in real terms by slightly more than 2 percent per annum during the period 1960-65, i.e., at a rate exceeding our estimate of GDP growth in Nigeria.

Chapter 2

THE POST-CIVIL WAR PERIOD:
1970-1975

Economic Development Orientation

Nurture-capitalism continued to constitute Nigeria's basic economic development orientation as it embarked in January 1970 upon its post-Civil War period. The private sector was to remain crucially important in both the short and the long run.[1] Gross private fixed investment was to increase from 48.6 percent of total fixed investment in 1970-71 to 60.2 percent in 1973-74 and was expected to continue to increase thereafter.[2] In the private sector, the foreign investor was pivotal. Foreign direct investment was projected at slightly more than half (50.6 percent) of gross fixed private investment for the Second Plan Period.[3] Foreign enterprises were to be relied upon to perceive investment opportunities, to establish their commercial viability, and to undertake (alone or in partnership with Nigerian public or private interests) most medium- or large-scale economic activities in the modern sector. With the reliance on private investment in general and particularly on foreign private investment went a constellation of related approaches and measures, a private-investment ecology, so to speak. There was a call to avoid uncertainty ("which

---

[1]There was recognition of "the importance of the private sector. But what is even perhaps more significant for development policy is that these proportionate contributions [of the private sector to GDP and employment] may tend to increase in the future." *Second National Development Plan 1970-74* (Lagos: Federal Ministry of Information, 1970); hereinafter referred to as *Second Plan*, p. 275.

[2]These gross fixed investment figures exclude defense capital expenditures, but adding these makes little difference. Including these reduces private investment from 52.9 percent to 51.1 percent of the total for the 1970/71-1973/74 period as a whole. *Second Plan*, p. 48.

[3]*Second Plan*, p. 48. The way in which the external account for oil is recorded might tend to overstate the importance of foreign investment. On the other hand, there have been substantial omissions which have resulted in understatements of the foreign-investment figure, perhaps by as much as 50 percent. Edwin R. Dean, *Plan Implementation in Nigeria, 1962-66* (Ibadan: Oxford University Press, 1972), p. 209. The exact definition of the concept of foreign investment in Nigerian government documents is not made clear. See Dean, p. 226.

scares away private investment") and instability.[4] There was stress on cooperation and consultation with private enterprise.[5] Government was committed to multifaceted assistance to private business.[6]

The particular form of Nigeria's postwar nurture-capitalism was shaped by a postwar ebullience compounded of the surprisingly good economic—and political—state of the country at the end of the war, of a flowering of national self-confidence, of a bright postwar idealism, and of a more assertive nationalism.

The economic situation at the end of the war was promising. The war, with its attendant import restrictions, had stimulated substantial growth in industry. Petroleum had clearly become a major factor in the economy. Production of petroleum increased more than fourfold between 1962-63 and 1966-67, and despite wartime setbacks the Second Plan projected more than a further doubling again by 1973-74. As a percentage of GDP, oil production rose from 2.0 percent to 5.1 percent in the four years from 1962-63 to 1966-67 and was expected to climb to 12.5 percent by 1973-74. Oil exports amounting to almost two-thirds of total exports were foreseen by 1973-74.[7]

The encouraging economic situation and the flush of victory in the Civil War gave rise in most of the country to a mood of buoyant confidence. "The war has helped to generate greater confidence in the basic strength and resilience of the Nigerian economy and enhanced its potential credit worthiness abroad. The origin of this confidence . . . [must be ascribed to] the overall natural endowments of the country in the fields of agriculture, livestock, forestry, fishing, water resources, mineral oil, solid minerals, fuel and energy. It must derive from the quantity and quality of its manpower, the innate ability of its people and their determination to transform their country politically, economically and socially. The Nigerian economy has emerged from the war as probably the most promising in Tropical Africa."[8]

A bracing postwar idealism manifested itself. The post-Civil War approach to economic development displayed verve, confidence, and a sense of idealism and purpose previously lacking.

What Nigeria lacked most in the past has been the national sense of purpose particularly in economic matters. The Federal Government will, therefore, oc-

[4]*Second Plan,* p. 67.
[5]The plan emphasized "the need to bring various interested groups [i.e., private interests involved in industrial development] into smooth and harmonious working relationship with Government bodies responsible for industrial matters." The Government was to set up new administrative machinery "to ensure regular and adequate consultation with representatives of the private sector." *Second Plan,* p. 145.
[6]*Second Plan,* pp. 145-146, 151, 231-233, 236, 293 and passim.
[7]*Second Plan,* pp. 50, 52, 56.
[8]*Second Plan,* p. 29.

cupy the commanding heights in the quest for purposeful national development
and provide the leadership and honest administration necessary for the attainment
of a national sense of purpose.[9]

The plan presented a resoundingly idealistic statement of goals:

(i)   a united, strong and self-reliant nation;
(ii)   a great and dynamic economy;
(iii)   a just and egalitarian society;
(iv)   a land of bright and full opportunities for all citizens; and
(v)   a free and democratic society.[10]

There was also a stronger, more assertive expression of nationalism, a
desire to be freed of dependence upon foreign investors. "Experience has
shown through history, that political independence without economic independence is but an empty shell . . . . The interests of foreign private
investors in the Nigerian economy cannot be expected to coincide at all
times and in every respect with national aspirations . . . a truly independent nation cannot allow its objectives and priorities to be distorted or
frustrated by the manipulations of powerful foreign investors."[11] There
was a fierce national yearning for greater "economic independence" that
could be ignored only at great peril, for "explosive socio-political consequences . . . are bound to arise in future with foreign-absentee control
of the nation's industrial sector."[12]

One facet of the nurture-capitalism engendered by this postwar ebullience was heightened emphasis on income distribution and the welfare of
the common man. The plan spoke of the need to "reduce the areas of
unearned incomes," to "broaden the social base of capital ownership in
the economy," to "reduce the high degree of concentration . . . of holdings of stocks and shares," and to "enable Nigerians to share in the
increasing profit generated in the country."[13]

The income-and-wealth redistribution and the other idealistic goals, as
well as the anticipated healthy growth and development, were to be
achieved through two other distinctive facets of postwar nurture-
capitalism: an intangible change in national spirit and attitude and a tangible change in economic policy.

The intangible change was envisioned as a shift to a leadership of integrity and dedication to development and the general welfare, and the good
results that would flow therefrom (e.g., "in stimulating a greater sense of

[9]*Second Plan*, p. 32.   [10]*Second Plan, p. 32.*
[11]*Second Plan*, p. 289.   [12]*Second Plan*, p. 144.
[13]*Second Plan*, pp. 75, 71. One of the major objectives of fiscal policy was to "minimise
existing inequalities in wealth, income and consumption standards which may tend to
undermine production efficiency, offend a sense of social justice and endanger political
stability." *Second Plan*, p. 68.

sacrifice in [the] community"). The government would "provide the leadership and honest administration" necessary for development. "Honest and dedicated leadership can go very far" in achieving self-reliant economic advance.[14] The Second Plan alluded often to the essentiality of a government led by dedicated men.

The major tangible innovation was to be the implementation of economic policy that would shape and hopefully even control the allocation (and perhaps also the magnitude) of investment. Indicative planning was to be used to influence "the quantum and composition of investment undertaken in the private sector in order to ensure that such investment activities are in consonance with national objectives and priorities."[15] This influence was to be achieved mainly through the differential application of investment incentives. Those who invested in priority fields were to be favored in the administration of the incentive programs; "only carefully selected industries which meet the requirements of national priorities will qualify."[16]

Aside from the differential application of incentives, government was to mobilize a range of other controls to improve the allocation of investment. There was considerable stress on government and indigenous private ownership in partnership with foreign investors. Statements about government ownership were much firmer and more insistent than similar pre-Civil War statements. Government was to insist on at least 55 percent ownership in a projected iron-and-steel complex, in petrochemical industries, in fertilizer production, and in petroleum products. Moreover, government and indigenous private equity together were to amount to at least 35 percent in a number of other important industries.[17] There was also strong reiteration throughout the plan of the long-standing stress on Nigerianization,[18] not only in employment at all levels, including technical and managerial positions, but also in partial ownership of foreign-run companies.[19] The government even raised the possibility of nationalization.[20]

---

[14]*Second Plan*, pp. 32, 33.

[15]*Second Plan*, p. 280.

[16]*Second Plan*, p. 144; see also pp. 279-286. Priority status was to depend primarily "on the value-added potential of proposed industries. . . . Priority status cannot be conferred indiscriminately on broad industry groups, but rather on those specific industrial activities within each group that are in consonance with the value-added maximization principle." Related but not identical criteria were also indicated. Priority status was to be accorded to "those industries that will consolidate the industrial achievements of the past decade through the provision of intermediate and capital goods" and those in which "the summation of the forward and backward linkages" is expected to be high. *Second Plan*, pp. 286, 281.

[17]*Second Plan*, pp. 145-146.

[18]*Second Plan*, pp. 144-145, 226-227, 230, 233, 288ff.

[19]*Second Plan*, p. 289.

[20]"The Government will not embark on indiscriminate nationalisation of existing or future

The government could also marshal other controls. It intended to require "honest accounting operations" by large firms, to discourage monopoly, and to control the repatriation of dividends and capital to encourage reinvestment in the Nigerian economy. It could apply various formal and informal pressures regarding such matters as licensing and permissible quotas of foreign personnel. It could even withdraw "authority granted for the establishment and operation of a business" and thus force a firm out of the country altogether.[21]

In brief, the economic development orientation set forth for the post-Civil War period differed slightly from the stated and actual orientations of the prewar period. With the stress on income and wealth distribution and on the well-being of the common man and the heavy emphasis on honest government dedicated to idealistic national goals, there was once again a welfare tendency. The heavy reliance on foreign investment outweighed nationalist pressures, so that the orientation was internationalist. A new element was the emphasis on guiding foreign investment through controls. Thus, the orientation was guided internationalist nurture-capitalism with a welfare tendency.

Performance

Nigeria departed from the economic development orientation just delineated in substantial respects, but discussion of the divergences between the actual and intended orientations is best left to the end of this section on the performance of the economy.

There was, according to official figures, considerable economic growth in the postwar period, and this growth started from a level that had not been significantly depressed by the Civil War. Real gross domestic product in 1970-71, the first postwar year, was 30.5 percent above the average for 1964-65 through 1966-67, the final three years of the prewar period.[22]

From 1970-71 growth proceeded as shown in Table 7.

---

enterprises in the country. Where any nationalisation is deemed necessary . . . compensation arrangements will be made in accordance with internationally accepted norms of equity and fair play." *Second Plan*, p. 289.

[21] *Second Plan*, pp. 288-289.

[22] GDP at factor costs, 1962-63 prices, calculated from *Second Plan*, p. 50 and Federal Republic of Nigeria, *Scond National Development Plan 1970-74, First Progress Report* (hereinafter referred to as *Second Plan, First Progress Report*) (Lagos: Federal Ministry of Economic Development and Reconstruction, 1972), p. 10. (The 1970-71 GDP was 47 percent above the average for the three subsequent war years, 1967-68 through 1969-70, according to an unofficial but well-informed source which based its calculations on official figures. However the GDP figures for these years were depressed both by the war and by exclusion of the output of the three eastern states originally encompassed in secessionist territory.)

TABLE 7

Gross Domestic Product[a] at Constant (1974-75) Prices

	₦ million	Percent growth
1970-71	9,442.1	—
1971-72	11,177.9	18.4%
1972-73	11,993.1	7.3%
1973-74	13,135.5	9.5%
1974-75	14,410.7	9.7%

SOURCE: Federal Republic of Nigeria, *Third National Development Plan 1975-80*, I (Lagos: Federal Ministry of Economic Development, 1975), p. 19.

[a]GDP at factor cost.

Average annual growth of GDP for the three years up to 1973-74 was 11.7 percent, according to official figures, and for the four years until 1974-75 it was 11.2 percent.[23]

Overall growth was accompanied by considerable expansion in manufacturing and construction. Starting from a very small base, manufacturing grew at better than 10 percent per annum since independence in 1960 and growth continued at that rate in the post-Civil War period. Manufacturing and crafts production together rose by 3.1 percent in 1971-72, 23.9 percent in 1972-73, 9.9 percent in 1973-74, and 9.2 percent in 1974-75.[24] Construction output increased even more rapidly but was unable to keep up with demand; increases were 41.2 percent in 1971-72, 23.2 percent in 1972-73, 25.3 percent in 1973-74, and 15.6 percent in 1974-75.[25]

Nigeria's balance of payments also improved. Deficits in the balance on current account of ₦270 million, ₦325 million, and ₦242 million in 1970, 1971, and 1972 were converted to an estimated surplus of ₦402 million in 1973; and in the 1974-75 fiscal year the estimated surplus soared to ₦3,616 million.[26]

---

[23]The use of 1974-75 prices overvalues petroleum through 1973. As petroleum production was increasing relatively rapidly, Table 7 exaggerates economic growth up to 1972-73. For example, the 1970/71-1971/72 increase in GDP was 12.0 percent in 1962-63 prices (calculated from *Second Plan, First Progress Report*, p. 10) while it was 18.4 percent in 1974-75 prices. The table then understates growth in the next two years, particularly 1974-75, by masking the impact in those years of the petroleum price increases.

[24]Federal Republic of Nigeria, *Third National Development Plan 1975-80* (hereinafter referred to as *Third Plan*), Vol. I (Lagos: Federal Ministry of Economic Development, 1975), p. 20.

[25]*Third Plan*, p. 20.

[26]*Third Plan*, p. 60; and International Monetary Fund, *Balance of Payments Yearbook* (Washington: International Monetary Fund, various years).

However, the record of the economy was less impressive than the foregoing official figures may suggest.

For one thing, the economy's growth performance was not nearly as good as it appeared to be. First, the fortuitous oil boom provided most of the increase in GDP. Excluding oil, GDP expansion was as follows, according to official figures:

1971-72	7.5%	1973-74	6.2%
1972-73	0.0%	1974-75	8.9%

Annual growth averaged 4.6 percent for the three years to 1973-74 and 5.7 percent for the four years to 1974-75.[27] Second, the unreliability of official economic statistics, already discussed, and the consequent penumbra of indeterminacy and unverifiability nurture the natural tendency of those at the helm to tilt the official growth rate upwards. For example, knowledgeable unofficial estimates indicate that the impact of the West African drought on agricultural output caused a decrease in GDP in 1972-73 and a much smaller increase than 6.2 percent in 1973-74. Third, the oil boom imparted a significant stimulus to the rest of the economy. It is not a coincidence that the economic growth rate increased after the 1974 surge in oil revenues.

Growth aside, there was a confidence-undermining series of other keenly felt problems. These relate to plan fulfillment, income distribution, agricultural performance, unemployment, inflation, and corruption.

1. The degree to which government and government bodies carried out the projects of the Second Plan was disappointing. Tables 8 and 9 present actual and planned capital expenditures for the four years 1970-71 through 1973-74. Table 8, with a year-by-year breakdown for each State and for the Federal Government, is more detailed, but Table 9 is more conveniently summarized for the discussion in the next few paragraphs. By the end of the four-year plan's third year (March 31, 1973) capital expenditures amounted to ₦1,300 million out of a sum of planned projects that then totalled ₦3,202 million.[28] Three-fourths of the way through the original four-year-plan period, then, expenditure was 40.6 percent of that planned for the four-year span.

By the end of that span (although the Second Plan had by then been extended another year), capital expenditures had reached ₦2,237 million.

[27]Calculated from *Third Plan*, p. 19; constant (1974-75) prices.

[28]There are minor discrepancies in the figures stated in different places, e.g., capital expenditures for 1970-73 are shown as ₦1,302 million on p. 26 of Federal Republic of Nigeria, *Second National Development Plan 1970-74, Second Progress Report* (hereinafter referred to as *Second Plan, Second Progress Report*) (Lagos: Federal Ministry of Economic Development and Reconstruction, 1974), but these are small enough to be disregarded. Minor discrepancies of this kind will not be mentioned hereafter.

TABLE 8

Actual Public Capital Expenditures
Second National Development Plan
(₦ millions)

(1)	(2)	(3)	(4)	(5)	(6)
	1970/71	1971/72	1972/73	1973/74	1970/74
Total	243	432	625	937	2,237
Federal Govt.	124	237	332	539	1,232
All States	119	195	294	397	1,005
Benue Plateau	9	13	22	24	68
East Central	5	14	11	32	62
Kano	19	26	37	34	116
Kwara	5	7	16	26	54
Lagos	5	11	34	36	86
Mid-West	16	20	29	34	99
North Central	5	15	26	51	97
North Eastern	9	16	24	30	79
North Western	7	14	23	31	75
Rivers	5	14	26	40	85
South Eastern	11	13	21	26	71
Western	23	33	23	34	113

SOURCES: Columns 2, 3 and 4: Federal Republic of Nigeria, *Second National Development Plan 1970-74, Second Progress Report* (Lagos: Federal Ministry of Economic Development and Reconstruction, 1974), pp. 106-108. Column 6: *Third Plan*, p. 23. Column 5: column 6 minus columns 2+3+4.

NOTE: There are slight discrepancies because of rounding.

This was 66.8 percent of planned capital expenditures for the 1970-74 plan period,[29] which were then listed as ₦3,350 million.[30]

Speaking of this expenditure proportion of two-thirds, the government stated: "This must be regarded as a satisfactory performance especially

[29]The plans make a distinction between the "nominal" and the "effective" capital programs. This will be discussed in Chapter 3. Here it is sufficient to note that we are following the *Third Plan* (pp. 10-11) in assessing Second Plan performance, by comparing actual capital expenditure with the sum of the capital costs of the planned projects. This is what the plans call the nominal program; actual capital expenditures compared to the "effective" program would show a better result.

[30]Planned capital expenditures were listed as ₦3,272 million on p. 10 and as ₦3,350 million on p. 25 of the *Third Plan*. From the context, the latter figure appears to be the more correct. The reasons for the increase in the figure for planned capital expenditure from ₦3,202 million to ₦3,350 million will be discussed shortly.

TABLE 9
Actual and Planned Capital Expenditures
Federal Government and State Governments
1970-73 and 1970-74
(₦ millions and percentages)

(1)	(2)	(3)	(4)	(5)	(6)	(7)
	Actual 1970-73	Planned for 1970-74[a]	Actual as percent of planned	Actual 1970-74	Planned for 1970-74[a]	Actual as percent of planned
Government						
a) Total	1,300	3,202	40.6%	2,237	3,350	66.8%
b) All States	608	1,271	47.8%	1,005	1,418	70.9%
c) Fed. Govt.	693	1,932	35.9%	1,232	1,932	63.8%

SOURCES: Columns 2 and 3: *Second Plan, Second Progress Report*, pp. 109 and 105. Columns 5 and 6: *Third Plan*, pp. 23, 25.

[a]Columns 3 and 6 both represent capital expenditures planned for the Second Plan period. The slight difference in the figures presumably results from minor adjustments in costing. See footnote 35 of this chapter.

when it is realised that it took quite sometime for the governments of the new States to establish a proper administration."[31]

In fact, execution of the plan could not really be considered satisfactory, and this was recognized by knowledgeable persons. Officials were well aware of and concerned about a deficiency of executive or implementation capacity and particularly an inability to prepare projects or to work with foreign experts in doing so.[32] In fact, government departments sometimes seemed hardly aware of the plan even as it applied to their own operations; "in some of the executive Ministries officials are not quite familiar with the content of their programmes under the Plan."[33]

Plan fulfillment during 1970-74 was actually considerably less than two-thirds. Expenditure figures do not bespeak physical performance. This is mentioned in passing in the plan: "It is appreciated, of course, that physical indices of performance are better guides to growth and development than financial outlays."[34] However, the necessary adjustment for substantial increases in project costs was not attempted. For example, in the year prior to the drafting of the Third Plan, the capital investment figure of the Second Plan was raised from ₦3,202 million to ₦3,350 million, an increase of 4.4 percent.[35] Encompassed in this 4.4 percent are four kinds of increases in costs: those arising from added projects or project enlargements, those caused by the rise in the general price level in a year of substantial inflation, those due to the considerable relative increase in the costs of construction and capital goods beyond the general pace of inflation, and those resulting from initial "gross under-estimation of costs" of projects[36] which had nothing to do with inflation but which were the result of superficial preliminary estimates.[37] Any of the 4.4 percent that may be left after allowing for additional projects and project enlargements does not even begin to cover the 1973-74 increases in project costs arising from the other three causes. In the face of rising project

[31]*Third Plan*, p. 11 (speaking of the Second Plan period). It is perfectly proper to regard the plan document as an expression of the views of the government. A draft document was reviewed sentence by sentence at the highest level of power before the final plan was issued. "The Plan has now been approved by Government after exhaustive discussion by both the Federal Executive Council and the Supreme Military Council . . ." General Yakubu Gowon, "Speech on the Third National Development Plan," (Lagos) *Daily Times*, March 31, 1975, p. 3.

[32]See, e.g., *Second Plan, Second Progress Report*, pp. 101-102.

[33]*Second Plan, Second Progress Report*, pp. 101-102. The document continues: "It is the duty of every head of department and all his senior staff to take greater interest in, and be constantly informed of progress in the implementation of his Ministry's plan projections . . . Every official should always be ready to discuss his Ministry's projects with confidence."

[34]*Third Plan*, p. 9.

[35]See Table 9. The former figure is from the *Second Plan, Second Progress Report*, the latter from the *Third Plan*. These two documents were prepared and published a year apart and presumably represent a costing of capital projects as at March 31, 1973, and March 31, 1974.

[36]*Second Plan, Second Progress Report*, p. 25.

[37]In some cases, project costs were exaggerated, but underestimation predominated.

costs, expenditures at two-thirds the planned level purchased physical performance substantially less than two-thirds of that planned. If we make the reasonable assumption that physical achievement was not more than 75 percent of expenditure (i.e., that projects valued at ₦75 required on the average something more than ₦100 to carry out), then aggregate physical achievement during the 1970-74 period was less than half of what was planned.

It should be mentioned that the administrative problems of the new State governments did not constitute a primary cause of the shortfall in plan achievement, as the plan stated (see the third preceding paragraph). The calculations in Table 9 show that State plan fulfillment was higher than Federal.

There was also plan distortion, by which is meant relative "over-expenditure on low priority sectors and under-expenditure on high priority sectors."[38] This was a matter of considerable concern to the Government,[39] but no assessment is attempted here. Furthermore, the intention of controlling foreign investment through indicative planning was unfulfilled, but this will be discussed later.

2. Rather than achieving the proclaimed goal of reducing income and wealth disparities, inequality probably increased. This aroused broad and bitter disillusion and anger by 1974, and in recognition of the "sensitive" and "explosive" nature of the issue, the Third Plan stressed the goal even more strongly than had the Second.[40]

Data are not available to allow one to speak with precision,[41] but retrogression on the income and wealth distribution issue is widely recognized. Official publications noted this retrogression rather cautiously. In 1973, it was observed that "not much has been done. Government is probably waiting for the Udoji Public Service Review Commission to complete its work before embarking on a major policy to reduce existing disparities between earnings in the public and the private sectors on the one hand, and between the low and high income workers within each sector, on the other."[42] Similar observations were made in 1974. "Unfortunately, Nigeria has never had an articulate and deliberate incomes policy."[43] "It is possible to record a high growth rate in per capita income while the masses of the people continue to be in abject poverty and

[38]Dean, p. 84. Speaking of plan distortion during the first plan period, Dean (p. 87) shows that "even within the limits of actual expenditure [which was considerably less than planned] there was excessive spending on low priority sectors and inadequate spending on high priority sectors, during the first four years."

[39]*Third Plan*, pp. 8, 402.

[40]pp. 31, 33.

[41]"Given the complete absence of data on both inter-factoral and inter-personal distribution of incomes it is not feasible to assess the extent to which the [income-distribution] objective was achieved between 1970 and 1974." *Third Plan*, p. 14; see also p. 33.

[42]*Second Plan, Second Progress Report*, p. 30.

[43]*Third Plan*, p. 33.

lacking in the basic necessities of life, particularly in a situation, such as in Nigeria today, where the momentum of growth derives from a sector whose direct impact on the bulk of the population is small."[44]

Unofficial comments were more blunt. In uncontrolled growth in a private enterprise economy, said one leading economist, "the tendency is for the rich to grow richer and for the poor to grow poorer. This appears to be what has been happening in our economy. Our economy has so far betrayed the third objective of a just and egalitarian society. The growing pattern of income and wealth distribution between the high and the low, between the urban and the rural areas, between the employed and the unemployed, between the military and civilian population and even between the Federal Government and the state governments is anything but just or egalitarian. The economically strong has been growing stronger and the economically weak growing weaker, buttressed by the increased abundance of the resources available to the governments."[45]

Said another prominent economist, discussing indigenization of business ownership, "although indigenisation may have succeeded in redistributing wealth between expatriates and Nigerians, it surely has created more inequalities in the distribution of wealth among Nigerians."[46]

The rural-urban income disparity was surely aggravated. There was a decrease in aggregate agricultural output from 1970-71 to 1974-75 and an even greater reduction in output per farmer.[47] The rural-urban gap was further widened by the Udoji wage increases of 1974-75. These not only substantially boosted urban incomes relative to rural incomes, but acted to reduce agricultural output by raising the price of hired farm labor.

The Udoji wage increases at the beginning of 1975 had mixed effects on income distribution.[48] Major increases were awarded throughout the public sector of the economy and these spilled over into the private sector as well. Except for those at the very top, the relative gap within the modern sector narrowed. Those at the bottom of the government pay scale got increases of 122 percent (from ₦27 to ₦60 a month) while most of the others received increases in the neighborhood of 30 percent.[49] On the other hand, the disparity increased between the modern-sector workers,

[44]*Third Plan*, p. 27.

[45]Sam Aluko (Professor and Head, Department of Economics, University of Ife), "Third National Plan," (Lagos) *Daily Times*, April 21, 1975, p. 14.

[46]G. O. Nwankwo (Professor and Head, Department of Finance, University of Lagos), "The Success and Failure of a National Development Plan," (Lagos) *Sunday Times*, December 15, 1974, p. 7.

[47]See the discussion of agriculture that follows.

[48]These were public-sector wage and salary increases resulting from the report of the Public Service Review Commission chaired by Jerome Udoji and modified by the Military Government. Indications were that the Udoji increases raised the annual wage bill by 50 to 60 percent.

[49]Increases at the very top were up to 100 percent, so for a small number of people the income gap did not narrow.

who constitute only 7.1 percent of the labor force and who were already a relatively privileged group anyway, and the rest of the population, particularly those in the rural areas. This increased gap was attacked by an energetic process of inflation as wholesalers and retailers, farmers, and others attempted to win a share of the income increase, but the enlarged disparity could only be eroded and not eliminated by this process.

3. Agriculture performed poorly. Agricultural output actually decreased during the period under review, according to official figures (see Table 10). The reductions occurred despite population growth and despite the "bringing back into cultivation of large tracts of land in the war affected areas."[50] As 70 percent of the population lives in rural areas, the poor showing in agriculture was a major problem.

TABLE 10

Agriculture and Related Output[a]

at Constant 1974-75 Prices

Year	₦ million
1970-71	3,399.7
1971-72	3,575.3
1972-73	3,351.8
1973-74	3,246.5
1974-75	3,372.7

SOURCE: *Third Plan*, p. 19.

[a]Listed as agriculture, etc.; includes livestock, forestry, and fishing.

4. As the agricultural problem generated rural unrest, unemployment in the cities engendered urban unrest. Given the national objectives of "a just and egalitarian society" and "a land of bright and full opportunities for all citizens," it is not surprising that the Second Plan explicitly adopted a "commitment to a full employment policy,"[51] but that commitment was not realized.

The official estimates of unemployment were low: 4.5 percent of the labor force in 1975 and a projection of 3.0 percent by 1980.[52] However, these estimates cannot be taken seriously. Official publications themselves suggest that unemployment is a much more troublesome problem than the 4.5 percent figure indicates. "The inability of economic growth

[50]*Second Plan, Second Progress Report*, p. 101.
[51]*Second Plan*, p. 34.
[52]*Third Plan*, pp. 368-370.

to generate adequate employment opportunities for the masses" was noted by the *Third Plan*,[53] while an earlier report lamented the "small growth of wage employment."[54]

When we turn from cautious official publications, assessments of unemployment were graver. Even high-level officials spoke of the "large scale unemployment in the country."[55] Professor Aluko wrote of "an economy plagued by increasing unemployment" and stated: "It is much more difficult to find jobs for the jobless today than it was in 1970, even without demobilization of soldiers, because the economy has been pumping out more job-seekers than it has been providing for."[56]

A careful scrutiny of the official statistics, weak as they are, supports the more dramatic statements. Official unemployment occurs almost exclusively in the cities; "overt unemployment is essentially an urban phenomenon. . . ."[57] The rural counterparts—underemployment and seasonal idleness—are not counted as unemployment. Therefore, as official unemployment relates essentially to the nonagricultural labor force, only this labor force should be considered in determining the unemployment percentage. In such a calculation (Table 11, row 5) unemployment amounted to 11.7 percent. Even this figure painted a sanguine picture of the unemployment problem. Aside from unemployment survey shortcomings, particularly with regard to staffing, which may well have caused undercounting, the official unemployment figure does not encompass the superabundance of hawkers of all kinds, of infrequently employed casual labor, and of the other underemployed, nor the large numbers not actively seeking jobs, particularly women, who would gladly take jobs if they were available. These omissions unduly reduce the size of the unemployment-percentage numerator; at the same time the denominator may be too large. Unemployment statistics refer essentially to those seeking *wage* employment. If these are compared to the *wage* labor force (those in or seeking wage employment), 1975 unemployment would amount to 37.5 percent, as shown in Table 11, row 8. (This calculation leaves aside any adjustments for possible understatements of the numerator.)

[53]*Third Plan*, p. 367.

[54]*Second Plan, Second Progress Report*, p. 35. The Report goes on to say: "Large scale enterprises in the private sector do not appear to have expanded their labor force in anything like the degree which could be wished. Labour Exchange statistics seem to indicate that the number of registered job seekers continues to rise. This situation is consistent with the increasingly massive outflow of potential wage-earners from educational institutions. The improvement achieved and projected in the availability of school-places is far from being matched by an equal availability of wage-employment opportunities in the country at large. The overall employment situation cannot be said therefore to provide any particularly good grounds for satisfaction."

[55]The Governor of Kano State, Police Commissioner Audu Bako, speaking to the Nigerian Economic Society: (Lagos) *Daily Times*, April 18, 1975, p. 1.

[56]Aluko, p. 14.

[57]*Third Plan*, p. 380.

TABLE 11

Unemployment, 1975 and 1980

	1975		1980 (projected)	
	Number (millions)	Percent	Number (millions)	Percent
1. Labor force	29.22		32.74	
2. Unemployment	1.31	4.5	0.98	3.0
3. Nonagricultural employment	9.85		12.55	
4. Nonagricultural labor force (2+3)	11.16		13.53	
5. Unemployment as percent of non-agricultural labor force (2÷4)		11.7		7.2
6. Wage employment	2.18		2.76	
7. Wage labor force	3.49		3.74	
8. Unemployment as percent of wage labor force (2÷7)		37.5		26.2

SOURCE: *Third Plan*, p. 372, and author's calculation based on these data.

While 37.5 percent may be an overstatement, for the denominator used in calculating it (the wage-labor force only) may be questioned, it has a more real "feel" than the official figure of 4.5 percent. In this regard, a Western State study of unemployment among primary and secondary school leavers (graduates) is informative. Table 12, row 3, shows that in 1969 38 percent of the school leavers were still unemployed a year after graduating, and this had increased to 43 percent in 1972. A more accurate figure is found by omitting those who continued in school and counting only those who were, presumably, in the labor market; then the unemployment figures are 62 percent in 1969 and 78 percent in 1972 (row 4).[58]

In addition to the problems of overt unemployment with which the unemployment calculations are concerned, there are also the problems already mentioned of underemployment, seasonal unemployment, and extremely low-income and low-productivity employment.

5. Pleased by a subsidence of inflation by 1972, the public was subsequently distressed by a sharp inflationary resurgence in 1974 and 1975. The war and postwar inflationary rates of 10 to 16 percent per annum

[58]Because school leavers have relatively high expectations, their unemployment rate was probably especially high.

TABLE 12

Activity of Primary and Secondary School Leavers
Western State, 1969 and 1972

Activity	Percentages	
	1969	1972
1. Continued in school	39	45
2. Employed one year after graduating	23	12
3. Unemployed one year after graduating	38	43
4. Unemployed one year after graduating as a percentage of those in the	100	100
labor force (3÷[2+3])	62	78

SOURCE: Calculated from *Third Plan*, p. 380.

slowed to less than 3 percent by 1972, according to the official figures shown in Table 13. But then a reversal of accelerating magnitude set in, the consumer price index rising by an estimated 20 to 25 percent in 1974. This was particularly painful to the more politically active and volatile urban areas, where public-sector wages rates, with private wages largely following suit, had been frozen since April 1972. The large price-level rise in 1974, coming as it did before the new oil revenues could make themselves widely felt and before the Udoji wage increases of 1975, was "indeed frightening and considered unacceptably high by most Nigerians."[59] This rise was then dwarfed by the price-level increases of 1975, estimated by the author at 75 percent.

6. Although one of General Gowon's major postwar goals was "the eradication of corruption in our national life," dishonest practices continued on a widespread basis and this was corrosive of national morale.

Encouraged by the partial success of an affidavit sworn by a Lagos businessman named Godwin Daboh charging the Commissioner (military government equivalent of Minister) of Communications, Joseph Tarka, with specific corrupt practices,[60] a campaign against corruption quickly gathered momentum among the public and in the press in mid-1974. The public was gleeful about the charges and exposures. People began to speak of "Dabohing" someone, i.e., exposing his wrongdoings. Many persons swore affidavits alleging corruption. By August 1974, the more independent newspapers were crowded with stories on official dishonesty, to the sour satisfaction of a disillusioned and angry public. There

[59]O. Teriba and S. I. Ajayi, "Inflation and Budgetary Policy in Nigeria," Mimeographed paper presented at the Symposium on Inflation, Nigerian Institute of Social and Economic Research, Ibadan, November 22-23, 1974.

[60]The Commissioner resigned from his post, but no further action was taken.

TABLE 13

Consumer Price Index[a]

1968-1974

Year	Index (1960=100)	Percent change in index
1968	120.3	− 0.4
1969	132.3	+10.0
1970	150.6	+13.8
1971	174.7	+16.0
1972	179.6	+ 2.8
1973	189.3	+ 5.4
1974	—	+20 to +25
1975	—	+75

SOURCES: Central Bank of Nigeria, *Annual Report and Statement of Accounts*, various years, as presented by O. Teriba and S. I. Ajayi, "Inflation and Budgetary Policy in Nigeria," mimeographed paper presented at Symposium on Inflation, Nigerian Institute of Social and Economic Research, Ibadan, November 22-23, 1974. The increase in 1974 is the estimate of Teriba and Ajayi. The 1975 increase is our own rough guesstimate.

[a]This consumer price index is a weighted average for the nine largest cities of price indices based on the household budgets of urban workers with basic annual earnings not exceeding N 800.

was a dual target: pervasive venality in high places ("A ravenous and greedy elite, so anxious to enlarge themselves by any means, may destroy the bright promise of this new nation")[61]; and a more general "corruption [that] had eaten deep into the fabric of society."[62]

The government soon moved, however, to repress the outcry against corruption. Mr. Daboh was put under intensive police investigation and was subsequently arrested and charged with extortion. Another prominent businessman who had sworn an affidavit charging the Military Governor of the Benue-Plateau State with corrupt practices was detained (jailed) for months without formal charges or trial. Journalists who overstepped unspecified bounds were on occasion interrogated by the police and sometimes detained.[63] The judiciary was instructed that corruption-charging affidavits were illegal, although there was some disagreement

[61](Lagos) *Sunday Times*, August 11, 1974, p. 8.
[62](Lagos) *Daily Times*, September 7, 1974, p. 28.
[63]The detention threat was a severe one indeed. Witness the case of journalist Kanayo Benny Esenulo, detained without charges since September 25, 1973, and mentioned in the press almost two years later because he was in a maximum security prison and was ill. (Lagos) *Daily Times*, July 22, 1975, p. 1.

about this. There was a crescendo of official warnings to the press, and to others, about irresponsibility. In a four-day period in September 1974, four stern statements by high-level authorities in the Military Government were issued. One warned that "anybody caught in the act of writing fictitious letters or spreading unfounded rumors would be dealt with by the law enforcement agencies."[64] Another said that "there were political undertones in affidavits being sworn to against individuals in responsible positions in the country and . . . it was up to judges to stop courts being turned into a political forum."[65] Another stated that the "current wave of affidavits-swearing alleging wrong doings against some public office holders cannot solve the problem of corruption in the country . . . [and that such affidavits] were mischievous acts capable of throwing the nation into chaos."[66] And General Gowon himself "warned both the courts and the Press not to allow themselves to be used as instruments of blackmail against highly-placed public officials with a view to tarnishing their image. He warned that the Federal Government would resist any attempt by any person in this country to discredit the military regime."[67]

The public campaign abated, but the private conviction was unshakable. After the coup of July 29, 1975, the new government, disclosing "plans to seize ill-gotten assets from whoever is found to have used his public office to enrich himself,"[68] publicly declared corruption to be a major problem.

In the post-Civil War period as in the preceding periods, we see that the actual economic development orientation diverged from the stated. First, there were divergences relating to the idealistic qualities of the orientation. (a) The equalitarian and welfare tendencies were not achieved; unemployment remained high and, more important, inequalities in income and wealth probably widened. (b) There had not been a discernible change in the degree of honesty and dedication in government. Second, guidance of foreign private investment through indicative planning, differential application of incentives, and other government levers of control was nonexistent. This was publicly admitted by indirection in the Third Plan, which discussed the need to articulate—note well, not to strengthen or revise, but to articulate—investment policies.[69] There was, evidently,

[64](Lagos) *Daily Times,* September 6, 1974, p. 1.

[65](Lagos) *Daily Times,* September 6, 1974, p. 5.

[66](Lagos) *Daily Times,* September 9, 1974, p. 2.

[67](Lagos) *Daily Times,* August 16, 1975, p. 1.

[68](Lagos) *Daily Times,* September 8, 1974, p. 1. General Gowon felt that the press was selective and vindictive. Jean Herskovits, "Nigeria: Africa's New Power," *Foreign Affairs* LIV (January 1975): 330. In this he was no different from government leaders the world over whose governments are under criticism by the press.

[69]"Given the need to ensure that private business decisions are in consonance with the objectives and priorities of the nation as expressed in the National Development Plan it is

not even an attempt to implement such policies during the Second Plan period.[70]

The actual economic development orientation thus remained essentially what it had been from the mid-1950s to the Civil War, i.e., throughout most of the period of Nigerian control of government. As neither the welfare nor the foreign-investment-guidance elements materialized, the stated orientation (guided internationalist nurture-capitalism with a welfare tendency) failed to dislodge the actual orientation of, simply, internationalist or dependent nurture-capitalism.

Overall, the performance of the economy was wanting. The attempts to improve upon the development orientation miscarried. And despite the already ongoing miniboom in oil, growth was less than satisfactory and the record with respect to plan fulfillment and inflation was disappointing. Discouragement, however, was swept aside by the new surge in oil revenues, which revived morale and restored optimism.

---

imperative that policies be articulated as a necessary adjunct to the direct investment programmes of the governments of the Federation." *Third Plan,* p. 31.

[70]Investment codes have been tried in a number of African countries, such as Ghana, Guinea, Mali, and Senegal, and have not worked.

Chapter 3

THE PERIOD OF
OIL AFFLUENCE

Economic Development Orientation

By reviving optimism and confidence, the new oil wealth gave rise by 1975 to an exuberant form of the familiar economic development orientation.[1] The Third Plan continued the basic nurture-capitalism division of responsibilities. Public investment programs heavily stressed the infrastructure. "The main thrust of the public sector programme under the Plan is the further development of essential infrastructural facilities. . . . In this sense the public and private sectors are largely complementary."[2] Government complemented private enterprise also by providing a business and economic climate and a set of programs and policies intended to encourage and assist the "very dynamic"[3] productive sphere of the economy. To avoid unsettling ambiguity for foreign investors, the areas reserved for indigenous enterprise and those in which foreign investment was welcomed were "clearly defined by law."[4] Business interests also were brought into the planning process. "The Plan has been prepared in

---

[1]The central economic role of the Third Plan continued after the coup of July 29, 1975. The Head of State, Brigadier Murtala Mohammed, told the members of the new Federal Executive Council: "The Third National Development Plan launched early this year will claim the prior attention of this council . . . I have great faith in the ability of this council and the public services as well as our citizens to accomplish the programme with courage and industry." Quoted in (Lagos) *Daily Times,* August 14, 1975, p. 5.

[2]Federal Republic of Nigeria, *Third National Development Plan 1975- 80* (hereinafter referred to as *Third Plan*), Vol. 1 (Lagos: Federal Ministry of Economic Development, 1975), p. 349. See also pp. 28-29: "The overall strategy of the Plan is simple. . . . it is the development strategy of the government to utilise the resources from oil to develop the productive capacity of the economy and thus permanently improve the standard of living of the people. In the relatively short time that the economy will enjoy a surplus of investible resources it is intended that maximum effort will be made to create the economic and social infrastructure necessary for self-sustaining growth in the longer run. . . ."

[3]*Third Plan,* p. 349.

[4]General Yakubu Gowon, "Speech on the Third National Development Plan," March 29, 1975, (Lagos) *Daily Times,* March 31, 1975, p. 29. See also a similar concern in Federal Republic of Nigeria, *Second National Development Plan 1970-74* (hereinafter referred to as *Second Plan*) (Lagos: Federal Ministry of Information, 1970), p. 67: "It is uncertainty, not controls, which scares away private investment."

close consultation with the private sector. . . . [This is] meant to ensure that the interests of the private sector are fully taken into account in the Development Plan."[5] Similar intentions had been stated in earlier years but the actual degree of private participation was considerably greater than had occurred before. "If my analysis of current trends and thinking is correct, the Government is happily becoming more and more responsive to the constructive suggestions which the organised private sector of the economy is privileged to make from time to time. For the first time, the sector has been deliberately and meaningfully involved with the development planning processes and the indications are that it will be even more closely associated with the implementation process."[6]

Directly productive investment remained primarily a private responsibility, although the Plan also projected substantial public investment in industrial activities in partnership with foreign corporations.[7] Private enterprise continued in a crucial role: "The Third National Development Plan offers to our indigenous entrepreneurs and to private foreign investors a tremendous opportunity to play an important part in the development of the Nigerian economy . . . Private investment activity is welcome in most sectors of the economy. . . ."[8] The projected magnitude of private investment (₦10 billion) was more than triple actual private investment (₦3.1 billion) during the four years of the original Second Plan period.[9]

The development orientation's balance between nationalism and internationalist dependence is difficult to characterize. On the whole, there was a rough and unsteady equiponderance of the two tendencies.

On the one hand, nationalistic forces were strong. Paradoxically, the implementation of a partial indigenization decree in 1974 increased the clamor for further indigenization. Strategically placed persons and other Nigerians who hoped to gain had self-interested motives for pressing

[5]*Third Plan*, p. 7.

[6]Chief Henry Fajemirokun, President, Chamber of Commerce, (Lagos) *Sunday Times*, March, 9, 1975, p. 7.

[7]Ojetunji Aboyade's characterization of the period up to 1970 still held: ". . . whatever the relative share of investment or of aggregate national expenditure borne by the public sector, the mixed economy system followed in practice by Nigeria both during the colonial period and in the decade after Independence, was really in essence a private enterprise system." The "unquestioned dominance of private enterprise ideology" that Aboyade saw as prevailing in 1973 continued. "Nigerian Public Enterprises as an Organizational Dilemma," in *Public Enterprises in Nigeria: Proceedings of the 1973 Annual Conference of the Nigerian Economic Society* (Ibadan: Nigerian Economic Society, 1974), p. 34.

Public investment in directly productive activities is examined near the end of this section in a discussion of affluence-induced modifications of the stated development orientation.

[8]Gowon, p. 29. The plan itself speaks of "the enormity of the challenge which this plan poses for the private sector . . ." *Third Plan*, p. 353.

[9]*Third Plan*, p. 10. On the proportions of public and private investment, see the discussion below of affluence-induced modifications of the stated development orientation. "Billion" as used here means a thousand million.

further. Moreover, the crucial role of the foreign investor, particularly in the more complex and technologically advanced fields, was a constant irritant. Government thus not only continued to assist Nigerian business as a means of promoting economic development, but also inclined toward advancing indigenous business interests even at the expense of retarding development so long as the cost was not believed excessive. The Plan placed considerable emphasis both on business-assistance programs for Nigerians and on indigenization.[10]

On the other hand, the internationalist or dependent tendency also continued and intensified. Policy-makers had been inclined in early work on the Third Plan to reduce dependence on foreign investors. However, after the oil-revenue-inspired increases in investment targets, they turned again to foreign business as a necessary source of investment. Government, for example, looked to foreign corporations to provide the know-how for a number of ambitious, directly productive ventures—in liquefied natural gas, other petrochemical products, petroleum products, fertilizers, and other industries—that were to be undertaken in partnership with foreign business, usually with government as the major partner. In the Second Plan period, foreign investment had been projected at slightly more than half of all private fixed investment; and while no comparable projections were made for the Third Plan period, the expected foreign proportion of private investment was probably greater. Although some fields were reserved for Nigerians, in the others "the foreign businessmen in our midst are as welcome as ever before. . . ."[11] In this welcoming attitude, important elements of the Nigerian business community concurred, for in a context of nationalist pressure and indigenization many were predominantly beneficiaries rather than competitors of foreign enterprise.[12] Foreign firms were to be relied upon for *development*—for the establishment of new techniques and new products, for innovation, for extending the Nigerian economy into new economic territory.

We have spoken of the exuberance of Third Plan nurture-capitalism, induced by the 1974 surge in oil income. The new prosperity modified the

---

[10]The programs will be discussed later in this chapter under "Reliance upon Indigenous Business."

[11]Gowon, p. 29.

[12]See, for example, the remarks of the President of the Lagos Chamber of Commerce: "It is true indeed that there are still abundant opportunities here for foreign private investment. In spite of the country's indigenisation policy, Nigeria still needs foreign investment and rapid manpower development in managerial, technical and technological skills. However, the present uncertainties regarding the remittance of technical management and advisory fees could constitute a disincentive to the transfer of technology and the provision of such essential services which the country badly needs. Nigeria should not only be prepared to pay for such services but it must also be seen to be so prepared. This is why we would like government to draw out specific guidelines promptly so as to facilitate the attraction of the much needed foreign private investment." Chief Henry Fajemirokun, "Private Entrepreneurs are Prepared to Cooperate," (Lagos) *Daily Times*, December 7, 1974, p. 7.

approach embraced in the *Third Plan Guidelines* and enhanced the possibility of attaining previously stated objectives. The expansive effects of the oil affluence are discussed in the remainder of this section.

1. Most striking was the impact of oil affluence on the ambitiousness of the development attack, as shown by the huge increase in the magnitude of planned investment. "The size of the Plan is meant to ensure a radical transformation of the economy during the Plan period."[13]

Public investment was projected at ₦32.1 billion or ₦20 billion, depending on how it was reckoned.[14] A distinction was made between a nominal investment program (the larger) and an effective program. The "Nominal Programme . . . is a simple summation of all the financial allocations made to all the projects . . . the Effective Programme is obtained by netting out . . . assumed underspending from the nominal programme."[15] The latter "level of investment by public agencies is considered the maximum feasible having regard to executive and absorptive capacity constraints. . . ."[16] The Plan's macro-economic analysis and public discussions both focused on the effective program as if this were the *real* investment program while the nominal program was without substance, as of course the very terms imply. However, the nominal program is actually the more real. It is the sum total of all the investment projects incorporated in the Plan. It is the list of projects that public agencies are committed to carrying out, and *implementation of these projects is to be their major goal.* The "government has decided to adopt the degree of Plan fulfillment by each ministry, corporation or state-owned company as the main criterion for measuring the efficiency of each organisation and of its principal officers."[17] The economic planners, aware of the more essential nature of the (nominal) program, do state at one point that the nominal program "represents in fact, the *operational* programme since it is the sum total of the estimated costs of the concrete projects. . . ."[18] In contrast, the "effective" program is simply a macro-economic projection.

---

[13]*Third Plan,* p. 8.

[14]*Third Plan,* p. 363. Plan magnitudes are actually larger than these figures indicate. Aside from general inflation, and even aside from particular rises in the prices of the goods or services to be purchased, project costs are commonly underestimated in Nigeria. As a consequence, at prices prevailing at the time the Third Plan was formulated, ₦32.1 billion and ₦20 billion are underestimates. This issue is discussed later in this chapter.

[15]*Third Plan,* p. 363. Also netted out in arriving at the effective program are intergovernmental transfers, but this is a minor adjustment and it can easily be and is carried out for the nominal program as well. The nominal-program figure used here embodies this adjustment.

[16]*Third Plan,* p. 363.

[17]*Third Plan,* p. 375.

[18]*Third Plan,* p. 395, emphasis added. See also the statement in Federal Republic of Nigeria, *Second National Development Plan 1970-74, Second Progress Report* (hereinafter referred to as *Second Plan, Second Progress Report*) (Lagos: Federal Ministry of Economic Development and Reconstruction, 1974), p. 19, that while macro-economic magnitudes are useful analytically, "it should be remembered that it is concrete projects which constitute

No matter how one approaches it, the Third Plan embodies an enormous expansion of investment ambitions. Comparisons with the past are complex, for there are many relevant magnitudes. Comparing investment programs, the Third Plan operational (nominal) program is more than nine times as large and the Third Plan effective program is almost six times as large as the upward-revised investment program (₦3.35 billion) for the five years of the extended Second Plan period.[19] Compared with *actual* investment during the four years of the original Second Plan period (₦2.237 billion), the Third Plan effective program is almost nine times as large and the operational (nominal) program is more than fourteen times as great.[20] These comparisons can be refined by making two adjustments: first, as the Second Plan initially spanned a four-year period while the Third encompassed five, per annum figures are preferable; second, because of rising price-levels, an adjustment for inflation is needed.[21] Actual public investment of ₦2,237 million for 1970-74 averaged ₦559 million per annum. The price level at the time of the Third Plan's final formulation was roughly 31 percent (between 28 and 34 percent) above the average price level during the Second Plan period.[22] Thus actual annual public investment during the 1970-74 period stated at the Third Plan price level averaged ₦732 million. Third Plan effective investment of ₦4,000 million per annum was approximately five and a half times as large and Third Plan operational (nominal) investment per annum of ₦6,426 million was almost nine times as large.

Finally, let us make a forward-looking comparison to supplement those just made with past magnitudes. The *Third Plan Guidelines* set a "huge" public investment target, which it considered overoptimistic and quite unlikely to be fulfilled, of ₦4.3 billion.[23] A year later, the Third Plan

---

the core of any development plan. Sectoral expenditure is the sum of expenditure on individual projects incorporated in the sector. Ultimately therefore, the progress of the Plan depends on progress made in the implementation of the hundreds of projects which constitute the Plan."

[19]For Second Plan investment magnitudes, see Tables 8 and 9. Note that the Second Plan investment figure of ₦3.35 billion is *nominal* investment.

[20]Of course, actual Second Plan investment continued during the added fifth year, and probably at a faster rate than in the first four years, so that these multiples would be smaller for the extended Second Plan period.

[21]V.P. Diejomaoh of the University of Lagos made somewhat similar adjustments in comparing total investment magnitudes (public plus private) for the Second and Third Plan periods. While his adjustment procedures were mistaken in this writer's view, and yielded quite different figures from those the approach employed here would generate, his article was interesting and perceptive. V.P. Diejomaoh, "Comparative Analysis of Second and Third Plans," (Lagos) *Daily Times*, May 8, 1975, p. 8.

[22]Calculated from Table 13.

[23]Federal Republic of Nigeria, *Guidelines for the Third National Development Plan 1975-80* (hereinafter referred to as *Third Plan Guidelines*) (Lagos: Federal Ministry of Economic Development and Reconstruction, 1973), p. 8: "But, given the fact that executive capacity continues to be a binding constraint on the growth of the economy, it is unlikely that the public sector would be able to implement such a huge investment programme."

presented an operational (nominal) investment program approximately seven and a half times as large as that of the *Guidelines* and an effective program more than four and a half times as large. This expansion was clearly indicative of the impact of the new oil prosperity.

Private investment projections were also increased sharply over Second Plan magnitudes, although not nearly so much as those for public investment. Third Plan nominal private investment was ₦12,870 million. This was truly a nominal figure, lacking the concrete meaning of nominal public investment; it did not refer to the sum of any set of projects that private firms intended to execute, but was simply the result of a disaggregated projection. The private sector "effective investment programme" was ₦10,000 million, a figure which was also simply a projection.[24] In the case of private capital formation, effective investment should be considered the more real planning figure, for it was the one generally used throughout the Third Plan, while the nominal figure was treated rather parenthetically.[25]

Effective private investment projected in the Third Plan (₦10 billion) was 3.2 times as great as the actual private investment of ₦3.1 billion during the Second Plan period 1970-74. On a per-annum basis adjusted for price-level changes, it was slightly less than double.[26] In the "forward-looking" comparison, it was 50 percent greater than the ₦6.7 billion target in the *Third Plan Guidelines.*[27]

The expansion set forth for private investment in the Third Plan was, therefore, much more restricted than that for public investment. The private investment multiples of 3.2, 2.0, and 1.5 described in the preceding paragraph contrast with parallel multiples for operational (nominal) *public* investment of approximately 14.0, 9.0, and 7.5.[28] The expansion of public investment targets was almost five times as great.[29]

2. In a second affluence-induced modification in development orientation, the Third Plan laid out a greatly enhanced relative role for public investment. In the earlier conception of the Third Plan, the private sector was to be the major source of capital formation. Private investment was

[24]*Third Plan,* p. 358 for both nominal and effective private investment.

[25]Businessmen considered both investment projections overoptimistic. "According to the Commissioner [of Economic Development and Reconstruction], the reaction from sections of the private sector to these figures was that of cynicism." (Lagos) *Daily Times,* December 7, 1974, p. 25.

[26]On a per annum basis, actual private investment during 1970-74 averaged ₦775 million; adjusted to the Third Plan price level this amounts to ₦1,015 million. Third Plan effective private investment of ₦2 billion per annum was slightly less than double.

[27]*Third Plan Guidelines,* p. 8. Making the same comparisons for *nominal* private investment projected in the Third Plan, the multiples were 4.2 (instead of 3.2), 2.5 (instead of 2.0), and 1.9 (instead of 1.5).

[28]For effective public investment, the multiples were approximately 9.0, 5.5, and 4.5.

[29]Accompanying the high investment targets were high projected growth rates in real gross domestic product for the Plan period: 9 percent per annum in the aggregate and 6.5 percent per annum on a per capita basis. *Third Plan,* p. 27.

projected at ₦6.4 billion.[30] This private investment ratio, in excess of 60 percent, exceeded the private investment proportion, whether projected or actual, of the Second Plan period. Projected Second Plan investment was 51 percent private and 49 percent public. Actual Second Plan investment (1970-74) was 58.4 percent private and 41.6 percent public.[31] However, the originally projected growth in the Third Plan private investment proportion was swamped by the exuberant expansion of planned public investment. Public capital formation in the final formulation of the Third Plan amounted to two-thirds of the total.

3. The oil affluence also afforded increased substance and attainability to the long-standing government intention to share with foreign investors in the ownership of nationally important projects. Stress on government and indigenous private partnership with foreign investors had gradually increased. Statements in the Second Plan about government ownership had been firmer and more insistent than pre-Civil War declarations.[32] Then, with the availability of ample oil funds, progress in government negotiations with foreign firms became more definite and the prospects of government participation on a wide scale became more real. The enterprises with shared ownership were generally to operate as any other profit-oriented private enterprises, and important officials conceived of increasing government participation in ownership as a process of developing "state capitalism."

4. Finally, greater income permitted a more promising resumption of emphasis on welfare. ". . . serious effort has been made to emphasize those sectors which directly affect the welfare of the ordinary citizen. These include housing, water supplies, health facilities, education, rural electrification and community development. The aim is that by the end of the Plan period every Nigerian should experience a definite improvement in his overall welfare."[33] Plan chapters on health, social development, water, sewerage, housing, town and country planning, community development, and education projected substantial program expansions in all these areas. ". . . one of the most far-reaching policy decisions in the Plan is . . . the introduction of free universal and compulsory primary education. . . ."[34] The broad welfare-oriented objectives of the Second Plan—including the development of "a just egalitarian society" and of "a land of

---

[30]*Third Plan Guidelines,* p. 8.

[31]*Third Plan,* p. 10.

[32]*Second Plan,* p. 289. "Government will not embark on indiscriminate nationalisation of existing or future enterprises in the country. Where any nationalisation is deemed necessary . . . compensation arrangements will be made in accordance with internationally accepted norms of equity and fair play."

[33]*Third Plan,* p. 8. See also pp. 27, 29, and passim.

[34]Primary education was to be free throughout Nigeria from September 1976 and was to be compulsory from September 1979. More broadly, government embraced a commitment to "the creation of an educational system capable of ensuring that every citizen is given full opportunity to develop his intellectual and working capabilities for his own benefit and that

bright and full opportunity for all citizens"—were readopted and were explicitly interpreted as requiring a "more even distribution of income."[35] Geographical and rural-urban income disparities were also to be narrowed.[36] Another strongly stated goal was the reduction of unemployment.[37]

The economic development orientation declared at the final-quarter-century mark, then, was one of nurture-capitalism without a pronounced leaning toward either nationalism or internationalism. This Third Plan nurture-capitalism was characterized by a highly ambitious program of accelerated development, an enhanced government investment-role with an element of state capitalism, and a concern for mass welfare, particularly for the reduction of income disparities and also of unemployment. We can call this orientation one of nurture-capitalism with state capitalist, welfare, and accelerated-development tendencies.

Probable Performance

The period of affluence produced an ambitious development plan. As a first step in assessing probable performance, we examine the nature of the planning process.

The government had every intention of constructing the Third Plan more realistically, thoroughly, and solidly than had been the practice in the past. "This is the first Plan in Nigeria to be prepared by a professional planning body—the Central Planning Office of the Federal Ministry of Economic Development and Reconstruction. The creation of this office in 1971 followed a realisation that the planning exercise had become in-

---

of his community. In this pursuit, the Educational Programme for this Plan period will seek in a very radical way to transform the educational scene of this country . . ." *Third Plan*, pp. 243, 244.

[35]*Third Plan*, p. 27. The Plan also states: "The main concern of policy will be the need to effect a more equitable distribution of income and to control inflation. . . . a major attempt will be made, beginning with the Third Plan period, to translate economic growth into meaningful development through income redistribution" (p. 31). Welfare and income redistribution measures were linked. "With respect to income distribution the Plan strategy adopted is for the public sector to provide subsidised facilities for the poorer sections of the population, including electrification, water, supplies, health services, co-operatives and community development programmes in the rural areas and housing in the urban areas for the low income groups. These programmes will directly raise the level of living of the poorer classes and constitute a more practical means of income redistribution than other more direct measures." *Third Plan*, p. 29. See also p. 27: "The primary objective of economic planning in Nigeria is to achieve a rapid increase in the standard of living of the average Nigerian . . . An important objective . . . is to spread the benefits of economic development so that the average Nigerian would experience a marked improvement in his standard of living."

[36]*Third Plan*, p. 28. See also *Third Plan Guidelines*, p. 34.

[37]See, e.g., *Third Plan*, pp. 27, 29, 369ff.

creasingly technical and could no longer be left to general administrators who are more concerned with broad matters of policy. . . . The Central Planning Office has expanded rapidly and now has an establishment of about 140 professionals. It is expected that this expansion and professionalism of the planning staff will be increasingly reflected in the quality of the plans formulated by the government of Nigeria."[38] Planners consulted with numerous organizations in the private sector. Federal and State officials who were to participate in plan formulation were enrolled in an intensive course. Consultants were engaged to study a number of strategic sectors, including agriculture, industry, health, education, and transport, and to assist in articulating projects. The Third Plan was postponed a year partially to allow more thorough preparation.[39]

The sudden surge of oil revenues, however, swamped the judgment of those responsible for the Plan. The diligent preparations and carefully considered procedures were brushed aside. There ensued a process that can best be described as *euphoric planning*.

Projects involving huge sums were added hastily, with little investigation or appraisal. Issues of project interrelation and coordination were ignored in the belief that rapid economic growth would ensure the utility of whatever was undertaken. Economic reasoning gave way before economic enthusiasm.[40] Problems of executive capacity (the ability to carry out the Plan) were ignored during the euphoria.[41] The outcome of the euphoric planning process was an unrealistic plan.

The runaway nature of the planning process inevitably aroused some uneasiness. The distinction between nominal and effective investment programs was a manifestation of this concern, but it constituted only a superficial approach to the problem. The use of the effective investment figure could have the cosmetic effect of diminishing the apparent degree of subsequent plan underfulfillment, but it did not come to grips with the inability of the public agencies to carry out the specified investments. The economic planners attempted to salvage some degree of real planning by providing for subsequent annual planning, but this proposal was finally rejected, probably because of opposition by the Ministry of Finance, which would have had its power curtailed. Other efforts were made to strengthen the role of the Ministry of Economic Development and Reconstruction, but the impact of these was marginal.[42]

---

[38]*Third Plan*, p. 7.

[39]*Third Plan*, p. 7.

[40]One example: "Table 6.4 shows a large gap between supply and demand for various crops during the Plan period. Consequently high growth rates have been projected for the output of various agricultural commodities . . ." *Third Plan*, p. 350.

[41]*Third Plan Guidelines*, p. 8.

[42]For example, if any public agency wished to add new projects outside the already enormous Plan, it was required that such proposals should be "submitted to, and discussed with the Ministry of Economic Development." *Third Plan*, p. 396.

Thus, although plan formulation for the Third Plan began more solidly than for past plans, the new oil prosperity engendered euphoric planning. The result was the astonishing enlargement of plan targets already described.[43] This brings us to the first of several probable divergences between stated and actual economic development orientations.

1. Government will not come close to reaching its ambitious public investment targets, but the costs of aiming so unrealistically high will be substantial. The long-standing deficiencies of "executive capacity" are too great. Decisions at all stages of project preparation (e.g., engaging consultants, review and approval or modification of proposals by consultants, suppliers, contractors, etc., negotiations on major and minor terms of proposed contracts) are made and carried out in a slow, halting, intermittent way that is both time-consuming and inexpert enough to allow poor choices to be made. Land-acquisition difficulties are formidable; suitable arrangements with indigenous firms are difficult to make; and there are many other early-stage delays: "most delays in project implementation occur even before a project reaches the stage of contract award."[44] Once contracts are negotiated, the government bureaucracy tends to be negligent, cumbrous, and even impeditive, interposing unnecessary obstacles, failing to provide agreed-upon assistance and facilities, hindering through lack of cooperation or antagonism between government agencies, etc. Then there are all the other, nongovernmental difficulties in the economic environment delineated later in Chapter 6. In the face of such executive-capacity problems, real public investment cannot be raised to a level almost nine times (for effective investment, 5.5 times) the rate achieved during the original Second Plan period.

Prediction of plan fulfillment is highly speculative and should no doubt be avoided between the preserving covers of a book, but we will be foolhardy. Our forecast refers to real fulfillment rather than investment expenditures, for project costs will almost surely increase.[45] Inflation of construction and capital-goods costs can be expected to continue. Infla-

---

[43]The criticisms made here of the magnitude of the Third Plan should *not* be construed as criticisms of an ambitious approach to investment. There is great merit, I believe, in striving to attain the maximum feasible rate of investment. As a matter of fact, this writer's basic criticism of the First Plan was for unconcern on this score; "Nigeria's First National Economic Plan, 1962-68: An Appraisal," *Nigerian Journal of Economic and Social Studies* V:2 (July 1963): 221-236. The writer's more general explanation of this approach is presented in "The Role of Capital Accumulation in Economic Development," *Journal of Development Studies* 5:1 (October 1968): 39-43. The Third Plan, however, goes far beyond any feasible investment target.

[44]*Third Plan*, p. 396.

[45]The real degree of plan fulfillment is necessarily an imprecise concept. Suppose only projects contained in the plan are carried out and also that we knew the final cost of each of those projects. Then an approximation of the degree of plan fulfillment would be a weighted average of the proportion of actual expenditures (A) to expenditures finally required (R) for each project, i.e., of $A_1/R_1, A_2/R_2 \ldots A_n/R_n$. (Actually, this would not fully reflect the effect of *rising* prices.) A simpler approximation would be the sum of actual *expenditures* as a proportion of the sum of required final expenditures, *i.e.*, $\Sigma A/\Sigma R$.

tion aside, project costs in Nigeria are commonly sharply underestimated because of either inadequacies in the original costing of projects or conceptual inadequacies that require subsequent changes in project scope. "It happens fairly frequently, that the estimated cost of a project as indicated in the Plan documents differs from the costing obtained at the stage of contract award."[46]

We will set forth probable maximum and minimum levels of plan fulfillment before hazarding a most-probable estimate. Our maximum plausible estimate is that government will fully carry out the ₦20 billion effective investment program. This amounts to 62.5 percent of the ₦32 billion operational program set forth in the Third Plan. Our minimum plausible estimate is that government will achieve the ₦4.3 billion target set forth in the *Third Plan Guidelines*. At the Third Plan price level, this amounts to ₦5.4 billion or 16.9 percent of the Third Plan operational target.[47]

Our most probable estimate must be placed somewhere within the plausible range, 16.9 to 62.5 percent. The lowest part of the plausible range, or even a figure below it, is suggested by the facts that the *Third Plan Guidelines* considered its ₦4.3 billion target overoptimistic, and that Nigerian public investment plans have always substantially exceeded subsequent performance. Nothing fundamental changed in the government apparatus or the economy after the *Guidelines* were established except for the increase in oil revenues, so it would seem that the same problems that caused skepticism about the *Guidelines* target would still apply.

On the other hand, a higher most-probable estimate is suggested by government efforts to ease or circumvent executive-capacity problems in order to raise the actual rate of investment. Many procedures were relaxed to gain time.[48] Competitive tendering (bidding) on construction and other contracts was to be dropped or moderated on a large proportion, by value, of the contracts, "particularly for implementing high priority projects over a limited period of time."[49] Some contract awards were to dispense with prior appraisal of project design, allowing "the design and construction stages [to] proceed simultaneously,"[50] both done by the same firm. Other tendering and monitoring safeguards were also to be eased to accelerate implementation. Review of proposed contracts was to be hastened; if a concerned ministry "fails, within four weeks, to react to a memorandum [on a capital project] sent for clearance, it will be pre-

---

[46]*Third Plan*, p. 395.

[47]This may seem overly ample for a minimum figure because it allows neither for underexpenditure, which the *Guidelines* clearly expected and which has occurred in all Nigerian plans, nor for increases in project costs. However, investment-facilitating considerations to be discussed shortly appear to make this a safe minimum.

[48]*Third Plan*, pp. 395-400.

[49]*Third Plan*, p. 399.

[50]*Third Plan*, p. 399.

sumed that the ministry has no comment to offer" and the contract-award procedure would continue.[51] Also to be relaxed were intended intragovernment procedures for monitoring the validity of project-cost increases submitted by implementing government agencies, and for subjecting to examination the introduction of proposed new projects not included in the Plan.

Other methods of increasing executive capacity were also adopted. In a move, already mentioned, to heighten internal incentives and pressures, public agencies and their officials were put on notice that they would be judged primarily by their plan-implementation ratios. Cumbrous procedures for land acquisition were simplified. The assistance of foreign governments was to be invoked in negotiating contracts with foreign construction companies. Restrictions on the use of foreign personnel were to be moderated.[52] Reliance on foreign investors was to be increased, particularly in partnership with Nigerian governments in large industrial ventures.

Weighing all the foregoing considerations, we conclude that actual fulfillment of the operational public investment plan will be in the lower part of the plausible range. Our most-probable estimate is 25 percent.[53] This is 40 percent of the effective program. It entails an annual rate of investment, adjusted for price-level changes, two to three times that achieved during 1970-74[54] and 1.5 times the target that the *Third Plan Guidelines* considered overoptimistic. To some degree the rate of plan fulfillment will depend on the price that Nigeria is willing to pay for acceleration. A higher fulfillment rate can be achieved, at a cost, by a greater relaxation of the procedures intended to ensure probity and effectiveness. Even 25 percent fulfillment can be attained only at considerable cost.[55]

We make no parallel attempt to forecast plan fulfillment in the private sector. There is strong reason to believe that the fulfillment ratio will be much higher.

[51]*Third Plan*, p. 397.

[52]*Third Plan*, pp. 400-401.

[53]The reader is reminded that we refer to real fulfillment, after allowing for increases in project costs caused not only by inflation, but also by initial underestimation of project costs resulting from inadequate costing and inadequate conceptions of the projects.

[54]The multiple is inexact because one cannot say precisely what the cost (in 1975 prices) would be of 25 percent fulfillment of the operational investment program of N32 billion. If there were *no* project cost increases caused by inadequate costing or conceptions of projects, the cost would be N8 billion and 25 percent fulfillment would entail a real investment rate 2.2 times that achieved from 1970 to 1974. If, however, inadequate project-costing and project conceptions raised the cost (in 1975 prices) of the operational investment program by one-fourth to N40 billion, then 25 percent fulfillment would require a real investment rate 2.75 times that achieved from 1970 to 1974.

[55]The degree of plan fulfillment will be difficult to ascertain, so a suggestion may be in order regarding a method of approximating it. The *Third Plan* presents estimates of material inputs required for public-sector plan implementation (p. 403). These are rough and, since

The consequences of euphoric planning extend beyond the simple fact that planned projects will go unimplemented. If that were the only effect and if actual investment were to be essentially the same as under a more realistic plan, the euphoria would have only public-relations and political costs. However, several substantial economic costs can also be expected.

First, rational allocation of investment resources, i.e., selection of those projects which promise the greatest national benefit, will suffer. The combination of an unrealizably large program and strong pressure on government agencies to maximize plan-fulfillment ratios cripples the planning process as a reasoned consideration of national priorities. Ease of implementation will become the major criterion determining just which projects materialize out of the many slated for each agency. Plan fulfillment will be heavily tilted toward roads and other kinds of construction that are relatively easy to contract out to foreign firms. Imports of expensive equipment such as locomotives may also proceed beyond the capacity of the importing organizations to make effective use of the goods. As the degree of plan fulfillment has been judged in Nigeria primarily by the ratio of actual expenditures to planned, agencies will be drawn to those projects that entail the largest outlays. Throughout the bureaucracy, implementability and fulfillment ratios will subordinate national utility.

The planners, mindful of potential allocation problems, established procedures that could have forestalled many of the problems under ordinary circumstances. Plan distortion, i.e., relative overexpenditure on low priority projects and underexpenditure on high, had been a matter of long-standing concern.[56] Thus, the Third Plan declared that "great importance will be attached to the maintenance of Plan discipline. No departures from the approved Plan without due authorisation as specified in the Plan will be allowed. For this purpose appropriate sanctions have been devised and will be applied to any agency which is found guilty of Plan distortion."[57] Control was to be maintained by requiring the approval of the Ministry of Economic Development and Reconstruction for changes in project scope and requiring appraisal by that Ministry before proposals for projects outside the Plan were submitted to the Supreme Military Council.[58] However, the ability of these control measures to ensure that investment resources would be directed to the highest utility projects was undermined by the lengthy list of projects within the Plan that each government agency could choose from.

Second, the combination of large plan and pressure to implement will also cripple the coordination of projects, all inevitably interrelated, car-

---

project scope is often underestimated in Nigerian plans, they are probably understated. Nevertheless ratios of materials used (domestic production plus imports) to materials projected as required might serve as an index of fulfillment.

[56]See Chapter 2, at footnotes 38, 39.

[57]See *Third Plan*, p. 8; also p. 402.

[58]*Third Plan*, pp. 395-396.

ried out by different government agencies. There was less motivation than ever to induce project coordination between the various ministries, corporations, and other government agencies, which have generally tended to regard themselves as separate and even antagonistic organizations and have had a poor record in cooperating with one another for the national benefit. Each agency will tend to proceed on the basis of implementability, neglecting interrelations with undertakings of other agencies. This will turn out to be mutually impeditive, for implementation by one agency will hinge partially upon other-agency investments. For example, virtually all Third Plan projects will be impeded by extreme and continuing port congestion, caused partially by Port Authority delays in implementing previous port-construction projects. Furthermore, in the absence of careful coordination of projects, the utility of those investments that are carried out will be undermined.

Third and fourth, the pressure to implement will encourage waste and corruption. The levels will depend on the degree to which affluence and haste induce a relaxation of government vigilance and standards of efficiency. Large construction contracts can be let relatively easily if government sufficiently slackens its concerns about the benefit-cost ratio, the suitability, the quality, and the cost of the job done.[59] Expensive equipment can also be imported relatively easily under similar conditions, including abated concern about effective use and maintenance of the equipment by the importing agency. It is a simple matter to negotiate partnership agreements with foreign investors if concern about the terms of the agreement and about subsequent performance of the joint enterprise is sufficiently tempered.[60] It is a matter of willingness to trade money for time. All investment-accelerating abatements of procedural safeguards and vigilance allow further leeway for both inefficiency and corruption.

Despite Nigeria's oil affluence these costs are consequential; the country cannot afford to squander its revenues. They will not be unlimited and cannot be expected over the long run to provide sufficient saving to cover Nigeria's investment needs. Third Plan savings during the Plan period are

[59]This is recognized by the planners. For example, "the absence of competition may result in higher contract prices. These limitations may be outweighed in certain cases by the savings in time." See also, "This method of awarding ['design and build'] contracts can reduce implementation time considerably since the design and construction stages may proceed simultaneously. For example, final engineering in respect of a major road project may take from 12 to 24 months. This period . . . can be reduced or almost eliminated if a 'design and build' strategy were adopted. Project implementation can be further accelerated by 12 to 18 months through the elimination of lengthy tender procedures. The main disadvantage of this approach, is that it tends to tempt contractors to take the line of least resistance even when such an action compromises the standard and quality specified for the job." *Third Plan*, p. 399.

[60]See, e.g., Schatz, "Crude Private Neo-Imperialism: A New Pattern in Africa," *Journal of Modern African Studies* 7:4 (December 1969): 677-688.

expected to be more than sufficient to sustain planned investment. Nevertheless, the Plan cautions: "It should be noted, however, that this surplus of investible funds declines steadily over the Plan period as the economy rapidly expands its absorptive capacity. . . . This means that the resource surplus may not be permanent and it is important to ensure that resources are used efficiently for purposes which would contribute to long term growth."[61] The Plan also projects a continual accumulation of foreign exchange reserves, but again cautions: "it is important to note that the tendency of the economy to build up reserves declines steadily throughout the Plan period."[62] The costs of euphoric planning must be a matter of serious concern.

2. A second divergence to be expected between stated and actual economic development orientations relates to the projected reversal in relative importance of public and private investment, with public investment surging from two-fifths to two-thirds of the total.[63] If our investment predictions are correct, the shift in investment dominance will not materialize. A similar abortion occurred in the preceding decade of a planned reversal of investment proportions. The First National Development Plan, 1962-68, targeted public investment at two-thirds of the total, but the actual public investment proportion for the four years, 1962/63-1965/66, was 36.7 percent.[64] Whatever the Third Plan share of public investment turns out to be, a significant portion will be carried out in association with foreign investors in joint undertakings run as private firms.

3. The announced intention of reducing income and wealth disparities will in all likelihood be frustrated. This probable divergence between stated and actual development orientations (and also other divergences in unemployment and corruption to be discussed shortly) are to be attributed not to euphoric planning, but to the basic nature of nurture-capitalism, which does not appear capable in Nigerian society of bringing about the desired changes.

[61]*Third Plan*, p. 44.

[62]*Third Plan*, p. 45. The Plan's assumptions regarding the petroleum sector were more sanguine than performance as the Third Plan got under way. While predicted oil exports were to rise steadily from ₦6,458 million in 1974-75 to ₦10,633 million in 1979-80, actual oil revenues declined sharply over a six-month span at the transition from the Second Plan to the Third and in May 1975 were only about two-thirds the rate expected for 1975-76 and about 45 percent of that projected for 1979-80. If oil revenues were to continue at the May 1975 rate, and if the effective (i.e., the smaller) investment program were implemented, balance-of-payments deficits would emerge in 1977-78 and savings deficits (i.e., national savings below projected investment) would emerge by 1979-80, and the shortfalls would increase thereafter. There is strong reason to believe that the sharp decline in receipts from oil is temporary, but the figures do point up the uncertainty of the oil revenues.

[63]This refers to the smaller "effective" public investment program.

[64]Edwin R. Dean, *Plan Implementation in Nigeria, 1962-66* (Ibadan: Oxford University Press, 1972), pp. 206-208. The public investment target was 67.1 percent or 63 percent according to two different sets of calculations in the Plan.

On the one hand, income and wealth disparities will be reduced by the planned extension of education, and by programs for water supplies, health facilities, rural electrification, and other amenities and welfare measures mentioned in the preceding section of this chapter. On the other hand, in a country where increases in income, including raises not only in wages but also in the producer prices of export crops, have been determined largely by government, there is strong reason to expect that the rural population will continue to fall still further behind the more politically articulate and effective urban dwellers. In particular, the well-placed elite, who purchased shares of stock paying dividends of 50 percent and more in foreign-owned companies as a result of the indigenization program, who have other connections with affluent foreign firms, and who have strategic positions in the Nigerian polity and economy, can be expected to forge further ahead. Incomes derived from corruption may grow. Most important, in the face of the powerful income-differentiating tendencies in Nigeria's early-capitalist society, little direct income policy was even proposed. The Third Plan proposed only the gathering of data and the formation of an Incomes Analysis Unit.[65]

4. Economic growth and the expansion of education will absorb some of the additions to the labor force. However, with the increased turnout of school leavers (graduates) to be expected from free and expanded primary and secondary education, with the youngish age distribution of the population and the continuing rapid population growth to be expected, with the probable continuing exodus of rural youth in response to higher incomes aand more attractive possibilities in the cities, with the evidently increasing distaste for life as a peasant farmer, the prospects are that urban unemployment will increase. The dismaying 78 percent unemployment rate among school leavers in Western Nigeria one year after graduation has already been cited.[66] The Nigerian National Council for Adult Education, in its fourth annual conference, predicted unemployment of approximately one million primary-school leavers in 1980 "when the first prod-

---

[65]"Unfortunately, Nigeria has never had an articulate and deliberate incomes policy." To deal with this, government appointed a National Accounts Study Team late in 1973 which expected to provide, inter alia, data on income distribution. "Furthermore, an Incomes Analysis Unit will be established . . . to analyse on a regular basis statistical information . . . on the basis of which it will make recommendations to the public and private sectors on permissible adjustments in salaries and wages . . . [A] Pay Research Unit [is] to be set up for the public services . . . The work of these two organisations should contribute to the formulation of an operational incomes policy during the Plan period." Third Plan, p. 33.

Income distribution will surely be a major focus of tension and discord. As Green has correctly said: "A general verbal commitment to a more equitable income distribution that is not seriously supported by policy probably soon becomes worse than nothing . . ." Reginald H. Green, "The Role of the State as an Agent of Economic and Social Development in the Least Developed Countries," Journal of Development Planning 6 (1974): 24.

[66]Chapter 2, Table 12.

ucts of the Universal Primary Education scheme (UPE) complete their term."[67]

5. At least until the coup of July 29, 1975, it appeared likely that accumulation of wealth and income through corrupt practices would increase in absolute and perhaps also in relative dimensions. Then the new government, in its early phase at any rate, attacked the problem energetically. Nevertheless, the multiplication of government expenditures will enhance the absolute amounts from which a corrupt tithe can be deducted. The emphasis on implementation, with its relaxation of controls over tendering, contracting, and other spending procedures, will enhance the opportunities for a take relatively as well as absolutely. The surge in oil wealth and the resultant Udoji wage increases unleashed a veritable frenzy of acquisition. The prospects for expunging corruption were discouraging until the coup and unclear thereafter.

In sum, the actual development orientation can be expected to diverge in a number of respects from what has been stated. It appears that the welfare and idealistic elements—income and wealth redistribution, alleviation of unemployment, and possibly the elimination of corruption—will atrophy, that the public investment role will not expand significantly, and that the acceleration of development will fall far short of what is envisaged. Thus, the orientation's modifying tendencies, described in the previous section, will not materialize; the actual orientation will be, simply, nurture-capitalism.

Reliance upon Indigenous Business

Nigeria's development orientation at the final-quarter-century mark clearly depended heavily on the expected dynamism of the private sector. A capitalist ethos was reinforced by the profit-seeking nature of a significant portion of public investment. Directly productive undertakings established in partnership with foreign interests, and heavily dependent upon the expertise and direction of the foreign investor, were to be run as private firms. Similarly, public utilities were instructed to operate on a profit-seeking basis.

Looking beyond the Third Plan itself, one can be confident that reliance upon private enterprise will be reinforced by government economic performance that will be disappointing when compared with the Plan. A drastic shortfall in public-sector plan fulfillment (even if obscured by misleading financial figures) will contrast with a much better relative investment performance by the private sector. Problems in government investments can be expected to surface because of poor allocation and lack of

---

[67]The conference recommended that "UPE products, should on graduation, be enlisted in a programme of National Youth Service; should be accommodated in camps and subjected to a form of strict discipline . . ." Reported in the (Lagos) *Daily Times,* July 22, 1975, p. 11.

coordination between government agencies. Poor quality jobs, sanctioned because of haste and possibly because of corruption, will be seen as wasteful. Possibly massive corruption will be exposed. All these will tend to further a disposition toward reliance on private enterprise.

Although substantial dependence on foreign corporations will necessarily continue, antagonism toward such reliance is powerful. This was expressed, for example, in the *Second Plan:* "Experience has shown through history, that political independence without economic independence is but an empty shell. . . . the interests of foreign private investors in the Nigerian economy cannot be expected to coincide at all times and in every respect with national aspirations . . . A truly independent nation cannot allow its objectives and priorities to be distorted or frustrated by the manipulation of powerful foreign investors."[68] The intensity of the demands by Nigerian businessmen for highly favorable treatment can be expected to continue unabated and even to increase. For example, despite the frequently poor performance of indigenous contractors, government reserved all contracts below ₦200,000 for them and gave them a 5 percent preference on all others. Nonetheless, a spokesman of the Nigerian Chamber of Indigenous Contractors charged that government was deliberately destroying their morale and "aiding their exit from business." The organization demanded as compensation for rising costs a 60 percent increase in government payments retroactive for a year and a half on all government contracts.[69] As the indigenous business class grows in numbers and wealth, its ability to assert such claims becomes more potent. The strength of this class is further reinforced by continuing entry of new members from the governing groups. These factors, particularly in a climate of new-country nationalism, assure an important place for indigenous business in the development of the economy.

Nigeria's inclination to rely on indigenous business has been further buttressed by, as well as reflected in, a wide range of extant and proposed programs to assist indigenous investors. Such programs have been set up in increasing number since 1949. Although many were little, or nothing, more than paper projects, the robustness of the business-assistance approach has grown. The Third Plan continued the trend. Measures to aid indigenous business were sprinkled throughout the Plan, with some emphasis on industrial production and employment. "It is . . . government policy to encourage private investment in these areas [i.e., small-scale industrial production, particularly in sectors with the highest growth targets] through the provision of a wider range of industrial incentives."[70]

---

[68]*Second Plan,* p. 289.

[69](Lagos) *Daily Times,* May 15, 1975, p. 2. The increase was to be retroactive to January 1, 1974. In July 1975 the ₦200,000 cut-off figure was raised to ₦300,000; all contracts up to the higher figure were thereafter reserved exclusively for indigenous contractors: (Lagos) *Daily Times,* July 28, 1975, p. 3.

[70]*Third Plan,* p. 351.

Small indigenous enterprises[71] hopefully might, in turn, "provide the main opportunity for the expansion of employment."[72]

Among Nigeria's earliest and longest-standing programs for indigenous business were those affording or facilitating credit,[73] an approach carried over into the Third Plan period. At the state level, government credit institutions such as the Industries Credit Schemes[74] were to be strengthened by financial assistance from the Federal Government;[75] on the Federal level, indigenous industrial enterprises were to receive loans from a department of the Nigerian Industrial Development Bank especially set up for this purpose[76] or from the Nigerian Bank for Commerce and Industry, while primary product-processing enterprises were to receive loans from the Nigerian Agricultural Bank;[77] in the private sector, government established commercial bank guidelines mandating provision of more short-term loan funds for indigenous business on easier terms.[78] In general, credit was to be available for indigenous enterprises with commercially viable projects in virtually any field of activity.[79] A strengthened network of training programs was proposed, designed to assist indigenous firms with training at every level: for the entrepreneur himself, for his managerial staff, for supervisors, and for his labor force. Nigerian enterprises were also to be offered advice on their training needs and help in establishing their own programs. A battery of agencies was to provide assistance: Industrial Development Centres already in existence or to be established during the Third Plan period; Trade Centres; Vocational Improvement Centres; a National Apprenticeship Scheme; an Industrial Training Fund; the Manpower Board which, among its other duties, was to coordinate a Comprehensive Training and Retraining Programme; the Nigerian Council for Management Education and Training, and other bodies.[80]

---

[71]"Thousands of small-scale enterprises each of which does not usually employ many persons. . . . wood and metal works; weaving, pottery, and ceramics; retail trade and dressmaking; mechanic and repair workshops; brick and blockmaking, etc." *Third Plan*, pp. 382-383.

[72]Also, "From the employment point of view, the attraction of small-scale enterprises lies in their high-employment potential." *Third Plan*, pp. 382-383.

[73]The development of these programs is discussed in Chapter 12.

[74]*Third Plan*, p. 153.

[75]*Third Plan*, p. 383.

[76]The N.I.D.B. was to pay much more careful attention to indigenous business needs and was alloted a substantial appropriation for this purpose. The Bank was to reduce the degree of concentration on foreign-owned projects and "make more meaningful investments in various industries controlled by Nigerians or with at least 55 percent Nigerian ownership." *Second Plan*, pp. 231-232, 293.

[77]E.g., *Third Plan*, pp. 124, 125.

[78]*Third Plan*, p. 186.

[79]Besides references already cited, see, e.g., *Third Plan*, p. 351, and *Second Plan*, pp. 146, 231-233, 293.

[80]*Third Plan*, pp. 382-383, 390-393, and passim. See also *Second Plan*, pp. 146, 236.

Government has undertaken to provide industrial extension and consultancy services to indigenous business on the design and quality of products, on the determination of specific equipment needs, on the purchase and installation of equipment, and on other matters. The Federal Institute of Industrial Research, which had been instructed to pay particular attention to "the design of products for small-scale industry,"[81] was to be expanded during the Third Plan period.[82] A Centre for Management Development, an Indigenous Business Advisory Unit, and the Industrial Development Centres had responsibilities in this sphere. Indigenous enterprises were to be aided in other ways: industrial estates and layouts,[83] commercial estates,[84] the establishment of more effective machinery for regular and meaningful business-government consultation, export duties on raw materials to promote domestic processing, trade fairs to promote domestic and foreign markets for indigenously produced goods, provision of special storage, processing, and distribution facilities, purchase preference programs favoring domestic producers and contractors.[85] Other provisions for indigenous business are mentioned throughout the Plan; indigenous business occupies a fundamental place in the country's development orientation. "The emerging entrepreneurial group in the country is dynamic and capable of exploiting the [great] potential in both the domestic and world markets. . . . and it is government's determination to ensure that these potentials are [realized]."[86]

The role of Nigerian private enterprise is strengthened not only by business-assistance programs but also by indigenization. Indigenization in the private sector is a policy of extending Nigerian ownership and control by government fiat or pressure.[87] Government leverage is employed either to exclude or to evict foreign concerns from certain fields of economic activity or to require direct sale of partial or complete ownership of existing foreign firms.

In Nigeria the policy has a history going back to 1949, when the objective of "maximum participation by Nigerians themselves" in the trade and industry of the country was first enunciated.[88] Indigenization only

---

[81]*Second Plan*, p. 146.

[82]Third Plan, pp. 351, 383, 390-391. See also *Second Plan*, pp. 145-146.

[83]"The Federal Government will finance the creation of a model industrial estate in each state of the Federation. All the states have also submitted ambitious plans for the development of industrial estates." *Third Plan*, p. 153.

[84]"Preferences would be given to Nigerian operators in allocating space in these urban commercial estates." *Second Plan*, p. 233.

[85]*Third Plan*, pp. 111, 123, 124, 128, 145, 151-152, 153, 390-391.

[86]*Third Plan*, pp. 382-383, 390-393, and passim. See also *Second Plan*, pp. 146, 236.

[87]"Indigenisation should be seen as an ongoing process of acquiring increased Nigerian involvement in the ownership, control and management of productive enterprises at all levels." S. O. Asabia, "The Meaning of Indigenisation," Remarks prepared for a Seminar on The Impact of Indigenisation on the Nigerian Economy, October 29, 1974, p. 1. Mr. Asabia was Deputy Governor of the Central Bank of Nigeria and Chairman of the Capital Issues Commission, which was deeply involved in implementing the Indigenization Decree.

[88]See Chapter 1, under "Economic Development Orientations."

gradually picked up momentum, mainly in the distributive sector and primarily through informal government pressures, but a major move was made with the Nigerian Enterprises Promotion Decree (the Indigenization Decree) of February 1972 with an implementation deadline of April 1974.[89]

The decree established two categories of firms. Schedule I in its final form listed twenty-six activities, mainly in small-scale industry, services, and retail trade, that were reserved exclusively for Nigerian ownership after April 1, 1974.[90] Existing foreign-owned firms were required either to sell out to Nigerian buyers or to liquidate. Schedule II consisted of another set of twenty-seven economic activities that were typically carried out on a larger scale than those listed under Schedule I or were technologically or organizationally more complex.[91] In these fields, most foreign-owned concerns were required to sell 40 percent of the equity capital to Nigerian interests. For small firms, however, with total equity capital below ₦400,000 and annual turnover below ₦1 million, a complete transfer of ownership to Nigerian hands was required, just as for Schedule I firms.

Substantial categories of private economic activity were not covered by the Indigenization Decree. Some types of enterprises transferred partial ownership to government.[92] Others had not been subjected to indigenization at all. The latter group, including the manufacturing of such items as motor tires, carpets, textiles, and blankets, encompassed more than half of the country's manufacturing activity in terms of value-added.[93] There was little doubt, however, that indigenization would ultimately go further.

The transfer of ownership to Nigerians did not start from scratch, for the Nigerian stake was already substantial. It was estimated that Nigerian

[89]*Nigerian Enterprises Promotion Decree 1972* (Lagos: Nigerian Enterprises Promotion Board, December 1973).

[90]Small-scale industrial activities included the manufacturing of cement blocks, bricks, and ordinary tile, of candles, jewelry and related articles, singlets, and ordinary garments. Also included were bakeries, rice-milling, tire-retreading, production of alcoholic beverages, and assembly of radios and record players. Services included hairdressing, laundering and drycleaning, municipal bus services, advertising and public relations, lotteries and pools, casinos, newspaper publishing, and radio and television broadcasting. *Third Plan*, p. 17. Olu Akinkugbe, "Nigerian Enterprises Promotion Decree and Its Implementation," in Nigerian Economic Society, *Nigeria's Indigenisation Policy: Proceedings of the November 1974 Symposium Organized by the Nigerian Economic Society* (Ibadan: Nigerian Economic Society, 1975), pp. 38-39.

[91]Schedule II included industrial activities such as the manufacture of soaps and detergents, beer-brewing, paper conversion, and fish and shrimp trawling and processing, service activities such as road haulage and clearing and forwarding agencies, and wholesale distribution. *Third Plan*, p. 17.

[92]Government acquired a 40 percent equity interest in the nation's three major commercial banks and a 40 to 49 percent equity interest in the principal foreign-owned insurance companies. Government also acquired at least a 55 percent ownership stake in the oil-producing companies.

[93]Data for the predecree year 1971.

ownership in 1967 amounted to 56 percent of the equity of Schedule I enterprises and 32.4 percent of the equity of firms on Schedule II.

By late 1974, 430 foreign-owned Schedule I concerns had been Nigerianized. Most of the transfers were arranged privately.[94] Among Schedule II firms, most was known about the relatively few public companies.[95] Equity transfers for twenty-four such firms were closely regulated by the Capital Issues Commission, which among other things set the prices for ordinary shares (common stock). More than 95 percent of the Schedule II companies, with perhaps five-sixths of the assets, were private.[96] By late 1974, 427 of these had complied with the Indigenization Decree; 82 involved 100 percent transfers while 345 involved 40 percent sales. Another 514 private companies had not yet complied.[97] Private company transfers were arranged privately, without Capital Issues Commission supervision.

Not all the transfers were to private owners. State governments and quasi-government organizations "bought up large quantities of shares under private treaty arrangements before such shares were made available for public subscription."[98] Information on the magnitude of governmental acquisitions was not available, but it is known that they were sizeable.[99] Such acquisitions were seen by some as activity directed "against the objective of encouraging private indigenous investment"[100] and by others as support for orderly indigenization.[101]

Indigenization provided a windfall for a sprinkling of fortunate Nigerians. Share prices of public companies were undervalued by the Capital Issues Commission. By October 1974 the average share price of the thirteen manufacturing companies rose 50.7 percent above the transfer price set by the Capital Issues Commission approximately six months earlier; for the eight companies in commerce, appreciation was 29.6 percent; and

[94]S. O. Asabia, "Share Valuation: The Nigerian Experience," Paper presented to the Symposium on Indigenisation, in Nigerian Economic Society, *Nigeria's Indigenisation Policy: Proceedings of the November 1974 Symposium Organized by the Nigerian Economic Society* (Ibadan: Nigerian Economic Society, 1975), pp. 19-25. Also (Lagos) *Daily Times,* November 23, 1974, p. 15.

[95]Joint stock companies; in American terminology, corporations. Private companies are permitted to have only a limited number of stockholders and are not permitted to offer their shares for public subscription, while public companies are not restricted in these ways. However, private companies are permitted considerably greater confidentiality regarding financial affairs than are public companies.

[96]Rough estimate by the author based on partial data in Asabia, "Share Valuation," pp. 19-21.

[97]Asabia, "Share Valuation," pp. 19-21; Asabia, "Meaning of Indigensation," pp. 3-4; *Third Plan,* p. 17.

[98]Asabia, "Share Valuation," p. 21.

[99]Asabia, "Share Valuation," p. 21. See also Akinkugbe, p. 42: ". . . there is enough evidence to indicate that government activity in this area has been substantial."

[100]Akinkugbe, p. 42.

[101]Asabia, "Share Valuation," pp. 20-21.

for the service companies, appreciation was 33.9 percent.[102] Moreover, dividend rates in the neighborhood of 50 percent were common soon after indigenization.[103] In private-company transfers, it was clear that Nigerians were often rewarded lucratively for cooperating in transfer arrangements advantageous to the foreign firms.

The indigenization windfall went mainly to strategically placed or wealthy Nigerians, but possession of adequate funds was not a prerequisite. Private acquisitions were financed primarily by credit. The major sources were the Bank for Commerce and Industry, a government institution established expressly for the purpose of helping to finance indigenization; the commercial banks; and in the case of the private companies, credit advanced by the foreign owners themselves in arrangements which often enabled them to maintain control.[104]

In all, implementation proceeded reasonably smoothly. The foreign companies generally went along with the decree; the Government acknowledged "co-operation of the alien companies affected."[105] On its side, government was willing to ease compliance problems by granting considerable extensions of time. This is not to say that all were happy or that no criticisms were expressed. Vocal critics included those who felt they did not get enough of a good thing, i.e., that "the future sum of dividends and capital gains have been spread [too] thinly among so many Nigerians."[106] A major criticism was that indigenization of private companies, which constituted the vast majority of the companies affected by the decree, was not accompanied by Nigerian control. The transfer arrangements in many of these cases, involving credits, deferred-payment agreements depending upon future dividends, pledging of stock certificates, and the like, were such that "effective control probably remains with the vendors."[107] Another major criticism was that the indigenization windfall benefited mainly a narrow group and "tended to widen the gap between the rich and the poor."[108]

A period of quiescence was expected after the 1974-75 implementation of the Nigerian Enterprises Promotion Decree. ". . . The intention of Government is to consolidate and not to advance compulsory ownership indigenisation in this Plan period."[109] However, the firm intention is, in due course, to push indigenization further.

---

[102]Asabia, "Share Valuation," p. 30.
[103](Lagos) *Daily Times*, March 28, 1975, p. 5.
[104]Asabia speaks of the prevalence in private company transfers of "nominal credits contrived by individuals, anxious to give the appearance of compliance without relinquishing effective ownership and control." See his "Share Valuation," p. 29.
[105]*Third Plan*, p. 17.
[106]Akinkugbe, p. 42.
[107]Asabia, "Share Valuation," p. 31.
[108](Lagos) *Daily Times*, November 23, 1974, p. 15.
[109]*Third Plan*, p. 153. See also General Yakubu Gowon, "Speech on the Third National Development Plan," (Lagos) *Sunday Times*, March 30, 1975, p. 29.

The indigenization and the business-assistance programs, the nurture-capitalism orientation of which they are a part as well as the probable divergences between stated and actual orientations, and the increasing power of the Nigerian capitalist class all support and strengthen Nigeria's inclination to rely upon and promote indigenous business. Having discussed the economy as a whole under nurture-capitalism in Part I of the book we turn our attention in Part II to the performance of the indigenous private sector. Part III will then examine the operation of the government programs to assist that sector.

PART II

Indigenous Private Enterprise

Chapter 4

CAPITAL

If the overall performance of the Nigerian economy up to the 1974 surge in oil revenues was not impressive, the performance of indigenous private business was weak indeed. Although data on investment by indigenous business are unavailable, it is clear that Nigerian businessmen generated little of the motive power for development. This is not to say that Nigerian businessmen lacked entrepreneurial attributes; they possessed at least some of these in abundance. Nevertheless, that "Nigerian ownership and control of industrial investments are extremely low"[1] has been a continuing concern. The disappointing record of indigenous businessmen was reflected in the tacit reorientation during the latter 1950s toward government and foreign enterprise as the means of generating modern-sector growth and development, an orientation that has since been maintained. During the 1970s the reliance upon foreign and government enterprise continued and the *Second Plan* and *Third Plan* manifested little confidence in the Nigerian business sector's ability to increase its own ownership and control in the modern sector.[2]

Part II of this study is concerned with analyzing the disappointing performance of indigenous private enterprise.[3] It examines the major ostensible impediments to development in this sector. Chapter 4 deals with the first of these: a shortage of capital.

The reason most often given for the limited expansion of the Nigerian

[1]Federal Republic of Nigeria, *Second National Development Plan 1970-74* (hereinafter referred to as *Second Plan*) (Lagos: Federal Ministry of Information, 1970), pp. 143-144.

[2]For example, the Second Plan stressed the urgency of Nigerian control and then stated: "It is vital therefore, for *Government* to acquire and control on behalf of the Nigerian society, the greater proportion of the productive assets of the country. . . . In order to ensure that the economic destiny of Nigeria is determined by Nigerians themselves, the *Government* will seek to widen and intensify its positive participation in industrial development." (*Second Plan*, p. 289; emphasis added.) The reliance on government action to foster Nigerianization reflected not an ideological preference but a belief that it was the only realistic means.

Indigenization constituted the principal means of increasing the Nigerian role in the private sector, and despite the indigenization of 1974 foreign firms were relied upon for the major share of private investment during the Third Plan period, and particularly for the more development-propelling investments.

[3]Effects of the new oil affluence beginning in 1974 are discussed in Chapter 14, under "Potential Sources of Modern-Economy Investment."

business sector is capital shortage; a shortage of funds is identified as the main obstacle. This has long been the explanation that most Nigerian businessmen offer. Such a belief emerges vividly in work with Nigerian entrepreneurs,[4] and it is found in systematic surveys[5] and in the work of other scholars.[6] This view has also been reiterated for many years by political and governmental spokesmen for Nigerian businessmen.[7] Even writers of scholarly works have been reluctant to forego this explanation entirely, although they have often qualified it.[8]

This chapter presents a contrary thesis: that a capital shortage is not a major impediment to indigenous private investment; that this conception is an illusion created by a large false demand for capital; and that the major problem for indigenous enterprise is actually a shortage of viable projects. (The concept of viability used here is a broad one; when a project is not commercially successful for any reason—whether the project itself is badly conceived, or because the entrepreneur has insufficient ability, or because conditions external to the enterprise are unfavorable—then the project is "not viable.")

[4]In author's interviews with Nigerian businessmen in 1961-65, 1968, and 1974-75, this view was consistently expressed.

[5]See, e.g., the survey-based finding that "most Nigerian businessmen believe that inadequate capital is their main or sole business handicap." Sayre P. Schatz and S. I. Edokpayi, "Economic Attitudes of Nigerian Businessmen," *Nigerian Journal of Economic and Social Studies* IV:3 (November 1962): 266. Another survey of 626 smaller enterprises (employing five or fewer workers) found that virtually every respondent espoused this belief. (Survey carried out in 1961 by the Western Nigeria Ministry of Economic Planning and Community Development.)

[6]Peter Kilby also found that "The Nigerian entrepreneur insists that lack of capital is the only obstacle retarding his progress." Peter Kilby, *The Development of Small Industry in Eastern Nigeria* (Lagos: United States Agency for International Development, 1962), p. 12. See also his *Industrialization in an Open Economy: Nigeria 1945-1966* (Cambridge: Cambridge University Press, 1969), p. 338; and E. Wayne Nafziger, "The Market for Nigerian Entrepreneurs," in Sayre P. Schatz (ed.), *South of the Sahara: Development in African Economics* (Philadelphia: Temple University Press, 1972), p. 70; and John R. Harris, "Industrial Entrepreneurship in Nigeria," Unpublished dissertation, Northwestern University, Evanston, Illinois, August 1967, Ch. 8, pp. 16-18.

[7]See, e.g., the vigorous complaint in 1952 of Alhaji S. O. Gbadamosi that government was not doing enough to remedy the scarcity of capital funds: "I would like to mention something, Sir, about provision of capital for industrialisation. Anyone who has had a loan from the Government will know that it is easier to pass through the eye of a needle than to obtain a loan for industrial development . . . private capital ought to be encouraged to come out of its hiding places. Here the role of the banks is very important. Quite a lot of small businessmen are at home with the African owned banks. Whatever views one may hold on the question of the control of banking activities in this country, there is no doubt, Sir, that one or two African banks would satisfy the most rigorous tests. What is the Government doing to encourage those banks? *African banks with sound financial backing will go a long way to encourage more African industrial adventurers* [i.e., entrepreneurs]." Nigeria, House of Representatives, *Debates, First Session, March 19, 1952*, p. 275 (my emphasis).

[8]For example: "experience . . . has shown that supervised credit for small-scale entrepreneurs can work but only with adequate technical and managerial assistance and favourable government policies and incentives." Gerald Faust, "Small Industries Credit Scheme in Northern Nigeria: An Analysis of Operational and Lending Patterns," *Nigerian Journal of Economic and Social Studies* XI:3 (July 1969): 205-206. "Many projects no doubt came up in loan applications which with adequate and able staff could be designed to produce accept-

False Shortage of Capital

The impression that capital shortage is a major impediment to indigenous business expansion arises primarily from what may be called a false demand for capital.

A false demand for capital exists when an entrepreneur or an aspiring entrepreneur seeks capital for a venture that does not have a reasonably good chance of business success. Unless a prospective lender has good reason to deem a project likely to succeed, the potential borrower has only a desire for capital, but not an effective demand. Just as demand for a commodity must be backed by purchasing power, so must demand for capital be backed by an acceptable project.[9]

False demand for capital is widespread in Nigeria. Vigorous and even impassioned calls for funds to finance chimerical undertakings are commonplace. A large proportion of the entrepreneurs this writer interviewed described projects that were clearly unrealistic. In many cases the pleas for capital simply come up in casual conversations. Many businessmen, however, go to considerable time and trouble to submit loan applications that are, in fact, hopeless: the cigar producer, for example, who applied for a loan to purchase machinery that could produce more cigars in a day than the firm had been able to sell in a year; another cigar producer with annual sales of 110,000 cigars who proposed to acquire equipment with an annual capacity of more than 3 million;[10] the applicant who described himself as an industrial consultant who had invented many types of plant and equipment and who applied for £ 50,000 to construct a new versatile plant for both drying fish and processing rubber;[11] the applicant who indicated that he ran a tailoring shop and who proposed a fanciful project for setting up simultaneous operations for fish-canning, bolt-and-nut manufacturing, gum manufacturing, glass-making, pottery-making, and ink manufacturing; the firm that applied for £ 45,000 (and later scaled its request down to £ 10,000) to expand its existing "umbrella-assembly

---

able offers [i.e., business ventures]." C. C. Onyemelukwe, *Problems of Industrial Planning and Management in Nigeria* (New York: Columbia University Press, 1966), p. 230.

[9]"Bankers' criteria for granting loans are numerous, and vary from time to time, country to country, and even bank to bank, but two are likely to be prominent in all times and places: (1) a reasonable prospect that the loan will be repaid when due, which may take the form of a pledge of marketable collateral, or may take less tangible forms, such as a demonstrated high rate of profit or trust and confidence in the borrower based on long personal acquaintance or, possibly, ties of kinship; and (2) a reasonable expectation that the loan will be part of and will contribute to a continuing profitable relation between the banker and the customer, which again may be based on previous experience, or on evidence of whatever nature that the proceeds of the loan will be used profitably . . ." Rondo Cameron, *Banking in the Early Stages of Industrialization* (New York: Oxford University Press, 1967), p. 13.

[10]Neither had the slightest idea of how he could even *begin* to sell the enlarged output he proposed, according to the investigator for the Federal Loans Board. This application and the others discussed in this paragraph are all drawn from the files of the Federal Loans Board.

[11]The investigator found that the proposal was completely unrealistic.

plant" into a relatively large-scale operation;[12] the applicant for £ 50,000 to establish a Pioneer Oil Mill for processing palm fruit and who withdrew his application when apprised of the annual interest and amortization payments and submitted instead an application for £ 19,000 for producing gari (a local food); the £ 35,000 application of a "tailoring enterprise" that was found on investigation to consist of the proprietor, one boy, and one girl, with one dilapidated sewing machine in an eight-by-ten-foot room.[13]

There were many other farfetched loan applications, but it should be stressed that most were much more sober. Even these, however, were generally for projects that could not be adjudged commercially promising. This is reflected, for example, in the record of the Federal Loans Board, the source of the most complete and detailed evidence on the false demand for capital. After careful investigation of potential viability and security, 82 percent of the applications that reached the Board, representing 89 percent of the loan funds sought, were turned down. Approximately 86 percent of the amount applied for was rejected on the grounds that the ventures would not be viable and 3 percent because the applicants were unable to provide adequate security.[14] In addition, a large number of applicants dropped out before a formal decision was made because the investigation officials made it clear that there was no hope of Federal Loans Board approval of their projects.[15]

The torrent of false demands for capital afflicts all institutions that make loans. The Regional Loans Boards were always swamped by applications for unviable projects.[16] Requests for loans for unpromising projects also pour into the commercial banks. Both Nigerian and foreign officials report this problem. And it arises equally in indigenous-owned and foreign-owned banks.[17]

It is this false demand for capital—which tends to be erroneously accepted at face value[18]—that creates the impression that Nigerian

[12]On his visit, the investigator found that the plant consisted of two sewing machines and a glue pot, with four operators at work in cramped premises.

[13]The applicant had little or no security for the loan, and moreover had no conception of what he was proposing.

[14]Loan applications were appraised nonpolitically. This is documented in Sayre P. Schatz, *Development Bank Lending in Nigeria: The Federal Loans Board* (Ibadan and London: Oxford University Press, 1964), pp. 37-39. See also Chapter 11 of the present work. The Federal Loans Board operated from 1956 to 1966.

[15]Including the dropouts, perhaps 95 percent of the applicants had projects adjudged not viable. Rejections discussed here do not include loan requests denied because they were outside the Federal Loans Board's jurisdiction or for similar administrative reasons. Schatz, *Development Bank Lending*, pp. 89-92.

[16]For a detailed discussion, see Sayre P. Schatz, *Economics, Politics and Administration in Government Lending: The Regional Loans Boards of Nigeria* (Ibadan and London: Oxford University Press, 1970), pp. 119-120.

[17]The Governor of Western Nigeria, Chief Odeleye Fadahunsi, "appealed to Nigerian businessmen to conduct their business in such a way as would make it possible for banks to afford them banking facilities." (Lagos) *Daily Times*, April 28, 1964, p. 5.

[18]Acceptance at face value of the false demands is a major cause of bad debts, which

businessmen are shackled by a lack of capital. The shortage, however, is unreal; it is a false shortage of capital.[19]

Availability of Capital

This is not to say that *all* the unsatisfied quests for capital arise from a false demand. There are certainly instances of good projects that cannot find financing. However, a frictional problem of this nature, which occurs in all economies, does not constitute a fundamental or major impediment to indigenous private investment. For the most part, Nigerian entrepreneurs who have profitable uses for capital have been able to secure it.[20]

As in the more-developed economies, the major source of capital for Nigerian firms has been profits. While general data are unavailable, most economists who have studied Nigerian enterprise, including this one, have found this to be the case. Reinvestment of profits has been the means of expansion for most Nigerian firms.[21]

---

constitute an unremitting problem. For example, the Plateau State government suspended its loans scheme for indigenous producers "because of the large sums of money owed to the board by some beneficiaries." Thirty-six of the defaulters were to be prosecuted. (Lagos) *Daily Times,* June 27, 1974, p. 22. The large private foreign-owned Standard Bank also described an overburden of uncollectible loans to indigenous borrowers. The other banks, indigenous and foreign-owned, also indicated they had the same problem, as did the Nigerian Industrial Development Bank, a government lending institution. (Lagos) *Daily Times,* June 29, 1974, p. 13.

[19]See, e.g., the concurring statement of a leading Nigerian economist, subsequently appointed Federal Commissioner (Military Government equivalent of Minister) of Finance, in August 1975: ". . .lack of capital funds is not the cause of continued lag in the economic take-off of the backward economies. . . . This has also been true of Nigeria. . . . [Lending agencies] were adequately funded to make loans available to Nigerians for business purposes." A. E. Ekukinam, "Management Problems, Accountability and Government Control of Public Enterprises in Nigeria," in *Public Enterprises in Nigeria: Proceedings of the 1973 Annual Conference of the Nigerian Economic Society* (Ibadan: Nigerian Economic Society, 1974), p. 131.

[20]On the amount of credit going to the private sector, see G. O. Nwankwo, "Causes of Inflation and the Relative Importance Between External and Internal Causes," Paper for the Nigerian Institute of Social and Economic Research Symposium on Inflation, Ibadan, October 1974, p. 23.

[21]E.g., John Harris found that profit reinvestment was by far the most important means of financing growth in sawmilling. Of the 43 firms that had expanded 40 indicated that reinvestment of profits was a major source of the necessary capital. John R. Harris, "Industrial Entrepreneurship in Nigeria," Ch. 4, p. 34. See also John R. Harris and Mary P. Rowe, "Entrepreneurial Patterns in the Nigerian Sawmilling Industry," *Nigerian Journal of Economic and Social Studies* VIII:1 (March 1966): 67-96. With his study of the shoe industry as a starting point, but speaking more broadly of Nigerian entrepreneurs, Nafziger generalized that "most successful firms have access to retained earnings." Nafziger, p. 70. See also by Nafziger, "The Effect of the Nigerian Extended Family on Entrepreneurial Activity," *Economic Development and Cultural Change* (October 1969). Similarly, speaking not only of the bakeries he investigated but also of Nigerian firms more generally, Kilby says, "the great majority of all firms have grown on the basis of reinvested earnings." Peter Kilby, *African Enterprise: The Nigerian Bread Industry* (Stanford: The Hoover Institution

Commercial banks have been a more important source of capital for Nigerian businesses than is popularly supposed. The major banks were frequently criticized, with good reason, for their performance of this function. Simple discrimination was practiced. "Probabilistic discrimination" sometimes made it difficult for Nigerians to get loans: the repayment record of Nigerians on the whole has been unsatisfactory, so that a Nigerian not well-known to the banker encountered the presumption, based on probabilities, that he constituted an unacceptable repayment risk.[22] Moreover, bank practices were usually based on foreign standards, and even the fairest application of such alien standards created difficulties for Nigerians. For example, the British-owned banks in Nigeria were reluctant to charge more than a very small risk premium, and since lending to Nigerians was risky the banks could not make many such loans.[23] Again, Nigerian businessmen have only gradually adopted the practice of keeping their money in banks; since banks favored their own depositors, this made it harder for Nigerians to get loans.

Despite all this, the banks have been a significant source of funds for the more successful Nigerian entrepreneurs. Here, too, hard data are unavailable, and the matter is partially obscured by the tradition of banking secrecy, but the investigations of a number of capable economists provide support for this judgment with respect to the 1960s and even the 1950s.[24] As the Minister of Commerce and Industry, a Nigerian, said in 1956, speaking of bank credit, "I think that some big businessmen in this House will bear me out. If an African is running his business on well-established lines, and has proper accounts, I think he will definitely get credit like anybody else."[25] An expansion of indigenously owned banking also widened the flow of bank funds to Nigerian businesses. These banks were more lenient than foreign-owned banks in making loans to Africans and, unlike the foreign-owned banks, they have often been willing to provide credit on a long-term basis.[26] In 1968 power was conferred upon the Central Bank to prescribe minimum ratios of credit which each commercial bank should extend to indigenous borrowers, and this power was used to increase loan funds to Nigerian business.[27] By 1974 approxi-

---

on War, Revolution, and Peace, 1965), p. 102. Garlick discusses the other uses traders made of their profits but indicates that the expanding trading firms in Ghana expanded on the basis of reinvested earnings. Peter C. Garlick, "African Traders and Economic Growth: A Case Study in Ghana," in Schatz (ed.), *South of the Sahara,* p. 83.

[22]On probabilistic discrimination, see Chapter 6 below on the economic environment.

[23]Charles V. Brown, Jr., "The Development of Monetary and Credit Institutions in Nigeria," Unpublished dissertation, London University, 1964, chapter 4.

[24]O. Olakanpo, "Indigenous Enterprise in Distributive Trades," Preliminary manuscript, unpublished, pp. 22, 26-29; Brown, chapter 4; Harris, chapter 4, p. 33.

[25]The Honourable R. A. Njoku in Nigeria, Federation, *Debates of The House of Representatives,* March 15, 1956, p. 563.

[26]Brown, chapters 3, 7.

[27]C. E. Enuenwosu, "The Role of Monetary Policy in the Control of Inflation in

mately half the credit provided by the large foreign-owned banks went to Nigerians.[28]

Other sources of funds for indigenous businesses include personal savings, loans from relatives and friends, small gifts from members of the family (it is common to give gifts of ₦50 to ₦1000, depending on the affluence of the family, to start a man off in business), traditional community saving and credit societies, hire-purchase (installment) credit, and, of course, government lending agencies.[29]

Shortage of Viable Projects

The important barrier to indigenous-business investment is not a shortage of capital for good projects, but a shortage of viable projects. There is a good deal of evidence to support this proposition.

There was, for one thing, the limited magnitude of Federal Loans Board lending. The Board's jurisdiction was broad. Within a ten-mile radius of the Federal Territory of Lagos it could make loans up to a £ 50,000 maximum. In the rest of the country the maximum was the same, but there were restrictions for some years on small loans because these were considered the responsibility of the Regional Loans Boards. There was a minimum of £ 30,000 from 1956 to 1958, of £ 10,000 from 1959 to 1961, but no minimum thereafter. The Board made conscientious and reasonably capable efforts to cultivate loanworthy projects, providing substantial help with applications, revising proposed projects to separate out a worthwhile core, financing ventures unacceptable to commercial banks. Despite all this and despite availability of funds, it could find few loanworthy proposals. It was able to make only 44 loans for slightly more than £ 400,000 in its first five and a quarter years.

The paucity of potentially profitable ventures is indicated further by the poor record of the firms that did get Federal Loans Board loans. This was a select group of firms. They were carefully chosen because they had the most promising prospects; they went through a non-political selection process that sifted out all but a small proportion of the applicants. They

Nigeria," *Symposium on Inflation of the Nigerian Institute of Social and Economic Research* (Ibadan: October 1974): 13.

[28](Lagos) *Daily Times,* June 29, 1974, p. 13.

[29]Olakanpo; Margaret Katzin, "The Role of the Small Entrepreneur," Preliminary unpublished manuscript, pp. 22ff.; Archibald Callaway, "Crafts and Industries," Paper prepared for seminar in Ibadan on the Changing Nigerian Scene, University of Ibadan, February 28 to March 1, 1964, p. 5; Harris, chapter 4, pp. 33-34. There is also the stock market. The availability of Nigerian venture capital for blue-chip projects was suggested by the more-than-doubly oversubscribed new stock offerings of £ 87,500 (Tate and Lyle) and of £ 500,000 (the Standard Bank [Nigeria] Limited) issued in 1969 and 1971 respectively. J. O. Odufalu, "Indigenous Enterprise in Nigerian Manufacturing," *Journal of Modern African Studies* 9:4 (December 1971): 602. However, given Nigerians' skepticism about their own businessmen, this source would be difficult for even the best Nigerian firms to tap.

came to a substantial extent from the most advanced areas of the economy. They were already established businesses rather than the new firms that provide most of the business mortality in developed economies. They also received other government assistance once they were approved for loans.[30] Nevertheless, of the projects that had loans long enough for an assessment to be made at the time of the Federal Loans Board study, only 38 percent were judged to be operating successfully, and there was considerable reason to believe that some of these would not continue to do so.[31] Thus, even among the most promising loan applicants, successful ventures were not typical.[32]

The lending operations of the Regional Loans Boards were so thoroughly enmeshed in political and other noneconomic considerations that one cannot isolate solid data on the frequency of potentially profitable ventures among their applicants. Familiarity with the operations of these boards indicates quite clearly, however, that such ventures were uncommon.[33] This accords with the judgment of the civil servants and others involved in the activities of the boards, who have always stated emphatically, publicly and privately, that a shortage of viable projects was a chronic major problem.[34] Certainly the Regional Loans Boards produced relatively few business successes.[35]

The work of other analysts studying particular groups in Nigeria also

[30]Nafziger has contended that the borrowers cannot be considered an economically select group because many Nigerian firms lacked access to the Federal Loans Board for noneconomic reasons, and because many prospering firms chose to raise funds from sources other than the Board. E. Wayne Nafziger, "A Reconsideration of 'Capital Surplus' in Nigeria," *Nigerian Journal of Economic and Social Studies* X:1 (March 1968): 111-116. This argument is faulty. First, the Federal Loans Board study included a substantial discussion of the firms lacking access to the Board and presented specific reasons for concluding that each of these "impeded-access groups" had relatively few loanworthy projects (Schatz, *Development Bank Lending*, pp. 103-105). Second, the ability of many profitable firms to finance expansion by profit reinvestment and in other ways supports the thesis that few viable projects were stillborn for lack of capital. It in no way denies that the Federal Loans Board borrowers were a select group among those who sought Loans Board financing.

[31]Schatz, *Development Bank Lending*, pp. 92-97.

[32]Ekukinan has also noted that "Some loan boards, like the Federal Loans Board, ceased to function because there were no creditable businessmen to whom to lend." He attributed the paucity of potentially sound loans, which he considered to be a continuing problem, to managerial deficiencies. Ekukinan, p. 131. See also the statement of the Chairman of the Nigerian Industrial Development Bank, a government institution that provides development capital to private firms: ". . .I regret to say that many of them [the Nigerian firms] have portrayed bad management and poor response to their debt servicing obligations." Quoted in (Lagos) *Daily Times*, June 29, 1974, p. 13.

[33]Schatz, *Economics*, pp. 119-121.

[34]See the statements quoted or referred to in Schatz, *Economics*, pp. 119-121. The Minister of Commerce and Industry, in response to a question about the Regional Loans Boards, made a statement about this in 1952: "The main obstacle to the wider issue of loans is not insistence on the provision of security by applicants but the scarcity of well-considered viable schemes." Nigeria, House of Representatives, *Debates, First Session*, April 4, 1952, p. 898.

[35]Schatz, *Economics*, chapter 6.

suggests that the fundamental impediment to indigenous private investment has not been capital shortage but a shortage of viable projects. Thus, in a study concentrating on sawmilling, furniture-making, and rubber-processing, but also dealing with several other industries, John Harris found for the types of industrial activity he surveyed: "Although a shortage of capital is frequently asserted to be a major impediment to the development of indigenous industry, and our respondents claimed inability to raise capital as their most serious problem we are loath to accept this proposition . . . capital shortage is not a principal barrier. . . ."[36] Wayne Nafziger, on the basis of his study of the Nigerian shoe industry and his survey of other work, including that of this author, agrees that the fundamental problem is a paucity of profitable ventures.[37] In his work on a small-industries credit scheme in Northern Nigeria, Gerald Faust found that "finance is not the major problem inhibiting the growth of small scale industries. . . ."[38] M. G. Smith depicted the successful Hausa trader in Zaria as accumulating capital faster than he could find productive use for it.[39] In general, those involved in promoting the indigenous private sector, whatever their vantage point, continually encounter this paucity of viable projects. Thus, a year after the onset of the new surge in oil revenues, the Managing Director of the Nigerian Bank for Commerce and Industry "appealed to indigenous businessmen and women to embark on viable large scale projects in order to benefit from the credit facilities offered them by the bank."[40] And on the capital-receiving side, an articulate business leader concluded: "Perhaps the most critical factor impeding the emergence of a strong indigenous business sector in our country is the lack of sophisticated indigenous entrepreneurial opportunities."[41]

The lack of commercially viable projects turns out to be the fundamental problem in country after country in Africa which has tried to promote development by providing capital to indigenous businessmen. Peter Garlick found this to be the case in Ghana.[42] It was also true in

[36]Harris, *Industrial Entrepreneurship,* Chapter 8, pp. 16, 18.

[37]Nafziger, "Market," p. 66. See also E. Wayne Nafziger, *Nigerian Entrepreneurship: A Study of Indigenous Businessmen in the Footwear Industry,* University of Illinois Ph.D. dissertation, 1967, Urbana, Illinois, pp. 189-190.

[38]Faust, p. 215.

[39]M. G. Smith, *The Economy of Hausa Communities of Zaria,* Colonial Research Studies, No. 16 (London: HMSO, 1955), pp. 100-101, 163. See also Kilby, *Industrialization,* p. 336.

[40](Lagos) *Daily Times,* November 15, 1974, p. 13. The Nigerian Bank for Commerce and Industry is a major government lending institution charged with the responsibility of making funds available for Nigerian business ventures.

[41]Olu Akinkugbe, "Nigerian Enterprises Promotion Decree and Its Implementation," in Nigerian Economic Society, *Nigeria's Indigenisation Policy: Proceedings of a November 1974 Symposium Organized by the Nigerian Economic Society* (Ibadan: Nigerian Economic Society, 1975), p. 38.

[42]Garlick, p. 66. See also Peter C. Garlick, *African Traders and Economic Development in Ghana* (Oxford: Oxford University Press, 1971), where this is discussed at greater length.

Uganda, where more than one investigation has found "more capital available to help the industrial entrepreneurs than can at present be effectively used," and that the difficulty lies in finding worthwhile schemes to finance.[43] The Industrial Development Bank of Sudan could find in its first year only three small projects (producing spaghetti and air coolers, and maintaining motor cars) that it could support with loans.[44] An investigation in Liberia found that an appreciable portion of the outflow of profits made from primary product exports would be reinvested in the country if only attractive opportunities could be found in other sectors of the economy.[45] In Sierra Leone, the problem was a paucity of promising investment projects,[46] and this also appears to have been the situation confronting the African Loan and Development Company of Southern Rhodesia.[47] Similarly: "The experience in Ethiopia would indicate . . . that while private investment capital is available there is a definite scarcity of clearly located and demonstrable investment opportunities."[48] And in a survey of banking in Africa *The Economist* concluded that "even the development banks have found it difficult to dispose of their funds in profitable manufacturing enterprises at reasonable rates without too great a risk of default."[49]

That a paucity of commercially viable ventures is a basic problem in underdeveloped economies generally is indicated by the work of a number of other analysts. Thus, Eugene Staley maintained that until other measures are taken to make indigenous industrial enterprises more profitable, "no purely financial solution will really help."[50] The United

---

The findings cited in this paragraph with respect to Ghana, Uganda, Liberia, Sierra Leone, and Ethiopia accord with the author's own findings in 1968 (Ghana, Uganda, Liberia, Ethiopia) and 1975 (Liberia and Sierra Leone).

[43]Henry B. Thomas, "African Entrepreneurs in Industrial Pursuits," in Warren H. Hausman (ed.), *Managing Economic Development in Africa* (Cambridge, Mass.: MIT Press, 1963), p. 103. Cf. Nyhart's conclusion after investigating the two major government-backed agencies financing individual Africans: "Both have more money available than they are able to place in sound loans or investments." J. D. Nyhart, "The Uganda Development Corporation and the Promotion of Entrepreneurship," East African Institute of Social Research conference paper, Makerere University College, 1959.

[44]"The Role of Banks in Emerging Africa," in *Africa Report* XI:5 (Washington: May 1966); reprinted from *The Economist* (London).

[45]James R. Brooks and William C. Ladd, *A Liberian Bank for Industrial Development and Investment*, Report prepared for the International Co-operation Administration (Washington: 1960), p. 10.

[46]Philip E. Beach, "Industrial Development Banks: Operating Practices," in Hausman (ed.), pp. 114-116.

[47]D. S. Pearson, "African Advancement in Commerce and Industry," *Journal of Modern African Studies* III:2 (August 1967): 247.

[48]A. H. Hanson, *Public Enterprise and Economic Development* (London: Routledge and Kegan Paul, 1959), p. 37, quoting a United Nations conference report.

[49]Quoted in *Africa Report* XI:5 (May 1966).

[50]Eugene Staley, "Development of Small Industry Programmes," in A. Winsemius and J. A. Pincus (eds.), *Methods of Industrial Development: With Special Reference to Less Developed Areas* (Paris: Organisation for Economic Co-operation and Development, 1962), p. 222.

States Agency for International Development, in an internal document, emphasized the importance of creating investment opportunities, "and when that is done, the money or the development bank almost takes care of itself. In our experience, no desirable investment opportunity has died because of lack of funds."[51] Albert O. Hirschman stated that the industrial credit section of the Bank of North-East Brazil was "slow in expanding the volume of its operations, largely because of difficulties encountered in locating industrial investment opportunities."[52] A. H. Hanson, dealing with the less-developed countries, discussed the problem of "capital unable to find profitable outlet."[53] Milton Friedman concluded: "In short, if any generalization is valid, it is that the availability of capital while an important problem is a subsidiary one—if other conditions for economic development are ripe [so that there are good investment opportunities], capital will be readily available; if they are not, capital made available is very likely to be wasted."[54] Finally, Edward Nevin also found that profit is usually too uncertain or too far off in most underdeveloped economies to attract private funds. "In a word, an economy is underdeveloped precisely because the greater part of its productive capacity has not proved an attractive investment for private funds."[55]

If the problem is a shortage of viable projects rather than a shortage of capital, we must seek an explanation for the low rate of indigenous private investment in conditions that prevent the emergence of a large flow of profitable business ventures. This brings us to a consideration in the next two chapters of Nigerian entrepreneurship and of the economic environment.

[51]U.S. AID, "Memo to Area and Technical Officers of A.F.E." (Washington: January 1962): 1.

[52]Albert O. Hirschman, *Journeys Towards Progress: Studies of Economic Policy-Making in Latin America* (New York: Twentieth Century Fund, 1963), p. 69. See also U.S. AID, *Report of the Cento Conference on Industrial Development Banking* (Washington: 1961), p. 70, on the Industrial Development Bank of Turkey.

[53]Hanson, pp. 36-38.

[54]Milton Friedman, "Foreign Economic Aid: Means and Objectives," in Gustav Ranis (ed.), *The U.S. and the Developing Economies* (New York: Norton, 1964), p. 30.

[55]Edward Nevin, *Capital Funds in Underdeveloped Countries: The Role of Financial Institutions* (London: Macmillan, 1961), p. 74.

Chapter 5

ENTREPRENEURSHIP

The limited emergence of profitable indigenous business ventures can be attributed to either or both of two causes. The problem may be one of entrepreneurship, i.e., shortcomings of the Nigerian businessman, or it may be caused by adversities in the economic environment, i.e., impediments arising out of the set of conditions with which the businessman must contend.

It is a common belief in Nigeria that the main problem is deficiencies in entrepreneurial capacity. A Nigerian economist has written: "What I would call 'drone capitalism' prevails in the Nigerian economy (the private indigenous sector) not only now but in the foreseeable future. . . . The ability of Nigeria's capitalist class to modernize the economy in the ways and at the levels envisaged in national development policies is, in my view, very much in doubt. . . . I find the vast majority of Nigerian businessmen (even most of the so-called business tycoons) to be very inadequate indeed. . . . The economy cannot forever absorb the inefficiency and the exploitative activities of 'drone capitalists' who simply fatten themselves upon existing national wealth without doing much to augment that wealth . . . the adaptive capacity of Nigeria's capitalist class is low. . . ."[1] This is an expression of a widely held and long-

---

[1] E. O. Akeredolu-Ale, "Some Thoughts on the Indigenization Process and the Quality of Nigerian Capitalism," in Nigerian Economic Society, *Nigeria's Indigenisation Policy: Proceedings of a November 1974 Symposium Organized by the Nigerian Economic Society* (Ibadan: Nigerian Economic Society, 1975), pp. 68, 70, 71, 72. A dozen years earlier another Nigerian economist wrote: "A typical Nigerian businessman is a man with many weak parts. He is inadequately equipped with capital and technical know-how. He is apt to imitate known skills and methods but is least ingenious in innovating new ones. He is invariably conservative in the ideas of economic change. He is low in business morals, greedy for quick returns and pompous in living habits. . . . He is basically distrustful of others in business deals, his family group not excepted. . . . As an entrepreneur his greatest weakness is his organisation inertia. . . ." S. I. Edokpayi, "Economic Individualism: A Study of Nigerian Entrepreneurial Problems," Unpublished paper, Ibadan, Western Nigeria Ministry of Economic Planning and Community Development, no date indicated (approximately 1962), pp. 1-2. Kilby also expresses a critical view. "With few exceptions, Nigerian industrialists are unwilling to provide continuous surveillance of their business operations, in terms of both physical supervision in the factory shop and in utilizing the principal instrument of management control, written records. This disposition is combined with a general lack of

established opinion.[2]

The present chapter is an examination of Nigerian entrepreneurship with a view to helping us understand the performance of the indigenous private sector of the Nigerian economy.[3] In this examination, it will be useful to adopt a broad definition of entrepreneurship: the businessman's ability, based on personal attributes, knowledge, and experience, to establish and operate a business. The higher the degree of entrepreneurship

---

interest in production efficiency and in possibilities for improving product quality. Nigerian entrepreneurs are generally slow to move when their operations hit a snag. They show little propensity to undertake innovations. . . . Finally, Nigerian businessmen are typically unaware that their managerial performance is in any way wanting." Peter Kilby, *Industrialization in an Open Economy: Nigeria 1945-1966* (Cambridge: Cambridge University Press, 1969), p. 338. Kilby is a strong advocate of the view that the principal reason for the inadequate performance of Nigerian private business is deficient entrepreneurial capability (pp. 336-342). He attributes this to "traditional socio-cultural factors common to all of Nigeria's ethnic groups" (p. 341). G. Akin Ogunpola, while not attributing the business difficulties of Nigerian contractors to this cause alone, is also quite critical of Nigerian entrepreneurship. "Most Nigerian contractors are still to adopt similar efficient management control, and it is not until they do this that they will gain parity with their expatriate counterparts." Speaking of medium- and small-size Nigerian firms, he says that "most of the contractors in these categories lack managerial ability, business acumen and integrity, all of which are prerequisites of a successful enterprise." G. Akin Ogunpola, "The Pattern of Organization in the Building Industry: A Western Nigerian Case Study," *Nigerian Journal of Economic and Social Studies* X:3 (November 1968): 350, 358; also 351-353, 357.

[2]See, e.g., International Bank for Reconstruction and Development, *The Economic Development of Nigeria* (Baltimore: The Johns Hopkins Press, 1955), p. 141; Basil Davidson, "And Now Nigeria," *New Statesman* LX:1542 (October 1, 1960): 465-468 at 468; J. D. Nyhart, "Notes on Entrepreneurship in Africa," Paper given at Development Seminar, Center for International Affairs, Harvard University, November 11, 1961 (unpublished), pp. 20-22; Gerald K. Helleiner, *Peasant Agriculture, Government and Economic Growth in Nigeria* (Homewood, Illinois: Richard D. Irwin, 1966), pp. 265-266. This is also the typical view of government officials concerned with Nigerian business.

[3]A great deal of capable work has already been done on Nigerian entrepreneurship, see, inter alia, John R. Harris, "Industrial Entrepreneurship in Nigeria," Unpublished dissertation, Northwestern University, Evanston, Illinois, August 1967, and his "On the Concept of Entrepreneurship, with an Application to Nigeria," in Sayre P. Schatz (ed.), *South of the Sahara: Development in African Economies* (Philadelphia: Temple University Press, 1972); E. Wayne Nafziger, *Nigerian Entrepreneurship: A Study of Indigenous Businessmen in the Footwear Industry,* University of Illinois Ph.D. dissertation, 1967, Urbana, Illinois, and "The Market for Nigerian Entrepreneurs," in Schatz (ed.), *South of the Sahara;* S. A. Aluko, "The Educated in Business: The Calabar Home Farm—A Case Study," *Nigerian Journal of Economic and Social Studies* VIII:2 (July 1966); O. Olakanpo, "A Statistical Analysis of Some Determinants of Entrepreneurial Success," *Nigerian Journal of Economic and Social Studies* X:2 (July 1968), and "Distributive Trade: A Critique of Government Policies,"*Nigerian Journal of Economic and Social Studies* V:2 (July 1963); Archibald Callaway, "Crafts and Industries," Paper prepared for seminar on Ibadan on the Changing Nigerian Scene, University of Ibadan, February 28 to March 1, 1964, and "Nigeria's Indigenous Education: The Apprentice System," *Odu: University of Ife Journal of African Studies* 1:1 (July 1964): 1-18; P. T. Bauer, *West African Trade* (Cambridge: Cambridge University Press, 1954); Peter Kilby, *African Enterprise: The Nigerian Bread Industry* (Stanford: The Hoover Institution on War, Revolution, and Peace, 1965), and *Industrialization in an Open Economy;* E. O. Akeredolu-Ale, "Values, Motivations and History in the Development of Private Indigenous Entrepreneurship: Lessons from Nigeria's Experience, 1946-1966," *Nigerian Journal of Economic and Social Studies* XIII:2 (July 1971): 195-220; Omafume F. Onoge, "Indigenisation Decree and Economic Indepen-

the more successfully this can be done.[4] The general argument of the chapter is that Nigerian entrepreneurial deficiencies are real enough but that their importance tends to be exaggerated.

The Leap

Nigerian entrepreneurs, possessed of considerable drive and vitality, have established multitudes of very small enterprises.[5] Such undertakings have been easy to start, even by men and women with little education, training, or business experience. Barriers to entry into such businesses have been negligible. The technical knowledge required is usually simple and many have acquired it as workers or apprentices in other small firms or through experience in large firms or in government. Capital requirements are also frequently minimal, and in fact traders have often operated with virtually no capital of their own, relying instead on advances from their suppliers. Requirements for skilled labor are usually negligible, and unskilled and semiskilled labor is cheap and abundant. On the eve of independence in 1960, officials estimated that there were already more than one and a quarter million enterprises in Nigeria, which some social scientists believed was an understatement.[6]

Once these enterprises are started, Nigerian entrepreneurship is adequate for carrying on. The market for the output of these enterprises is relaxed about product uniformity, product specifications, and regularity of production schedules. It is therefore possible for a firm to get by despite serious deficiencies in production, delivery, services, and sales promotion. In fact, with their willingness to persist despite trifling incomes, Nigerian entrepreneurs are in many ways particularly well-suited to sustaining such enterprises.

The very small enterprise that proves successful, however, is soon likely to grow to a critical size at which a new and qualitatively different set of problems emerges. Such enterprises cannot continue to grow by slow degrees, incrementally, gradually becoming large. If this were possible, Nigerian entrepreneurial drive would have begot by now a much greater number of large-scale Nigerian businesses. Alfred Marshall's title-page maxim was that nature does not make jumps. Be that as it may,

---

dence: Another Case of Bourgeois Utopianism," in *Nigeria's Indigenisation Policy: Proceedings of the 1974 Symposium*. This writer has also written several articles on the topic.
[4]Similar broad definitions of entrepreneurship are also employed by Harris, "Concept," pp. 5-6, and Nafziger, "Market," pp. 61-62, both in Schatz (ed.), *South of the Sahara*.
[5]The personal attributes of Nigerian entrepreneurship are discussed near the end of this chapter. Of course, one cannot generalize about all the peoples of Nigeria. See, e.g., the discussion of the way in which the Tiv social structure has made it "quite difficult for a larger Tiv entrepreneurial class to emerge." Justin Iyorbee Tseayo, "The Integration of the Local into the National Economy: The Tiv Case," *Nigerian Journal of Economic and Social Studies* XV:3 (November 1973): 434.
[6]J. D. Nyhart, "Notes on Entrepreneurship."

the problem confronting the successful and ambitious African entrepreneur is precisely that he *does* have to make a jump. He soon reaches the brink of a necessary leap—a technological, organizational, and marketing leap—if he is to continue to expand his enterprise. It is the difficulty of this leap that accounts for the commonly observed scarceness of indigenous as opposed to foreign ownership of large-scale enterprises in Nigeria and in less-developed economies generally.[7]

One aspect of the leap—or perhaps it would be more accurate to conceive of several interrelated leaps—is technological. The level of technology required often changes dramatically. It may be necessary to adopt an entirely different scale of operations and/or an entirely different set of qualitative standards. In Nigerian tin mining, for example, there was a fairly definite limit to the size of the operations that could be conducted along the labor-intensive, technologically simple lines employed by indigenous mine-owners. Such operations could make use of a maximum of perhaps £ 10,000 in capital. Further expansion, however, required equipment of a different order of complexity (involving investment on the order of £ 50,000 to £ 100,000) and an entirely different set of techniques, entailing new and forbidding technological and other demands upon the entrepreneur. At the time of this writer's investigations, even the most successful and highly regarded indigenous mine owner did not feel he was yet able to cope with such an enterprise.[8]

The technological leap also involves more demanding production standards. The growing firm cannot get by with gradual improvements in quality, for it must penetrate a more exacting market, in which higher quality is required by the product users or distributors. Even more difficult, the firm must forgo relaxed attitudes to meet rigorous requirements regarding uniformity of output, conformity with samples or specifications, and assured and regular delivery schedules. In sawmilling, for example, "sawing for export is demanding in control of quality and requires an ability to fill rather large orders in a reasonable time." These difficult requirements constituted one of the major reasons that less than 10 percent (6 out of 65) of the Nigerian sawmilling firms studied by John Harris had made the leap from exportation of logs to the exportation of timber.[9]

---

[7]The necessity for a leap is implied by a number of other writers on Nigeria. See, e.g., Wayne Nafziger, "Market," in Schatz, p. 7, and C. C. Onyemelukwe, *Problems of Industrial Planning and Management in Nigeria* (New York: Columbia University Press, 1966), pp. 196-197.

[8]Based on interviews with officials of the Association of African Miners in Jos and with Nigerian mine-owners, February, 1963. Tin mining has been dominated by large, foreign-owned companies. There were also a large number of individual Nigerian operators, mostly members of the A.A.M., but they produced in the early 1960s only about 6 percent of the total output. "Nigeria's Tin Resources," *Nigeria Trade Journal* 11:22 (April-June 1963): 64.

[9]Harris, *Industrial Entrepreneurship*, Ch. 4, p. 18. In 1976 a ban was placed on the export of timber: *West Africa*, February 16, 1976, p. 214.

An organizational leap is also necessary—from an enterprise personally supervised by the owner on the basis of close personal familiarity with all of the firm's operations to a more complex establishment requiring the use of more modern, impersonal management devices and techniques. The small firm gets by on the basis of "the flexibility that comes from intimate personal management where the craftsman-entrepreneur is in everyday association with his suppliers, customers and production workers."[10] It is difficult to establish a management system to compensate for the loss of flexibility as the firm grows. Thus, Nafziger found in Nigerian shoe firms that at some point, as output expanded, "the entreprener can no longer rely on supervising the production process directly on an *ad hoc* basis. The organization of the firm needs to be more complex than before, with a greater necessity for delegation of responsibility, advanced planning of work tasks, and a system of communication. In his previous apprentice training, the entrepreneur was not prepared for management and organizational problems of a firm of this complexity."[11]

The business encounters other organizational and managerial problems. Very small enterprises rarely keep books at all and even the more successful firms often have inadequate accounts. The lack or inadequacy of accounts soon becomes an impediment to growth, hampering rational control of internal operations and virtually eliminating the possibility of raising capital from outside sources. The adoption of a relatively sophisticated accounting system becomes imperative. The firm will also probably have to deal with labor in a new way as the size of the work force grows and demanding government labor regulations are applied. The difficulty of establishing a management system to compensate for the loss of intimate personal management is a universal problem in less-developed economies. "The transition from personal supervision is, according to many observers, the most difficult single problem with which a manager has to cope."[12]

A leap to new marketing methods is also often necessary for the expanding firm. Small firms depend on haphazard means of selling their goods. They sell to customers in their immediate area. They make small wholesale sales to personally known traders with whom dealings are flexible and informal. They get along on the basis of their feel for the market, knowing little about broader prospects, especially outside their immediate

[10]Archibald Callaway, "Crafts and Industries," p. 7.

[11]Nafziger, *Nigerian Entrepreneurship*, pp. 162-163. See also John R. Harris and Mary P. Rowe, "Entrepreneurial Patterns in the Nigerian Sawmilling Industry," *Nigerian Journal of Economic and Social Studies* VIII:1 (March 1966): 79.

[12]Joseph E. Stepanek, *Managers for Small Industry: An International Study* (Glencoe, Illinois: The Free Press, 1967), p. 71. See also Peter Kilby, *The Development of Small Industry in Eastern Nigeria* (Lagos: U.S. AID, 1962), pp. 15-16; Guy Hunter, *The New Societies of Tropical Africa* (London and Ibadan: Oxford University Press, 1962), pp. 322-325; Harris, "Concept," p. 12, and Nafziger, "Market," p. 71, both in Schatz; and Harris and Rowe, "Entrepreneurial Patterns," pp. 79 and 80.

areas. They are not concerned about transport of their goods and transport costs. But the enlarged firm, with the higher level of production and of fixed costs that accompany the new technology, must penetrate wider markets. This may require the company to develop a sales organization, a difficult task given the frequent lapses in commercial morality characteristic of all people moving from a traditional to a modern business society. Or the firm may seek regular outlets through one of the large trading chains, a relationship that is prized but difficult to establish.

Shortcomings in Making the Leap

It is in negotiating the leap that the inadequacies of Nigerian entrepreneurship emerge.

Technological

One frequently encounters in Nigerian businessmen a bland naiveté regarding the difficulties of modern business operations, a striking tendency to underestimate the technological (as well as organizational) complexities of business expansion. It is assumed that, with modern machinery, a supply of raw materials or intermediate inputs, and easily available local labor, production will proceed virtually automatically. This naive faith in modern machinery is illustrated by the action of a large printing firm which deliberately misapplied a government loan and, rather than buying the authorized equipment, used the funds as partial payment on a more expensive, highly advanced, but highly specialized photogravure rotary printing machine. The entrepreneur's reasoning appeared to be simply: the more technically advanced and complex the equipment, the better. In the Nigerian market, however, the costly specialized equipment could then be used for one purpose only, printing beer-bottle labels, and was therefore generally idle. It could be adapted for other purposes only by purchasing expensive ancillary equipment, and at the time this writer's study of the Federal Loans Board was completed, the Board was debating whether it should possibly throw good money after bad by financing the purchase of the ancillary equipment.

Cheerful confidence regarding the operation of technologically complex enterprises is usually not sustained in practice. Matters of overall plant organization and work flow are not generally handled competently. Productivity tends to be low relative to the level of capital and technology, and it is often clear that output would be increased by simple alterations in plant organization.[13] Moreover, maintenance, adjustment, and repair of

---

[13]Peter Kilby, "Organization and Production in Backward Economies," *Quarterly Journal of Economics* LXXVI:2 (May 1962): 304-7; see also his *Industrialization*, pp. 336-8. On technological inadequacies in Nigerian sawmilling, see Harris, *Industrial Entrepreneurship*, Ch. 4, pp. 3, 29.

equipment is a frequent problem. In visits to Nigerian firms one often finds machinery that is not in working order. In a not atypical case with which this writer was familiar, a sawmill operator requested deferment of his loan repayment because of a breakdown in the modern bench saw purchased with a Federal Loans Board loan. Investigation by a government industrial officer showed, however, that the problem was caused by damaged and worn-out parts which could be obtained immediately from local distributors. The entrepreneur had simply been unaware of this, and the machinery was soon restored to working order. In John Harris' study of sawmilling, he found that "most Nigerian sawmills are producing only about 10-20% of the lumber that the installed machines are capable of producing" (although this was only partially attributable to technological mismanagement) and that foreign-operated sawmills consistently operated at higher levels of utilization.[14] E. E. Enabor attributed "the generally low level of efficiency of Nigerian forest industries" to, inter alia, "nonexistence of mill maintenance facilities, poor training of operators and low entrepreneurial performance."[15]

Organizational

Nigerian businessmen suffer from organizational (or managerial) deficiencies for a number of reasons. One has been the limited opportunities for Nigerians to acquire business experience, an essential ingredient in the creation of entrepreneurship.[16] Another has been the limited opportunities for most would-be major entrepreneurs to participate in the modern society that provides the social as well as the economic setting for businesses of any size. All-round "modernization" is an important factor in business success in this milieu.[17] Striving Nigerian entrepreneurs are also impeded by lack of education, for there is a positive correlation between education and degree of business success. Compare, for example, entrepreneurs in very small scale industry in Eastern Nigeria (average firm employment of 10.9 persons) studied by Kilby with major entrepreneurs of large industrial firms studied by Nafziger. Only 10 percent of the former had any post-primary schooling and twice that number had no formal schooling at all, while the latter had an average of 10.2 years of education.[18]

[14]Harris, *Industrial Entrepreneurship*, Ch. 4, pp. 23-24. See also Onyemelukwe, *Problems*, p. 213.
[15]Ephraim E. Enabor, "Nigeria's Foreign Trade in Forest Products," *Nigerian Journal of Economic and Social Studies* XV:2 (July 1973): 193.
[16]The role of experience in creating entrepreneurship is discussed in Chapter 7.
[17]See the discussion of the alien social and economic milieus in Chapter 6.
[18]Kilby, *Development*, p. 15; and Nafziger, "Market," in Schatz, pp. 68-69. See also Nafziger's *Nigerian Entrepreneurship*, pp. 81 ff.; Peter C. Garlick, "African Traders and Economic Growth: A Case Study in Ghana," in Schatz, p. 80, and Hunter, *New Societies*, p. 135. However, Kilby maintains that there is only a "weak correlation between education and entrepreneurial success." Kilby, *Industrialization*, pp. 339-40. On the basis of a more

Organizational deficiencies make the leap difficult. With inadequate bookkeeping practices, already mentioned, most Nigerian entrepreneurs have only a hazy knowledge of costs other than direct outlays for materials and labor. They may well neglect depreciation in their calculations, an oversight that may be inconsequential when tools are simple and inexpensive but that becomes important for the firm trying to expand and modernize. They often do not even have any clear idea of gross receipts. Where it is feasible, they often determine their own pricing policies by reference to those charged by large foreign firms.[19] Nigerian businessmen tend to cling to one-man management, exhibiting an unwillingness to delegate real authority. This not only threatens long-run survival and growth through failure to create a successor to the owner-manager, it also makes it impossible to run efficiently a firm of any size and complexity. It is particularly difficult for most Nigerian businessmen to make useful estimates of potential costs and receipts when contemplating expansion. This problem is clearly manifested in the great bulk of the applications to government lending agencies.[20] Managerial shortcomings impinge in many other ways upon the internal efficiency of the firm.[21]

---

rigorous analysis of data originally published by O. Olakanpo, Adamu concluded: "There is a high level of significance between no education (group 1) and some sort of education (the other groups). There is no significant difference [in business success] between the educational levels as long as the trader does have some education." S. O. Adamu, " 'A Statistical Analysis of Some Determinants of Entrepreneurial Success: A Nigerian Case Study'—A Theoretical Consideration and Extension," *Nigerian Journal of Economic and Social Studies* XI:1 (March 1969): 40.

[19]An executive of one of the leading accounting firms in Nigeria states that virtually none of the Nigerian-owned firms, not even the most successful, have adequate accounts, and that the accounts are particularly deficient for determining costs. See also Onyemelukwe, *Problems,* pp. 223-24.

In his study of 65 sawmilling firms, John Harris found that 13 kept no books at all while another 32 had only rudimentary cash-in-and-out accounts. More than one-third prepared no annual summaries of any kind and only 10 had any kind of cost accounts. Even those with better accounts generally failed to use them as a management tool. Less than one-third of the entrepreneurs had an adequate understanding of depreciation, very few even had any idea of their previous year's gross receipts, and only about one-fourth could give a reasonable estimate of the minimum daily production required to break even. Harris, *Industrial Entrepreneurship,* Ch. 4, pp. 25-26.

It is the general opinion of knowledgeable observers, including government officials who have worked with Nigerian businessmen, that accounting deficiencies constitute a serious handicap. It is this writer's impression, however, that for small firms, and perhaps even for large ones, the importance of improving accounting practices may be overestimated. This writer's investigation of Federal Loans Board borrowers suggested that adequacy of bookkeeping was not a particularly important factor in their success or failure. Sayre P. Schatz, *Development Bank Lending: The Federal Loans Board* (Ibadan and London: Oxford University Press, 1964), pp. 42-43.

[20]Schatz, *Lending,* Ch. 6, and *Economics, Politics and Administration in Government Lending: The Regional Loans Boards of Nigeria* (Ibadan and London: Oxford University Press, 1970), Ch. 2.

[21]This writer is by no means alone in finding managerial deficiencies. Virtually all studies of Nigerian businessmen have made the same point, often much more emphatically than here and in considerable detail. See, e.g., J. D. Nyhart, "Notes on Entrepreneurship," pp.

They also make for difficulties in relations with other organizations. All but the most sophisticated and successful Nigerian businessmen are often at a loss in dealing with modern firms as suppliers or customers, with banks, and with government agencies. For example, they have usually been unaware of potentially helpful government programs. A survey of Western Nigerian businessmen indicated that most business-assistance programs were unknown to most businessmen and the majority of the programs were known to less than 15 percent of the respondents. Some 60 percent of the respondents had not taken advantage of any programs.[22] Nigerian businessmen have also often had difficulties in clearing goods through customs, in implementing import licensing procedures, in dealing with exchange regulations, and in other commercial transactions.[23]

Marketing

The marketing leap is also difficult. Establishing a widespread sales organization entails distribution costs not borne when a firm sells to customers in the immediate area. There are also expensive problems of control of untrustworthy sales agents. Thus, Kilby has found that the marketing disadvantages of the technologically superior large Nigerian bakeries offset their cost-of-production advantages and allow the smaller bakeries to thrive.[24] The establishment of regular outlets through one of the large distribution chains requires a constellation of production standards which, as has already been mentioned, Nigerian firms find hard to meet. In the early years of Nigerian independence some chains deliberately favored Nigerian producers, but their experiences were not successful and as concern over possible political repercussions subsided most of these relationships were terminated.

"Our Government" Approach

Nigerian businessmen have commonly displayed what may be called an "our government" approach. This attitude developed as political control passed from colonial into Nigerian hands, reached a peak a few years after independence, and has gradually diminished in the latter 1960s and into the 1970s. Its essence is the belief that Nigerian governments ("our government") should go far beyond simply creating a congenial climate and providing conventional programs to aid business—that government should aid Nigerian businessmen in direct, personal, day-to-day, and im-

---

21-22; Gerald K. Helleiner, *Peasant Agriculture,* pp. 265-266; Onyemelukwe, passim; Harris, *Industrial Entrepreneurship,* passim; Nafziger, *Nigerian Entrepreneurship,* passim; Kilby, *Industrialization,* Ch. 10.

[22]Sayre P. Schatz and S. I. Edokpayi, "Economic Attitudes of Nigerian Businessmen," *Nigerian Journal of Economic and Social Studies* IV:3 (November 1962): 259-262.

[23]See Nigeria, *Annual Report of the Department of Commerce and Industries* (Lagos: Government Printer) for various years.

[24]Peter Kilby, *African Enterprise,* Ch. 6.

mediately tangible ways and deal with the individual problems of each particular firm.

This attitude is a natural outcome of nationalist agitation for independence. It was a nationalist strategy to convert individual economic grievances into a collective national grievance against the colonial government.[25] The Government was blamed for all economic troubles.[26] A belief that the Government could dispel these troubles if only it wished to carried over into the period of effective Nigerian control.[27] Moreover, the view that government was an instrument for serving important business interests appeared to accord with Nigerian observations of colonial practice.[28]

The constellation of demands of the tenants at the Government's Yaba Industrial Estate illustrates the "our government" approach. A large

---

[25]See, e.g., James S. Coleman, *Nigeria: Background to Nationalism* (Berkeley and Los Angeles: University of California Press, 1958); Thomas Hodgkin, *Nationalism in Colonial Africa* (London: Frederick Muller, 1956).

[26]For example, the failure of the African-owned and -operated Industrial and Commercial Bank—which examination showed to be the result of gross mismanagement and probable fraud—was widely blamed on the British authorities. W. T. Newlyn and D. C. Rowan, *Money and Banking in British Colonial Africa* (Oxford: The Clarendon Press, 1954), pp. 97-98.

[27]A Nigerian economist remarked: "The present feeling throughout the country is that social and industrial amenities fall like manna from heaven, with Government as the channel for transmission." J. Amadi-Emina, "Presidential Address" [to Nigerian Economic Society], *Nigerian Journal of Economic and Social Studies* IV:1 (March 1962): 6. Similarly, a member of Parliament decried "the public notion that money available to the Government is inexhaustible . . . People go about thinking that the Government is such a big father that he should not hesitate to give his son what the son wants." Nigeria, Federation, *Debates in the House of Representatives, Session 1959-60* (Lagos: Government Printer, 1960), p. 211. Such expectations were expressed even by members of Parliament. Speaking of the Federal Minister of Commerce and Industry, one member of Parliament remarked: "I know the Minister is so bold, so strong, so powerful . . . He recently returned from a world tour, and I wish the Minister to see that we now have some industries within the country, and I wish him to extend the number of industries in Nigeria. Those that are not productive, I would like him to make them productive . . ." Nigeria, *Debates, Session 1960-61*, p. 146. Other MP's censured the same Minister because of low and falling prices of groundnuts and of palm oil. Nigeria, *Debates, Session 1959-60*, pp. 504-506.

This attitude has been common in countries of recent independence. See, e.g., Dunduzu Chisiza, "The Outlook for Contemporary Africa," *Journal of Modern African Affairs* I:1 (March 1963): 30. In Uganda, a Government commission remarked: "We deplore the general attitude that the money of the Uganda Credit and Savings Bank is Government money and therefore fair game." Uganda Protectorate, *The Advancement of Africa in Trade* (First Meeting of the Commission, March 30, 1954) (Entebbe: Government Printer, 1955), p. 35. Another observer commented that businessmen in Uganda "think that now that they are about to gain political independence these things [power, status, money] are to be theirs automatically . . ." Henry B. Thomas, "African Entrepreneurs in Industrial Pursuits," in Warren H. Hausman (ed.), *Managing Economic Development in Africa* (Cambridge, Mass.: MIT Press, 1963), p. 107.

[28]Post has pointed out that government has to a significant extent been popularly conceived of as a bestower of benefits. K. W. J. Post, *The Nigerian Federal Election of 1959; Politics and Administration in a Developing Political System* (London: Oxford University Press, 1963), p. 390.

proportion were consistently behind in their rental obligations, and many had left surreptitiously owing substantial unpaid back rent. While tenants agreed that the rate was a bargain, they asserted that, as participants in a special government effort to aid indigenous businessmen, their rent should be reduced or eliminated altogether. Among other things, moreover, the tenants wanted the government to undertake the following: to give priority in some manner to the industrial estate in the supply of electricity so that tenants would not suffer the same power failures as other users in the Lagos area; to extend loans with totally inadequate security; to help them sell their goods; and to purchase government supplies from the tenants whenever possible.

Nigerian tin-mine owners also expected a great deal from government. They wanted differential royalties on tin, lower for Nigerian than for foreign-owned companies with, furthermore, a provision for reduction when an indigenous company was not profitable. As one owner put it: "Because, after all, we're beginners. Why shouldn't Government try to help us by giving this concession. After all, we pay rents, royalties, tax." They also wanted the Mines Department to reduce its fee on the prospecting equipment it rented to small proprietors who could not afford their own. Highly unrealistic hopes for government aid were also revealed in a Western Nigeria survey of 626 small handicraft and manufacturing establishments employing less than five workers. There were requests for, among other things, the prevention of raw-material price increases, the making of business loans almost automatic upon request, and guaranteed government patronage regardless to the quality of output.[29]

Loan programs have frequently been abused. Leaving aside politically motivated loans, repayments have often been difficult to collect unless the borrowers were forced to pay through threats or compulsion, as when the Federal Loans Board achieved a flurry of hurried payments during 1961 and 1962 by notifying delinquents of the pending sale of the property they had pledged as security.[30] As one highly educated and articulate

[29]The converse of unrealistic expectations of government were severe criticisms when hopes were dashed. The charge has been repeatedly expressed to this writer by both large and small Nigerian businessmen that government favored foreign-owned businesses. As one respondent in a survey of Western Nigerian businesses remarked: "It appears as if our Governments of Nigeria are giving more cooperation and patronage to those foreign firms and thereby enriching their pockets at the expense of we Nigerians and to the detriment of we indigenous businessmen . . ." (These charges were not always without foundation, as when payoffs to venal politicians were involved.) Businessmen also complained that hire-purchase agreements for lorries were one-sided and unfair; that the Ministry of Commerce and Industry was not giving sufficient aid to African importers; and that competition caused expatriate produce buyers to pay the peasants more than the stipulated minimum price for their goods, thus forcing the African produce-buyers to do the same.

[30]Federal Loans Board, *Sixth Annual Report, 1961-62* (Lagos: Government Printer, 1962), p. 9. This attitude carried over to some degree to the banks. As a highly capable political leader remarked in Parliament: "You know the mentality in this country today is that if you want money of course the money is there in the bank. The bank seems to be able to grow money out of the ground." Nigeria, Federation, *Debates of the House of Representatives, Session 1958-59* (Lagos: Government Printer, 1959), p. 870.

businessman rationalized: "We feel no moral obligation to repay loans, because we see the colossal waste and corruption in government." Borrowers have also had no compunctions about misapplying loans (i.e., spending the money for purposes different from those specified in the loan agreement) and other evasions of Loans Board obligations.[31]

The effects of the "our government" attitude are difficult to appraise. They may diminish businessmen's ability to make the leap by engendering passivity and by inhibiting the self-reliance needed for Schumpeterian entrepreneurship.[32] An attitude survey found that Nigerian expectations of government were "very much higher than customary,"[33] and it expressed the apprehension that disappointment about government "might spill over into a mood of individual frustration, pessimism and despair at the personal level."[34] However, observations by this writer and many others of the fierce struggle for business success in Nigeria suggest that the negative effects of the "our government" approach on Nigerian entrepreneurship are probably small.

Financial Trustworthiness

One of the most passionate criticisms of Nigerian businessmen is for lack of trustworthiness. It comes from all sides. In a survey of 419 Western Nigerian businessmen, an open-ended question about the obstacles to the formation of partnerships or joint business ventures with other Nigerians elicited the response in 74 percent of the cases that partnerships were difficult or undesirable because of financial untrustworthiness. Some characteristic answers were: ". . . the spirit of cheating reigns supreme among us"; "the only reason is that honesty is still wanting among the indigenous businessmen"; "most of our businessmen are not honest"; "established businessmen prefer to stick to their assured small profit than to risk losing all to a dishonest partner. This conviction will not change until morals improve, both in the business and the social sphere." A

---

[31]There is ambivalence, however. Coexisting with excessive expectations is excessive gratitude when government does use its tax revenues to provide services. The latter emotion was played upon in a speech by the Western Nigerian Housing Corporation chairman: "This new scheme . . . is a fine gesture on the part of the Government and an act for which she should be highly praised. It is an act that can never be forgotten by whoever comes to be benefitted by it, because it is not easy to forget anyone who provides shelter for one and for one's family." Western Nigeria Housing Corporation, *Building for the People* (no place, no date [1962?] given), p. 3.

[32]"The government has done so much to help the Nigerian businessman. But the Nigerian businessman seems to be absorbing all the facilities without 'delivering the goods.' " Akin Mabogunje, "Discussion," in Nigerian Economic Society, *Nigeria's Indigenisation Policy: Proceedings of a November 1974 Symposium Organized by the Nigerian Economic Society* (Ibadan: Nigerian Economic Society, 1975), p. 75.

[33]Lloyd A. Free, *The Attitudes, Hopes and Fears of Nigerians* (Princeton, N.J.: Institute for International Social Research, 1964), p. 38.

[34]Free, p. 71.

similar attitude is expressed by bankers,[35] by other foreign businessmen,[36] and by Nigerian political leaders.[37]

Commercial immorality (and its possible exaggeration, to be discussed
shortly) tends to diminish the possibility of making the leap. It reduces the
likelihood that joint business ventures pooling capital or talents will be
established and discourages the formation of large impersonal corporations over which investors may have little direct control. Some observers
have considered this a major problem.[38] It may also occasionally impede
viable plans for expansion by making it more difficult for Nigerians to get
credit from ordinary commercial sources.

Since such strong feelings are expressed by both Nigerians and foreigners about the problem of business dishonesty, let us digress briefly to
consider the causes of the problem and also the possibility that it may be
exaggerated.[39]

The problem is a common one. A disregard of commercial morality is
often simply one facet of economic underdevelopment. "A society in
which the acceleration of growth has occurred only in very recent decades
always displays many incongruities. People take a long time to adjust
themselves to a money economy. . . . They need a new pattern of morality, which may take a long time to be created; for they cease to live in a
community where obligations are based upon status, and move into one
where obligations are based upon contract, and generally upon market
relationships with people with whom there are no kinship ties. . . . rapid
change causes old beliefs and institutions to disintegrate more rapidly
than new beliefs and institutions can be integrated in their place."[40]
Frustration over tremendous income disparities, over the gulf between
small and large (especially foreign-owned) companies, and over the irritat-

---

[35]". . .Lending to Africans is a business fraught with great risks owing to the comparative
financial unreliability of African businessmen and the lack of adequate and acceptable banking collateral." O. Olakanpo, "The Loynes Report and Banking in Sierra Leone," *Bankers'
Magazine* CXCIV, No. 1420 (July 1962): 19-27. See also Hunter, p. 137.

[36]In the Western Nigeria survey just mentioned, a typical expatriate response to a question about the suitability of Nigerian businessmen as partners in joint business ventures was:
"In general, contracts are honoured only when profitable and flagrantly dishonoured when
they prove to be inconvenient or unprofitable to execute. Also, indigenous businessmen in
general are notoriously unwilling payers of debts due, and such protection as is offered by
the Courts is inadequate."

[37]Said a leading member of Parliament, a Federal Minister, "One thing lacking in this
country is honesty. We have men capable and intelligent, determined to help the progress of
the country, but one thing is missing and that is integrity." Nigeria, Federation, *Debates of
the House of Representatives, Session 1958-59* (August 9, 1958), columns 2321 and 2322.

[38]"It would probably be difficult to over-emphasize the degree to which the prevailing
mutual suspicion" prevents the establishment of larger, more impersonal, but more permanent enterprises in Nigeria. J. D. Nyhart, "Notes on Entrepreneurship." See also Ogunpola, pp. 351, 358.

[39]See Schatz and Edokpayi for a fuller discussion of this point.

[40]W. Arthur Lewis, *The Theory of Economic Growth* (Homewood, Ill.: Richard D.
Irwin, 1955), pp. 144-145. See also the *Report of the Advisory Committee on Aids to African*

ing adversities of the economic environment strengthen the tendency to cut moral corners. The tendency is reinforced by the belief that respectable European firms have prospered through exploitation.

However, the degree of financial unreliability appears to have been exaggerated, and by Africans themselves. Most have had a rather unrealistically virtuous image of the European, arising out of colonial experience and education. In colonial schools, ideals came to be regarded as descriptions of the way Europeans actually behaved. In the textbooks, especially those written for Africans, "Europeans appeared in a very favourable light. Explorers, statesmen, inventors, scientists and so forth marched across the pages in a glorious procession. . . . there was excessive emphasis on the outstanding figures; not enough was conveyed to the children about the humdrum everyday lives of millions of whites. . . ." African pupils came to believe that "All Europeans are trying to improve their country" and "Europeans always do or die." The misleading impression that such ideals were in fact the prevalent norms "put before the African children an impossibly high standard to emulate. . . ."[41]

Experience tended to strengthen this picture of European virtue and superiority. Europeans held positions of dominance and prestige, had higher incomes, greater education, and greater skills than all but a few Africans. And European feelings of superiority inevitably tended to be transmitted to their subordinates.

European business sophistication also buttressed this impression. Businesses the world over encounter temptations to cut moral corners, and many succumb to the temptation. To whatever extent foreign-owned firms operating in Nigeria engage in such practices, however, they are more adept in camouflaging them than their less experienced African colleagues. As a result a smaller proportion of European than of African malpractices are discovered.

In contrast with the flattering image of European behavior, the real day-to-day behavior of Africans has been seen as shameful. Among Europeans "there is a tacit recognition that many of [the generally accepted] norms are directional ideals, which ordinary people could not be expected even to approach; self esteem is therefore not appreciably lowered . . . But Africans cannot, within the alien set of values they have been taught, make these fine discriminations between directional and operative norms, although they can and do within their own traditional

---

Businessmen (Lagos: Federal Government Printer, 1959), which quite correctly maintains that with economic development, the African trader "will, like other people, soon develop the correct attitude to [inter alia] . . . business integrity" (p. 4).

[41]Gustav Jahoda, White Man: A Study of Attitudes of Africans to Europeans in Ghana before Independence (London: Oxford University Press, 1961), p. 99. My discussion relies heavily upon this study.

value-system."[42] They have therefore tended to exaggerate their own shortcomings.

Apprehension about financial unreliability is heightened by the low income level. "It is only natural that a man whose life savings amount to a trifle should be reluctant to invest it in an enterprise the management and control of which are in other people's hands."[43] Moreover a cultural tradition among many of the people of Nigeria that inclines people to attribute misfortunes to malevolent personal intervention has the same effect.[44] For example, when excessive delays caused the spoilage of large amounts of gari, the Gari Traders Union charged the Nigerian Railway Corporation with intentionally damaging behavior.[45] Sales by foreign-owned companies of used cars brought the charge by the Nigerian second-hand-car dealers' association that this was "another way of killing off our trade and making life difficult for us."[46] Procedural delays in government or other disappointments are commonly attributed to laziness or the need for a bribe. In the same way, business misfortunes that occur in dealing with other Nigerians are commonly attributed to someone's dishonesty.

Because of the entrepreneurial shortcomings just discussed, and perhaps others as well, Nigerian businessmen are less capable of making the leap than their advanced-economy counterparts. There is an entrepreneurial gap.

This gap, it may be noted parenthetically, is partly[47] responsible for the frequent complaints about unfair competition. As a case in point, the basic premise of Nigeria's Committee on Aid to African Businessmen was "The African businessman lacks capital, managerial experience, and technological skill. He is as a result engaged in an unequal competition with those who have behind them a tradition of wealth and business technique."[48]

[42]Jahoda, p. 126.

[43]*Report . . . on Aids to African Businessmen*, p. 4.

[44]I am indebted for this point to John Boston, an anthropologist with long experience in Africa.

[45](Lagos) *Daily Times*, August 16, 1963, p. 13.

[46](Lagos) *Daily Times*, August 8, 1963, p. 3.

[47]There are other important reasons. One is the existence of differential difficulties in the economic environment working to the disadvantage of the indigenous firm, to be discussed in the next chapter. Another is the tendency for antagonisms between small and big business to be seen in colonial and post-colonial settings in terms of imperialist exploitation and therefore unfair competition. (See Jahoda, pp. 72-3, for a discussion of a related process.) Then, of course, there is the actual use of practices that would generally be considered unfair.

[48]The committee elaborates upon this position at some length, *Report . . . on Aids to African Businessmen*, pp. 3-4. The charge of unfair competition has had a long and vigorous life; the following comment is representative of many that can be found in the parliamentary debates and the press. "An open competition between the small African farmer and the big

On the Other Hand

Despite the entrepreneurial gaps (and despite, also, economic-environment difficulties to be discussed in the next chapter), the leap is not impossible. Virtually all of the successful Nigerian entrepreneurs have started small and made the leap successfully.[49] The deficiencies of Nigerian businessmen are usually exaggerated, and Nigerian entrepreneurship has certain strengths as well.

Exaggerations

The exaggerations of African entrepreneurial deficiencies arise from an assortment of misconceptions and misapprehensions. Sometimes it is a matter of definition. Entrepreneurship is in effect defined or conceived of as that quality or combination of qualities that generates economic development. If, then, development is lagging, it is a result of poor entrepreneurship. (An exception may be made: that grossly bad government might hamstring even potentially superior entrepreneurship.) An example of this fallacy is found in a study of development banking in India, Pakistan, Iran, and Turkey. The author explained the relatively high level of industrial investment in India and Pakistan, the low level in Iran, and the intermediate level in Turkey in the following way: India "has a larger proportion of experienced entrepreneurs" than the other countries of the study; "Pakistan men of means have been much more progressive in venturing into industry with their capital than is true of Iran"; "In contrast with India and Pakistan, Iran suffers from a shortage of venturesome entrepreneurs"; "Turkish capitalists appear to have been more willing to enter industry than those of Iran but possibly less so than the Indian and Pakistani entrepreneurs."[50]

---

alien plantation owner or the rivalry between the Nigerian petty trader and manufacturer on the one hand and the vast phantasmagoric of alien multi-millionaires and 'Big Business' on the other hand is rightly regarded with alarm. . . . a fight between the elephant and the ant." Nigeria, Federation, *House of Representatives Debates, First Session, 1952* (Lagos: Government Printer, 1952), p. 244. (Minor typographical errors were corrected.)

[49]In his intensive study of handicraft and industrial production in Ibadan, Callaway also found many instances "of individual Nigerians winning their way through to high income as traders and then branching out to invest within the motor transport and building industries. A few have emerged at the head of promising but small industrial enterprises." Archibald Callaway, "Crafts and Industries," p. 2. The initial capital of 5 small manufacturing firms in Onitsha examined by Katzin was £ 30, £ 50, £ 70, £ 265, and £ 2,000. Margaret Katzin, "The Role of the Small Entrepreneur," Preliminary unpublished manuscript, p. 4. A study of businesses in India indicates the same pattern. In a study of 52 medium-size light-engineering firms and manufacturing firms, Berna found that 85 percent of the firms surveyed were established as small units—many very small indeed—and grew into medium-size enterprises. James A. Berna, *Industrial Entrepreneurship in Madras State* (London: Asia Publishing House, 1960), pp. 146, 213.

[50]Nathaniel H. Engle, *Industrial Development Banking in Action: A Study of Organisation, Operations and Procedure of Private Development Banks in India, Iran, Pakistan, Turkey* (Pakistan Industrial Credit and Investment Corporation, 1962), pp. 282, 285, 287

Sometimes the African entrepreneur is, implicitly, measured against an image of the highly capable businessman falsely believed typical of advanced economies (an entrepreneur who, in economic theory, always produces at the lowest possible costs).[51] This kind of comparison is often made by relatively young and inexperienced foreign academics and business and government personnel, and also by African officials with little or no experience of managerial practices outside their own countries. African officials, moreover, are somewhat inclined to make unfavorable comparisons because of their role and their situation. They have both a parochial predisposition to believe that the business-assistance programs they administer will be effective and also a patriotic predisposition to believe that the national economic environment will sustain adequate development—if only businessmen responded properly.

Experienced observers have been less impressed with entrepreneurial and managerial practices in advanced economies. "From the standpoint of economic analysis, organizational behavior is not always 'rational'. Indeed, the economist who studies any form of management soon finds out that business organizations are surprisingly 'inefficient'. The decision-making processes in the modern enterprise are not so precise or so rational as the economic theorist might presume, and a great deal of energy within the organization is absorbed in clearly noneconomic activities."[52]

Surveys of American business consistently reveal entrepreneurial inadequacies. One indicated that 89.4 percent of failures were due to management deficiencies. The survey also showed that only one manager out of twelve realized that he was at all responsible for the difficulty. The United States Small Business Administration stated: "Statistics show that over 60% of new businesses never last over five years and the reason for the majority of failures is lack of management know-how. In fact, poor management is the reason for most business failures. Many of these men who failed believed that more money would solve their problems, but found it did not."[53] Even *successful* small businesses are generally entrepreneurially deficient. A study of the characteristics of successful small businesses found, for example, that the firms rarely engaged in long-run planning, that they had no aggressive plans for expansion, and that though

(mimeographed). Harris also discusses the tendency to make entrepreneurship important by definition. J. R. Harris, "Concept," p. 7.

[51] For an interesting discussion of some implications of this assumption, see Harvey Leibenstein, "Allocative Efficiency vs. X-Efficiency," *American Economic Review* 56:3 (June 1966): 392-415.

[52] Frederick Harbison, "Entrepreneurial Organization as a Factor in Economic Development," *Quarterly Journal of Economics* (August 1956), reprinted in Bernard Okun and Richard W. Richardson (eds.), *Studies in Economic Development* (New York: Holt, Rinehart and Winston, 1961), pp. 316-317.

[53] Stepanek, p. 3.

the typical chief executive felt that he delegated considerable authority and responsibility his subordinates and independent interviewers as well indicated he did not.[54] Another study of active small business indicated: "In general, the picture was one of complacency among most of the businessmen and confusion among those who saw a need for improvement."[55] Still another study of small American manufacturers found that many paid little attention to marketing and failed to make strong growth efforts; "they accept new customers but make little or no effort to uncover additional business." Only 27 percent said that they had clearly formulated objectives for market planning.[56]

Some criticisms of Nigerian entrepreneurs have arisen from the unrealistic expectation that they act in ways considered most productive of economic development rather than in ways that promise the best returns.[57] The Federal Minister of Transport stated: "The fact is that in these long term investments the Nigerian is never very keen on putting in his money: he wants quick returns. . . . That is why the government has to take the initiative, reluctantly. Government would be much happier if Nigerians would be able to do it themselves."[58] Even a highly sophisticated indigenous businessman spoke disparagingly of the fact that Nigerian businessmen "won't take risks; they prefer to invest in real estate." Such criticisms are common throughout Africa. However, one cannot expect entrepreneurs to pass up lucrative and safe investment in real estate (in which the annual return on investment was frequently 20-25 percent or more, and in which three or four years' rent in advance was paid), or to forgo investments in trading activities when they expect large returns, or to relinquish lucrative political plums in contracting to sink their limited capital into long-term industrial projects, which are not only riskier and lower yielding but in which they will also have a much smaller

[54]Kenneth Lawyer and Associates, *Small Business Success: Operating and Executive Characteristics* (Cleveland, Ohio: Bureau of Business Research, Western Reserve University, 1963), summarized in Small Business Administration, *Management Research Summary* (Washington, D.C.: Small Business Administration, 1963).

[55]L. J. Crampon and Stewart F. Schweizer, *A Study of the Informational Needs and Problems of Small Businessmen* (Boulder: Bureau of Business Research, University of Colorado, 1961), summarized in Small Business Administration, *Management Research Summary* (Washington, D.C., 1962), p. 3.

[56]R. J. Holloway, *Marketing Research and Market Planning for the Small Manufacturer* (Minneapolis: School of Business Administration, University of Minnesota, 1961), summarized in Small Business Administration, *Management Research Summary* (Washington, D.C.: 1961), p. 1.

[57]Unrealistic expectations of this kind have constituted a common failing of foreign personnel in Africa. See, e.g., Peter F. M. McLoughlin, "Land Reorganization in Malawi, 1950-60: Its Pertinence to Current Development," in Schatz, *South of the Sahara*, pp. 133-38; and R. H. Green and S. H. Hymer, "Cocoa in the Gold Coast: A Study in the Relations Between African Farmers and Agricultural Experts," *Journal of Economic History* XXVI:3 (September 1966): 299-319.

[58]Nigeria, Federation, *Debates of the House of Representatives, Session 1958-59* (November 25, 1958), columns 2565-2566.

chance of evading or avoiding taxes. If any criticism is rational in such cases, it is not a criticism of the quality of entrepreneurs but of the social consequences of rational entrepreneurial behavior.

Another criticism is based on the diversified nature of the undertakings of many of the more successful businessmen in Nigeria. It is argued that this reflects entrepreneurial inability to run large enterprises.

It is true that the multifaceted one-man enterprise is common in Nigeria. Typically, the entrepreneur has been successful in one line but, instead of enlarging operations in that line, has branched out to other fields. Each of the activities is a separable one-man business, linked through the common person of the entrepreneur. The most frequent aggregations are trading combined with transport, construction, and/or manufacturing. Some of the profits have also often gone into real estate. There tend to be frequent transfers of funds between the different activities, even if they are separately incorporated. The successful Nigerian entrepreneur has thus flourished typically not by expanding one line of activity, but by establishing many virtually unrelated businesses.[59]

To attribute this pattern to a lack of entrepreneurial ability, however, does not seem sensible. More energy, drive, and ability are required to run a multifaceted business than to run a single-faceted business of the same size.[60] The diversified pattern is most easily explained by the limited markets, the flood of competing new entrants attracted by success in any one line,[61] and other problems in the economic environment that make it very difficult to enlarge an existing line of activity.

The entrepreneurs themselves explain their diversification in this way. A capable and successful diversified Northern Nigerian businessman (construction, cigarette distribution, truck transport, and two petrol stations) explained to this writer that there was a limit to potential earnings in any one line, and that "I have four wives and ten children so I need more money than I can make" in any of his business activities. Similarly, Northern Nigerian builders and suppliers of building materials explain that they are involved in an assortment of different activities because the amount of building work is so limited relative to the number of competitors in the business. This was confirmed by an examination of government records (the Northern Nigerian Government having been the major client of such firms). The number of contracts awarded annually averaged only about two-fifths of the number of government-registered

[59]Nyhart, p. 20.

[60]Berna's appraisal of Indian entrepreneurs who diversified production seems pertinent for Nigeria: "The conclusion seems warranted that the entrepreneurs under study are a rather enterprising group of men, willing to abandon traditional activities and accept the risks in entering new fields and possessing considerable ability to adapt to changing conditions and circumstances." Berna, p. 208.

[61]See, e.g., J. O. Odufalu, "Indigenous Enterprise in Nigerian Manufacturing," *Journal of Modern African Studies* IX:4 (December 1971): 603.

contractors. Contractors continually besieged the office of the Senior Quantity Surveyor in the hope of getting even a small job.[62] In rubber processing, too, Harris found: "As competition had increased in the activities through which they had prospered, [most of] these relatively wealthy and experienced entrepreneurs were seeking new industrial opportunities for diversification and expansion."[63]

The way that severe competition for limited profit opportunities deflects successful Nigerian entrepreneurs into a variety of activities is common elsewhere in Africa and in less-developed economies generally. In his study of Indian light-engineering firms, Berna found that nearly half of the firms that entered new lines of production did so "to compensate for the loss of traditional markets or severe competition from rivals."[64] Stepanek has also found that the ability of the entrepreneur in less-developed economies may outstrip the ability of the economy to sustain expansion in most lines of activity. "A few managers have developed their ability to organize at a faster rate than the economy allows the enterprise to expand. Perhaps the limit of the market has been reached. The more able and ambitious managers may then diversify their first company or establish additional companies. . . . This type of managerial development is not at all uncommon."[65]

Positive Attributes

Nigerian entrepreneurs also have attributes and advantages that partially compensate for the deficiencies.

They tend to possess in high degree the pure personal qualities of entrepreneurship. They tend to be highly responsive to the possibility of gain, to pursue economic advantage vigorously and strenuously. They are flexible and venturesome, are willing to seek far and wide and to take risks in the quest for profit. Any venture that has the remotest prospect of success attracts them. Applicants to government loans boards have sought loans for an enormous variety of business ventures, ranging from the commonplace to the imaginative to the far-fetched.[66] More than one-third of 626 very small entrepreneurs surveyed indicated willingness to abandon their present ventures for others which appeared more promis-

---

[62]See also Ogunpola, p. 354: "Many of them [Western Nigerian contractors] even engage in businesses which have no bearing whatsoever with the building industry. This apparent lack of specialization at these levels is due essentially to the fact that these contractors do not get contract work regularly and that the work they get at any given time is not big enough to occupy them fully."

[63]Harris, *Industrial Entrepreneurship*, Ch. 5, p. 17. Harris' finding of a negative correlation between sawmill operators' rates of return on sawmilling and the size of their real estate holdings might also be interpreted as evidence that diversification results from limited profit possibilities in an existing line of activity: Ch. 4, p. 41.

[64]James J. Berna, p. 206.

[65]Joseph E. Stepanek, p. 71.

[66]Schatz, *Bank Lending*, pp. 70-72.

ing.[67] They surge quickly into any line that is profitable. "It is particularly noticeable that where opportunities arose for African participation in economic activities in West Africa, Africans were always quick to seize them."[68]

Most students of Nigerian economic affairs agree with P. T. Bauer's characterization in the first substantial study of West African entrepreneurship. "The general impression I formed was always the same: exceptional effort, foresight, resourcefulness, thrift and ability to perceive economic opportunity."[69]

Nigerians are sometimes able to make good use of detailed knowledge that a foreigner is not likely to have. Thus, owner-drivers are at an advantage in the casual road-transport business, in which a regular run may be made but in which charges are a matter for bargaining and in which passengers and goods are picked up and discharged anywhere along the way. They can deal more knowledgeably and effectively with the tendency of drivers to pilfer a substantial part of the receipts, to fabricate expensive repairs, and to overstate the amounts needed to "quench police troubles." Unique opportunities can sometimes be found, as in the case of a successful Nigerian trucker, under contract to a petroleum concern, who was able to make use of salvaged parts and materials scrounged from various places to construct a semi-trailer at a cost of approximately one-fourth of the normal purchase price. He was also able to effect similar savings by using his not always fully utilized work force to rebuild a scrapped engine block he managed to acquire. Sometimes thorough familiarity with Nigerian tastes is important. Thus, a phonograph record dealer was able to survive in the face of severe competition from well-financed, foreign-owned firms "because it was difficult for them to know the choice of Africans in music."[70]

Indigenous entrepreneurs can often work within and make use of complex social patterns that constitute obstacles for outsiders. Consider, for example, a case in which intense, and sometimes violent, resistance prevented the working of a stone quarry in an Eastern Nigerian community because the quarry was inhabited by a snake that had religious signifi-

---

[67]Unpublished survey carried out in 1961 by the Western Nigeria Ministry of Economic Planning and Community Development.

[68]E. K. Hawkins, *Road Transport in Nigeria* (London: Oxford University Press, 1958), p. 93. See also *Development: The ENDC Quarterly Magazine* 6:18 (April-June, 1962): 27.

[69]One could easily draw up a long list of similar observations. Bauer, p. 30.

[70]This incident and the one related in the next paragraph are drawn from a series of seminars on Nigerian entrepreneurship conducted by Dr. R. S. Rungta while he was Lecturer at the University of Nigeria, Nsukka, during the academic year 1963-64. At monthly meetings well-known businessmen discussed papers on the growth of their enterprises with a group of business managers, senior civil servants, and academicians. Dr. Rungta and the present writer subsequently worked on this material together. Some other materials in this section as well as occasional points elsewhere in the book are also drawn from this source.

cance for the people of the community and quarrying operations killed the snake. Although the Nigerian Railway Corporation and other large organizations had been stymied by the resistance, a sensitive Nigerian entrepreneur with the appropriate knowledge of local ways was effective. By "inventing" a story of his consanguineous relationship to the community, by becoming familiar to and with the local people, and by working out special arrangements with local religious leaders, he was able to get the quarry operating again, at a nice profit for himself.

The use of intricate social interrelationships is also exemplified by the kola trade. The distribution of kola nuts is characterized by considerable complexity, substantial risks, a wide variety of alternatives to consider at any one time, a need for extensive but detailed knowledge of continually changing conditions, and the absolute necessity for far-flung credit arrangements. To handle these requirements, "the Hausa have managed to develop an extensive, intricate business organization which covers every stage of the trade." Abner Cohen describes the elaborate, large-scale, tribally based network in fascinating detail.[71]

To sum up, Nigerian businessmen manifest various entrepreneurial deficiencies, particularly in attempting the leap to relatively large, impersonally managed enterprises. These deficiencies are often exaggerated; moreover, indigenous entrepreneurs tend to possess certain strengths and advantages. Nevertheless, the Nigerian economy is trammeled by an entrepreneurial gap. This constitutes one set of reasons for the paucity of profitable business ventures discussed in Chapter 4. We move in the next chapter to another set of reasons, the environment in which Nigerian businessmen operate.

[71]Abner Cohen, "Politics of the Kola Trade," in Edith H. Whetham and Jean I. Currie (eds.), *Readings in the Applied Economics of Africa; Volume 1: Micro-Economics* (London: Cambridge University Press, 1967), p. 155.

Chapter Six

THE ECONOMIC ENVIRONMENT

It has been maintained so far that the major impediment to indigenous private investment in industry and commerce is not capital shortage but rather a paucity of profitable business ventures, that this paucity is partially attributable to the entrepreneurial gap, but that the importance of entrepreneurial shortcomings tends to be overstated. This brings us to the economic environment.

"Economic environment" refers here to all the factors impinging upon the operation of a business other than the availability of capital and the ability of the businessman himself—problems of securing proper equipment in reasonable time and in good working order, problems of human resources, of infrastructure, of supplies, of adequate markets, etc. It is the thesis of this chapter that special difficulties are encountered in the economic environment of a poor country that make success for a businessman there considerably more difficult to achieve than for an equally well-financed and talented counterpart in a more developed economy. Many of the environmental adversities of the Nigerian economy hinder impartially all firms, whether foreign or indigenously owned, but many affect mainly or exclusively indigenous entrepreneurs, making success particularly difficult for them to attain.

The major part of this chapter is devoted to delineating the special adversities in the Nigerian economic environment, those that are not likely to be encountered in the more developed economies. In the second and third sections, the relationships between the economic environment and entrepreneurship are considered.

Adversities in the Economic Environment

Acquiring Capital Goods and Supplies

Enterprises operating in Nigeria encounter many cost-increasing difficulties in acquiring the capital goods, intermediate goods, and raw materials they need.

1. Frequently ordering at long distance and without good contacts, and buying in a world that generally does not design equipment for African conditions, indigenously owned firms often find it virtually impossible to order the best equipment for their purposes. Thus, a Nigerian cement company found after installation of its equipment that the wet-grinding process the company was going to utilize was not suitable. It was necessary to convert the plant to a dry-grinding process, and this was a major cause of a two-year delay in initiating production. After the conversion, a residue of problems remained which contributed (to a minor degree, it must be said) to such continuing production difficulties that the company was producing at less than 15 percent of planned capacity in 1975 despite Nigeria's severe shortage of cement. Even careful consultation might not help. A Nigerian printing firm in which an American management advisor and investor had a substantial interest placed an order for a sizeable package of interrelated printing equipment from an American manufacturer. The precise kinds of equipment to order were carefully decided in close consultation by the Nigerian entrepreneur, the American management advisor, and the equipment manufacturer's representative in Nigeria. Fortunately, before the equipment order was filled, the American (for reasons not related to the equipment purchase) made a trip back to the United States and took the opportunity to visit the equipment manufacturer. There he learned that he had not ordered the best equipment for the printing firm's purposes. Following the manufacturer's advice, he was able to purchase equipment that was not only more suitable but that also saved approximately 15 percent on the original £ 108,000 purchase. Most African firms, however, do not have the opportunity to rectify mistakes in this manner. One of Nigeria's leading indigenous industrial firms of the 1960s, for example, ordered a machine for producing camelback (a necessary component in the tire-retreading process) that they were told was large enough to supply all three of their plants. After laying out the money for the equipment (and after a series of expensive difficulties in setting up and installing the equipment), the firm discovered that the capacity of the machine was actually insufficient for even one of its factories. The firm therefore had to undertake the additional expense (£ 28,000) of ordering more equipment.

A firm operating in Nigeria often has less precise knowledge of and control over the exact nature of imported supplies than does a firm operating in an advanced economy where it is aided by highly developed international marketing facilities. As a result the entrepreneur in Nigeria is more likely to order supplies that are not fully suited to his purposes.[1] An

---

[1]This particularly affects the businessman who is setting up modern operations. "A modernized and expanded enterprise may require raw materials of a type or quality different from that of a very small company. A cobbler can use leather of a quality unacceptable to a shoe factory. Yarn imperfections that would be permissible for a hand loom would not be

example was provided by a modern Nigerian factory for rubber-soled shoes, which suffered expensive and protracted delays because raw material imports proved unsatisfactory.

2. Whether or not he orders suitable equipment or other inputs, the businessman operating in Nigeria not uncommonly finds that the goods specified are not delivered or do not arrive in good condition. Damage or deterioration and pilferage during transit, always problems,[2] became absolutely commonplace as a result of the overwhelming port congestion that developed in 1975 in Nigeria. Moreover, the equipment the entrepreneur finally gets may not be exactly what he desires or specified—as in the case of a printer who found that the machine that he understood was earmarked for him had been sold, with the result that he purchased an alternate costing 50 percent more.

3. The African firm, particularly the indigenous one, tends to pay a high price for its equipment and other inputs, even aside from importing costs. The printing firm whose American participant paid the fortunate visit to the equipment manufacturer saved approximately £ 25,000 on an original order of £ 180,000.[3] The African entrepreneur also loses out on the chance for special bargains that occasionally present themselves to a buyer on the spot. The ability of the indigenous firm to get special discounts, to buy below list price, to receive extra services that in effect shave the price a little, is very limited compared to that of firms operating in advanced economies; it is, in fact, more limited than that of foreign-owned firms operating in Africa, for these firms have extensive contacts in the equipment-producing countries.

The cost of constructing appropriate premises may also be very high. While the construction of standard types of structures was not expensive, it was the pattern that costs soared tremendously if anything unusual was to be done.[4] For example, while standard steel window frames were manufactured in Nigeria, frames of a special size or finish had to be imported. If carpentry was required except for doors and windows, little finished lumber was delivered to the job, and the labor force had to square

---

tolerated by a power loom." Joseph E. Stepanek, *Managers for Small Industry: An International Study* (Glencoe, Illinois: The Free Press, 1967), p. 72.

[2] Eastern Regional Development Board, *Second Annual Report, 1950-51* (Enugu: published by the Board, no date), p. 11, tells of a river transport firm that ran into serious difficulty because the launch it ordered from the United Kingdom was damaged during transit, and the damage was not fully covered by insurance.

[3] Equipment often turns out to be more costly than expected. See, e.g., Walter D. Gainer, "Nigerian Energy Policy: Planning and Performance in the Power Sub-Sector," *Nigerian Journal of Economic and Social Studies* XV:2 (July 1973): 265, 267. The causes are various.

[4] Even on ordinary jobs, contractor incompetence sometimes raised costs. Government spokesmen complained of severe cost-increasing problems with indigenous contractors "who could not cope" and who manifested "frivolous reasons for incompetence" (*West Africa*, January 19, 1976, p. 91, and (Lagos) *Daily Times*, August 4, 1975, p. 3). However, these were of a special nature; see Chapter 9 below.

and plane this material before use. Factors of this nature often doubled or tripled construction costs per square foot.[5]

4. Inordinate delays in getting equipment even after it has been ordered also increase costs. Always a common problem[6] and traceable to many causes, it was severely exacerbated by Nigeria's port congestion of the mid-1970s. For more complicated projects, the orders themselves are sometimes delayed because indigenous entrepreneurs cannot interest potential suppliers in submitting estimates until they can demonstrate that they already have a firm assurance of the funds.[7]

5. Delays in getting ancillary equipment or other appurtenances necessary to start operating the machinery are sometimes more excruciating than the wait for the basic equipment itself. Thus, a printer who bought a stitching machine from a local supplier found that the supplier did not have the wire necessary for using the machinery. The printer, at considerable cost to himself, had the supplier order the wire by air and received it in two weeks. This wire was found to be the wrong kind. Another delay ensued, while work piled up. During the entire period, until the correct stitching wire arrived, the equipment dealer maintained that he was not responsible for the wire needed for the stitching machine just as a car dealer is not responsible for the petrol needed for a car.

6. Equipment ordered from abroad encounters many expensive installation difficulties in Africa. For example, a large textile firm that did not supervise carefully enough found that its looms had been improperly installed and, partially for this reason, scrapped them and purchased new ones.[8] The printing firm with the American partner, already mentioned, also incurred unexpectedly high installation costs. Continuous and close consultation between the architect and the machinery supplier was impossible, for the former was in Nigeria while the latter was overseas. As a result, the building was not designed with precisely the right clearances for the machinery, and expensive changes in construction were subsequently required. Equipment of any size or complexity often requires the presence of an engineer or technician from the supplying country. This is not only costly but may cause delays until properly qualified

[5]Arthur D. Little, Inc., *Manufacturing Opportunities for Construction Products in Nigeria*, Report to the Ministry of Commerce and Industry, Federal Republic of Nigeria, April 1964, pp. 28-32.

[6]The pumps required in the 1950s for the Aba urban water system evidently took more than two years to arrive. Nigeria, Eastern Region, *Eastern House of Assembly Debates, 1956*, March 26, 1956 (Enugu: Government Printer, 1957), p. 536 (the Minister of Development).

[7]For a description of this problem in Pakistan, see Nathaniel H. Engle, *Industrial Development Banking in Action: A Study of Organisation, Operations and Procedure of Private Development Banks in India, Iran, Pakistan, Turkey* (Pakistan Industrial Credit and Investment Corporation, 1962), p. 102 (mimeographed).

[8]Peter Kilby, *Industrialization in an Open Economy: Nigeria 1945-1966* (Cambridge: Cambridge University Press, 1969), pp. 161-62.

personnel in the supplying country can be spared. Moreover, the technicians available for such overseas assignments are often not of the requisite ability. One large indigenous firm, for example, found after ten costly months that the German engineer hired to set up their German equipment was incapable of doing the job, and the firm therefore had to hire other technical personnel to do the installation properly.

Because of the difficulties and delays in getting, installing, and beginning operation of equipment, starting a project in Nigeria requires, in the words of one foreigner, "substantially more capital, especially working capital" than in a more developed economy. As a result of equipment-related delays and delays associated with the other economic-environmental adversities described in this chapter, the establishment of an enterprise may take years. Thus, a government official rather wistfully predicted to the author in 1975 that construction would begin that year or the next of a cement plant on which organizing efforts, intermittently intensive, had begun in 1962.

7. Once the equipment has started operating, there are problems in getting the supplies and replacement parts necessary to keep it operating. For one thing, slow and irregular deliveries and the frequent unavailability of substitutes force the producer in Nigeria to sink more capital than his advanced-economy counterpart into large stocks.[9] When the enterprise operates on a small scale, as is usually the case, and when at the same time a fairly large number of different materials and intermediate goods are used, maintaining such supplies is an expensive burden. This is particularly true when the firm has to import its supplies directly (e.g., an indigenously owned printing firm with specialized photogravure equipment, which was the sole importer of the specialized reels of paper and photogravure inks) and especiallly when the firm's orders are small (small orders are more troublesome at the docks and are subject to especially long delays). Supplies from domestic sources, incidentally, need stocking just as badly as do imports. A steady flow of uniform quality goods can no more be relied upon from domestic producers than from foreign suppliers.

Still, firms often find that their stocks have been inadequate to prevent the idling of equipment or even complete cessation of production. On one visit to a successful Nigerian mattress producer, the writer found the shop completely idle except for a few women combing out coir fiber by hand. The workers were there (and drawing their pay); the demand for the products of the firm was adequate; the equipment was in good working order. The trouble was that the stock of a seemingly insignificant ribbon which was used to bind the seams of the mattresses had run out. The ribbon had been ordered from abroad in plenty of time, according to the

[9]For example, one of the cement companies visited by the author spent ₦300,000 for spare parts in fiscal 1974-75, building up its total stock of spares to ₦500,000 even though in that fiscal year the company used only a (below average) ₦20,000 worth.

entrepreneur, with a substantial leeway for delays in delivery. However, because of difficulties that the entrepreneur did not yet fully understand, delivery of the ribbon had been delayed so long that the firm's supply was exhausted and production petered out to virtually nothing. The firm had made efforts to secure a substitute locally but these had not been successful. In another case, cement was lying unsold and deteriorating in a plant visited by the author despite severe shortages in 1975 because the firm could not get paper sacks to bag the cement. Bags were produced in Lagos, but a petrol and diesel-oil shortage prevented shipment of the bags to the cement plant in Sokoto. Another cement company had started earlier to manufacture its own bags because of supply problems and costs, but was experiencing difficulties in importing the needed kraft paper.[10]

Acquisition of replacement parts and materials for equipment constitutes perhaps an even bigger problem. A single example: one cement company had to wait two years for replacement kiln-lining bricks although delivery time was quoted as six months.[11]

8. The life expectancy of equipment is generally shorter in tropical Africa than in the more developed areas. The humid climate, the lack of skill and experience of the operators, the less expert maintenance services, careless handling, and similar factors all tend to shorten the working life of machinery. This is a costly problem experienced by virtually all businesses operating in Nigeria.[12]

Human Resources

The African firm's human resources difficulties—problems regarding the productivity, responsibility, availability, etc., of human inputs—take many forms.

1. The literature on African unskilled and semiskilled labor is voluminous, so the issue will merely be touched upon here. Despite what may be called European folklore to the contrary, careful studies suggest that it was not necessarily high-unit-cost labor. On the basis of his studies, Peter Kilby concluded that "we may dismiss a number of problems commonly claimed to be impeding the progress of industrialization in Africa. These include problems of labour recruitment, partial commitment to wage-earning, adverse effects of labour migration, impaired productive capacity as a result of excessive absenteeism, and barriers to the development of a skilled labour force as a result of labour instability."[13]

---

[10]Even raw materials that one might superficially expect to be abundant might be unavailable. See, e.g., Ephraim E. Enabor, "Nigeria's Foreign Trade in Forest Products," *Nigerian Journal of Economic and Social Studies* XV:2 (July 1973): 189.

[11]Replacement-part availability was a major problem for most of the cement companies operating in Nigeria in 1975.

[12]This may be the main reason that the depreciation rate of the Electricity Corporation of Nigeria is twice that of United States and Canadian operations. Gainer: 274.

[13]Gainer: 213. See also Robert Ward, "Economic Spotlight on Nigeria," *SAIS Review*

This is not to say that African labor productivity may not often be low—partly because of managerial and supervisory deficiencies,[14] and partly because of inexperience, illiteracy, language problems which hamper communication with fellow nationals of different ethnic groups and with Europeans, intertribal friction, debilitating diseases and malnutrition, and other problems.[15] Lower productivity was usually counterbalanced by lower wages—for example, while Nigeria's labor productivity in textiles was approximately half of Britain's, unit labor costs were lower because the hourly wage was one-sixth that of Britain[16]—but the wage differential was markedly narrowed by the whopping Udoji increase of 1975.

2. Higher-level manpower, however, constitutes a serious problem. Skilled labor is in short supply and tends to be inferior because of deficiencies in training, education, [17] and the problems mentioned in the preceding paragraph.

Supervisory and managerial personnel involve an even more serious problem. "With few exceptions among firms employing over twenty-five, the inadequacy of Nigerian supervisory performance was reported by management to be their chief problem in the labour field."[18] The unpredictable nature of some of the problems is illustrated by the experience of a Lagos electronics firm. Their production was interrupted by their production control supervisor who, after several quarrels with the foreman, petulantly withheld parts from the assembly line.[19] As for Nigerian managerial personnel, there is virtually universal testimony by businessmen,

---

(Spring 1967): 23: "where systems of production are similar, there has been nothing to suggest that the Nigerian [unskilled or semiskilled] worker is less capable than his counterpart in Europe. Most industrialists in Nigeria feel that with adequate training, supervision, and incentive payments, Nigerian labour can be about as productive as labour in Europe or the United States in repetitive and routine jobs." Ward then presents examples.

[14]Peter Kilby, *Industrialization*, pp. 225 ff.; and "African Labour Productivity Reconsidered," *Economic Journal* LXXI:282 (June 1961): 273-291.

[15]For example, the Federal Commissioner of Finance has deplored the attitude of Nigerian workers to their jobs and the Military Governor of Kwara State stated that the government was determined to "change the attitude of Nigerians toward work." *West Africa,* March 8, 1976, p. 322, and January 26, 1976, p. 122. See also T. M. Yesufu, "Employment, Manpower and Economic Development in Nigeria: Some Issues of Moment," *Nigerian Journal of Economic and Social Studies* XVI:1 (March 1974): 58, who believes that the poor quality of general labor was, at the time of his writing, one of Nigeria's two major manpower constraints.

[16]Kilby, *Industrialization*, p. 124; labor costs are discussed on pp. 123-128.

[17]Yesufu stresses the lack of technical and vocational education for middle-level manpower. Yesufu, p. 57.

[18]Kilby, *Industrialization*, p. 224. See also F. A. Wells and W. A. Warmington, *Studies in Industrialization: Nigeria and the Cameroons* (Ibadan and London: Oxford University Press, 1962), p. 88.

[19]Robert Waite, "Establishing an Electronics Industry in Nigeria," Unpublished M.B.A. thesis, New York University, 1964, p. 104. See also Yesufu, p. 58, on "the acute shortage of intermediate manpower."

indigenous and foreign, as well as by scholars, that it is deficient in supply and inadequate in quality.[20]

3. Overseas sources of higher-level personnel are often resorted to, but such sources have been generally unsatisfactory. For one thing, they are "fiendishly expensive."[21] As an inducement for overseas work, salaries of such personnel tend to be high; estimates range from an average of 50 percent to 100 percent greater than home-country salaries. Travel and other allowances must be paid. And there are other expenses as well. For example, the cost of constructing housing for the European personnel of a proposed company to be set up in Northern Nigeria was actually expected to be 50 percent greater than the cost of the proposed factory building. The housing amounted to approximately 40 percent of the total fixed capital of the firm.

Hiring foreign personnel involves substantial drawbacks besides the direct expense, especially for indigenous businessmen. Foreigners working for African firms are not so conscientious or so interested in the success of the enterprise as those working for European-owned firms. Their careers and personal interests are not usually so firmly bound up with the interests of an indigenous firm as with those of a foreign firm. Foreigners working for African firms expect to return to their own countries, often within two or three years' time,[22] and then will probably sever their connections with the indigenously owned enterprise, unlike employees of large foreign companies who are doing a tour of service in Africa. This may mean a devastating loss of managerial familiarity with the particular circumstances of the indigenous firm.[23] The quality of foreign personnel is often, even usually, disappointing. Indigenous firms, having limited contacts overseas, have often hired people who were incompetent. Several successful Nigerian businessmen have told me of such experiences, and some have forsworn foreign personnel completely.

[20]See, e.g., E. Wayne Nafziger, *Nigerian Entrepreneurship: A Study of Indigenous Businessmen in the Footwear Industry*, University of Illinois Ph.D. dissertation, 1967, Urbana, Illinois, pp. 149-150, 171; John R. Harris, "Industrial Entrepreneurship in Nigeria," Unpublished dissertation, Northwestern University, Evanston, Illinois, August 1967, Ch. 5, p. 13; Kilby, *Industrialization*, pp. 224-233; Enabor, p. 189; author's own interviews; and sources cited in the preceding footnotes.

[21]The phrase of the Chairman of the Commonwealth Development Corporation in an interview with the author.

[22]The leading Nigerian manpower economist confirms that ". . . a high rate of turnover has become characteristic of expatriate staff . . ." T. M. Yesufu, "Nigerian Manpower Problems (A Preliminary Assessment)," *Nigerian Journal of Economic and Social Studies* IV:3 (November 1962): p. 207.

[23]In one case a Nigerian employer hired a British technician for approximately two-thirds more than he was receiving in England. He proved successful, his salary was raised to more than double his original English salary, and the business was gradually built around him. However, after a few years he decided to leave Nigeria. The last information the author had was that the employer had offered a salary almost triple the initial English salary, but feared that even this would not be sufficient to induce the technician to stay.

Nafziger also relates the case of a Nigerian footwear manufacturing firm that "out of reaction to the ineptness of foreign managers in [another firm] . . . decided to rely only on Nigerian entrepreneurs."[24] Technical personnel can sometimes be secured for a limited period on secondment from an equipment-supplying firm. But if the Nigerian firm wants a per-. manent technical employee or a manager, it finds that the persons available "are often second-rate, but yet have to be paid very highly."[25]

4. The shortage of skilled and higher-grade manpower often imposes substantial training expenses upon firms operating in Nigeria. For example, a Nigerian company which purchased complex photogravure rotary printing equipment had to send some of its employees to England for a year's study. The training expenses were, of course, considerably greater than those that would have been incurred by a British firm, even assuming that the latter could not have employed workers already capable of operating the equipment. The services of the trainees are also completely lost for the training period. This was a serious problem for a cement company which sent nine of its "top officers" abroad for training in 1975 because the plant was converting from the wet-grinding to the dry-grinding process. Some firms find it necessary to establish expensive training facilities that would not be needed in an advanced economy. The cost of these programs is made greater by the substantial difficulty firms in Nigeria have in retaining their trainees. They are not only lured away by other employers, but a great many have used their additional training and savings from enhanced incomes as a springboard for entry into universities.

5. From the point of view of the firm, the human-resource problems discussed so far are primarily internal, but there are also difficulties that are mainly external. The problems of servicing and repair of equipment may be either, depending on whether such jobs are performed by employees or by outside firms. In any case, it is difficult to find competent personnel for servicing or repair jobs that are somewhat out of the ordinary. The writer has seen cases in which equipment breakdowns have idled entire plants for more than a week. Larger firms sometimes turn to

[24]Nafziger, p. 27. T. M. Yesufu, "Manpower Problems," p. 207.

[25]Yesufu, "Manpower Problems," p. 207. Testimony regarding the high cost and unsatisfactory nature of foreign high-level personnel comes from all sources: the largest non-African companies, virtually all Nigerian firms large enough to employ foreigners, Nigerian government officials, foreign government personnel concerned with Nigerian economic affairs, and internationally financed development organizations. Written sources include Yesufu, "Manpower Problems"; Harris, Ch. 5, p. 13; Nafziger, pp. 151-152, 155-157; Charles H. Olmstead, "Private Investment in Nigeria," in Warren H. Hausman (ed.), *Managing Economic Development in Africa* (Cambridge, Mass.: MIT Press, 1963), p. 97; *British Aid—I, Survey and Comment* (London: Overseas Development Institute, 1963), p. 49; and Sayre P. Schatz, "Crude Private Neo-Imperialism: A New Pattern in Africa," *Journal of Modern African Studies* 7:4 (December 1969): 681-685.

the expensive alternative of hiring foreigners for maintenance and servicing at salaries far above their remuneration at home.[26]

6. Consultants, specialists, subsidiary services of all kinds, and sources of advice and information are often lacking altogether in Nigeria, and when available they are frequently of low quality and are more expensive than in more developed economies.[27] Market research services are inadequate; capable accounting services may be unavailable; consulting engineers and architects are few. These services are often crucial for firms operating in the difficult economic environment of Africa.[28]

A substantial array of subsidiary sources of information and advice, available, and often free, to businessmen in developed economies, may be unavailable in Nigeria. Financial institutions in advanced economies have "usually provided technical advice and maintained close continuing relations with the enterprises in which they invested."[29] Suppliers of machinery and materials are often in close contact with their domestic customers and offer useful advice and information. Managers in advanced economies benefit from the counsel of expert and broadly experienced directors and advisors.[30] Many entrepreneurs in advanced economies receive a great deal. of highly useful information from trade and business associations.[31] Universities, government agencies, and other organizations in advanced economies also provide valuable advice and information.[32] Unfortunately, assistance from these sources is usually unobtainable in Nigeria.

The lack of technical expertise and advice is perhaps the most keenly felt. Modest technical jobs may be prohibitively expensive. A small Nige-

---

[26]Wells and Warmington, p. 38.

[27]Many of the indigenous consulting and specialized-services firms that emerged after the oil revenue surge were established primarily as means of benefiting from government pressures on foreign companies performing such services to associate with indigenous firms. They had little real capability. It might also be mentioned that a large portion of the terribly expensive advice provided by foreign consultants was of little value; see below.

[28]W. Arthur Lewis, e.g., mentions the need to provide consulting services for small businessmen in less developed economies: *Development Planning: The Essentials of Economic Policy* (New York: Harper and Row, 1966), p. 271.

[29]William Diamond, *Development Banks* (Baltimore: published for the International Bank for Reconstruction and Development by the Johns Hopkins Press, 1957).

[30]See Everett E. Hagen, "The Allocation of Investment in Underdeveloped Countries," in Massachusetts Institute of Technology, Center for International Studies, *Investment Criteria and Economic Growth: Papers Presented at a Conference Sponsored Jointly by the Center for International Studies and the Social Science Research Council, October 15, 16, and 17, 1954* (Cambridge, Mass.: MIT Press, 1954), pp. 63-64.

[31]"Many businessmen look on these associations as their most important sources of information." L. J. Crampon and Stewart F. Schweizer, *A Study of the Informational Needs and Problems of Small Businessmen* (Boulder: Bureau of Business Research, University of Colorado, 1961), summarized in Small Business Administration, *Management Research Summary* (Washington, D.C.: February 1962). Of the businessmen surveyed, 38 percent belonged to one or more associations.

[32]Stepanek, p. 63.

rian businessman producing simple science equipment for schools cited examples in which local costs were literally fifty times greater than those in advanced economies. The choice between alternate sets of equipment has to be made blindly. The most important obstacle to business success in Nigerian sawmilling, according to Harris, may have been the difficulty of "obtaining technical information that will enable the entrepreneur to select the appropriate equipment and supervise its operation." This difficulty "explains a good bit of the low quality of sawing and poor maintenance of equipment."[33]

Foreign consultants, like managerial personnel, have proved costly and unsatisfactory. An internal report on the Nigerian Public Works Department (applicable to the private sector as well) delineated some of the problems. First, foreign consultants "insist on high standards in order to maintain their professional reputations and tend to impose European standards" inappropriately. Second, they "need to be briefed by [busy local personnel] with a knowledge of the local background and needs." Third, "all the knowledge and experience of local conditions gained from their work . . . departs with them. . . ." Fourth, "their recommendations at all stages normally take the form of alternatives," and overworked local personnel must then take the time to make the decisions. Foreign consultants have often given bad advice.[34] Sometimes they simply have been unwilling to allot enough time to do an effective job.[35]

Governmental Problems

1. Attitudes of government personnel are frequently unaccommodating or impeditive. A survey of business in 1961 revealed strong feelings on this score:[36]

Both internal and external business would be much facilitated if departmental staffs (particularly those junior grades with whom the public has most contact) were to be made to understand the importance of business to the life of the country. The usual attitude at present varies between disinterestedness and delib-

[33]Harris, Ch. 4, p. 35. See also C. C. Onyemelukwe, *Problems of Industrial Planning and Management in Nigeria* (New York: Columbia University Press, 1966), p. 25, on the difficulties of securing information required for industrial development.

[34]See, e.g., G. K. Helleiner, "New Forms of Foreign Investment in Africa," *Journal of Modern African Studies* 6:1 (May 1968): 21-22, and Schatz, "Crude Private Neo-Imperialism," pp. 681-685. For a specific case, see the statement that one of the reasons for the difficulties of a relatively large ceramics firm in Western Nigeria was "that the expert advice [by foreigners] given to them on the outset did not allow for special circumstances of this country," Nigeria, Federation, *Proceedings of Commission of Inquiry into the Affairs of Certain Statutory Corporations (Coker Hearings)* (Lagos: 1962), Day 34, p. 23 (mimeographed).

[35]Waite, pp. 92-93. In contrast, Crampon and Schweizer found that most of the surveyed firms (in the United States) that used consultants were satisfied with the results (p. 2).

[36]See Sayre P. Schatz and S. I. Edokpayi, "Economic Attitudes of Nigerian Businessmen," *Nigerian Journal of Economic and Social Studies* IV:3 (November 1962): 262. This comment, while coming from a foreign firm, expressed Nigerian feeling as well.

erate obstruction. The question seems to be not 'How can I help this person?' but 'What can I do (exceeding the limits of my authority if necessary) to hold up this transaction?'

As a result, the simplest piece of business takes more time and trouble than it should and frequently requires the attention of a senior instead of a junior employee before it can be done at all. This adds considerably to the actual cost of operating a business and involves uneconomic use of manpower.

Fifteen years later the problems referred to were more acute than ever.[37] In particular, small-business proprietors, who are usually of modest social status, frequently encounter governmental contrariety. Foreign businessmen also find that friction and misunderstanding with African officials interfere with investment-incentive measures. Delays and palaver with respect to tax incentives, land acquisition, immigration quotas, etc., are commonplace and well known.

2. Nigerian proprietors of modest businesses often find government unwilling to extend business-incentive provisions to them. Government concessions to investors are intended for relatively large, hence usually foreign, investors. Although indigenous businessmen often feel that this involves an infuriating kind of neocolonialist discrimination against Africans, government policy-makers are probably correct in believing that the benefits to be derived from administering these complex programs for small business would not justify the costs.[38]

3. Finally, two widely discussed governmental problems deserve at least brief mention. The capability of the young governments in Africa is often still limited. This "in some instances . . . constitutes the most serious of all obstacles to economic development."[39] There generally has not been sufficient time to establish a solid government apparatus, manned by competent, experienced personnel and free of serious staff shortages. Bungling often results. For example, the Nigerian Ports Authority, in what businessmen consider typically feckless fashion, introduced new

[37]See, e.g., the critical remarks of the Federal Commissioner of Finance on the attitudes of Nigerian employees toward the public with whom they came into contact. *West Africa,* March 8, 1976, p. 322. See also the statement of General Ankrah, Chairman of the Ghana National Liberation Council, upon receipt of a report on the Ghanaian civil service, castigating civil servants for "slipshodness, laziness, apathy, improper practices, lack of integrity, and ineptitude seriously rampant among public servants." *West Africa,* January 13, 1968, p. 49.

[38]See Chapter 9. See also Sayre P. Schatz, "The High Cost of Aiding Businesses in Developing Economies: Nigeria's Loans Programmes," *Oxford Economic Papers* 20:3 (November 1968).

[39]A. H. Hanson, *Public Enterprise and Economic Development* (London: Routledge and Kegan Paul, 1959), p. 52. See also Guy Hunter, *The New Societies of Tropical Africa* (London and Ibadan: Oxford University Press, 1962), p. 188, for a brief discussion of the bureaucratic problems of African countries; and A. L. Adu, *The Civil Service in the New African States* (London: Allen and Unwin, 1965), pp. 228-229, for an interesting discussion of problems of African civil servants related to the problem discussed here.

regulations governing the handling of dangerous and hazardous goods, but neglected to give advance notice to users of port facilities, thereby causing considerable unnecessary expense and inconvenience.[40] Another common syndrome in newly developing countries—undergoing rapid social transformation, discarding old values and patterns before fully developing new ones, exposed to the personal-gain philosophy that is the mainspring of capitalism—is a proliferation of corruption and favoritism. Most small businessmen in Nigeria believe that they suffer from such practices.[41]

The Alien Social Milieu of Business

Nigerian businessmen have operated in a significantly alien economic network. They sold to or bought from foreign-owned enterprises; they competed with such enterprises; they exported or imported; they sought financing from foreign-owned banks; they dealt with foreign managers, engineers, accountants, or other consultants. Even if not in direct contact with foreigners, they dealt with companies and government agencies run by modern (i.e., European rather than traditional) standards. The rules and procedures of the economy, the personnel to a significant extent, the unspoken and unconscious presumptions and judgments, and even the language were of alien origin. While the problems arising out of the alien character of the milieu in which indigenous business must function are diminishing with the growth of the Nigerian business class, with indigenization and increasing pressure on foreigners to deal with Nigerians, and with the new oil prosperity and the boost it has given to government expenditures, and while conversely the advantages grow in being part of an African social network, nevertheless significant problems remain for the less sophisticated, less affluent, and less influential businessmen who constitute the great bulk of the Nigerian business population. Problems related to the alien social milieu are discussed in this section and those related to the alien economic milieu in the next.

1. Nigerian businessmen miss out on opportunities because of lack of social contact. In the relatively small expatriate business communities, foreign businessmen are likely to know one another personally or to have mutual friends. Even when not personally acquainted, "they share a

---

[40]Lagos Chamber of Commerce, *Quarterly Review* (September 1961):4. Business complaints are discussed in many issues of this publication (later called the *Quarterly Review of the Lagos Chamber of Commerce and Industry*). See, e.g., complaints about shortages of imported spare parts, June 1968, p. 2. On governmental ineptness, see also *Public Enterprises in Nigeria: Proceedings of the 1973 Annual Conference of the Nigerian Economic Society* (Ibadan: Nigerian Economic Society, 1974), particularly the already cited articles by Aboyade, Ekukinam, and "Government as a Surrogate Corporation," by Pius N. C. Okigbo, on pp. 105-118.

[41]Those who took power in the July 1975 coup took vigorous action against corruption and governmental incompetence but recognized the tenacious nature of the problems and made no promise to eradicate them. See, e.g., *West Africa,* February 16, 1976, p. 198.

common culture and a common knowledge of their society. Dress, manner, background, personal history are mutually intelligible . . . There are also clubs and informal social networks which facilitate and reinforce business relations."[42] For the African businessman the absence of this kind of rapport is an impediment. It is important, for example, in making sales, and it is particularly important when (as is frequently the case in Nigeria) those making the purchasing decisions lack the expertise required for judging the quality of many of the goods and services they have to buy and therefore rely on personal relationships. In general, many kinds of assistance, advice, and information—from bankers, suppliers, and other business colleagues—tend to flow less freely when business relationships are unlubricated by the camaraderie of ethnic similarity.

2. Noninvolvement in the social milieu also results in discrimination against capable Nigerian businessmen. Leaving aside blatant prejudice, which exists, there is also a more subtle form of discrimination, which may be called probabilistic discrimination. This may be practiced by men who are not prejudiced; more important, given the disparate social networks, it may be commercially justified.

Because of the social separateness, "all Africans look alike" in a figurative sense to many foreign firms, especially those without long experience in Africa. They find it extremely difficult to differentiate—to distinguish between those indigenous entrepreneurs who run their businesses capably and carefully and those who may be slipshod or dishonest. In these circumstances, Nigerian businessmen (including the capable ones) tend to be passed over in various business dealings simply on the basis of probabilities. Thus, an outstanding Nigerian firm that rewound electrical generators and did so as well as or better than any other firm in the country,[43] was simply ignored by some foreign-owned firms that were potential customers. Acting in accord with the general probability, they gave their work to an expatriate rewinder. (The proprietor tried to meet this problem by creating an image of a firm substantially capitalized and run by foreigners.) Even Nigerian consumers share this prejudice; they are predisposed in favor of imported rather than domestically produced goods.

3. The fact that the language of commerce and government is English, a foreign tongue, sometimes causes problems. Some African businessmen have not mastered the language; this is one of the reasons few Northern Nigerian merchants engaged in exporting or importing. Language problems also arise between Nigerians. While complex and delicate relationships can be sustained among businessmen of the same tribe, language barriers sometimes complicate dealings between different ethnic groups.

[42]Peter Marris, "The Social Barriers to African Entrepreneurship," *Journal of Development Studies* 5:1 (October 1968): 33.

[43]This represents the judgment of a knowledgeable foreign businessman.

In Nigeria's kola trade, for example, the many intricate matters of storing, packing, and shipping the kola nut, of securing credit, and of mutual confidence among those engaged in the trade are "made more difficult and complicated by the differences in language and cultural tradition between the centres of consumption in the North and the centres of production in the South—more specifically between Hausa and Yoruba respectively."[44]

The Alien Economic Milieu

The economic milieu of business is also significantly alien in Nigeria. Many of the conditions and parameters of the economy have been established by and adjusted to foreign participation. Being required to operate in this alien economic network entails difficulties for African businessmen.

1. There are personnel problems. To the extent that an indigenous firm requires upper- or even middle-level manpower, it has been faced with salary and perquisite levels arising mainly out of the colonial situation and subsequent political developments and inappropriate to the economic conditions of less-developed countries. Earnings have been based upon the relatively high inducements that were required during the colonial period to persuade Europeans to work and live in the tropics. Under conditions of nationalist agitation it was politically impossible to do anything but institute the same rewards for Africans and then to continue the relative salary standards after independence.[45] Foreign-owned firms have also been willing to pay high salaries for upper-level Africans because, under nationalist pressure, they have been buying not only managerial or other skill but also good public relations and political acceptability.[46] For indigenous businesses, the cost and difficulty of hiring capable personnel are further increased by the better prospects for further training and promotion in government or foreign firms,[47] although the exhilarating opportunities for rapid advancement are not as abundant as they were in the early years of Nigerianization.

2. Labor costs are also raised for the successful African firm because, as it grows, it encounters labor and social welfare codes designed for

[44]Abner Cohen, "Politics of the Kola Trade," in Edith H. Whetham and Jean I. Currie (eds.), *Readings in the Applied Economics of Africa; Vol. I: Micro-Economics* (London: Cambridge University Press, 1967), p. 156.

[45]An interesting reversal occurred with the large Udoji wage increases of 1975. Nigerian salaries led the way; foreigners got substantial raises to match the percentage increases awarded to Nigerians.

[46]Nafziger, p. 156.

[47]See, e.g., Theodore Geiger and Winifred Armstrong, *The Development of African Private Enterprise* (Planning Pamphlet 120) (Washington, D.C.: National Planning Association, 1964), p. 54: "African entrepreneurs have difficulty in recruiting sufficient employees in this latter category [middle managerial and technical personnel] particularly since the great majority of them do not offer opportunities for training and advancement commensurate with those provided by many government agencies and some foreign firms."

European enterprises. Nigerian employers find it hard to meet standards regarding working conditions, minimum wages, vacations, hospitalization, etc., originally intended for large foreign firms. "The Nigerian capitalist comes to play his part at a time when overtime pay, sick pay, casual leave, leave allowances and even pension fund have become part of his labourers' vocabulary."[48]

3. Then there is the special competitive problem that arises from the necessity of competing in the alien economic network. Compared with foreign-owned companies, indigenous firms suffer from entrepreneurial shortcomings and from differential economic-environmental difficulties, i.e., those difficulties that have a more pronounced impact on indigenous than on expatriate firms. Even if there were no competition from foreign firms, the entrepreneurial and environmental problems would constitute a heavy drag on the indigenous businesses. They would increase costs, reduce receipts, and render unattractive a broad margin of projects that would be profitable in the absence of these problems. Still, there would be many ventures that indigenous firms could undertake profitably. Returns would be lower than they might otherwise be, but nevertheless the undertakings would be viable. Since expatriate firms do in fact compete with indigenous firms, however, many of the projects that the latter could otherwise profitably undertake are preempted or are rendered more precarious by the superior competitive power of the former. The indigenous firm may be likened to an infant industry facing competition with mature foreign companies; but since the foreign competitors operate within the borders of the less-developed country, no tariff protection is possible.[49]

Severe Indigenous Competition

The competition faced by Nigerian businessmen is—even aside from expatriate competition—often unusually severe.

The problem arises from the large number of eager entrants into most lines of business, hopeful of earning even a small income. They are particularly attracted into any line in which some pioneers are prospering,[50]

[48]Omafume F. Onoge, "Indigenisation Decree and Economic Independence: Another Case of Bourgeois Utopianism," in Nigerian Economic Society, *Nigeria's Indigenisation Policy: Proceedings of a November 1974 Symposium Organized by the Nigerian Economic Society* (Ibadan: Nigerian Economic Society, 1975), p. 64. See also Geiger and Armstrong, pp. 99-100: ". . .these codes are often intended for large enterprises and do not take into account the inability of small entrepreneurs to meet the same wage and social benefit standards. In addition, compliance with these codes often involves a large amount of paper work, which may be burdensome for small entrepreneurs."

[49]This is not to say that the presence of European firms necessarily has a negative overall effect on development.

[50]"Private capital in [Eastern Nigeria] can be surprisingly quick to follow a successful lead, so that strong local competition may be encountered within a short space of time," stated the credit manager of the Eastern Nigeria Development Corporation. *Development: The ENDC Quarterly Magazine* (April-June 1962): 27.

but they are also willing to try any venture that has the remotest prospect of profit. Applicants to government loans boards have applied for loans for a vast variety of different business ventures.[51] Many Nigerian businessmen are ready to shift out of their existing businesses into others which appear to offer better prospects.

Excessive entry puts great pressure on all businessmen in the industry. A competitive equilibrium is reached in theory when pure profits disappear and the entrepreneur earns only a competitive return on his own capital, labor, and managerial services; in the absence of profit prospects, further entry is inhibited. Under Nigerian conditions, however, the minimum acceptable "wage of management" is so low that entry continues long after it would stop in a more-developed economy. Moreover, imperfect knowledge often causes continued entry even when minimum wages of management can no longer be earned. Under these circumstances, the competition sometimes tends to become pathological.[52]

The erosion of profits through excessive entry affects not only businessmen who approximate pure competitors, but also those who have managed to secure a pure profit by differentiating their output or through superior efficiency or some other competitive advantage. Even the large foreign firms are affected.[53]

Infrastructural Problems

The fact that inadequate infrastructures in less-developed economies increase costs and reduce potential receipts is thoroughly familiar and needs no extended discussion. In some ways, infrastructural difficulties have intensified with development. Their severity in 1975—with incredible port delays, stifling traffic jams, inoperative telephones, petrol shortages, railway breakdowns, strikes in essential services, etc.—constituted an important factor in the forces leading to the coup in that year. The following announcement may serve as a vivid illustration of the impact of infrastructural deficiencies in Nigeria: "The Nigerian Cement Company Ltd. regrets to announce that due to the failure of the Electricity Corporation of Nigeria to supply sufficient power to the cement works at

[51]Sayre P. Schatz, *Development Bank Lending: The Federal Loans Board* (Ibadan and London: Oxford University Press, 1964), pp. 71-72.

[52]The Secretary of the Nigerian Petroleum Operators Union vividly described to the writer the competition among Nigerian-run gasoline stations in the Kaduna area in 1965. The main forms of competition were sales at discount and on credit. Agreements to refrain from these practices were quickly violated and broke down. Between the reduced profit margins, the time spent chasing after collectible debts, and the losses on bad debts, the frazzled operators were in despair. (Of course, "cutthroat" or "destructive" competition is not confined to underdeveloped economies.)

[53]See Kilby, *Industrialization*, pp. 61-63, for a brief discussion of the way that, for large merchant firms, "entry of new sellers has far more than offset the growth in demand with consequent pressure on profit margins."

Nkalagu, production of cement has been drastically reduced . . . Effective immediately and until further notice, sales . . . are suspended. The Electricity Corporation of Nigeria is at present unable to give a firm date for resumption of full power to Nkalagu. We are therefore unable to give any indication as to when production will be back to normal."[54]

The frustration and rage generated by these difficulties is sometimes explosive. Citing a case in which seven carloads of gari were completely spoiled because they had been delayed for weeks by the railroad, the Kaduna Branch of the Northern Nigerian Gari Traders' Union demanded that the Federal Minister of Transport institute a full-scale inquiry into the Nigerian Railway Corporation's "deliberate infliction of losses to gari traders."[55]

Other Cost-Increasing Problems

There are many other cost-increasing problems, only some of which will be mentioned in this section.

There are site problems. As a direct or indirect result of traditional land-tenure relations, it is sometimes difficult to make satisfactory arrangements regarding a business site. There are often an assortment of time-consuming legal problems and lawsuits.[56] A Nigerian construction and civil engineering firm finally turned back a Federal Loans Board loan of £ 11,000 to finance expansion, more than three years after the loan was approved, because of such problems, despite assistance from a sympathetic government agency. The project "did not materialize owing to the inability of the company to obtain a good site. The original site obtained is being contested. . . ." The project was abandoned.[57] A firm might well

---

[54]*West Africa*, August 20, 1966, p. 951. See also I. I. Ukpong, "Economic Consequences of Electric Power Failures in the Greater Lagos Area," *Nigerian Journal of Economic and Social Studies* XV:1 (March 1973): 68: ". . . one consequence of power failures was dislocation in production programmes of majority of firms." In early 1976, there was a 40-hour electricity failure in central Lagos: *West Africa*, February 16, 1976, p. 222. Among innumerable articles containing examples of infrastructural problems, see R. A. Akinola, "Factors Affecting the Location of a Textile Industry—The Example of the Ikeja Textile Mill," *Nigerian Journal of Economic and Social Studies* VIII:3 (November 1965): 255; Gainer, p. 275; Iz. Osayimwese, "The Evacuation of Groundnuts in Nigeria: A Linear Programming Approach," *Nigerian Journal of Economic and Social Studies* XV:1 (March 1973): 105-106; Siyanbola Tomori, "The Financial and Commercial Policies of the Nigerian Railway Corporation," in *Public Enterprises in Nigeria: Proceedings of the 1973 Annual Conference of the Nigerian Economic Society* (Ibadan: Nigerian Economic Society, 1974), p. 140.

[55](Lagos) *Daily Times*, August 16, 1963, p. 13.

[56]See, e.g., Paul O. Proehl, *Foreign Enterprise in Nigeria* (Chapel Hill: University of North Carolina Press, 1965), ch. 7. For a discussion of changes in land tenure under the impact of economic development, see Sayre P. Schatz, "Implications of Economic Development," in John H. Hallowell (ed.), *Development: For What?* (Durham: Duke University Press, 1964), pp. 59-64.

[57]Federal Loans Board, *Annual Report, 1960-61* (Lagos: Government Printer, 1962), and internal materials.

encounter delays of this nature, as a result of locally instituted court actions, even though it has leased land from the government. And even for the Federal Government acquisition of sites has been a major problem: "Difficulties in land acquisition have been mentioned by virtually all public agencies as the most important single factor which frustrated the implementation of a number of their projects during the Second Plan period."[58]

There are credit problems. Long-standing customers, under strain because of social change, may suddenly and unexpectedly default on credit.[59]

There are knowledge problems. Aside from the already discussed problems in making information available, little may be known about the countries' natural resources and their manufacturing and processing qualities, about the applicability of various techniques of production under African climatic conditions, or about the climate or geography.[60]

The Market

The size of the market has always been considered critical in the literature on economic development. For Adam Smith, it governed the division of labor and thus the level of technology. Rosenstein-Rodan stressed the pivotal role of market magnitude in a seminal article published at the very beginning of the contemporary revival of interest in development.[61] Nurske stated his "modern variant" of Smith's thesis: "The inducement to invest is limited by the size of the market."[62] Many others have amplified the point.[63] Despite Nigeria's size, at Nigerian income levels, the national market has been too small for profitable production in the case of many products. More constraining, effective market size is usually greatly narrowed by high transport costs and transport difficulties, by paucity of knowledge, and by an assortment of marketing-network problems (discussed in the next section). While the new oil affluence has helped,[64] the problems remain.

[58]Federal Republic of Nigeria, *Third National Development Plan 1975-80* (hereinafter referred to as *Third Plan*), Vol. 1 (Lagos: Federal Ministry of Economic Development, 1975), pp. 396-397.

[59]See Hunter, p. 140.

[60]Gainer, p. 279.

[61]Paul N. Rosenstein-Rodan, "Problems of Industrialisation of Eastern and South-Eastern Europe," *Economic Journal* LIII:210-211 (June-September 1943): 202-211.

[62]Ragnar Nurske, *Problems of Capital Formation in Underdeveloped Countries* (New York: Oxford University Press, 1967), p. 6. See also chapters 1 and 4 in that book.

[63]For a quite interesting historical analysis, see H. J. Habbakuk, "The Historical Experience on the Basic Conditions of Economic Progress," in Leon H. Dupriez (ed.), *Economic Progress: Papers and Proceedings of a Round Table Conference Held by the International Economic Association* (Louvain: Institut de Recherches-Economiques et Sociales, 1955), p. 153.

[64]The effect of the 1974 increase in oil income is discussed in the concluding chapter.

The market may not only discourage investment, it may also be niggardly relative to the productive capacity existing at any given time. Considerable excess capacity was common in Nigeria during the 1960s. In visits to indigenously owned enterprises, the writer found it commonplace to see workers and equipment, some of it modern and technologically advanced, standing idle for lack of demand for the firm's output. This situation was encountered in printing, in cushions, pillows, and mattresses, in wooden furniture, rubber-soled shoes, leather shoes, sawmilling, gramophone recording, car servicing and repairing, tailoring, hotels, soap-making, modern production of chickens and eggs, banking, and other lines. Others, in intensive studies of particular industries, have made similar observations. In sawmilling, John Harris concluded "that demand is the most serious problem facing the industry today" and that "expansion [of productive capacity] has been faster than the growth of . . . markets."[65] In modern wooden furniture, he also found that marketing has been the major problem, and that (although there were conceptual difficulties of measurement) there appeared to be underutilization of capacity.[66] Nafziger similarly found that idle capacity because of demand limitations was important in the shoe industry.[67]

Marketing Channels

The underdeveloped marketing network impedes the expansion of domestic firms. Producers trying to reach the domestic market can generally do so adequately only through one of the large national trading companies. For many reasons, however, these organizations were reluctant to handle new locally produced goods. The regular suppliers of their big-selling, well-known lines tended to be antagonistic. The trading firms may have lacked the facilities to stock or display a larger variety of brands[68] and they were reluctant to sink money into larger inventories. Particularly in the case of indigenously produced goods, they often found that quality was uneven and delivery was uncertain.[69] Officials who tried to persuade the large sales outlets to deal with Nigerian suppliers had little success.

Capable salesmen, sales agents, or other dealers are hard to find. For example, a Nigerian firm signed a contract with a "van promotion contractor" who used sound-equipped vans to promote sales in "up-country" villages. The van salesman, however, tried to demonstrate the radios during the day in areas that received only inadequate daytime

[65]Harris, ch. 4, pp. 19, 42.
[66]Harris, ch. 7, pp. 7-8.
[67]Nafziger, pp. 134-35. The subject of underutilized productive capacity is further discussed below in Chapter 7.
[68]See, e.g., Waite, p. 110.
[69]One of the major trading firms gave a deliberate margin of preference to Nigerian-produced goods for political and public relations reasons, but it stopped this practice after a while.

transmission. He therefore did more harm than good, for the audiences thought that the radios were defective.[70] Sometimes the sales agents cannot be trusted. When Nigerian entrepreneurs were asked about obstacles to the formation of joint ventures with other Nigerian businessmen, 74 percent of those surveyed spoke of financial untrustworthiness.[71]

There are other marketing problems. Market information is inadequate.[72] Insurance of goods in transit is not yet highly developed although the risks are substantial.[73] Storage facilities are limited and often ineffective in preventing product deterioration. Extensive distribution is often hampered by the absence of uniform grades and measures.[74] Advertising costs were estimated to be triple those of similar advertising in the United States and, moreover, there has been a widely held belief (or guess) that advertising is not very effective.[75] Even the pattern of consumer preferences may inhibit expansion. Kilby has maintained that there is an extremely strong preference for the cheapest product even if it is of substantially poorer quality. "A producer must turn out a product whose quality is markedly greater than those of his competitors before the consumer is willing to pay a higher price."[76] If this is true, it tends to impede at least one method of expansion: producing a higher quality product.

Inadequacy of the marketing network is in many cases an important factor limiting expansion. It restricted the growth of Nigerian shoe factories[77] and hampered entrepreneurs in the sawmilling and wooden-furniture industries.[78] Marketing control problems were a critical factor curtailing company growth in the bread industry.[79] A leading indigenous druggist and distributor of pharmaceutical products was unable, on more than one occasion, to take up advantageous opportunities to become the sole distributor for Nigeria of imported pharmaceuticals because of the nonexistence of a national marketing network. The existence of a marketing organization is so important, in fact, that it even tends to determine

---

[70]Waite, pp. 108-109.

[71]Schatz and Edokpayi, pp. 262-263.

[72]See, e.g., C. O. Ilori, "Trade Constraints: A Barrier to Economic Cooperation in West Africa," *Nigerian Journal of Economic and Social Studies* XV:3 (November 1973): 413.

[73]Cohen, p. 156.

[74]Buying and selling is often "done in unit, volume, bundle and heap rather than by weight. This may be adequate when trading is confined to a limited area. But as the market is widened the system becomes a serious bottleneck." Ilori, p. 412.

[75]Waite, p. 113.

[76]Peter Kilby, *The Development of Small Industry in Eastern Nigeria* (Lagos: U.S.A.I.D. [United States Agency for International Development], 1962), p. 9.

[77]"It is rare for a footwear firm in Nigeria to have the requisite marketing knowledge and organization to warrant the establishment of a plant in which the value of assets is £ 100,000 or more." Nafziger, p. 135.

[78]Harris, ch. 4, p. 20; ch. 7, p. 7.

[79]Peter Kilby, *African Enterprise: The Nigerian Bread Industry* (Stanford: The Hoover Institution on War, Revolution, and Peace, 1965), p. 86.

the kinds of goods the largest firm in West Africa will undertake to produce. All but one of the twenty-eight industrial projects of the United Africa Company were directly related to already established marketing facilities of the company.[80]

Unexpected Difficulties

There is a fervent consensus among virtually all who have actually taken part in establishing businesses in Nigeria that, when one initiates a project, a rich and multivarious and enormously frustrating assortment of *unexpected* difficulties arise. Participants have commented on this ever since experience started to accumulate on setting up modern industries in Nigeria. An early government report speaks several times of "the exceptional expense and hazards of starting new industries under local conditions."[81] "Projects may look wonderful on paper, but all kinds of unexpected difficulties come up."[82] "Setting up an industry here is incredibly difficult." There are "so many snags that never occur elsewhere." Because of the unexpected problems, "one does become more cautious as he accumulates experience."[83] Unforeseen difficulties emerge at every stage: in getting a preliminary project description to a point at which an intelligent decision can be made on going ahead; in constructing the facilities, purchasing and installing the equipment, and setting up the enterprise; and in production and marketing once operations are under way.

These burdens sometimes submerge an enterprise. The long procession of unlooked-for complications that have bogged down attempts to establish what originally appeared to be the simple operation of manufacturing gari has been described by Kilby.[84] In fact, the sanguine expectations of government in undertaking a whole series of efforts to initiate domestic processing went unfulfilled; with the benefit of hindsight, Kilby concludes that "a majority of the projects in the field of processing, canning, and preserving of foodstuffs should not have been undertaken."[85] Even experienced businessmen are sometimes overwhelmed; for example, a number of European and other foreign entrepreneurs who were successful in the shoe industry in their home countries but who failed in Nigeria,[86] or the well-known Lebanese businessmen who invested in equipment for culling out "hand-selected" peanuts for the confection trade. Perhaps the

[80]Kilby, *Industrialization*, p. 78. This point was also made to the writer by the director of the United Africa Company.

[81]Nigeria, Federation, *Statement of the Activities of the Department of Commerce and Industries* (Lagos: Government Printer, 1953), p. 17.

[82]An industrial-development advisor of a foreign government aid mission.

[83]The foreign manager of a regional-development corporation.

[84]Kilby, *Industrialization*, pp. 191-195.

[85]Kilby, *Industrialization*, p. 195.

[86]Nafziger, pp. 24-25.

most striking example of an experienced firm being struck by an unforeseen disaster occurred in the sugar-growing and -processing operation established in Nigeria with the participation and under the management of
Bookers, one of the most experienced companies in the world. When they
cut the cane and brought it to the mill, it was found to be completely
desiccated. They had unknowingly waited too long to harvest the crop. In
Nigeria, ripe cane looks different from cane elsewhere.

The cumulative impact of such improbable inflictions was epitomized
by a businessman running a very large and very successful textile plant
near Lagos. In response to a query about why he did not expand further,
he replied that if he had known what he had to go through, he would not
have established the plant and he would not do it again. He had aged five
years in two.

The Significance of Foreign Investment

The first section of this chapter has presented a formidable array of
economic-environment difficulties beyond those encountered by the
businessman in an advanced economy. It has been our intention to show
that these difficulties do indeed constitute a major reason for the paucity
of profitable investment opportunities for Nigerian businessmen.

It might be argued, however, that the investment performance of the
foreign-owned companies contradicts this thesis. If the investment rate of
these companies was high, it might appear to indicate that profitable investment opportunities were developing at a satisfactory rate for firms
with adequate entrepreneurship, but that Nigerian firms, suffering from
entrepreneurial deficiencies, were unable to take advantage of them. According to this "indigenous entrepreneurial inadequacy thesis" then, it
was not the economic environment that closed off profitable investments
for indigenous businessmen, but rather their own entrepreneurial
shortcomings. This has been the contention of a number of writers on the
Nigerian economy.[87]

Investment by foreign-owned companies has been substantial. Table 14
shows that total private investment was a sizeable and increasing component of gross national product in the years immediately preceding the
Civil War. After fluctuating between 5.8 percent and 7.3 percent of GNP
from 1958-59 to 1962-63, it rose rather strongly from 6.9 percent in 1962-63
to 10.6 percent in 1965-66 and 1966-67. Then in the post-Civil War 1970s,
it maintained levels above the prewar high, according to the best estimates. After a postwar peak, gross private fixed investment was 11.7

[87]E.g., Gerald K. Helleiner, *Peasant Agriculture, Government and Economic Growth in
Nigeria* (Homewood, Illinois: Richard D. Irwin, 1966), pp. 265-266; Peter Kilby, *Industrialization*, pp. 340-42; Nafziger, p. 150.

TABLE 14

Gross Private Fixed Investment and
Gross National Product at Constant (1962-63) Prices
(millions of N £)
1958/59-1970/71

Year	Gross private fixed investment	Gross national product	G.P.F.I. as percent of G.N.P.
1958-59	68.9	1,089.4	6.3
1959-60	73.6	1,172.4	6.3
1960-61	77.7	1,329.0	5.8
1961-62	98.5	1,340.3	7.3
1962-63	95.4	1,392.6	6.9
1963-64	115.5	1,498.9	7.7
1964-65	141.0	1,559.7	9.0
1965-66	170.3	1,607.7	10.6
1966-67	174.6	1,647.4	10.6
1967-68[a]	134.4	1,368.1	9.8
1968-69[a]	143.3	1,409.4	10.2
1969-70[a]	n.a.	1,626	—
1970-71[b]	316	2,023	15.6

[a]Excluding Eastern States during the Civil War years 1967/68-1969/70.

[b]Provisional.

SOURCE: *Nigeria: Options for Long-Term Development* (Report of a mission sent to Nigeria by the World Bank) (Baltimore: Johns Hopkins University Press, 1974), p. 211.

percent and 11.2 percent of gross domestic product[88] in 1972-73 and 1973-74 respectively (Table 15). Although no figures are available, we know that most of this investment was carried out by incorporated businesses; in the Second National Plan's 1970-74 projections, approximately 85 percent of all private investment was to be by incorporated business.[89] We also know, again although no figures are available for

[88]As Nigeria's gross national product was approximately 93 percent of gross domestic product in 1972-73 and 1973-74 (*Third Plan*, p. 22), the investment percentages are slightly higher when related to GNP, specifically 12.6 percent in 1972-73 and 12.0 percent in 1973-74.

[89]Federal Republic of Nigeria, *Second National Development Plan 1970-74* (hereinafter referred to as *Second Plan*) (Lagos: Federal Ministry of Information, 1970), pp. 290, 295. The Third Plan contains no similar projections.

TABLE 15

Gross Private Fixed Investment and
Gross Domestic Product at Constant (1970/71) Prices
1970/71-1973/74
(millions of Naira)

Year	Gross private fixed investment	Gross domestic product	G.P.F.I. as percentage of G.D.P.
1970-71	823	5,320	15.5
1971-72	1,040	6,110	17.0
1972-73	756	6,481	11.7
1973-74	773	6,923	11.2

SOURCE: Federal Office of Statistics and other authoritative estimates.

overall corporate private investment, that most of this investment was carried out by foreign-owned firms. In the modern manufacturing sector, the division of ownership (as represented by official data on paid-up capital) between foreign and Nigerian-owned business was 88.7 percent to 12.3 percent in 1963 and 84.8 percent to 15.2 percent in 1965.[90]

Thus the data appear to indicate that capital formation by non-African firms was flourishing. However, the significance of this investment is not nearly as clear-cut as it seems. It is true that there is an entrepreneurial gap, as discussed in the last chapter. Nevertheless there are strong reasons for doubting that the higher investment by foreign-owned firms supports the indigenous entrepreneurial inadequacy thesis.

1. Economic environment difficulties are more severe and disabling for indigenous than for foreign-owned firms. This has been pointed out repeatedly in the preceding section and need therefore be stated simply here, but it is a weighty factor.

2. Probably even more important, the Nigerian government, in its desire to promote modern industry, encouraged foreign investors by offering a wide array of profit-increasing incentives and other measures. These affected foreign investors almost exclusively (for reasons that will be indicated shortly) and fostered investments that would not otherwise have been consummated.

a. There was the standard battery of tax incentives: income tax relief, rebates or forgiveness on duties levied on imported intermediate goods used in manufacturing (through the Import Duties Relief and Ap-

[90]Calculated from data collected by Philip Packard, "A Note on Concentration and Profit Rates within the Manufacturing Sector, 1963 and 1965," *Nigerian Journal of Economic and Social Studies* XI:3 (November 1969): 381.

proved Users Schemes), and accelerated depreciation allowances. These allowances had been freely granted and were very generous; for example, with accelerated depreciation a firm could write off 73 percent of the cost of a commercial vehicle in its first year.[91] The generosity of the allowances has been attested to by virtually all.[92] Although there were delays, arbitrariness, and inequities in operating the programs,[93] on the whole they appear to have been rather competently administered.[94] Most important, the programs appear to have had a significant investment-increasing impact. Phillips assessed the impact of the income tax relief program in two ways. Though he found that many investments that benefited from this program would have occurred without it, his data at the same time indicates its effectiveness. In his "survey approach" he found that income tax relief was a necessary incentive in at least one-fourth and perhaps more of the cases he surveyed.[95] In his "comparative profit approach" he came to the tentative conclusion that as little as 25 percent of the investment would have been undertaken *without* the encouragement of income tax relief.[96] Income tax relief, moreover, was only *one* of the incentives, and Phillips stressed his finding that Import Duties Relief was considerably more important as a precondition for foreign investment.[97] It thus appears clear that the package of tax incentives induced considerable investment.

b. Protective tariffs have usually been granted to foreign investors, particularly in manufacturing. In bargaining with government on this issue the foreign investor normally had the advantage of superior knowledge

[91]P. C. Asiodu, "Industrial Policy and Industrial Incentives in Nigeria," *Nigerian Journal of Economic and Social Studies* IX:2 (July 1967): 166. For a description of accelerated depreciation under Nigeria's Corporation Income Tax, see Adedotun O. Phillips, "Nigeria's Companies Income Tax," *Nigerian Journal of Economic and Social Studies* X:3 (November 1968): 326-327.

[92]"The unnecessary generosity of the allowances were [sic] criticised by visiting economists and other experts including those from international agencies." Asiodu, p. 166. This writer can vouch for this, having read and discussed with its author a confidential report by Ben Lewis to the government of Nigeria in 1961 stressing precisely this point. See also A. O. Phillips, "Nigeria's Experience with Income Tax Exemption: A Preliminary Assessment," *Nigerian Journal of Economic and Social Studies* X:1 (March 1968): 45, and "The Significance of Nigeria's Income Tax Relief Incentive," *Nigerian Journal of Economic and Social Studies* XI:2 (July 1969): 148ff.

[93]See, e.g., Asiodu, pp. 164-165; A. O. Phillips, "Nigerian Industrial Tax Incentives: Import Duties Relief and the Approved User Scheme," *Nigerian Journal of Economic and Social Studies* IX:3 (November 1967): 319-322, and "Nigeria's Experience with Income Tax Exemption," p. 38.

[94]See A. O. Phillips, "Nigerian Industrial Tax Incentives," pp. 319-322, and "Nigeria's Experience with Income Tax Exemption," pp. 36-37. Phillips carried out a careful investigation and study of the incentive programs.

[95]Phillips, "Significance," pp. 155-157.

[96]Phillips, "Significance," p. 161.

[97]". . . of 51 companies answering inquiries, 31 ranked relief from import duties highest among the tax incentives available to them. Sixteen ranked it second most important."

and expertise, so that the tariff agreed upon often provided a generous level of effective protection, not infrequently exceeding 100 percent.[98] For example, in the textile industry the 1964 level of effective protection was well over 100 percent for grey cloth and ranged as high as 155 and 191 percent for other processes.[99] For the fifteen products covered by Hakam, the median legal tariff rates (which are considerably below the effective rates) increased from 10 percent in 1961 (before domestic production started in most cases) to 33⅓ in 1963 and to 50 percent in 1965.[100] The two foreign-owned companies that established tire factories (Dunlop and Michelin) induced the Nigerian government to raise legal tariff rates from 20 percent to 33 percent and then 60-70 percent *and* to ban the importation of used tires. Protection of domestic production clearly induced investment that would not otherwise have occurred.[101]

The converse of the tariff inducement to invest is tariff pressure. There was pressure on foreign suppliers to establish domestic plants for fear that they would otherwise lose their established markets to firms who would set up in Nigeria under the inducement of a substantial protective tariff. Approximately two-thirds of the 51 firms surveyed by Phillips and three-fifths of the 68 firms surveyed by Hakam mentioned this as an important reason for establishing factories in Nigeria. "Many of the companies, particularly British ones, already had a long connection with Nigeria, and in fact had a ready-made market created by the export activity of their parent companies. The activities of competitors, coupled with rising tariff walls, were such that it was no longer rational to stick to the former pattern of manufacturing abroad (although this was more economical and less risky) and exporting to Nigeria . . . It would appear that 'defensive

---

Phillips, "Nigerian Industrial Tax Incentives," p. 317; see also his "Nigeria's Experience with Income Tax Exemption," pp. 47-48.

[98]The effective rate rather than the legal rate is a true measure of protection. It compares the tariff rate with the actual producing and distributing costs of the commodity in question (i.e., the "value added"). In a simplified illustration, assume that an imported commodity can be sold for $100, and assume that $75 of this covers raw material and intermediate inputs while $25 covers value added; assume also the same raw-material and intermediate-input costs for a domestic producer. If a legal tariff of 25 percent is imposed so that the imported commodity is sold for $125, the effective rate of tariff protection is 100 percent. The domestic industry can meet the price of the imported good if it can produce and distribute the commodity for $50, 100 percent more than was needed for the imported item. A concise definition of the effective tariff rate is presented by Healey: "The percentage by which the value added in the course of production, valued at domestic prices, exceeds the value added at world prices, allowing for differences between domestic and world prices for both inputs and outputs." Derek T. Healey, "Development Policy: New Thinking About an Interpretation," *Journal of Economic Literature* X:3 (September 1972): 762.

[99]Peter Kilby, *Industrialization*, pp. 46-48.

[100]Ali N. Hakam, "The Motivation to Invest and the Locational Patterns of Foreign Private Industrial Investments in Nigeria," *Nigerian Journal of Economic and Social Studies* VIII:1 (March 1966): 63.

[101]Kilby, *Industrialization*, p. 74.

investment' constitutes a major share of the investment by these companies."[102]

Considering the tax and tariff measures together, Hakam concluded that these incentives were a necessary condition for most modern-sector investment in Nigeria.[103]

c. Processing operations were sometimes established with the inducement of substantial subsidization through the privilege of purchasing Marketing Board export crops at prices below the world market level. In a number of cases, this subsidization exceeded the world market value added by domestic processing, so that "effective subsidization" (parallel to effective protection) exceeded 100 percent. In the case of cocoa butter, this arrangement not only promoted an otherwise unprofitable activity but also an activity that actually *decreased* the value of Nigeria's output. An Arthur D. Little feasibility study found that cocoa butter produced in tropical areas sold on the world market at a 5 percent discount because of inferior quality. "This fact alone means that value-added in processing at world prices is negative."[104]

d. There was also a variety of other inducements sometimes provided to foreign investors. Industrial and other business sites were made available. Liaison was arranged with government agencies responsible for electricity, water, and other services. Government promised non-nationalization and noninterference. Government sometimes furnished substantial amounts of loan capital to new enterprises on extremely favorable terms. There were also public-financed technical investigations and feasibility studies, either by government agencies (e.g., various pilot projects of the Department of Commerce and Industries and the Federal Institute of Industrial Research), by foreign organizations working under government agencies (e.g., Arthur D. Little, Inc.), or by organizations financed by foreign foundations (e.g., the Rockefeller Brothers Fund).[105] Special assistance of various kinds was sometimes provided. In the case of the Bacita sugar plantation and factory, the government undertook the expense of a soil survey and analysis, an aerial survey, and the construction of a twelve-mile access road, as well as offering all of the ordinary

[102]Phillips, "Significance," p. 153, and Hakam, p. 50. See also Harris, *Industrial Entrepreneurship*, ch. 3, pp. 30-32, "Many industrial ventures have been undertaken by important exporters to Nigeria who feared loss of this market to import substituting domestic manufacture; loss of a potentially large market rather than immediate profitability has frequently been the primary consideration of these firms." See also S. R. Dixon-Fyle, "Economic Inducements to Private Foreign Investment in Africa," *Journal of Development Studies* 4:1 (October 1967). Kilby also discusses this phenomenon at considerable length and in interesting detail: *Industrialization*, chapters 3 and 4.

[103]Hakam, p. 55.

[104]Kilby, *Industrialization*, p. 178.

[105]Nigerian officials felt a real lack of feasibility studies of projects suitable for Nigerian investors.

incentives. When regional rivalry for industrial firms reached fever pitch, the package of inducements offered to foreign investors was sometimes extremely generous indeed.[106]

The combination of all these investment incentives and related measures was extremely important in promoting otherwise reluctant foreign investment. Murray Bryce, an economist intimately involved in Nigeria's investment-promotion processes, was correct in stating: "without some protection or incentives few new industries would be established."[107] These incentives affected mainly investment by foreign-owned firms. They greatly magnified the significance and impact of the foreign investors' economic-environment and entrepreneurial advantages. Moreover, Nigerian businessmen widely asserted that foreigners were deliberately favored, and there was probably truth to these allegations in some instances. Aside from a general predisposition in favor of foreign capability, special arrangements were sometimes made for non-African companies for venal reasons.[108]

3. In addition to the two major sets of reasons just discussed for the differential investment performance of foreign and indigenous firms, some other, more minor, factors are worth mentioning. The first of these may be called the "network effect." Long established, multifaceted "expatriate firms" like the United Africa Company benefit considerably from their already existing network of activities in Nigeria. Any new investments they undertake have the cost-free use of a functioning organization that provides supporting services and advice and assistance, and can make use of a widespread, effective marketing system. The available knowledge, experience of Nigeria, personnel, and complementary facilities help in appraising a potential new activity and then may easily make the difference between success and failure. Managers of two of the largest companies indicated that this network effect was a significant factor in their investment decisions.[109] An international network effect, supporting the activities of multinational corporations, also obtains. Hakam found that multinational firms undertook investments in Nigeria despite "an initial small market in the hope that with their experience elsewhere, their intricate raw material and marketing outlets, their economies of scale and the growth of the internal and export market, they can eventu-

[106]Hakam, pp. 57-58. For a vivid description of regional rivalries over a steel mill, see also O. Aboyade, "Industrial Location and Development Policy: The Nigerian Case," *Nigerian Journal of Economic and Social Studies* X:3 (November 1968): 288-292.

[107]Murray D. Bryce, "Creating a Practical Industrial Development Programme," *Nigerian Journal of Economic and Social Studies* IV:3 (November 1962): 232-233, 236. Bryce was the head of the Arthur D. Little team working in the Federal Ministry of Commerce and Industry.

[108]See Schatz, "Crude Private Neo-Imperialism," on "bilateral swindling."

[109]A tendency of the large foreign-owned firms to invest in ventures which benefit from their already existing activities is also reported by Hakam, p. 54, and Kilby, *Industrialization*, p. 65.

ally become not only dominant in their respective industry but will be highly profitable.''[110]

4. In the case of some foreign investments, there were peripheral reasons not directly related to the projects' expected profitability. Some projects (euphemistically referred to in the *Second Plan* as "industrial projects whose viability was not assessed before execution and some of which have now turned out to be 'white elephants' ''[111]) were undertaken not because they were expected to be profitable but because someone could pull down a substantial take even out of a financial disaster. By overpricing the equipment, managerial services, or other inputs sold to the new venture, and by manipulating the capital structure and expenditures of the firm, an unscrupulous equipment supplier or promoter (perhaps with the collusion of an African political figure) could write off his own participation in the investment and still make an attractive profit on a dead-end venture.[112] Reasons other than profitability also motivated some investments by perfectly legitimate foreign-owned firms. Some highly visible, long-established firms undertook such investments reluctantly "under extreme political pressure" (to quote the manager of one of these companies) and subsequently regretted them. Somewhat smaller firms also responded to such pressures. A significant cause of investment "was redeployment from trade to industry by Lebanese and other expatriate firms that were in Nigeria prior to the industrial venture [i.e., the new venture surveyed by Hakam]. With some firms such as U.A.C. and John Holt redeployment into industry is a professed policy."[113]

5. Finally, one must be wary of the investment figures: investment growth appears more impressive because it started from a very small base; this base probably underestimated indigenous investment; and we must recall the discussion in Chapter 1 of the general weakness of Nigerian statistics.

The special factors discussed above affecting foreign-firm investment performance (and statistics)—the economic-environment differential, the investment incentives and other benefits government provided to foreign investors, the network effect, the peripheral reasons for investment, and the statistical qualifications—rebut the thesis of indigenous entrepreneurial inadequacy considered in this section. The higher investment rates of the foreign-owned firms do *not* demonstrate that there was an abundance

---

[110]Hakam, p. 51.

[111]*Second Plan*, p. 140.

[112]See, e.g., Schatz, "Crude Private Neo-Imperialism." For an interesting discussion by a top-level civil servant, see also A. A. Ayida, "Contractor Finance and Supplier Credit in Economic Growth," *Nigerian Journal of Economic and Social Studies* VII:2 (July 1965): 180-182. The capital invested by government agencies in such projects was not included in the private investment figures.

[113]Hakam, p. 52.

of profitable opportunities, and that therefore the chief reason for the paucity of profitable indigenous investment was inadequate entrepreneurship.

These special factors, however, do not necessarily support the converse thesis—that economic-environment adversities constitute the major cause of the paucity of profitable opportunities for indigenous business.[114]

Economic Environment and Entrepreneurship

In one sense, argument about the relative importance of the economic environment and entrepreneurship is meaningless. For one thing, it appears impossible to measure the relative investment-inhibiting effects of economic environment and entrepreneurial capacity. One cannot describe these factors in measurable enough terms to say with any clear or easily agreed-upon meaning that one is more important than the other. For example, there is no clear or workable idea conveyed in the statement that, say, a greater increase in investment will result from an X percent improvement in the economic environment than from a like improvement in entrepreneurship. Or, if we assume that some enhancement in the economic environment will generate as big an increase in investment as some enhancement in entrepreneurship, one cannot say that the enhancement in one was greater than that in the other.

Moreover, the economic environment and entrepreneurship are not separate and distinct matters. They are positively interrelated; amelioration in one causes amelioration in the other. The more entrepreneurship there is—in other words, the more businesses of all sorts there are in an underdeveloped economy and the better they are run—the better is the economic environment. The exercise of entrepreneurship constitutes one facet of the economic environment for other entrepreneurs. Conversely, the more favorable the economic environment, the greater the number of thriving businesses that will emerge, and therefore the more entrepreneurship there will be.[115]

Yet there *is* validity in the economic environment-vs.-entrepreneurship issue. The issue is meaningful in the arena of economic policy. If entrepreneurial inadequacy is considered the main barrier, then development policy will deal with ways of improving entrepreneurship and coping with

---

[114]Although entrepreneurship is more commonly emphasized, one can find strong support in the development literature for this thesis. A considerable number of references are cited in footnotes 6, 18, and 21 of John R. Harris, "On the Concept of Entrepreneurship, with an Application to Nigeria," in Schatz (ed.), *South of the Sahara: Development in African Economics* (Philadelphia: Temple University Press, 1972), pp. 24, 27.

[115]This point is also made in Harris, "Concept," pp. 22-24.

entrepreneurial deficiencies. Policy will tend to concentrate on training and education. If the economic environment is stressed, policy will tend to focus on means of improving that environment and of increasing investment despite the paucity of profitable ventures in an unmanipulated market. The former approach tends to be associated with greater policy passivity; the latter tends to be associated with greater policy activism.

Chapter 7

DIVERGENCES
BETWEEN PROFITABILITY AND
NET SOCIAL BENEFIT

The main obstacle to investment and development in the indigenous private sector of the Nigerian economy, according to the preceding three chapters, was not a shortage of capital. Rather, the conjunction of entrepreneurial and economic-environment problems—the entrepreneurial-environmental symphysis—caused a scarcity of profitable investment opportunities, i.e., of opportunities that Nigerian businessmen could perceive and carry out profitably. In an essentially private-enterprise economy, and leaving aside for the time being the role of foreign investment,[1] this is ordinarily taken to mean that, under the existing conditions, there is a paucity of directly productive ventures that can be undertaken usefully. The absorptive capacity for capital in the directly productive sphere is seen as limited and thus investment and development must proceed slowly.

In this chapter we examine (and criticize) the rationale for this interpretation, which accepts profitability as an index of the social utility of directly productive investments. This rationale is rather complex and it is dealt with rigorously in the appendix to this chapter. The chapter itself presents a less than fully rigorous explanation and critique but one that is intended to be comprehensible to persons who are not economists.

Rationale of the Price System

The rationale of the profit-oriented price system, i.e., of the linking of the profitability and the social utility of economic activities, rests on two basic propositions. The first is that a firm's money receipts from the sale of an increment of its product[2] measures the real benefit to society of that

---

[1] To the extent that advantages in entrepreneurship and economic environment favor foreign investors, there may be an additional margin of sufficiently profitable investment opportunities for them in the directly productive sphere of the economy. The role of foreign investors is discussed in Chapter 14, where, inter alia, it is suggested that this margin is not wide enough to warrant reliance on private foreign investment as the engine of development.

[2] Strictly speaking, we have to consider an increment of product (the marginal product) in dealing with the rationale of the price system. This is done in the appendix, but no great harm is done in this layman's presentation if we ignore this consideration.

output. This holds whether the output is produced by existing capacity or is a result of investment that expands the capacity of a firm or establishes a new firm. The reasoning is that the consumers pay for the product what it is worth to them, and the utility of the product to the consumers constitutes the benefit to society.[3]

The second basic proposition is that the money cost of producing a product measures the real cost to society of that output. The chain of reasoning is more complex than for the first proposition (and the reader who finds the remainder of this paragraph confusing need keep only the foregoing sentence in mind as he reads the rest of the chapter). Money costs are the payments of the producing firm (call it Firm A) for the necessary inputs in the production process. It is assumed that Firm A pays no more than the amount required to attract the inputs from their most productive possible alternative uses in Firms B, C, D, etc.[4] To do this, Firm A pays an infinitesimal amount more than the maximum Firms B, C, D would be willing to pay if they had to. Under competitive pressure in bidding for inputs, each of Firms B, C, D would be willing to pay an amount up to the net addition to the firm's output and therefore to its money receipts attributable to the last increment or decrement of an input.[5] Thus, the money cost to Firm A of an increment of output is an infinitesimal amount (so small it can be disregarded) more than the net addition to output that Firm A's inputs would produce in their best possible alternative uses. The latter—the amounts of products B, C, D that Firm A's inputs would have produced if they had been optimally utilized in their best alternative employments—is the real cost to society of producing product A.

It follows that profitability and social utility coincide. To maximize profit (the difference between money receipts and money costs) is also to maximize net social utility (the difference between the real benefits to society of a firm's production and the real costs). Activities or investments that are profitable are socially beneficial; conversely, those that are unprofitable entail an excess not only of money costs over money receipts but also of social costs over social benefits and thus are harmful to soci-

---

[3]Intramarginal consumption, the consumption of a product which is more intensely desired than the marginal or least desired purchase of the consumer, yields a satisfaction bonus to the consumer. On such purchases he gets more than his money's worth in the sense that he would be willing to pay more for the product if he had to. This "consumer's surplus" is ignored in this discussion, but its inclusion would tend to strengthen rather than weaken the thesis presented here. That is to say (for the more economically sophisticated reader), the divergences between profitability and net social utility to be discussed in this chapter and its appendix exist at the margin and are not related to consumer's (or producer's) surplus.

[4]Or to attract the inputs from idleness (leisure) if that is worth more to the worker or input-owner than employment in some other firm.

[5]A reminder that this applied to the marginal input. The intramarginal inputs would, under conditions of increasing marginal costs and/or decreasing marginal revenues, yield a surplus to Firms B, C, D.

ety. Here then is the importance of profitable investment opportunities. A paucity of such opportunities signifies a paucity of socially beneficial uses of capital and so enforces a slow rate of development until the conditions causing the want of profitable investment are changed.

Critical Examination
of the Rationale: Divergences

There are flaws in this rationale. There are divergences[6] between money receipts and real benefits to society and between money costs and social costs, and thus between profitability and net social utility. Because of these divergences, profit maximization does not coincide with maximization of net social utility. This section undertakes to explain the nature of the profitability-social utility divergences and to suggest their importance with the aid of illustrations drawn primarily from Nigerian, and sometimes other African, conditions and sources. Depicted here are only positive divergences, i.e., those causing net social utility to exceed profitability, although there are negative divergences as well.[7] It is the writer's belief that the former tend to predominate in a developing economy (like Nigeria's), but this is not a necessary condition for the conclusions that will be drawn. A comprehensive listing or delineation of the kinds and sources of divergences, positive or negative, is not attempted.

Benefits Besides Those to the Consumer

Let us assume for the time being that the price the consumers pay and thus the money receipts of the firm for an increment of product measures the utility of that product to the consumers.[8] In addition to consumer utility, however, there may be a great many other uncaptured benefits from production or investment,[9] i.e., benefits that are not comprehended in the money receipts of the firm. These benefits, which create positive divergences, are depicted here at some length.

Human Productive Capabilities   There is enskilment. The operation of an enterprise, whether a factory, a pharmacy, an accounting firm, or a bank, creates and enhances human productive capabilities. Skills and job abilities are created primarily through experience, perhaps supplemented by on-the-job training, rather than through formal educational or training

[6]Even at the margin.

[7]For example, pollution.

[8]This compound assumption is subjected to considerable criticism, which will be dealt with later in this chapter.

[9]A reminder: the increment of product we are considering may be produced either by existing facilities or by means of an investment that expands the capacity to produce those goods.

programs.[10] The author saw this in all kinds of manufacturing enterprises in Nigeria: from large, relatively modern textile plants which transformed large numbers of unacclimatized and unskilled new employees into semiskilled and even skilled workers—to a small factory, producing wooden furniture of modern design, which hired young men with some education and perhaps even vocational training and developed them into rather skilled operatives. One also saw it in a spectrum of nonmanufacturing enterprises, ranging from a successful Nigerian wholesale and retail druggist (chemist) who relied for fairly demanding work on pharmacist's assistants who had learned through job experience, to a relatively large foreign accounting firm which served virtually as a school for bookkeepers and accountants for Nigeria.[11] Most of the bookkeepers and clerks employed by small Nigerian firms had acquired their skills primarily through experience in large enterprises.

The formation and improvement of skills is a continuing process; there is evidence that the productivity of those who begin as unskilled workers may continue to rise for years. For example, it was found that the average output per worker in the urban sectors of Uganda's economy had been increasing between 5 and 6 percent a year in the 1960s, and that one of the major causes "has simply been increasing efficiency . . . due to longer experience in production."[12]

Valuable supervisory capacities are also created by experience. Generally, the Nigerian enterprises that were most effective in developing labor skills also developed their own supervisory labor.[13] Needed managerial capability is also formed in this way.[14]

[10]Some firms operating in Nigeria, such as the United Africa Company and Shell-BP, have run substantial training programs of a rather formal nature. For example, there were 610 Nigerians in departmental training for Shell-BP at June 30, 1962, 224 in general executive training, 337 in technical training, 30 taking courses abroad, and 161 with scholarships. Shell-BP Petroleum Development Company of Nigeria Limited, *Training for Industry in Nigeria* (Lagos: Shell-BP . . ., [1965]).

[11]The firm hired secondary school graduates and trained them on the job. Opportunities elsewhere for these employees were great. A number had become qualified accountants, having earned certificates by passing the examination of the Association of Certified and Corporate Accountants (United Kingdom), and about four times this number, without certificates, had left for good accounting jobs in other firms.

[12]Paul G. Clark, "Development Strategy in an Early-Stage Economy: Uganda," *Journal of Modern African Studies* IV:1 (March 1966): 58. See also Baldwin's conclusion that increased productivity of African labor in the Rhodesian copper mines was realized during the 1950s because the employees' work ability had been increasing gradually since the thirties . . . A job that required 10 laborers in earlier years could now be accomplished with [say] 7 workers." Robert E. Baldwin, *Economic Development and Export Growth: A Study of Northern Rhodesia, 1920-1960* (Berkeley: University of California Press, 1966), p. 99.

[13]"Most existing Nigerian foremen have worked their way up from the lower grades." C. C. Onyemelukwe, *Problems of Industrial Planning and Management in Nigeria* (New York: Columbia University Press, 1966), p. 307.

[14]"In short, managers and administrators are produced in employment." Jacob Oser, *Promoting Economic Development: with Illustrations from Kenya* (Evanston: Northwest-

In the formation of entrepreneurship as well, experience is widely recognized as a major ingredient. Most of the successful Nigerian entrepreneurs interviewed by this writer indicated that their work experience was a crucial element in their success.[15] The ways in which entrepreneurship is created are diverse, indirect, and unpredictable. Thus, Malawi migrant workers ("many thousands of motivated, relatively sophisticated, and by no means unskilled adult males") whose accustomed access to nonagricultural jobs in countries to the south was impeded became an important source of agricultural entrepreneurship in Malawi.[16] Entrepreneurship may even be developed by unsuccessful experience. An important Nigerian manufacturer who pioneered in the production of foam-rubber products and failed in the venture because of technical and marketing difficulties nevertheless "learned in this unsuccessful venture [lessons] which were turned to good stead in an enterprise manufacturing plastic foam."[17]

Other benefits   Enterprises may bring into being not only the human capabilities just discussed, but also scarce capital. A profitable firm generates saving and investment. The owner often devotes a significant portion of his profits to the expansion of his company. Thus, in an example which is surely typical, for Nigerian crepe rubber producers the most important source of capital was found to be reinvested profits.[18] Sometimes a firm provides overhead capital for other firms and for the general public. For example, the Amalgamated Tin Mines of Nigeria, with only a small subsidy from government, constructed a whole network of roads over the Jos Plateau. The operation of one firm may also engender capital formation by generating profitable investment opportunities for other firms; this brings up the concept of linkages.

A linkage occurs when the establishment of a firm or activity creates

ern University Press, 1967), p. 57. See also references cited in Paul O. Proehl, *Foreign Enterprise in Nigeria* (Chapel Hill: University of North Carolina Press, 1965), p. 215.

[15]This is confirmed repeatedly in John R. Harris, "Industrial Entrepreneurship in Nigeria," Unpublished dissertation, Northwestern University, Evanston, Illinois, August 1967, passim, and E. Wayne Nafziger, *Nigerian Entrepreneurship: A Study of Indigenous Businessmen in the Footwear Industry*, University of Illinois Ph.D. dissertation, 1967, Urbana, Illinois, passim. See also Theodore Geiger and Winifred Armstrong, *The Development of African Private Enterprise (Planning Pamphlet 120)* (Washington, D.C.: National Planning Association, 1964): ". . . most existing African entrepreneurs have acquired their technical and managerial skills more through on-the-job experience than through formal vocational training," p. 49; also pp. 73, 133. Also P. T. Bauer and B. S. Yamey, *The Economics of Underdeveloped Countries* (Chicago: University of Chicago Press, Cambridge Economic Handbooks, 1957), p. 109.

[16]Peter F. M. McLoughlin, "Land Reorganization in Malawi, 1950-60: Its Pertinence to Current Development," in Sayre P. Schatz (ed.), *South of the Sahara: Development in African Economies* (Philadelphia: Temple University Press, 1972), p. 139.

[17]Harris, ch. 5, pp. 16-17.

[18]Harris, ch. 5, pp. 16-17.

profitable opportunities for other enterprises either to supply the first firm (a backward linkage) or to make use of its product (a forward linkage). There are many Nigerian examples. The introduction during World War II of modern, relatively hygienic pig-farming in Nigeria and its subsequent development encouraged the establishment of a modern pork-products processing enterprise in 1959.[19] Reciprocal linkages then arose, for the expanded domestic processing facilities induced further expansion and improvement of pig raising.[20] The establishment of a cigarette factory created both backward and forward linkages; it encouraged substantial tobacco raising by farmers and opened opportunities for businessmen in marketing the tobacco products.[21] The establishment of domestic textile factories gave rise in similar fashion to trading enterprises that handled the textiles.[22] Rubber-creping factories encouraged the expansion of existing rubber plantations and the development of new ones.[23] Tire-retreading operations engendered domestic production of the necessary camelback.[24] The operation of breweries brought into being facilities that produced bottle caps, cartons, and other supplies.[25] The manufacture of tires generated local production of the cotton cord used in the tires.[26] Oil drilling and refining operations encouraged the development of domestic transport and civil engineering firms. The establishment of the linked undertaking entails capital formation, as mentioned in the preceding paragraph; it may give rise in addition to the other uncaptured benefits associated with the formation of new enterprises discussed in this section. Although disappointment has sometimes been expressed that linkages in Nigeria were not greater, they are likely to become increasingly frequent and important as the economy develops and becomes more complex. Moreover, potential linkages that are not acted upon may entail positive divergences. The creation of the market or the supply may be a necessary condition for the effectuation of another investment even though, at the existing state of the economy, it may not be a sufficient one.

The economic environment improves as a country develops. As the number and complexity of economic activities increase, they call forth a widening circle of supporting firms and services. Supply channels improve. The druggist already mentioned, for example, described how he

[19]"This decision was due to the fact that the quality of locally-bred pigs was such as to give confidence for investment in such an industry." "Nigeria's Pig Industry," *Nigeria Trade Journal* 11:3 (July/September 1963): 115.

[20]A number of other benefits or positive divergences were said to have resulted: foreign exchange savings and earnings; provision of foundation stocks for extensive improvement of pig-raising in Nigeria; diffused nutritional and health benefits and others. "Nigeria's Pig Industry," p. 115.

[21]"The Tobacco Industry," *Nigeria Trade Journal* 11:3 (July-September 1963): 110-111.

[22]Arthur D. Little, Inc., *A Study of the Kaduna Textile Mills, Limited,* Report to the Ministry of Commerce and Industry, Federal Republic of Nigeria, December 1962, p. 9.

[23]Harris, ch. 5, pp. 11-12.   [25]Onyemelukwe, p. 192.

[24]Harris, ch. 5, pp. 11-12.   [26]Onyemelukwe, p. 192.

benefited from the emergence of several wholesale organizations that had good stocks locally and that relieved him of the necessity of ordering directly from abroad.[27] Better maintenance and repair facilities develop. Thus, growth in the number of rubber-creping mills "made economical the establishment of a service organization by the principal machinery manufacturer. Worn rollers can be machined in Nigeria and expert service obtained quickly. . . ."[28] Other supportive activities spring up: accounting firms, architectural firms, technical services, specialists and consultants, and subsidiary services of all kinds. The infrastructure improves. To the extent that each new enterprise helps to call forth this increasing division of labor and specialization, it helps to create an economic environment that is congenial to and supportive of further development—and thus creates a social benefit not reflected in its own money receipts.

Although a complete catalogue is not intended, there are many other kinds of uncaptured benefits and a few more will be mentioned here. There are the products which benefit not only the purchaser but also the general public, such as those which improve hygienic or health conditions for the consumer and thereby for others who come into contact with the consumer. Investment creates income, a social benefit if an expansion of aggregate demand is salutary for the economy. New investments may entail improved technologies which are then transmitted to other firms. Sometimes the new technology is transmitted through demonstration and imitation; sometimes a modern enterprise provides assistance to suppliers; sometimes it provides in-plant training for employees of other firms;[29] sometimes a firm raises standards in other firms by influencing the quality of the products demanded by consumers.[30]

Finally, there are the broad social effects of investment. An interesting study of modernization in six countries including Nigeria showed considerable "modernizing effects of the factory" involving "substantial changes in a man's . . . attitudes, values and basic orientations." The study found that: "Education is the most powerful factor in making men modern, but occupational experience in large-scale organizations, and especially in factory work, makes a significant contribution in 'schooling'

[27] In like fashion, this druggist established regular supply channels to the smallest retailers, who purchased from him, relieving them of the necessity of traveling to a major city for supplies. Another example: A furniture producer who once had to accept whatever furniture fabrics happened to be available described happily the appearance of buying agencies which would "search for the appropriate materials through the world."

[28] Harris, ch. 5, p. 16.

[29] See, e.g., Joseph E. Stepanek, *Small Industry Advisory Services: An International Study* (Glencoe, Illinois: The Free Press, 1960), p. 89.

[30] The output of the furniture company previously mentioned induced architects and other large purchasers to insist that other furniture producers meet its standards of quality.

men in modern attitudes and in teaching them to act like modern men."[31] The pace and nature of technological progress are probably also affected. Such broad effects are intangible and difficult for the economist to take into account, but it seems clear that they may be highly important. As W. Arthur Lewis has said in speaking of a developing country's rural inhabitants: "The potential effect of a small investment in broadening their experience, widening their horizons and releasing their energies is incalculable."[32]

Divergences Between Price and Utility[33]

In the preceding section we temporarily assumed that the price a consumer pays for a product measures its utility for him. This assumption is now discarded. In fact, utility sometimes exceeds the price people are able or willing to pay, so that the real benefits of production exceed the money receipts of the producing firm. In a society characterized by wide disparities of income, the utility of an increment of output for the poor who cannot afford to buy more would exceed the utility forgone through an equal (in money terms) decrement of output for those who are affluent. Thus, stating it oversimply, the utility of additional output of the goods the poor would buy if income were more equal would exceed the price. Similarly, useful goods which are shunned because of ignorance[34] may have a real utility in excess of the price that the product can command on the market.

Monopolistic Divergences

Any degree of monopoly power (i.e., any deviation from the rigorously defined and rarely found conditions of pure competition) in buying or selling give rise to what may be called monopolistic divergences between profitability and net social utility. A firm with some degree of monopoly power maximizes its profits by raising the price of its product and restricting output. Similarly a firm with monopsony power in buying its inputs maximizes its profits by deliberately restricting its use of them (and therefore production) to exert downward pressure on their prices. Additional production or investment in productive capacity by such firms would reduce monopoly profits, in other words the increment would be money-losing but would nevertheless yield a net social benefit.

Monopolistic divergences are of some importance in Nigeria. In an

---

[31]Alex Inkeles, "Making Men Modern: On the Causes and Consequences of Indirect Change in Six Developing Countries," *American Journal of Sociology* 75 (September 1969): 215, 216, 208.

[32]Lewis, *Development Planning: The Essentials of Economic Policy* (New York: Harper and Row, 1966), p. 85.

[33]These are the VMP-MU divergences of the appendix.

[34]See, for example, the discussion of eggs in the VMP-MU section of the appendix.

exhaustive survey, Miracle has shown that a considerable degree of monopolistic restraint prevails in the marketing of virtually all major commodities in tropical Africa.[35] Profit maximization by the traders tends to curtail purchases from and hence production by the peasants and to restrict sales to the consumers below socially desirable levels. Additional production and sales would give rise to a net real benefit, although the effect on pecuniary profitability would be negative.

Costs

There are also the divergences between the monetary measures of costs and the real or social costs of additional production. Negative divergences, when social costs exceed private costs to the firm (e.g., pollution), are widely discussed, but positive divergences may be very large. The most important positive divergence arises when inputs are utilized that would otherwise be inactive. For example, while the money cost of employing otherwise unemployed labor is the wage paid, the real cost is small. The alternative goods that the labor would otherwise have produced would be virtually nil; if the labor was not employed in the productive activity in question, the alternative would be idleness.

The Nigerian economy has been continually characterized by substantial underutilization of productive resources of all kinds:[36] ordinary labor, arable land, and the valuable skilled, supervisory and managerial labor, the entrepreneurship, and the capital in the many firms producing well below capacity.[37] Thus the positive divergence associated with the use of underemployed resources is a major one in Nigeria.

Implications

The significance of the paucity of profitable investment opportunities discussed in Chapters 4, 5, and 6 can now be assessed in the light of the foregoing delineation of divergences between profitability and net social utility. The paucity of profitable projects would signify a corresponding

[35]Marvin P. Miracle, "Market Structure and Conduct and Tropical Africa: A Survey," in Schatz (ed.), *South of the Sahara,* pp. 88-107.

[36]Underutilization was also characteristic of the early stages of development of economies now advanced. The acceleration of capital formation and economic growth in Western Europe, the United States, Russia, and Japan before 1914 did not reduce consumption, according to Habakkuk, mainly because "there were at the start of the process reserves of unused capacity which could be brought into use with relatively little additional capital." H. J. Habakkuk, "The Historical Experience on the Basic Conditions of Economic Progress," in Leon H. Dupriez (ed.), *Economic Progress: Papers and Proceedings of a Round Table Conference Held by the International Economic Association* (Louvain: Institut de Recherches Economiques et Sociales, 1955), p. 162.

[37]The underutilization of Nigeria's productive resources is described in Chapter 14. See also the discussion of firms producing below capacity in Chapter 6.

lack of socially useful investments if profitability were a good index of social utility. It is not a good index, however; there are many positive divergences between net social usefulness and pecuniary profitability. Therefore, there are many potential ventures that would be socially though not privately profitable or, to say it differently, that would be profitable in real though not in monetary terms.

Once this is recognized (and policy-makers in Nigeria have long recognized, at least implicitly,[38] the distinction between profitability and social utility), getting such projects under way becomes an important policy consideration. Two major approaches are possible. One is to establish, in the directly productive sector of the economy, public enterprises that would be guided by considerations of net social utility rather than profitability.[39] Nigeria, by and large, has not adopted this approach. Its public enterprises have always been instructed to act on the basis of the profitability criterion (i.e., to act essentially like private enterprises), although assorted measures have tended to moderate the verdict of an unmanipulated market.

The second approach, which Nigerian governments have employed extensively, is to assist, nurture, and subsidize private business to enhance the profitability of undertakings that would not be profitable without government support. The implicit assumption is that most of the private undertakings so nurtured would create a net social utility even though they would be unprofitable in the absence of public assistance. Governments in Nigeria have carried out a range of business-assistance programs. Part III of this book is devoted to an examination of the operation of these programs in the period up to the Civil War.

Appendix to Chapter 7:
Externalities, Divergences, and the Profitability Criterion*

This appendix sets forth a distinction between a narrow or "pure" concept of externalities and a broader concept of divergences between profitability and net social utility, and delineates the broader concept. It then explores some implications of this emendation.

There has been persistent haziness regarding the meaning of exter-

---

[38]Explicitly, too. Government officials sometimes spoke of "development projects" which were not likely to be profitable but which were nevertheless considered socially desirable.

[39]There are ways of modifying the functioning of the price system to this end through the use of shadow or accounting prices.

*This appendix originally appeared as an article by the author in *Quarterly Review of Economics and Business* 13:4 (Winter 1973): 19-26.

nalities.[1] In particular, there have been conflicting tendencies regarding
the breadth of the concept. Many writers have attempted to broaden the
concept in one way or another,[2] but these broadening thrusts have often
been vigorously resisted, e.g., by Mishan who complains of the problems
caused in the theory of externalities "in consequence of misapplications
or, in another interpretation, of arbitrary extensions of the original meaning."[3]

One of the basic reasons for the ambiguity has been the use of the
externalities concept in dealing with two quite different situations:[4] in
discussion of the equilibrium-price-theory model, it has signified unpriced
effects of economic activities on production and welfare; in discussion of
the real world, it has been related to the broader idea, discussed here, that
there are divergences between private profitability and social utility.[5]

I suggest that it would promote clarity and a better assessment of the
significance of the phenomena under discussion if we reserve the term
"externalities," as Mishan wishes, for those "relevant effects on production or welfare which go wholly or partially unpriced" in the equilibrium-
price-theory model,[6] and use the term "profitability-social utility divergences" (or simply "divergences") to refer to all real-world differences between profitability and net social utility.[7]

[1]The opening sentences of Scitovsky's well-known article still apply: "The concept of
external economies is one of the most elusive in economic literature . . . full clarity has
never been achieved." Tibor Scitovsky, "Two Concepts of External Economies," *Journal
of Political Economy* 17 (1954): 143. A few years later Bator spoke of the "rich but confusing" literature in this area. Francis M. Bator, "The Anatomy of Market Failure," *Quarterly
Journal of Economics* 72 (August 1958): 356. The 1962 article by Buchanan and Stubblebine
opens with the remark that despite the importance of externalities, "rigorous definitions of
the concept itself are not readily available in the literature." James M. Buchanan and
William Craig Stubblebine, "Externality," *Economica* 29 (1962): 371. Finally Mishan remarks that the concept of externalities "is far from being unambiguous." E. J. Mishan,
"Reflections on Recent Developments in the Concept of External Effects," *Canadian
Journal of Economics and Political Science* 31 (February 1965): 3-34; reprinted in E. J.
Mishan, *Welfare Economics: Ten Introductory Essays* (New York: Random House, 1969),
p. 183.

[2]E.g., P. W. Rosenstein-Rodan, "Problems of Industrialisation in Eastern and South-
Eastern Europe," *Economic Journal* 53 (June-September 1943): 202-211; Ronald Coase,
"The Problem of Social Cost," *The Journal of Law and Economics* 3 (October 1960): 43
(where he argues that in appraising alternate economic activities, "the total effect . . . in all
spheres of life should be taken into account"); and articles already cited by Scitovsky,
Buchanan and Stubblebine, and Bator, particularly the latter at p. 362.

[3]He continues: "If the cutting edge of this powerful analytic tool is to be restored, some
attempt must be made to chip away much of the accumulating accretions of meaning that
have attached themselves to this term over time." Mishan, p. 183; see also p. 197. In accord
with his own injunction, "all such extensions of the original concept are ignored" in his
review of the literature on externalities. E. J. Mishan, "The Postwar Literature on Externalities: An Interpretative Essay," *Journal of Economic Literature* IX:1 (March 1971): 7.

[4]This has been pointed out by Scitovsky in the article cited.

[5]E.g., the articles by Rosenstein-Rodan, Scitovsky, Bator.

[6]Mishan, *Welfare Economics*, p. 184. In his "Postwar Literature" he adds that these
effects should be "unintended or incidental."

[7]"Profitability" refers here simply to the private profitability of the firm. "Net social

To delineate the divergences, it is necessary first to specify the conditions under which profit maximization and social optimization would coincide. We can do this by considering the relations between the following economic magnitudes resulting from an increment of output and the associated increment of input:

$$MSC:MOC:VMF:MC:MR:VMP:MU:MSB.$$

The abbreviations represent, respectively, marginal social cost, marginal opportunity cost, value of marginal factors, marginal cost, marginal revenue, value of marginal product, marginal utility, and marginal social benefit.[8]

Consider first the equilibrium-price-theory model in general equilibrium. Profit and social-utility maximization coincide if all of the incremental magnitudes listed above are equal. Every firm is maximizing profits by equating MC and MR. For social optimization it is necessary to assume universal perfect competition, so that MR for a given increment of production equals VMP, and the MC entailed in producing that increment of output equals the VMF. The price of the marginal factors is equated to the productivity in their best alternate uses, so that the VMF equals their MOC. The VMP, we can say, relates to the degree to which consumer preferences are satisfied, and perhaps the simplifying statement will be allowed in this context that in some sense this means that the VMP measures (or perhaps we can say equals) the utility of the marginal goods to the consumers (MU).[9] The equality of MSC and MOC and of MSB and MU are also required for optimal equilibrium. MSC = MOC indicates that opportunity costs constitute a full representation of the social costs of production; MSB = MU indicates that the satisfaction of consumer preferences constitutes a full representation of the social benefits of production. Under these circumstances, profit maximization by equating MC and MR also entails social-utility maximization by equating MSC and MSB.[10]

Now consider the single firm in a context of partial equilibrium

---

utility" refers here to the difference between the social benefits and the social costs of an economic activity. The social benefit and social cost concepts will be discussed shortly.

[8]The terms are defined in a way that differs from the usual textbook definitions, which associate some of the terms with a unit increment of output and others with a unit increment of input. Here we are talking of some (not necessarily a unit) increment of output and the associated increment of input. We are linking the increment of output with the increment of input which produces it. Thus, MC and MR refer to the increments in total costs and total revenues associated with the increment of input and output. VMF and VMP refer to the increments of physical input and output multiplied by the prices of the inputs and outputs. Similarly MU, MOC, MSB, and MSC refer to the effects of the associated increments of input and output.

[9]For simplicity's sake consumer's surplus, and producer's surplus as well, are neglected. Their inclusion, however, would only strengthen the thesis presented in this paper.

[10]If we omit MSC and MSB, the equality of all the relations involves a Pareto-optimal

analysis, assuming optimal conditions in the rest of the economy and assuming that the just-described relations between MC, VMF, MOC, and MSC and between MR, VMP, MU, and MSB hold for the disequilibrium firm. Then short-run profit maximization involves maximization (given the demand-and-supply conditions that underlie the disequilibrium) of short-run social utility; i.e., production at the level that equates short-run MC and MR also equates short-run MSC and MSB. Similarly, the firm's long-run profit maximizing adjustment (via changing capacity, i.e., investment) moves the firm to alignment in an optimal general equilibrium; i.e., when long-run MC and MR are equated, so are long-run MSC and MSB.

We can now delineate the real-world divergences between profitability and social utility. We will not attempt anything like a comprehensive listing of all significant divergences but will, nevertheless, present quite a few examples as a way of supporting a contention that divergences are more important, particularly in the less-developed economies, than most economists have been ready to believe.

In the real world the equalities discussed above do not hold; there are six types of divergences which add up to the overall divergence between social utility and profitability. These are classified as follows into two broad categories:

Divergence between:	*Label*
MC and VMF MR and VMP	monopolistic divergences
MSC and MOC MOC and VMF	money-real divergences (on the cost side)
MSB and MU MU and VMP	money-real divergences (on the benefit side)

situation. Inclusion of MSC and MSB broadens the definition of the optimum, the breadth depending on what we include in or mean by social costs and benefits. Taking social costs and benefits to include all economic effects, the optimum defined by the equations is broader than the traditional Pareto-optimality. See in this regard recent work on income distribution and optimality, e.g., E. O. Olsen, "A Normative Theory of Transfers," *Public Choice* 6 (Spring 1969): 39-58; H. M. Hochman and J. D. Rodgers, "Pareto Optimal Redistribution," *American Economic Review* 59 (September 1969): 542-557, and Comments by R. S. Goldfarb, P. A. Meyer, and J. J. Shipley, and R. A. Musgrave with a Reply by Hochman and Rodgers in *American Economic Review* 70 (December 1970): 988-1002; R. J. Zeckhauser, "Optimal Mechanisms for Income Transfer," *American Economic Review* 61 (June 1971): 324-334; G. M. von Furstenberg and D. C. Mueller, "The Pareto Optimal Approach to Income Redistribution: A Fiscal Application," *American Economic Review* 61 (September 1971): 628-637. If social benefits and costs are defined to comprehend *all* effects of an

The monopolistic divergences and the money-real divergences can occur together or separately. (The discussion that follows is confined to those divergences that cause net social utility to exceed profitability, called here positive divergences. There are, of course, negative divergences as well. The examples will relate to underdeveloped economies. It is my guess that positive divergences tend to predominate in an underdeveloped economy seeking the fundamental change required for economic development, while negative divergences tend to predominate in advanced economies.)

In the presence of any degree of monopoly, profit maximization will cause divergences between VMP and MR and between VMF and MC. These are the monopolistic divergences. The equality between VMF and MC breaks down to the extent that the firm's factors are supplied monopolistically or purchased monopsonistically. The equality between VMP and MR breaks down to the extent that the firm's output is sold monopolistically or purchased monopsonistically. If more than one of these four conditions occur together, the effects are additive. It is evident that in the real world the monopolistic divergences may be substantial.

Probably more important than the monopolistic divergences are money-real divergences. On the benefit side of our set of magnitudes, the money-real divergences are those between MSB and MU and between MU and VMP. The VMP-MU divergences tend to arise for various reasons. For one thing, VMP and MU can be called equal only if we assume that consumer preference and consumer satisfaction jibe perfectly, a problem raised by Alfred Marshall. Unfortunately, the perfect link between preference and satisfaction breaks down in the face of consumer ignorance of various kinds—e.g., about the properties of the product itself or of one's own probable reactions upon using the product. This VMP-MU divergence can be of considerable importance in underdeveloped economies. For example, in parts of Nigeria, where protein-deficiency diseases are rampant, a strong superstition inhibits the eating of eggs. Since poultry farming and egg production appear to be relatively easy and feasible ways of producing high-protein foods in Southern Nigeria, governments have encouraged private enterprises to produce eggs by modern methods and have also invested directly in relatively large-scale government egg-producing undertakings. However, the prejudice against eggs has severely limited the markets and the prospects of these enterprises. One can say that the price or VMP of eggs, especially for any substantial expansion of egg production, is less than the MU of egg production.

---

economic activity, then the overall equality would produce an *optimum optimorum*. The broadest definition of social costs and benefits offers an opening for the interpenetration of other disciplines.

Another VMP-MU divergence that may be particularly important in underdeveloped economies relates to income distribution. Let us allow ourselves interpersonal comparisons of utility and the assumption of a diminishing marginal utility of income. Then products for which the poor would increase demand if their incomes were augmented would have a higher marginal utility relative to their price (or VMP) than luxury goods for the wealthy. There is a differing relative VMP-MU relationship depending on income.

MU-SMB divergences (which can conveniently be called social benefit divergences) constitute the other component of the money-real divergences on the benefit side.[11] Economic activities usually have effects beyond the product's utility for the consumer. The MU-SMB divergences comprise many significant effects of economic activity. Let us examine some of these, using an investment in a modern factory to illustrate. These illustrations are intended partially to clarify and partially to persuade the reader that, particularly in developing economies, the positive divergences of economic activities may be very important.

There is enskilment, the creation of increased labor productivity through experience, acclimatization to the routine and regularity of modern production methods, on-the-job acquisition of skills, etc. The increase in productivity can be divided into three parts. First, there may be an uncompensated increase in productivity. This may have been expected and taken into account in the initial investment and hiring decisions, and there may also have been some uncompensated increase in productivity that was unexpected. The firm presumably adjusts to this increase in productivity by re-equating MR and MC. Second, there may be a compensated increase in productivity, i.e., a rise in the marginal productivity of the labor curve matched by a proportional increase in wages. This would leave MR and MC equal at the same output, so there would be no effect on production. Nevertheless the workers are better off because their wages have increased; MSB has increased beyond MU; there has been a social-benefit divergence. Third, a similar social-benefit divergence emerges when an increase in labor productivity is transferred to other firms through labor turnover, assuming that the transferring workers are paid commensurately with their increased productivity. The benefits from enskilment occur for all types of labor, including technically advanced, supervisory, and managerial labor.

Experience also increases the level of entrepreneurship (defined broadly as the ability to establish and operate a business successfully). The level increases among those who already have entrepreneurial re-

---

[11]Some of the social-benefit divergences to be discussed below could be thought of as lying on the cost rather than the benefit side. Where a divergence is placed, however, is unimportant.

sponsibility. More important, probably, investigation of the backgrounds of successful entrepreneurs in underdeveloped economies makes it abundantly clear that a major formative element in the creation of new, modern-sector entrepreneurs is job experience in modern enterprises. Here is a MSB-MU divergence that may be of substantial importance, although its magnitude is extremely difficult to assess.

A familiar social-benefit divergence arises when the use of a good benefits not only the consumer but also others in the general public, for example, products or services that improve the external appearance of a building, or (more important for less-developed economies) that improve hygienic and health conditions for the consumer and consequently for others who come into contact with him.

Each investment contributes, to some degree, to increasing division of labor and specialization. Economic development tends to be cumulative and self-reinforcing in many ways. As an economy grows, there emerge specialized firms and skills for servicing and repair of equipment, accounting services, architectural services, technical services, specialists and consultants, and subsidiary services of all kinds. Geographically closer, better and more reliable sources of input-supply arise. Facilities appear which enable the domestic entrepreneur to order foreign goods more knowledgeably. The infrastructure improves. To the degree that each investment contributes to this development-enhancing enlargement and differentiation of the economic structure, the investments are creating positive social benefit divergences.

To the extent that investments contribute to the growth and development of the economy, they tend to make the economy more inviting to foreign investors. Foreign capital, managerial and professional and technical labor, and know-how are attracted. If such foreign resources are productive of development, we have another positive social benefit divergence.

A related social benefit divergence may arise in a growing economy. Investment generates an expansion of money income which is a necessary but not sufficient condition for growth of the economy. If the other requisites of growth are present, the necessary expansion of aggregate demand may be considered a social benefit.

To the extent Hirschman is correct in valuing the forward and backward linkage effects of investments, and if these are something different from the benefits of increasing division of labor and specialization, they constitute another set of positive social benefit divergences.

As a final example of social benefit divergences, we may mention modernization and other broad social effects of development. These are intangible effects of investment on society about which the economist has little to say but which are nevertheless exceedingly significant. An economist as much concerned with measurement as Tinbergen believes that the unmeasurable effects of investment—the "almost invisible influences"—may be vitally important.[12]

Money-real divergences on the cost side, like those on the benefit side, also comprise two subsidiary sets of divergences: between VMF and MOC, and between MOC and MSC. Given the unemployment and underemployment not only of labor but also of arable land and modern capital goods common in underdeveloped economies, the payment for marginal factors (VMF) may well exceed the opportunity costs. For those factors that would otherwise remain idle, the opportunity cost might approach zero. The VMF-MOC divergence is a substantial one in many underdeveloped economies.

There may also be divergences between MOC and MSC; social costs are not necessarily equal to other production forgone as a result of an economy activity. Negative divergences (e.g., pollution) come more readily to mind and are probably more important, but positive divergences may occur. Consider an economic activity set up in a coal-mining region that draws workers out of the mines. The opportunity cost of attracting these workers from the mines is the coal forgone. But let us assume that coal mining also engenders other real costs in the form of accidents and sickness, costs borne partially by the workers and partially by the rest of society in the forms of increased need for hospital and other medical facilities, welfare payments for those who were made destitute or were widowed or orphaned, social costs of broken families, etc. The net social cost of attracting workers from coal mining into a safer occupation would then be less than the opportunity cost; it would be the opportunity cost minus the social costs of the hazards of coal mining.

This article has distinguished between the narrow equilibrium-price-theory concept of externalities and the broader real-world concept of divergences between profitability and net social utility. It has set forth a classification of the component types of divergences that make up the overall divergence in the real world, a classification that suggests that in many countries divergences are of major importance.

Two broad conclusions are suggested, one for applied economics, the other for economic theory. In applications of economic theory, particularly in less-developed economies, economists generally manifest an unjustified degree of overreliance on the profitability criterion. If positive divergences predominate in less-developed economies, as suggested here,

[12]Jan Tinbergen, "The Relevance of Theoretical Criteria in the Selection of Investment Plans," in Massachusetts Institute of Technology, Center for International Studies, *Investment Criteria and Economic Growth: Papers Presented at a Conference Sponsored Jointly by the Center for International Studies and the Social Science Research Council, October 15, 16, and 17, 1954* (Cambridge, Mass.: MIT, 1955), pp. 9-12.

this overreliance reinforces tendencies to restrict unduly the rate of capital formation, particularly in the directly productive sectors of the economy where investment projects are almost invariably judged on the basis of profitability. One may legitimately wish to recommend that policies be based on profitability because of the dangers and difficulties involved in departing from this criterion, but in making such a recommendation the economist should be clear about the potential importance and magnitude of the real-world divergences. For economic theory, it is the writer's hypothesis that the overall divergence may be so great as to cast doubt on the real-world usefulness of the micro-economic foundation of economic theory and on much of the superstructure erected on this foundation.

Nurture-Capitalism and Business-Assistance Measures

Chapter 8

THE POLITICAL ENVIRONMENT

The problems of indigenous enterprise discussed in Part II gave rise to an assortment of public business-assistance measures. In Part III we examine the operation of these programs in the period up to the Civil War. The present chapter delineates the political setting in which the programs were carried out.

Despite the subsequent imposition of military rule, the uses of the state, discussed in the second section of this chapter, remained essentially the same in the years after the Civil War.[1]

The Nigerian political class achieved political power in a setting that was conducive to the abuse of that power. Four aspects of the colonial economic-policy heritage were influential in this regard. First, nurture-capitalism involved the state directly in the activities of the individual units of the economy; one of the functions of government after World War II was to nurture and assist not only business in general but also individual businesses. Second, this economic approach was being carried on in a political and social milieu which, in reaction to Nigerian feelings of discrimination and deprivation under colonialism, was intensely concerned with Nigerianization in every sphere of life. It was therefore natural that the state apparatus should be used for the promotion of Nigerian economic interests. Third, while such an approach could have been directed single-mindedly toward the general welfare, the power-achieving Nigerians were accustomed to a different government orientation. They perceived a colonial pattern in which government had accorded primacy to British interests, i.e., in which the interests of those who controlled government rather than the general welfare had first priority. Fourth, economic development had not been a matter of urgency. This is not to say that colonial officials had not desired development, but it is fair to say that it was not usually considered an undertaking of pressing urgency.

Such a setting was conducive to the self-interested use of the government machinery by those with political power. And, by and large, those to

---

[1]This study does not attempt to assess possible effects of the coup of July 27, 1975, which may be taken as the study's cut-off date.

whom the British relinquished power responded in a self-interested way. Let us now examine the nature of this new Nigerian political class.[2]

The Emergent Political Class

The crucial events in the formation of Nigeria's political class were those centering on the elections of August 1951, including the competition and campaigns beforehand and the competition and accommodations reached afterward. Sophisticated Nigerians recognized that the constitutional changes that brought about the elections entailed the transfer of a significant and attractive degree of power to those who proved to be politically successful.

Under the Macpherson Constitution of 1951, the three Regional Houses of Assembly (Eastern, Western, and Northern) were to have elected Nigerian majorities. Nigerian Regional Ministers were to be chosen from among the members of the Houses, and the Regional Houses were to have genuine power regarding finances, education, public health, agriculture, and local government. The central House of Representatives, to be composed of Nigerians selected by the Regional Houses from among their membership, was to have genuine power to deal with transport, communications, and commerce. Central Government Ministers were to be chosen from among the membership of the House of Representatives. There was also a clear prospect that the 1951 transfer of power was only a first instalment and that Nigerian power would increase over the years.

The processes of power acquisition and the nature of the groups that were politically successful differed in the North and the South. Let us first discuss the South, i.e., the Eastern and Western Regions.

The South

The political class in each of these regions was formed mainly out of three already existing elites. Let us briefly examine these somewhat overlapping elites separately before discussing their fusion into a political class. First, there was the educated group, which can well be divided into two subgroups. The less important comprised Nigerians with a limited degree of education, frequently employed in clerical capacities by government and foreign firms. They provided considerable vitality and support to the nationalist drive for self-government and independence. Moreover, such people had frequently been included on local government councils because the District Officers needed literate persons to whom they could

---

[2]The concept of the political class is discussed at the very end of the section on the South in this chapter.

explain their ideas for improvement of the town between their infrequent visits.[3] But the important subelite among the educated group was composed of those with substantial educations. These persons were in relatively prestigious and high-income occupations. They constituted "an exceedingly small group of European- or American-educated professional men (lawyers, doctors, journalists, teachers)" who were "at the top of the new social structure" in the years preceding the devolution of power to Nigerians.[4]

The second elite was made up of Nigerian businessmen, all small by international standards.[5] This petty capitalist class had a longer history than the educated group. It had been developing, with various vicissitudes, at least since the early nineteenth-century shift in emphasis by the British from slave trade to legitimate trade in palm oil.[6]

Until 1949, the development of a Nigerian petty capitalist class was hampered in some ways. In general, the prevailing colonial philosophy, implicit in indirect rule, embraced the desirability of promoting only "organic" growth or development of the native societies, which were, by and large, to be sheltered and preserved. British colonial emphasis on primary production, opposition to tariff protection, and adoption on occasion of other measures inimical to domestic industry, along with the formidable competition of the large expatriate trading companies, constituted substantial problems. License fees were imposed that indigenous businessmen found extremely burdensome. Nevertheless, within the general framework of colonial policy, indigenous businessmen were for the most part allowed to make their way without substantial hindrance, and the class waxed and waned depending mainly on the competition of the large expatriate companies and the degree of general prosperity. Despite the difficulties caused by the Great Depression of the 1930s, the capitalist class entered the postwar era with some strength and wealth. By the late 1930s many ambitious traders had amassed considerable capital through growth of the cocoa industry,[7] and they augmented this wealth during the war and the postwar prosperity. Then, with the adoption of the nurture-capitalism orientation in 1949, aiming for the development of a modern economy with growing participation of Nigerians in that economy, this

[3]Peter C. Lloyd, "The Integration of the New Economic Classes with Local Government in Western Nigeria," *African Affairs* 52:209 (October 1953): 332.

[4]James S. Coleman, *Nigeria: Background to Nationalism* (Berkeley and Los Angeles: University of California Press, 1958), p. 410.

[5]Some of the keenest political analysts of Nigeria have considered the educated and capitalist elites together as one "new middle class" (Hodgkin's term) or "rising class" (Sklar's term). See, e.g., Thomas Hodgkin, *Nationalism in Colonial Africa* (London: Frederick Muller, 1956), p. 116; Richard L. Sklar, *Nigerian Political Parties: Power in an Emergent Nation* (Princeton: Princeton University Press, 1963), pp. 480-481.

[6]K. Onwuka Dike, *Trade and Politics in the Niger Delta, 1830-1885* (Oxford: Clarendon Press, 1956).

[7]See, e.g., Coleman, p. 252.

class was (in policy declaration and sometimes in fact) actively aided by government.

The third elite consisted of the chiefs and other traditional authorities. They were important partly because of their traditional legitimacy as rulers and partly because many had also become members of the emerging modern elites by virtue of economic or, sometimes, educational attainments.

The authority of the customary rulers, although curtailed in some respects by the British, had in other respects been enhanced. The validity of some shaky regimes may have been bolstered. For administrative convenience and sometimes out of ignorance of indigenous patterns, the powers of the customary authorities were increased in some ways. In particular, chiefs and councils were freed by British support and protection from many of the traditional checks on their authority. As a result, Busia has pointed out, they were often able to stifle the expression of the will of the majority and to flout it.[8] Like rulers everywhere, the traditional authorities did not always use their enhanced power for the common good, as for example when they alienated for their own personal gain uncultivated land that was regarded as a tribal heritage belonging to all the people of the tribe.[9]

The power, prestige, and privileges of the chiefs carried over with considerable vitality into the era of power-transfer from British to Nigerians. Even though the new elites were increasing their strength and status, most Yoruba towns, for example, were still governed in 1953 by their tribal kings and chiefs. Election and installation of kings and chiefs continued to generate a great deal of enthusiasm. Many of the traditional rulers were aged and illiterate, but an increasing number of younger men with wider experience were becoming chiefs.[10] Many of these traditional leaders had been able to use their strategic positions, despite fierce antagonisms between the modern elites and the chiefs, to become members of the business elite as well. Most prominent Yoruba chiefs had widespread trading interests and so had many Hausa emirs.[11]

Before turning to the elections of 1951 and the fusion of these three

---

[8]Kofi A. Busia, "The Gold Coast and Nigeria on the Road to Self-Government," in C. Grove Haines (ed.), *Africa Today* (Baltimore: Johns Hopkins Press, 1955), p. 293. See also Sir Alan Burns, *History of Nigeria*, 5th edition (London: Allen and Unwin, 1955), p. 296: "The chiefs have had little to complain of . . . their position was more assured and their incomes more certain."

[9]W. Keith Hancock, *Survey of British Commonwealth Affairs, Volume II. Problems of Economic Policy, 1918-1939, Part 2* (London: Oxford University Press, 1942; issued under the auspices of the Royal Institute of International Affairs), pp. 182-185.

[10]Lloyd, pp. 329-330.

[11]The Yorubas are the major ethnic group in what was then the Western Region of Nigeria. In Northern Nigeria also (discussed below), a similar pattern prevailed among Hausa emirs. P. T. Bauer, *West African Trade* (Cambridge: Cambridge University Press, 1954), p. 41.

elites into a dominant political class, a word is in order about the influence of the British. They were not neutral. They undertook to bolster those whom they considered the more responsible elements of the population. They also undertook to influence those whom they expected to become politically powerful. The need "to associate the more energetic and progressive elements of the community with [the colonial] administration" and to secure "an identification of interest between these elements of the local population and the . . . government" had been explicitly discussed and "fully endorsed" by the African Governors Conference in 1947.[12] Moreover, the colonial officials undertook to bolster those elements of the population they considered more responsible.

By responsible elements, Lee points out, the British meant persons with outlooks like those of the "official classes," i.e., the members of the Colonial Service and also businessmen, missionaries, teachers, doctors, and the like in the colonies. They governed according to British norms. "The idea of good government for the colonies rested very largely upon the middle class upbringing which so many of the participants themselves had experienced. . . . Good government was a collection of political attitudes accepted by general consent among those in positions of responsibility."[13] It was expected that the local people who would eventually take over should "reconstitute the official classes."[14] A responsible transfer of power required the official classes to replace themselves by "an indigenous elite which had enjoyed a political education similar to their own."[15] The process of developing a responsible indigenous group to assume power "was often described as creating 'a political class' . . . Wherever the local elite set the same standards of good government as British officials, the transfer of power had been [successfully] completed."[16]

The melding of the educated, business, and traditional elites into a dominant political class centered on the 1951 elections. The politically successful in those elections were generally members of the two modern elites, the educated and the businessmen. They were the people who had been successful in dealing with the modern world. They had seized the opportunity for a Western education and had moved into the professions or they had established profitable footholds in the economy. In general the modern elites were characterized "by four objective criteria: high-status occupation . . . , high income, superior education . . . , and the ownership or control of business enterprise."[17]

They were admired in their communities as a result of their attainments, and their opinions were respected. They were often members of

[12]United Kingdom, Colonial Office, *Record of Proceedings of the Conference of African Governors, 8th to 21st November, 1947*, p. 196 (mimeographed).

[13]John M. Lee, *Colonial Development and Good Government* (Oxford: Clarendon Press, 1967), p. 2.

[14]Lee, p. 13.   [16]Lee, pp. 13–14.

[15]Lee. p. 1.   [17]Sklar, pp. 480–481.

local councils and leaders of community organizations. Many had received honorary chieftancy titles in recognition of their accomplishments or for payment. "They were, in fact, a group which had made a success out of the rapidly changing conditions in Nigeria since the 1930s, and were looked up to because of their success and widely known in their home areas because of it. They were the people who would naturally be chosen in 1951 to represent the interests of their localities in the various legislatures."[18]

They carried out an "interpretative function." They explained the new ways to the traditional society and helped people meet the obligations imposed by the changing milieu. In return for the assistance they rendered, people respected and supported the new men. "The 'interpretative function' at a local level was thus one of the foundations of Nigerian politics."[19]

Some of the new men were nationalists, militants, radicals in their demands for rapid decolonization. Their desire for national independence was fervent and, for some, superseded their own personal interests. Some, as Sklar has suggested, may have been willing to "sacrifice their fortunes for the national interest."[20] But most had not been militant nationalists at all. They had accepted the status quo and had done well. Even those with strong nationalist aspirations frequently "were also people who had careers to make, people who had seen that politics was a new way by which they could improve or maintain their economic and social positions. Often party loyalty was regarded as an investment and standing for election as a business venture."[21] Party allegiance and changes in that allegiance were frequently determined not by deeply held beliefs or ideology but by pursuit of personal advantage, membership in the governing party being attractive while membership in the opposition party was particularly unattractive.[22]

The prospect and subsequent reality of power precipitated a fusion of the elites into a single dominant class in each region. The exercise of power was a serious and attractive business, and those with power set

[18]K. W. J. Post, *The Nigerian Federal Election of 1959; Politics and Administration in a Developing Political System* (London: Oxford University Press, 1963), p. 47.

[19]Post, p. 48.

[20]Sklar, p. 264.

[21]Post, p. 49.

[22]There are a surprising number of detailed, painstaking, insightful discussions of basic Nigerian political forces and of Nigerian classes. Among many good discussions of Southern Nigeria are Sklar, pp. 107, 213-215, 256-257, 262-264, 350-353, 390, 418, 480-487, 501-502; Post, Chapter 2; Hodgkin, particularly pp. 116-117; Thomas Hodgkin, "Towards Self-Government in British West Africa," in Basil Davidson and Adereka Ademola (eds.), *The New West African* (London: Allen and Unwin, 1953), pp. 57-61; Coleman, particularly pp. 48-51 and ch. 17; Martin Kilson, "Nationalism and Social Classes in British West Africa," *Journal of Politics* 20 (1958): 368-387; Lloyd, pp. 327-334; James O'Connell, "The Political Class and Economic Growth," *Nigerian Journal of Economic and Social Studies* VIII:1 (March 1966): 129-140.

about strengthening their hold on it while those on the outside sought to share in it. The politically successful leaders endeavored to broaden their support by wooing the legislators and influential supporters of the opposition party, and the latter generally responded eagerly, switching allegiance to the dominant party in each region.[23] The traditional authorities participated in this fusion although they had not generally run in the elections. They had strong backing based upon social patterns of continuing vigor. In any base-broadening sought by the political leaders, their support was an obvious goal. In their place, the chiefs and traditional authorities recognized that substantial changes were taking place and that power and privilege was to be increasingly dependent upon political strength. They were therefore quite ready to exchange their support for influence and membership in the governing group.[24]

Out of the jockeying for power there emerged in each region (Eastern and Western) a dominant class. Divergent groups influenced and accommodated to one another. The more conservative elements, including many of the chiefs and the new men who had been indifferent or antagonistic to the activities of the militant or radical nationalists, "imbibed the heady wine of nationalism; in turn, many of the radicals acquired attitudes and interests akin to those of a privileged class."[25] The groups blended into a governing class. "This class is an actual social aggregate, engaged in class action and characterized by a growing sense of class consciousness. It may be termed the 'political class' . . . in that its members have controlling positions in the dominant institutions of society . . . the leaders of the ruling parties constitute[d] the core of the political class."[26]

[23]The phenomenon of "carpet-crossing" in the legislature is discussed later in this chapter.

[24]Of course, this interpenetration of the political and economic elites is not unique to Nigeria nor to the developing countries. See, for example, Aitken's discussion of the closeness of the political and economic elites in Canada, and also the United States, in the nineteenth century. Hugh G. J. Aitken, "Government and Business in Canada: An Interpretation," *Business History Review* 38:1 (1964): 5ff.

[25]Sklar, p. 481.

[26]Richard L. Sklar, "Contradictions in the Nigerian Political System," *Journal of Modern African Studies* 3:2 (1965): 204. Sklar adds: "The value of this term [the political class] is magnified in the analysis of a developing country, like Nigeria, where it may serve to suggest that political power is the primary force that creates economic opportunity and determines the pattern of social stratification."

Pertinent here is the Marxian discussion of the factors which, given the economic and social position of an aggregate of individuals, cement that aggregate together into a class. Marx and Engels mention, inter alia: conflicts over the distribution of economic goods with another group (in Nigeria with the British colonial governing group and later with those elements in the Nigerian population, whether idealistic or leaders in the other regions, which threatened the hold of the regional political class on power and privilege); easy communication among those in the same class position, encouraging the dissemination of ideas and plans for action; growth of class-consciousness, i.e., of a feeling of solidarity and a consciousness of a common role in society. To stimulate the fusion process it is also necessary to have a class enemy (which in the Nigerian instance may perhaps be read as a political

The North

In the North as in the South a small ruling group took over the power the British relinquished, but the process differed in some significant ways from that of the South. Perhaps most noticeable at the time, the transfer lagged slightly and, particularly from 1952 to 1954, the North was considerably behind the South. Most fundamental, unlike their counterparts in the South, the Northern traditional authorities maintained unquestioned preeminence before, during, and after the transfer of power. As Sklar remarked in 1963, "Emirs still rule in the North, assuredly with limitations . . . while *Obas* merely preside in the West."[27]

The ruling class or alliance was formed from three elites parallel to those of the South. As already indicated, the "natural rulers" and aristocracy of the North constituted the dominant elite.[28] In most of the North, there was a hereditary titled ruling class of noble birth. This class was usually of Fulani origin but a similar pattern prevailed in most of the non-Fulani-ruled areas outside the Middle Belt (about which a word will be said shortly). The emirs and the hereditary aristocracy had in some ways been strengthened by the British and the philosophy of indirect rule.[29] Some writers even maintain that their hegemony was tottering and was saved by British colonization, although others are skeptical.[30] At the least, the British had avoided dismantling their power structure; "indirect rule had left intact the essential institutions of traditional government in the emirates."[31] Despite ultimate British authority, "due regard had to be paid to acquiring and maintaining the goodwill of the traditional rulers."[32]

During the period of transfer of power also, the British carefully buttressed the authority of the "natural rulers." In the advance to self-government, the British wanted "to introduce the required changes without dislodging traditional authority. . . ." Consequently "British officials made every effort to closely associate the emirs with constitutional developments as they affected the North." Colonial officials, in accord with

---

enemy, namely the opposing political parties, particularly those dominant in the other regions). Karl Marx and Friedrich Engels, *The German Ideology* (New York: International Publishers, 1939), pp. 16ff.

[27]Sklar, *Nigerian Political Parties*, p. 350. Three penetrating studies of the Northern Nigerian political and power systems are Sklar, *Nigerian Political Parties;* C. Sylvester Whitaker, *The Politics of Tradition, Continuity and Change in Northern Nigeria, 1946-1966* (Princeton: Princeton University Press, 1970); and Billy J. Dudley, *Parties and Politics in Northern Nigeria* (London: Frank Cass and Co., 1968).

[28]Dudley's enumeration shows that the top leadership of the North almost all came from aristocratic ruling-class families: Dudley, pp. 136-137.

[29]See, e.g., Dudley, pp. 16-17. Whitaker remarks that "the Pax Britannica eliminated important sources of resistance to the power of the emirs . . .": Whitaker, p. 263.

[30]See, e.g., Amanke Okafor, "West African Background: An Outline," in Davidson and Ademola, p. 46. For an example of the skeptical position, see Michael Crowder, *West Africa under Colonial Rule* (Evanston: Northwestern University Press, 1968), pp. 212-219.

[31]Whitaker, p. 28.

[32]Whitaker, p. 41.

the philosophy of indirect rule and out of concern for stability, used their influence to prevent erosion of "the extraordinary position of power which chiefs in Northern Nigeria occupied."[33]

There was, secondly, an administrative elite. It comprised mainly the literate functionaries holding executive and clerical jobs in the Native Authorities.[34] These were mainly the sons of noblemen, other members of aristocratic families, and their retainers, for British colonial policy had given educational priority to the "natural rulers." This elite clearly was closely linked with and dependent upon the dominant elite.

A third elite, also subordinate, comprised the capitalists, mostly petty businessmen: import and export merchants, licensed buying agents of the major export crops, road transporters, cattle dealers, contractors, etc. They were generally of a nonaristocratic class. While this group customarily had little political weight, its influence tended to increase throughout the pre-Civil War period.[35]

In the Middle Belt of Northern Nigeria, the pattern of leadership was more like that in the South. However, as they constituted a small minority in the North, the new men of the Middle Belt gravitated toward the dominant political party, the Northern Peoples' Congress (NPC).

In the process of devolution of power to Northern Nigerians the traditional, administrative, and business elites fused into a powerful political class—or perhaps it would be more accurate to speak of an incipient political class or a ruling alliance, for the persisting social distinctions between various groups were substantial. The focus of that fusion or alliance was control of the Northern Nigeria government, and the political instrument was the Northern Peoples' Congress. The NPC was originally conceived and organized as a vehicle for political cooperation among educated and progressive Northerners, who regarded the traditional power structure with misgivings; but it was rather quickly transformed from a means of questioning and challenging to one of upholding the power of the traditional rulers. In the course of its first two years, the emirs and other conservative forces were able to mold the NPC so that it served their own interests. Thus, unlike the Southern parties, the NPC was not regarded as a means of *attaining* power, but as a means of *defending* power already possessed from possible encroachment under the Macpherson constitution, with its Regional House of Assembly and Regional Council of Ministers.[36]

The emirs and traditional aristocracy continued to dominate the politi-

[33]Whitaker, pp. 297-298, 300.

[34]Former Prime Minister of Nigeria Alhaji Sir Abubakar Tafawa Balewa came from this class. Dudley, pp. 136-137.

[35]One member of the North's top leadership in the period before the coup of January 1966 was a wealthy merchant. Dudley, pp. 136-137.

[36]For an excellent concise description of the Northern Nigerian governmental structure during this period see Dudley, pp. 27ff.

cal alliance. They assumed the ministerial posts and the other highest positions in government. They completely controlled the House of Chiefs, which was considerably more powerful than is usual for such bodies. And even when not formally active in the NPC, they were nevertheless the actual power. They dominated the NPC nominating procedures for the House of Assembly; "it seemed highly improbable that any individual who was unacceptable to a major emir would be nominated by the NPC."[37] The business class generally undertook political roles not on their own initiative, "but in response to overtures on the part of leaders of the NPC who perceived the assistance . . . [they] could render in competition for the loyalty of the mass electorate."[38] They played an important role in the party. Springing from the common people, they were effective campaigners against more radical elements. The administrative elite provided most of the members of the House of Assembly and other political activists, but they were usually relatives or clients of the emirs and dependent upon them for their careers.

There were two subgroups among the adminstrative elite.[39] The conservative reformers were the larger of the two. The typical member of this group was "a high-born upper-echelon member of a local hereditary-bureaucratic hierarchy" who valued and benefited from traditional institutions. His regard for these institutions was tempered by desires for African self-determination and for economic development, however, so he favored reforms that would meet British conditions for self-government and that promised economic advance. Still, these reforms were to be limited "to ensure that the institutions of power and authority in the emirates would be disturbed as little as possible." The smaller subgroup, the Northern critics, lacked such a commitment to the existing power structure. For the typical member of this group, e.g., a trained clerk or elementary schoolteacher, "his own foothold in the traditional hierarchy was marginal and tenuous, enjoyed more by dint of special training and technical skill than through close blood or strong clientage relationships with his superiors." However, the criticisms of these critics were mild and self-censored and grew increasingly weaker. The critics were exposed to censure and retaliation. As a minority, they felt weak and ineffective in any case. They feared Southern domination as the British withdrew. And they were apprehensive about mass enfranchisement of the peasantry, fearing that they would support radical and irresponsible Southern political leaders. As a result of these fears and doubts, they threw in with the existing power structure, hoping thereby to enhance their influence and prestige. (The few members of the House of Assembly

[37]Sklar, *Nigerian Political Parties*, p. 388.
[38]Whitaker, p. 333.
[39]This paragraph is based primarily on Whitaker, pp. 58-67, and the quoted passages are from this source.

who came from very humble stations, incidentally, were for the most part in the opposition parties.)

The fusion of the three elites was mutually beneficial. The capitalists contributed financially and helped consolidate support among the common people. They gained through the good relationship with government that resulted, for government was the main source of contracts, directly oversaw most export trade via the Marketing Board, and controlled or influenced many other facets of economic activity. The administrative elite contributed by supplying a large part of the skills, ability, and even leadership necessary to run the political party and the regional government. They benefited in that politically loyal service was rewarded with security, promotion, association with the centers of prestige and power, and often by access to economic opportunities. The emirs and other traditional rulers contributed by dispensing the rewards to the other groups. They benefited by consolidating their control during a threatening period of change. They also profited economically through lucrative directorships, chairmanships, and similar posts in government corporations, and through the development of substantial interests in private economic undertakings.

The British were not unaware that those coming to power in the colonies tended to constitute an economic as well as a political class, but did not want to discuss it publicly. "The paternalism of colonial relationships prevented an open discussion of the economic status of the new national leadership. The ownership of the means of production was too embarrassing a subject in many colonies to be publicly debated."[40]

Use of the State

Once this essentially self-interested political class (speaking of the different regional groupings as different divisions of the one class) attained power it used that power to entrench and enrich itself.

Enrichment

The uses of government power for enrichment ranged from the completely legitimate to the thoroughly illegitimate.

Since many important members of the political class were outstanding businessmen and since in general there was a considerable infusion of businessmen in the political class, many of the benefits of business-assistance measures and of other government activities, such as land allotments, contract awards, etc., quite naturally and properly went to members of the political class. On the other hand, government programs were manipulated with varying degrees of flagrance, with abuses extending from mild pressure on civil servants to pay especially careful attention

[40]Lee, p. 98.

to loan applications of the politically favored to outright corruption and payoffs. Political manipulation and corruption are discussed at some length in Chapter 13; moreover, hundreds of pages of detailed examination of corruption have emerged from the various official investigations, so the topic will not be examined in detail here. Suffice it to say at this point that this phenomenon was widely observed and commented upon throughout most of the 1950s and 1960s.[41]

Members of the political class also made use of the authority of the state and its position as the representative of the Nigerian people to bolster their ability to make economically beneficial arrangements with foreign interests. In this arena, too, the methods ranged by imperceptible degrees from the perfectly proper to the thoroughly unscrupulous. Businessmen established legitimate linkages with foreign-owned firms, supplying goods and services to them and distributing their output. Sometimes there were good positions for educated members of the political elites or their families, opportunities to get in on good investments and other legitimate benefits. Some gains arose out of considerations that were less than pristine pure but that nevertheless did not involve any political manipulation. Foreign firms, motivated by a generalized desire to forfend possible hostile public reactions and antagonistic government actions, appointed Nigerians to their Boards of Directors or to window-dressing managerial posts,[42] established business connections with Nigerians, and even helped to set up Nigerian firms. In such actions they naturally favored influential Nigerians.

It was often difficult to tell whether more direct political considerations were involved. Shell-BP, for example, had construction, earth-moving, and similar contracts for up to £ 10,000 with a selected group of Nigerian firms. The agreements were based on direct negotiation or selective tendering rather than on open competitive tendering. In the nine-month period from June 1964 through February 1965 it had negotiated 44 such contracts with 10 firms for £ 231,977, not including petty contracts. Two

---

[41]For example, a member of the Western House of Assembly spoke in 1956 of "the phenomenal rise in affluence within the past five years of the Members of the Government Party . . . the landed property amounting to some five million pounds which has now been acquired by a few Members of the Government Party who five years ago could not pull together between themselves a sum of £ 1,000 . . ." Nigeria, Western Region, *House of Assembly Debates*, 4th Session, Omnibus Issue No. 6, December 21, 1956, columns 38-39. See also Aboyade's statement that "the political and economic power structure was such that a handful of the Nigerian middle class in collusion with powerful foreign interests increasingly gained control of the government apparatus largely for the promotion of their joint interests": Ojetunje Aboyade, "The Economy of Nigeria" in Peter Robson and L. A. Lury (eds.), *The Economy of Africa* (Evanston: Northwestern University Press, 1969), p. 191. Also O'Connell's statement that "There is no honest way of accumulating the wealth that the Nigerian politicians considered that they needed . . .": O'Connell, p. 136.

[42]Positions as public relations and personnel directors were often window-dressing posts (a term often used in Nigeria). In these positions, the Nigerian executives usually dealt with other Nigerians but had little real influence on important decisions of the firm.

contractors received 31 of these contracts for £ 196,602. Many of these entrepreneurs were or had been in politics, but Shell-BP officials stated that they required that these contractors do a good job or no renewals were forthcoming. They said that the proprietor of the firm with the largest number of contracts was a capable engineer who, however, had been focusing excessively on politics, but who then acceded to a Shell-BP demand that he devote his energies to doing a good job for them. In light transport, two of the three Nigerian firms they were still dealing with in 1965 got their original contracts through political connections. One was owned by the Chief Whip in the Nigerian House of Representatives and the other by a group of Eastern Nigerian ministers. Most cars, pickups, and other light-transport vehicles were hired by Shell directly from dealers (who were foreigners), but when they hired vehicles from Nigerians, whom they tried to favor, they paid a 15 percent premium because the Nigerians had to pay a higher price than the dealers for the cars. Shell-BP was frequently willing to give a price preference to Nigerian businessmen. The only successful Nigerian in heavy (truck) transport for Shell-BP had once been Deputy Speaker of the Eastern House of Assembly. He had been encouraged to establish the business, was advised and given contracts by Shell-BP, and then left politics to work full-time on his business. (The only other Nigerian in heavy transport for Shell had also been a politician, but his performance was unsatisfactory and Shell was trying to terminate its small contract with him in 1965.) Whatever the motivations of Shell-BP, there is no doubt that members of the political class were frequently favored in business relations and jobs with foreign firms for political reasons.[43]

Sometimes the political-class incomes from foreign firms were completely illegitimate. Venal politicians often colluded with unscrupulous foreign companies or promoters in schemes to swindle government or government corporations.[44] Sometimes venal elements in the political class were in a position to extort money from the foreign investors.

Entrenchment

The Nigerian political class used its hold on government to entrench itself in power. The benefits of office were far too attractive to many who otherwise would have had little glory or affluence to allow them to contemplate the forfeiture of these perquisites without carrying on the most effective possible fight regardless of means. Moreover, an authoritarian

[43]Esseks speaks of "a form of bribery employed by many American firms [in Ghana], a clear or tacit offer of lucrative employment upon leaving government service or politics . . ." John D. Esseks, "Government and Indigenous Private Enterprise in Ghana," *Journal of Modern African Studies* 9:1 (May 1971): 19.

[44]See, e.g., Sayre P. Schatz, "Crude Private Neo-Imperialism: A New Pattern in Africa," *Journal of Modern African Studies* 7:4 (December 1969): 681-685.

approach accorded with the colonial political heritage. The colonial regime's "power to crush those who opposed it impressed the Nigerian peoples generally and the nationalist leaders particularly."[45] To entrench itself, the political class used legal, extralegal, and illegal means of rewarding friends and punishing enemies.

Politicians and businessmen were highly amenable to these kinds of pressures. For those without strong ideological convictions the reward-deprivation choice was easy to make. Politicians were magnetized by the prospect of prestigious, lucrative positions as government ministers, chairmen or directors of public corporations, etc. The number of ministerial and other grand positions was multiplied far beyond any governmental need. As the Federal Minister of Communications and Chairman of the Western Working Committee said (at a time when regional governments had something like thirty ministers and junior ministers), "but for the mad rush for power all over the Federation, every region could do with 10 ministers."[46] By 1965 the federal government alone provided an amazing eighty ministerial and junior ministerial positions.[47] For minor political figures there were minor posts and privileges.

Consolidation of political support through the reward-punishment alternative found its clearest expression in "carpet-crossing," i.e., the crossing over of parliamentary representatives from the opposition to the party in power. Most frequently the carpet-crossers were "merely careerists and opportunists pure and simple. This type prefer to go with the winning side . . ."[48] and change parties in order to share in the perquisites of power. On the opposite side of the same coin, some switched party allegiance to avoid considerable unpleasantness. They often were "victims of persistent persecution, prosecution and other forms of victimisation . . . [One opposition member] knew neither political peace nor domestic rest. His business concern was compelled to close down. His means of transport was wrecked, they even attempted to deprive him of his wife. . . . He was ultimately compelled to seek membership [in the party in power]."[49]

Businessmen, like politicians, were eager to share in the bounty and were vulnerable to deprivation. Given the manifest determination of the political class to manipulate government programs for political advantage, adherence to the party in power seemed a necessary condition for partaking of the business benefits that government influenced or controlled.

---

[45]O'Connell, p. 129.

[46]Nevertheless, as a political leader he found that "The present state of Western Nigeria justifies the number of ministers in that region." *West Africa,* December 21, 1963, p. 1444.

[47]The costs of providing eighty federal ministerial posts was estimated in *West Africa,* April 10, 1965, p. 390.

[48]Increase Coker, "The Romance of Carpet Crossing," (Lagos) *Sunday Post,* July 22, 1962, p. 6. This is a highly perceptive newspaper article.

[49]Coker, p. 6.

Sometimes the business uses of government authority were intricate and the pressures were subtle.[50] Often the pressures were quite overt and heavy, as shown by the following newspaper report:

The Produce Buying Licenses withdrawn from three leading produce buying agents in Ilesha have now been renewed and returned to them following the declaration of the Directors of the Agents for the NNDP [the party then in power in Western Nigeria] last weekend. . . . Following the withdrawal over 500 workers (all Ijeshas) serving the agents were laid off. Last week-end, the men declared for the NNDP and on Monday their licenses were renewed and handed to them.

Addressing a rally of the NNDP in Ijesha, Mr. Lawrence Omole said he was not leaving the Action Group [the opposition party] because he had any reason to do so 'neither am I joining the NNDP out of my own personal conviction.' He said he was doing so following pressure. . . .[51]

In an earlier example in Eastern Nigeria, following an abortive attempt to oust Nnamdi Azikiwe from the leadership of the NCNC (the governing party), the produce-buying license of L.N. Obioha, the primary financial backer of the rebel group, was withdrawn.[52] Government could nurture or chastise businessmen also through control of titles for business sites, rents, permits, pioneer status, tax legislation, and in many other ways.

The reward-deprivation system was applied not only to politicians, businessmen, and other individuals, but also to entire communities. It was often stated quite explicitly that areas which supported the party in power could expect to receive "amenities" (roads, hospitals, dispensaries, schools, etc.), while those which voted for the opposition could expect few such benefits from the government.[53]

Other means were also used to consolidate power. There was outright bribery of the voters.[54] There was substantial intimidation and obstruction of persons and parties opposed to the governing party. Meetings,

[50]See, e.g., the way Hausa kola traders in Western Nigeria have made changing use of federal government power, depending on the circumstances, to protect their advantageous position. Abner Cohen, "Politics of the Kola Trade," in Edith H. Whetham and Jean I. Currie (eds.), *Readings in the Applied Economics of Africa; Vol. I: Micro-Economics* (London: Cambridge University Press, 1967), p. 162.

[51]*Nigerian Tribune*, September 18, 1964, p. 6. (Some brief paragraphs are run together.)

[52]Eme Awa, *Federal Government in Nigeria* (manuscript), p. 342.

[53]"Dr. M. I. Okpara [Premier of Eastern Nigeria] said it was strange that Onitsha people were 'going the Dynamic Party way' and warned that his Government would not erect industries in areas which were hostile to the Government party." (Lagos) *Daily Times*, February 12, 1962, p. 1. Other newspapers carried similar stories at various times. For example, the (Lagos) *Daily Express* (November 7, 1961, p. 1) reported: "Dr. Okpara is putting it clearly to the voters here—'Vote for the NCNC and you shall have your amenities. Vote against us and lose everything.' " And the *West African Pilot* (November 4, 1961, p. 8) reported that Dr. Okpara "warned that those who did not support the NCNC now 'should not hope to reap where they did not sow.' "

[54]See, e.g., the long parliamentary discussion of election expenses in Nigeria, Federation, *Debates of the House of Representatives*, Session 1959-60, August 11, 1959, pp. 164-170. There was much complaint that if a candidate "though he may be very brilliant and intelli-

processions, and other political activities were hampered, disrupted with the connivance of the authorities, or forbidden altogether. There were politically motivated criminal prosecutions and punishments including fines, jailings, and whippings.[55] The political classes also used their control of the government purse to finance their political parties. Important party workers were given well-paying sinecures; political jobholders kicked back part of their salaries to the party; and substantial outlays of the Development and Finance Corporations, the Marketing Boards, and the Statutory Corporations were used to finance party activities (with some of the money sticking to the hands of the individual politicians). ". . . there was a general failure in Nigeria to distinguish between public, party and private financial interests."[56]

---

gent and capable for the post, does not have the money to give, the next thing is that the crooks, his opponents, who have the money but not the ability for the post will have it" (p. 164).

[55]See, e.g., Post, and Sklar, *Nigerian Political Parties*. Intimidation of political opposition was widely written about from 1964 on.

[56]Post, p. 63.

Chapter 9

CONSTRUCTION

Demand-Channeling

One of the ways in which governments tried to assist indigenous firms was by channeling demand to those firms. These *demand-channeling* measures took various forms.[1] The most explicit were the systems followed by all the governments for awarding contracts for government construction (to be discussed in this chapter) and the Federal Government's Approved Manufacturers Scheme, which was intended to favor domestic over foreign producers as government suppliers (to be discussed in the next chapter).

The demand-channeling measures were national and regional. While the national Government followed the policy of favoring Nigerian or domestic firms over foreign-owned or overseas firms, the regional governments tended to favor businessmen from the region over Nigerians from another region. For brevity, we can say the national government favored Nigerians or nationals and the regional governments favored Northerners, Easterners, and Westerners, or regionals.

The demand-channeling programs favoring nationals or regionals were established for three main sets of reasons. First, there were powerful pressures brought not only by the businessmen who hoped to benefit

---

[1]At the urging of the government departments responsible for establishing handicraft centers, government agencies sometimes purchased handicraft goods, particularly textiles, produced at the centers. The handicraft-promoting departments (at the central, later the Federal and regional government levels) also made some attempts to promote sales to private purchasers. On occasion, attempts were made to generate government or private orders for other indigenous firms, such as printers, road transporters, and others. Assistance was provided with foreign trade and financing procedures, including provision of status reports on Nigerian businesses to foreign companies seeking business relations and, conversely, provision of "trade introductions" both ways, establishment of trade information offices in Britain and Nigeria, and inspection and grading of export produce. Government sometimes used its contacts and facilities to help indigenous firms procure supplies; efforts of this nature went back at least as far as the early post-World War II period, when special consideration was sometimes given to Nigerians in import licensing. Displays were sometimes set up for Nigerian producers at trade fairs and commercial exhibits. Designation of Nigerians as Licensed Buying Agents for Marketing Board produce could also be considered a form of demand-channeling, and there were other measures as well.

directly, but also by a public that wanted means of satisfying their growing nationalist (or ethnic or regional) and anticolonial feelings. These pressures were intense and long-standing. They erupted continually, for example, in the Parliamentary debates. There were calls for special favoritism for indigenous or domestic producers. In a typical speech urging strengthened government programs to purchase domestic products, a prominent political leader declared: "Let us not say that the cloth manufactured locally here is inferior to the ones imported. To a very large extent we know it is, but it is only by using this inferior cloth" that Nigerian production can be promoted.[2] There were hostile inquiries concerning the number of construction contracts going to Nigerian (or Regional) contractors as compared to foreign (or extra-Regional) firms, and defensive responses by government spokesmen indicating intentions to Nigerianize or Regionalize the personnel involved in awarding government contracts,[3] and explaining why the number of contracts awarded to nationals or Regionals was not larger, and reiterating government determination to increase this number.[4]

The second reason for adopting demand-channeling measures lay in the gains for political leaders. Aside from meeting the need to respond to the demands of their constituents (essentially a complement of the first reason), politicians gained the power and leverage realized by those with patronage to dispense and also gained tempting self-enrichment opportunities.

Third, any favoritism for Nigerians (and the point applies mutatis mutandis to Regionals) involved a cost: the differential between the Nigerian price and quality package and that of the foreign producer. It was correctly realized, although not necessarily in the form of a sophisticated

[2]Nigeria, Federation, *Debates of the House of Representatives* (Session 1958-59), February 25, 1958, p. 203. Said another prominent leader: ". . . with a young indigenous industry just starting it will be very difficult to have the prices compare favorably with the imported goods of the same quality. I am asking that the Government should have special consideration for these locally manufactured products because for about five or ten years it will be impossible for them to have competitive prices." Nigeria, Federation, *Debates of the House of Representatives* (Session 1959-60), August 12, 1959, column 1800. There were many other strong and even vivid statements. See, e.g., *Debates* (1959-60), columns 1799 and 1802.

[3]E.g., Nigeria, Northern Region, *House of Assembly Debates*, Second Legislature (Second Session, Second Meeting, July 30 to August 6, 1958), August 6, 1958, columns 815-16 (Government Printer, 1958).

[4]See, e.g., Nigeria, *House of Representatives Debates*, 1st Session, (1952), March 29, 1952, p. 699; Nigeria, Federation, *Debates of the House of Representatives* (Session 1959-60), August 5, 1959, column 1450; Nigeria, Federation, *Parliamentary Debates: House of Representatives*, 1st Parliament, 3rd Session, 1962-63, March 26, 1962, column 193, and April 9, 1962, columns 1122-23; Nigeria, Eastern Region, *Eastern House of Assembly Debates* (Third Session, First Meeting, 1956), March 14, 1956 (Enugu: Government Printer, 1957), pp. 243-244; *Eastern House of Assembly Debates* (Second Session, First Meeting, 1958), March 11, 1958, column 24. See also the well-documented discussion of such pressures in Richard L. Sklar, *Nigerian Political Parties: Power in an Emergent Nation* (Princeton: Princeton University Press, 1963), pp. 327-328, 386.

cost-benefit analysis, that despite such costs there were or might be net national benefits in such favoritism. Such a net benefit would occur if sufficient positive externalities or divergences would be created by promoting national firms. These positive divergences might take many forms, such as an enhancement of the skill, ability, and income-earning potentialities of Nigerians rather than foreigners, an enhancement of gross national product (which refers to output produced or income earned by nationals of a country) rather than gross domestic product (which refers to output produced or income earned by residents of a country, including foreigners) or other forms discussed at some length in Chapter 7 on Divergences.

The Construction Industry
in Nigeria

Construction was a type of economic activity particularly well suited to demand-channeling. Unlike products considered for purchase under the Approved Manufacturers Scheme, which might possibly be acquired more cheaply from producers abroad, construction had to be carried out domestically whatever the cost-increasing and quality-decreasing entrepreneurial and economic-environmental difficulties involved. The issue was one of the nationality rather than the geographic location of the producers.

Moreover, construction was a field in which Nigerian experience and capability had already existed as the nurture-capitalism phase of development got under way in 1949 and in which indigenously owned capacity had increased to a significant level during the 1950s. During the fiscal years 1957-58 to 1961-62 inclusive, for example, the Federal Ministry of Works and Surveys awarded 253 out of 403 building contracts to indigenous contractors. On projects for roads and bridges, which tended to be much larger, 3 of 46 contracts went to Nigerian firms.[5] During the years 1960 and 1961, the Federal and regional governments awarded indigenous contractors 10 contracts valued at £ 397,341 in the Eastern Region, 16 contracts worth £ 257,980 in the Western Region, 26 contracts amounting to £ 421,865 in the Northern Region, and 14 contracts worth £ 438,010 in the Federal Territory.[6] Of 267 Nigerian building and civil engineering contractors upgraded in the Federal Government registry during the period April 1, 1959, to December 31, 1961, 6 were placed in the highest contract category (over £ 100,000), 20 in the £ 50,001-100,000 category, and 60 in the £ 20,001-50,000 range.[7] In the Western Region Ministry of

[5]Nigeria, Federation, *Debates: House of Representatives,* 1st Parliament, 3rd Session, 1962-63, March 26, 1962, column 193.
[6]Nigeria, Federation, *Debates: House of Representatives,* 1st Parliament, 3rd Session, 1962-63, April 9, 1962, column 1123.
[7]Nigeria, Federation, *Debates: House of Representatives,* 1st Parliament, 3rd Session, 1962-63, April 9, 1962, column 1192.

Works registry, by 1960, 4 Nigerian companies were approved for contracts in the £ 50,001- £ 100,000 range and 2 for contracts in the highest category, over £ 100,000.[8] Nigerian capacity developed partially because of the necessarily domestic nature of construction activity and partially because of the relatively substantial importance of the construction industry in the Nigerian economy. From 1957 to 1962, 55 percent of gross fixed capital formation was produced by the construction industry and 22.3 percent of all recorded employment was in the construction industry.[9]

Furthermore, construction was also a particularly good field for demand channeling because a substantial part of government's capital expenditures were for construction. For example, in Northern Nigeria in the 1962-68 plan period, building alone constituted 27 percent (£ 44.6 million of £ 168.0 million) of planned capital expenditures.[10] This does not include heavy outlays for roads, bridges, and other types of construction. Particularly in the earlier years (although data on government expenditures are not classified in a way that enables one to show this), government's capital programs were largely concerned with construction and governmental capital expenditures were almost synonymous with construction.

The stipulated procedures for carrying out construction projects were basically similar for the Federal and the three regional governments, although there were minor differences from government to government and time to time. The essential elements of these procedures held also for most of the statutory corporations although variations were somewhat greater.

Government Construction-Contracting

In this section we deal primarily with stipulated procedures and later consider distortions in these procedures.[11]

Construction for government can be divided into three categories: government jobs, carried out by government itself; petty jobs, carried out by petty contractors; and major jobs, carried out by registered private contractors.[12]

---

[8]G. Akin Ogunpola, "The Pattern of Organization in the Building Industry: A Western Nigeria Case Study," *Nigerian Journal of Economic and Social Studies* X:3 (November 1968): 348.

[9]Ogunpola, pp. 339-341.

[10]Government of Northern Nigeria, *Report on Building Costs* by Robert Matthew, Johnson-Marshall and Partners (no date [1963?], no place given), pp. 17-18.

[11]The procedures described in this chapter are those of the Federal and Regional governments. Jobs controlled by local-government authorities were usually awarded in a less systematic fashion, with virtually no safeguards against political and other favoritism. See, e.g., Ogunpola, "The Pattern of Organization in the Building Industry," pp. 353-354.

[12]So called "major" jobs could be for as little as £ 1,000.

Many projects, particularly the smaller ones, were undertaken by government itself. For example, in Eastern Nigeria in the mid 1960s most jobs of less than £ 7,000 were carried out directly by the Ministry of Works using its own staff, although projects requiring a specialized kind of expertise (e.g., water resource projects), no matter how small, were contracted out to private firms. The Western Nigeria Ministry of Works and Transport also undertook a substantial portion of the regional government's building projects, carrying out most of the work itself and relying relatively little on private subcontractors.[13] This practice of government construction activity was subjected to constant pressure from private contractors and politicians who wanted to increase the number of contracts going to private firms. Construction by government agencies does not concern us in our discussion of business-assistance demand-channeling programs, so we turn to the privately done jobs.

Petty Jobs

Petty-contract jobs were those costing less than some maximum amount, usually £ 1,000. Most such jobs were for considerably less than that limit, perhaps for just two or three hundred pounds. Frequently these jobs were for repairs or painting or some other maintenance work. Special registries of petty contractors were established. These were maintained on a localized basis—province by province in the regions, and the Lagos City Council also kept such a registry.[14] Contractors in the lowest categories of the major-job registries were also eligible for petty contracts.

The procedures for awarding petty contracts were administratively simpler, less costly, and less carefully safeguarded than those attending the award of major contracts. Contractors were generally not asked to submit bids. Instead, price was established by the appropriate government agency or official, frequently the Provincial Engineer, with the approval of the Ministry of Works. The contract could then be let in various ways. At times, there was a quality or capability competition; all registered petty contractors were eligible to apply and a Provincial Tenders Board (presumably following the expert advice of the Provincial Engineer) chose the applicant who appeared most capable. At times, petty contractors were chosen on a simple rotational basis from among those registered in the province. After the lists of registrants grew to enormous length, a combination of these procedures was commonly used: a group of eligibles was chosen by rotation and from among these the most suitable applicant was presumably chosen by the Provincial Engineer and the

[13]Ogunpola, pp. 345-346.
[14]Nigeria, Federation, *Comments of the Federal Military Government on the Report of the Tribunal of Enquiry into the Affairs of the Lagos City Council for the Period October 15, 1962 to April 18, 1966* (Lagos: Federal Ministry of Information, 1966), paragraph 2.11.

Provincial Tenders Board. Other, less clearly defined procedures were
also used. The system was structured so as to favor regional (or at the
Federal Government level, Nigerian) inhabitants. Thus, the Parliamentary Secretary of the Northern Ministry of Finance spoke in 1958 of the
view that the Northern Regional government had awarded too few minor
contracts to Northerners and of the consequent reorganization of the
Provincial Tenders Boards to include two Northern nonofficials as
members.[15]

Large numbers of aspirants sought to share in the petty contracts. As a
result, a great many of the firms on the petty-contractor registries never
got any jobs at all or got them only exceedingly rarely. Moreover, registrants were frequently persons with no experience at all in construction or
related activities. If they were awarded contracts, they might take a
commission for themselves and subcontract the job to someone else, or
they might carry out the jobs themselves but often rather badly.

Major Jobs: Registration

To allot the major jobs, it was necessary first to establish an eligibility list,
a registry of those who could be considered for the coveted government
contracts. As a result of the clamor for Nigerianization and the eagerness
for government patronage, there was pressure to establish as broad and
inclusive a list of registrants as possible.

Contractors who wished to be registered were required to complete an
application form which served as a basis for appraising the capabilities of
the firm. This form elicited financial data, information on the technical
qualifications of members of the staff, a detailed report on construction
and transport equipment possessed by the applicant, information on the
length of the owner's experience as a contractor, a report on construction
engaged in currently or within the preceding three years. The form also
asked the applicant to state what he believed to be the appropriate size-
category for his company (to be explained shortly). Applicants were also
required to indicate the type of work they would bid for: road works; civil
engineering, including water resources, bridges, sewerage works, and the
like; buildings; and electrical works.[16]

The application was submitted to the Provincial Engineer of the Province in which the contractor's headquarters was located. The Engineer
was supposed to inspect the applicant's business premises and operations
and interview the applicant. The Engineer then submitted to the Ministry
of Works a confidential report on the firm's regular staff and labor force,

---

[15]Nigeria, Northern Region, *House of Assembly Debates* Second Legislature, Second
Session, Second Meeting, July 30 to August 6, 1958 (Kaduna: Government Printer, 1958),
August 6, 1958, columns 815-816.

[16]Described here is the mid-1965 procedure in Eastern Nigeria. Registration procedures at
other times and places were generally similar.

TABLE 16

Regional Government Registration Categories for Contractors
(in N £)

	Eastern Nigeria mid-1965	Northern Nigeria Sept. 1962		Western Nigeria 1968
A	1,001- 5,000	1,000- 6,000	A	501- 3,000
B	5,001- 10,000	6,001- 12,000	B	3,001- 6,000
C	10,001- 20,000	12,001- 25,000	C	6,001- 10,000
D	20,001- 50,000	25,001- 50,000	D	10,001- 20,000
E	50,001-100,000	50,001-100,000	E	20,001- 50,000
F	100,001 and over	100,001 and over	F	50,001-100,000
			G	100,001 and over

SOURCE: See footnote 17.

financial status, and suitability for undertaking work for the government. He also recommended a size category. The Ministry of Works then processed (essentially, summarized) the application forms and the confidential reports so that a Registration Board could deal with a large number of them expeditiously.

The Registration Board, a body consisting of politicians and civil servants but dominated by the former, made the final registration decisions. These boards met occasionally and briefly (perhaps two to four times a year for one to three days) and acted upon a large number of applications. A mid-1965 one-day meeting of the Eastern Nigerian Registration Board, for example, made decisions about the registration categories of 132 applicants. Given work loads of such magnitude, the Registration Boards generally approved the recommendations they received, but did not do so invariably.

The registration procedure classified contractors "according to their financial and executive capacity," i.e., according to the magnitude of the jobs they could effectively handle.[17] The regional-government classifications for roads, civil engineering, and building are shown in Table 16.[18] A contractor might be placed in different categories for different types of work. The categories were modified from time to time. For electrical works the categories were much smaller; Eastern Nigeria, for example,

[17]Eastern Nigeria, Ministry of Works, "Rules for the Registration of Contractors in Eastern Nigeria," (no date), p. 1 (mimeographed). See also Ogunpola, p. 347. Nigeria, Northern Region, *Report on Building Costs,* also deals with this matter but is oversimplified.
[18]Eastern Nigeria, "Rules for Registration," p. 2; Northern Nigeria, *Report on Building Costs,* p. 28; Ogunpola, p. 347.

had five classifications ranging from £ 500 and below to £ 5,000 and over.[19]

In general, firms were to contend for jobs within their own category. The purpose of this classification, discussed more fully below, was to reserve smaller jobs for smaller (hence indigenous) firms. However, firms might "also be invited to tender for contracts, the value of which is in one class or in special cases, at the discretion of the Honourable Minister of Works, within two classes below the class in which they are classified."[20] Provisions for flexibility similar to this Eastern Nigerian provision obtained also for the other regional and the Federal governments. The size of the contracts firms actually received could be, as a result, considerably smaller than that indicated by their registration category. The average value of the government contracts received by firms in the four highest of the six Northern Nigerian categories in 1961-62, for example, was less than half of the minimum contract size designated for that category (see Table 20).

Firms could move or be moved out of their categories. For poor work the Registration Board might put a contractor into a lower class or drop him from the register altogether. Conversely, for good performance and after some minimum period (eighteen months in Eastern Nigeria) a contractor could have his classification raised. There was also some tendency for the average size of firms to increase.[21]

As government contracts were highly prized, the number of registrants with the Federal Government and with the Regional governments was excessively large, particularly in the lower categories. In Tables 17 and 18, which show registrants with the Western and Northern Regional Governments, we see the relatively large numbers in the lowest categories. We see also that the number of registered contractors grew rapidly. There was a fourfold increase in the total number of registrants in Western Nigeria from 1960 to 1966 and an even greater increase in the three smallest classes. And despite the fact that a substantial number of registrants were pared off the list in 1963 because they had not received a contract in five years, Northern Nigeria experienced an increase from 375 to 585 in less than two years, with the sharpest rise occurring in the lowest category. It might also be pointed out that placing contractors into three size groups, as did Ogunpola, reveals an expected pattern that is obscured in Tables 17 and 18: the number of registrants tapers off markedly as size increases (Table 19).

The most striking evidence of the undue proliferation of registrants is shown in Table 20. Although 177 firms were registered in the lowest category in Northern Nigeria, only 5 regional-government contracts were

---

[19]Eastern Nigeria, "Rules for Registration," p. 2.
[20]Eastern Nigeria, "Rules for Registration," p. 2.
[21]Northern Nigeria, *Report on Building Costs,* paragraph 71.01.

TABLE 17

Distribution of Building Contractors by Classified Categories, 1960-1966
Western Nigeria

Category	Value of Contract (in N £)	1960 N	1960 F	1960 Total	1962 N	1962 F	1962 Total	1964 N	1964 F	1964 Total	1966 N	1966 F	1966 Total
A	501- 3,000	70	—	70	164	—	164	225	—	225	299	—	299
B	3,001- 6,000	32	—	32	73	—	73	121	—	121	159	—	159
C	6,001- 10,000	16	—	16	42	—	42	53	—	53	75	—	75
D	10,001- 20,000	7	—	7	17	3	20	25	3	28	34	3	37
E	20,001- 50,000	6	1	7	13	1	14	20	2	22	26	2	28
F	50,001-100,000	4	4	8	6	4	10	13	4	17	14	4	18
G	Over 100,000	2	19	21	3	29	32	3	38	41	3	39	42
		137	24	161	318	37	355	460	47	507	610	48	658

SOURCE: G. Akin Ogunpola, "The Pattern of Organization in the Building Industry: A Western Nigerian Case Study," *Nigerian Journal of Economic and Social Studies* (November 1968).

NOTE: N = Nigerian firms; F = Foreign firms.

TABLE 18

Distribution of Building Contractors by Classified Categories
Northern Nigeria, 1962 and 1964

Category	Value of Contract (N £)	Number of Contractors	
		September 1962	August 1964
A	1,001–6,000	177	319
B	6,001–12,000	89	110
C	12,001–25,000	21	29
D	25,001–50,000	13	24
E	50,001–100,000	21	30
F	100,001 and over	36	73[a]
Total		357	585

Source: Northern Nigeria, *Report on Building Costs*, and Ministry files.

[a]This includes 28 firms headquartered in Lagos, but registered with the Northern Nigerian government.

TABLE 19

Distribution of Building Contractors by Size
Western and Northern Nigeria

	Western Nigeria 1966	Northern Nigeria 1964
Small contractors[a]	533	429
Medium-size[b] contractors	83	83
Large contractors (over N £100,000)	42	73[c]
Total	658	585

Sources: Ogunpola, "Pattern of Organization," p. 352, and Northern Nigeria Ministry of Works.

[a]N £ 1001 to N £ 10,000 in Western and N £ 1001 to N £ 12,000 in Northern Nigeria.

[b]N £ 10,001 to N £ 100,000 in Western Nigeria and N £ 12,001 to N £ 100,000 in Northern Nigeria.

[c]Includes 28 firms registerd in the North but headquartered in Lagos.

TABLE 20

Number of Firms Registered, Classified by Registration Category,
Number and Value of Contracts Received
Northern Nigeria, 1961-62[a]

Registration categories eligible for contracts of	Number of registered firms[b]	Number of contracts received	Total value of contracts received (N £)	Average value of contracts received
N £ 1,001–6,000	177	5	13,040	2,618
N £ 6,000–12,000	89	4	24,080	6,020
N £ 12,001–25,000	21	9	40;230	5,470
N £ 25,001–50,000	13	3	34,400	11,460
N £ 50,001–100,000	21	4	50,140	12,535
over 100,000	36	28	1,218,320	43,510

SOURCE: Northern Nigeria, *Report on Building Costs,* pp. 28-29.

[a]The precise period is not clear. It might be the fiscal year 1961-62 or the two calendar years or something in between.

[b]On September 18, 1962.

awarded during 1961-62 to this group. Four contracts were awarded in the next category, which comprised 89 firms. In the next three categories 16 contracts were parceled among 55 firms. Only in the highest class did the number of contracts (28) even approach the number of firms (36). (It should be pointed out, however, that the small firms on the regional registry were also eligible, along with firms on the provincial registries, for petty contracts. It was estimated that petty jobs totalling £113,000 per year were distributed among all these firms.[22]

For many of the registrants, it was stretching things to call them contractors at all. "Many of these [small] firms exist in name only, as anyone who attempts to locate them finds to his amusement."[23] If ever awarded contracts, many simply sublet them, taking a cut for themselves. Most never received any government contracts at all. Such contractors were subject to being dropped from the registry[24] and on occasion this was done.

Major Jobs: Awarding the Contracts

Having a list of registrants, it was then necessary to select from this list a specific firm to do any given job. In this section we will discuss the contract-award procedure, primarily concerning ourselves with pre-

[22]Northern Nigeria, *Report on Building Costs,* paragraph 71.03.
[23]Ogunpola, p. 353.
[24]In Northern and Eastern Nigeria. With respect to the Federal and Western Nigerian registries, the procedure was not clear to the writer.

TABLE 21

Building Contracts Awarded, Classified by Contractor-Selection
Procedure
Northern Nigeria, 1960-62

Contractor-selection procedure	Number of contracts	Percent of total number	Value of contracts (N £)	Percent of total value
Open tender	41	24.7	703,127	17.1
Selective tender	4	2.4	142,150	3.5
Negotiation	121	72.9	3,262,917	79.4
Total	166		4,108,194	

SOURCE: Northern Nigeria, *Report on Building Costs*, pp. 56-57.

scribed practices and leaving until later any extensive discussion of distortions in the stipulated way of doing things.

Contractor selection was carried out by any of three methods: open tendering or bidding (open competition), selected tendering (limited competition), or negotiation. Although competitive bidding in one form or another is usually considered the normal procedure in contractor selection, and generally deemed the most desirable for an economy like Nigeria's, it was relatively infrequently used. For example, the two competitive selection procedures together (open and selective tendering) accounted in Northern Nigeria during the early 1960s for only slightly more than one-fourth (27.1 percent) of all building contracts awarded and for slightly more than one-fifth (20.6 percent) of the value involved (Table 21). The possibilities of political manipulation or other abuses inherent in the preponderance of noncompetitive contract awards hardly needs comment.

Under open tendering, the job was listed in the official government *Gazette* (and perhaps also a regional government might list in the Federal *Gazette*) and was advertised in the newspapers. Interested contractors could get a more complete job description with technical and other specifications from the Ministry of Works. The Ministry assisted the contractors by providing a questionnaire which was essentially a tendering form. By filling out this form, the contractor completed his bid. Government assisted also by undertaking responsibility for acquiring a site, preparing the architect's brief, designing the building, and specifying the materials needed.[25]

[25]Northern Nigeria, *Report on Building Costs*, paragraph 52.03, p. 19.

The interested contractors then submitted their bids. The next step was a sensitive one which the writer's informants were uniformly reluctant to discuss: the opening of the sealed bids. Even officials who were quite candid on most matters were deliberately obscure and ambiguous. According to the stipulated procedure, bids were to be opened in public, in the presence of the contractors themselves or their representatives, as well as high-level, nonpolitical[26] government personnel, on a predetermined date, and were to be publicly announced and recorded. The process was surrounded by a substantial array of safeguards.[27]

The opening of the bids was a sensitive step, and was subject to considerable abuse, because in open tendering the closeness of a firm's bid to the prior confidential estimate made by the professional personnel in the Ministry of Works was crucial in the selection process. Only bids that were close to this estimate were considered further and, ceteris paribus, the closer the bid and the estimate the more likely the firm was to be chosen.[28] Tampering with the bids at this stage could therefore substantially influence if not determine the outcome of the tendering process.

The opened tenders were evaluated by the technical personnel in the Ministry of Works. Contractors whose bids were reasonably close to the Ministry's cost estimate were put on a short list sent to the Tenders Board for final selection, although if only one or two firms had bid within the appropriate range the Ministry might list and report on others. The Ministry did not rely on price alone in making its recommendations, for an unqualified contractor might have hit upon the right price by luck or connivance.[29] The contractors' experience and capability were also appraised.

The Tenders Boards were politically controlled bodies, dominated by cabinet-level political leaders (ministers or junior ministers), usually from

---

[26]"So far, no Minister has ever been present when the tenders are opened in the Ministry of Finance by the Permanent Secretary, the Secretary of the Tenders Board and a representative of the Director of Public Works." Minister of Finance, Western Nigeria, Nigeria, Western Region, *House of Assembly Debates*, 4th Session, Omnibus Issue No. 6, December 19, 21, and 22, 1956 (Ibadan: Government Printer, 1957), December 21, 1956, columns 133-134.

[27]See, e.g., Nigeria, Federation, *Statement of Policy by the Government of the Federal Republic of Nigeria on the Relations between the Federal Public Corporations and the Legislature, the Government and the Public, and between the State Owned Companies and the Government* (Sessional Paper 7 of 1964) (Lagos: Federal Ministry of Information, 1964), pp. 8-9.

[28]Generally in open tendering, low bids were not considered an index of greater efficiency but of ignorance and probable incompetence.

[29]"Being conscious of this disability on the part of their experts [i.e., their actual inexpertness], they hang around the office of the Public Works Department and scout around junior clerks to find out how much money is allocated to this project. One way or another they get [a figure] . . . If they get the wrong information, they have had it; if they get the right information, there you are. They will then go and cook up the [detailed] figures." Minister of Development, Nigeria, Eastern Region, *Eastern House of Assembly Debates*, Third Session, First Meeting, 1956 (Enugu: Government Printer, 1957), March 26, 1956, p. 534.

the Ministry of Finance and/or the Ministry of Works, although the boards might have included one or two nonpolitical appointees. The Tenders Board was normally supposed to follow the expert advice of the Ministry of Works in making the final selection of the contractor. If further advice was needed, it could summon the Ministry engineers to its meetings. The Tenders Board, however, had the authority to disregard all recommendations. It could select a firm on the short list that was not recommended or even select firms that had not been short-listed at all. Here clearly was a route for political invasion of the selection process or for other abuse, but charges of such machinations were always strenuously denied in public.[30]

In selective tendering only a selected small group of firms are invited to bid on a government contract. These firms were chosen by the Ministry of Works from the appropriate registration categories either on a rotational basis (so that eventually all registered firms would have had an opportunity to bid) or because of special qualifications for the job to be undertaken. Thereafter the procedure was similar to that of open tendering. In theory this procedure has much to commend it, "and it should be a priority aim of any country to introduce this procedure as early in its development as conditions will allow."[31] Invited to bid is only "a short list of firms of established skill, integrity and responsibility, and with a proved competence for work of the character and size contemplated, any one of whom could be entrusted with the job. If this is achieved, then the final choice of the builder will be simple—the firm offering the lowest tender." As the cost of bidding is substantial, large tender lists significantly raise costs; "if the average length of tender lists is reduced, then building costs will be correspondingly lowered."[32] Limiting competition could have other advantages. It was maintained that it economized on input of overworked governmental personnel. When the registration procedure was first established, large numbers of unqualified aspirants registered as contractors, eligible to bid on government contracts. This posed a problem, said the Eastern Nigerian Minister of Development: "We want to do our work quickly and well . . . one contract document, be it just for an ordinary house costing £ 500, will take up to 10 to 15 pages, for specifications and drawings and everything."[33] Selective tendering, using less complete specifications, enabled economies here. Moreover, it was a speedier procedure than open tendering. There were also sometimes special reasons for

[30]For an early public dispute see Nigeria, Western Region, *House of Assembly Debates*, 4th Session, December 21, 1956. Replying to various recriminations, the Minister of Finance declared (column 341): "There has never been any occasion when the Tenders Board has ever thrown overboard the expert suggestion and recommendation of the Director of Public Works."

[31]Northern Nigeria, *Report on Building Costs*, paragraph 82.03, p. 57.

[32]Northern Nigeria, *Report on Building Costs*, paragraph 82.04, pp. 57-58.

[33]Nigeria, Eastern Region, *House of Assembly Debates*, Third Session, March 1956, p. 533.

limiting competition, as when a foreign-aid agreement required the use on aided projects of contracting firms owned by residents of the aiding country.

However, under Nigerian conditions there were two mutually reinforcing reasons for avoiding selective tendering. For one thing, there was "insufficient evidence" about building capabilities and costs of firms in different localities; "in fact the statistical data we collected to study this problem served only to confuse the issue." This made it impossible to specify the firms best qualified for any particular job. Second, the likelihood of political manipulation or other abuse was too great, a likelihood increased by the just-mentioned lack of solid information.[34]

The third contract-award procedure was through direct negotiations with an individual contractor in the appropriate size category who was believed to be particularly well qualified for the given job. With Executive Council permission the Ministry of Works was empowered to select a contractor who could presumably do the job effectively and economically. An appropriate price was estimated by Ministry technical personnel and then negotiated with the contractor. Smaller contractors usually accepted the price set by the Ministry, but larger ones were most likely to bargain. In any case, if the job proved more costly than expected, the Ministry usually made an adjustment.

In general, the advantages and disadvantages of selective tendering obtain, perhaps to a greater degree, for contract award by negotiation. In addition, the practice of negotiating tenders suffers from the major disadvantage that it eliminates competition. The contractor "has no incentive to offer a competitive price" and the government negotiator works within a "system which deprives him of a chance to develop a commanding knowledge of market conditions."[35] Because of the problems associated with negotiated tenders, a Federal Government statement issued two years before the 1966 coups expressed concern about "circumvention of the tenders procedure" and "the need for strict observance of the approved tenders procedure" for Public Corporations, and directed that contracts for £ 10,000 or more should be awarded on the basis of competitive tendering and that no contracts should be handled by negotiation save "in exceptional cases."[36]

Favoritism for Indigenous Contractors

Let us now take stock briefly of the ways in which the registration and contract-award procedures favored indigenous contractors (in the case of

---

[34]Northern Nigeria, *Report on Building Costs*, paragraph 82.05, p. 58. On the interrelationship between insufficient information and expertise and political manipulation, see Sayre P. Schatz, *Economics, Politics and Administration in Government Lending: The Regional Loans Boards of Nigeria* (Ibadan and London: Oxford University Press, 1970), pp. 123-126.

[35]Northern Nigeria, *Report on Building Costs*, paragraphs 82.10 and 82.11, pp. 59-60.

[36]Nigeria, Federation, *Statement . . . on Federal Public Corporations*, pp. 7-8.

the regional governments, indigenous to the region). Most important was the structure of the registration system itself. Separating contractors into noncompeting categories according to the size of the jobs they could handle was a way of reserving smaller jobs for smaller (hence indigenous) firms. The link between smallness and indigenousness was strong. For example, 39 of the 48 foreign firms registered in Western Nigeria in 1966 were in the highest (over £100,000) category. The lowest category in which there were any foreign firms registered was the middle one (jobs between £10,001 and £20,000), and in this class only 3 of 34 registrants were foreign (see Table 17). A similar pattern prevailed for the few registrants with the regional governments who were from other regions. For example, 5 of the 10 extra-regional registrants in Northern Nigeria in 1964 were in the highest category, and the others constituted a tiny proportion of the numbers of registrants in the other categories. The protective device of noncompeting categories was necessary because, on strictly cost and quality grounds, the larger contractors were superior. For at least as good a job, they could generally underbid the smaller contractors.

The preference for indigenous contractors built into the registration system was sometimes augmented by contract splitting. Larger jobs were split into a number of smaller jobs so that they could be alloted to smaller firms.

However, contract splitting as a legitimate means of assisting indigenous business[37] was tapering off by the mid-1960s. It had been primarily resorted to when there were few if any indigenous firms registered in the higher categories. For example, the North did a great deal of contract splitting in the immediate post-Independence years. Many of the projects at this time were quite large and virtually no Northerners were qualified to bid on such jobs. As indigenous capability developed, the need to subdivide jobs to award them to indigenous firms became less imperative. More weight was placed on the disadvantages of contract splitting: experience showed that it was more expensive; it entailed substantial pressure on limited staff (as a leading professional civil servant of Northern Nigeria remarked, it takes a great deal more work to develop ten contracts, get tenders on them, and then supervise the work, than to carry out the same project under one contract ten times as large).

There were also informal, unsystematized preferences given to indigenous firms. The view that an indigenous contractor who could render an adequate performance should get the contract even if his price or quality couldn't fully match those of a foreign company had widespread support and influenced the technical personnel in the Ministries of Works as well as the political and administrative personnel on the Tenders Boards. Sometimes this preference was stated as a more or less formal price

---

[37]It continued, as we will see, for illegitimate purposes.

preference (for example, a Federal Government 2½-percent price preference for Nigerian-owned firms, according to the Permanent Secretary in
the Federal Ministry of Works in June 1965); more often it was an informal manifestation of an implicit understanding pervading the government
structure that indigenous firms were to be favored.

Sometimes efforts were made to award contracts to smaller firms as
such even though the larger companies that would have otherwise received the contracts were indigenous companies. Thus, Northern Nigeria
revised its categories in 1958, creating a new £1,000-£3,000 class, to
assist small contractors.[38] Regional governments also resorted to contract
splitting to direct government construction spending to smaller firms. On
the other hand, government officials, anxious to get their work done and
to spend government funds effectively, often tended to avoid even the
more capable and promising small firms. They lacked confidence in the
ability of small contractors to handle any jobs competently. Moreover, it
was administratively more convenient to deal with larger companies. In
fact, proposals were made on more than one occasion to consolidate
registration categories, an action which would have reduced the registration system's built-in favoritism for small contractors.[39] On balance, efforts to direct government construction spending toward the smaller
indigenous contractors were dilatory and ineffective. We have seen earlier (Table 20) that such firms rarely received Federal or regional government contracts.

Non-Political Problems

The program to aid indigenous construction firms by funneling government contracts to them was more expensive and less effective than had
been hoped. There were political problems and economic and administrative problems.

1. A major problem lay in the low level of competence of most of the
Nigerian contractors. Many of the smaller firms had sprung up with virtually no capability at all. ". . . as soon as the former Minister of Works
invited people to come and register, more than 500 people registered as
contractors. They ranged from house-boys and stewards who had just left
their masters to big contracting firms. . ."[40]

Even the firms which started on a substantial basis usually manifested
serious deficiencies. At building sites one found an "absence of any indication of overall planning on the part of management. The work was
carried out on a day to day basis."[41] Materials and labor were used

---

[38]Nigeria, Northern Region, *House of Assembly Debates,* August 6, 1958, columns 815-
816.
[39]See, e.g., Northern Nigeria, *Report on Building Costs,* paragraphs 71.05-71.09.
[40]Nigeria, Eastern Region, *Eastern House of Assembly Debates,* March 26, 1956, p. 533.
[41]Northern Nigeria, *Report on Building Costs,* p. 43.

uneconomically; "there undoubtedly is excessive wastage of materials, and there is a surplus of labour on most sites."[42] There was misuse and inadequate maintenance of equipment; "some mechanical plant was damaged, especially the few excavators, due to mishandling by operators and lack of maintenance."[43] Simple labor- and cost-saving equipment was overlooked; "over 50 labourers were used to carry concrete for placing at ground level on one site. With the use of wheelbarrows this could have been reduced to a labour force of between 6 and 10 men." This would have enabled a direct saving and also a saving through more effective supervision of the smaller work force.[44] Accounts or financial records were entirely inadequate or missing altogether.[45] Most contractors were entirely unable to make reasonable cost estimates for bids and had to rely on some rule of thumb or inside information.[46] According to a Nigerian economist who made a study of the industry, indigenous contracting was characterized by frequent "lack of managerial ability and integrity" and "indolence and wastefulness" and, in all, considerably less competence than foreign contracting. ". . . the expatriate firms which pay relatively higher wage rates still produce more cheaply than the indigenous ones, bearing in mind that labour accounts, on the average, for about forty per cent of the total costs of building."[47]

2. There was extensive excess capacity in the industry which (aside from the waste of potential production forgone) tended to intensify the cost and quality problems associated with the generally low level of competence among indigenous contractors. Excess capacity was especially characteristic of the large number of small contractors, who received very few contracts[48] It also prevailed among most of the large and more capable contractors, who displayed "no lack of eagerness to tender,"[49] who often submitted bids in competition with one another when such opportunities arose, and who actively sought work price categories below the ones in which they were registered. *The Report on Building Costs* in Northern Nigeria estimated (conservatively, in the view of many) that "the industry could absorb an increased demand upon it of about 40%."[50]

The underemployment of the industry's capacity tended to raise costs and discourage efficiency-improving investments.[51] The industry had dif-

[42]Northern Nigeria, *Report on Building Costs*, p. 61; see also p. 33.
[43]Northern Nigeria, *Report on Building Costs*, p. 47.
[44]Northern Nigeria, *Report on Building Costs*, p. 47; also see p. 48 on similar kinds of inefficiency.
[45]Northern Nigeria, *Report on Building Costs*, p. 33.
[46]Northern Nigeria, *Report on Building Costs*, p. 139. See also *Eastern House of Assembly Debates*, March 14, 1956, p. 244.
[47]Ogunpola, p. 357; see also pp. 345, 349, 350, 353, 358.
[48]See earlier in this chapter under the heading "Major Jobs: Registration."
[49]Northern Nigeria, *Report on Building Costs*, p. 26.
[50]Northern Nigeria, *Report on Building Costs*, p. 26.
[51]Northern Nigeria, *Report on Building Costs*, p. 26, speaking of extra costs arising from

ficulty in attracting and retaining high-quality labor. It tended to neglect training of its workers, for much employment was intermittent and casual. And there were the other costs associated with intermittent hiring and consequent turnover of labor. Moreover, underemployment of the industry had other cost-increasing effects. The permanent staffs of capable and experienced supervisory and managerial personnel tended to be minimal. The owners frequently occupied themselves with other business affairs in addition to their contracting and did not devote sufficient attention to possible organizational or other improvements. With limited revenues, the underemployed firms tended to be undercapitalized and therefore unable to order sufficient materials in advance to assure a smooth flow of work. Moreover, possible cost-saving investments were neglected.

3. In view of the weakness of Nigerian contractors, many carefully considered recommendations were made for government advice and assistance,[52] for example, preparation of a simple handbook explaining how cost and other financial records should be kept and used; employment of a civil servant to assist contractors in the development and keeping of accounts; publication and circulation of simple technical advisory leaflets on such basic matters as concreting and lifting methods, etc.; provision of direct advice on ways in which a contractor could improve his organizational methods; preparation of a prepriced tendering form that would help contractors to submit realistic bids.

Government did provide some assistance. In Northern Nigeria (and perhaps in the other regions) a prepriced tendering form *was* developed for indigenous contractors. The government inspector of construction jobs often became virtually an unpaid supervisor-foreman for the contractor. The Ministries of Works advised contractors of claims they could submit for legitimate extras. But on the whole, because of staff shortages and limited funds and also because the award of construction contracts to indigenous firms came to be dominated by political rather than economic-development considerations, the amount of help given to indigenous firms was severely limited.

4. The Ministries of Works of the various governments lacked personnel and other resources to carry out their planning and supervisory functions adequately. "The responsibility of the Ministry [on works carried out by private contractors] . . . consists essentially in planning the project and supervising the contractors at work to ensure that they build according to the building drawings and specifications. However, the resources of the Ministry (especially with regard to personnel) seem inadequate to

underemployment of the industry finds "lack of continuity of work for contractors . . . retards the development of plant holdings and does not encourage them to improve their organisational methods."

[52]For example, knowledgeable recommendations are sprinkled throughout the *Report on Building Costs* for Northern Nigeria.

cope. . . ."[53] Often they were not able to do even essential preliminary work; sometimes "even the preliminary surveys and costing have to be left to the contractor, a situation which is open to obvious abuse."[54] Supervision of work done by private contractors, always a major function of the Works Ministries, was always a problem, and insufficient executive capacity for this function was officially singled out on several occasions as one of the major causes of lags in the various economic plans. As a direct consequence of such ministerial deficiencies, Nigerian firms frequently "get away with bad work done for these bodies"[55] and the governments got poor value for their expenditures. Moreover, "the incentive to improve and become more efficient is lacking . . . ";[56] an opportunity is lost to pressure indigenous firms into improving their competence.

5. Even governmental capacity to make judgments regarding appropriate registration categories for firms was very limited. Information regarding the assets, the output, or even the number of employees of firms was extremely unreliable, given the usually poor or nonexistent records and the meager investigatory capacity of the Ministries. Partially as a result (and partially because of political factors) many firms were registered in inappropriate categories.

6. Finally, it may be worth remarking briefly upon some other administrative problems related only tangentially to programs for channeling demand to indigenous contractors. Frequently waste arose from crash programs. Sometimes, because of protracted budgetary procedures, "late in the day the Ministry of Works has been asked to commence a number of buildings at great speed, of different sizes than originally intended, without sufficient time to plan them, provide thought-out specifications or (most important of all) to receive tenders in a form and atmosphere conducive to low costs."[57] There was also extravagance, for example in the construction of secondary schools, which consumed a very substantial portion of the total building expenditures of Northern Nigeria. "The type and standards of accommodation provided in these institutions derive from the boarding schools of the U.K. Indeed, the extent, variety and quality of the spaces provided in some of the schools visited, especially those for girls, surpassed that to be seen in some of our most expensive boarding schools. The U.K. certainly could not establish and maintain a state system of free secondary education at this level within its present resources."[58]

[53]Ogunpola, p. 345.
[54]Elizabeth Hopkins, "A Study of the Problems of Implementation of Western Nigeria's Six Year Development Plan, 1962-68," Unpublished M.Sc. (Econ.) dissertation, University of Ibadan, 1965, pp. 216-217.
[55]Ogunpola, p. 353.
[56]Ogunpola, p. 353.
[57]Northern Region, *Report on Building Costs*, p. 19.
[58]Northern Region, *Report on Building Costs*, p. 77.

Political Problems

It is not surprising that the process of awarding and carrying out construction contracts was permeated by politics. Large government expenditures were devoted to construction and large payments to private contractors were easily subject to clandestine manipulation. Moreover, as construction is a kind of activity that must be carried on domestically and one in which Nigerians had some experience and could therefore press a strong claim for Nigerianization or regionalization, government procedures were *designed* to accord a degree of favoritism for Nigerian or Regional firms as opposed to outsiders, and such procedures were easily turned to political purposes.

Widespread charges of political corruption[59] in the award of government contracts for construction go back to the assumption of power by Nigerian politicians in the early 1950s. Speaking of political corruption in 1952, a leading member of the Nigerian Parliament remarked: "No one would deny how rife it is in this country." However, "instead of being loathed it is regarded as an indispensable evil in practically all quarters."[60] These charges replaced—partially but not completely[61]—similar allegations that the British-dominated colonial government unduly favored foreign-owned firms.[62]

Corruption and political manipulation in contracting prevailed throughout the entire period covered by this book. Said a 1966 report: "award of contract has come to be regarded generally in this country . . . as a very lucrative transaction. So eager is everyone in the hierarchy of any organi-

[59]It would not be fruitful to get bogged down in a long and inevitably rather scholastic discussion of the meaning of the term. As the editor of a massive volume on political corruption has stated, "the word *corruption* has a history of vastly different meanings and connotations." He points out that most social science writers "relate their definitions of *corruption* essentially to concepts concerning the duties of the public office" and use a concept similar to the Oxford English Dictionary definition applicable to political contexts: "Perversion or destruction of integrity in the discharge of public duties by bribery or favour." This covers the basic meaning of the term "political corruption" (or, for short, simply "corruption") in the present volume. See Arnold J. Heidenheimer (ed.), *Political Corruption* (New York: Holt, Rinehart and Winston, 1970).

[60]Nigeria, *House of Representatives Debates,* 1st Session, March 17, 1952, p. 161. Nigerians continued to place on the public record innumerable strong condemnations of corruption in general and of corruption in contracting in particular. See, e.g., Nigeria, *Debates of the House of Representatives* (Session 1959-60), February 9, 1959, p. 59; February 12, 1959, pp. 187-188; August 11, 1959, columns 1763-1765; Nigeria, *Debates: House of Representatives* (Session 1960-61), January 19, 1960, pp. 127, 129; April 4, 1960, p. 121; Nigeria, *Eastern House of Assembly Debates,* March 26, 1956, p. 533; Nigeria, *Western House of Assembly Debates,* December 21, 1956, columns 24-204. See also a vivid statement by Chief Awolowo, (Lagos) *Daily Express,* November 4, 1961, p. 1. For a knowledgeable discussion of political influences in contract awards in the 1950s, see also Sklar, pp. 416-419, 451-452, 459, 501.

[61]See, e.g., the 1960 complaint that venal Nigerian politicians were directing large public works contracts to foreign building contractors. Nigeria, *Debates: House of Representatives* (Session 1960-61), April 2, 1960, p. 51.

[62]These allegations also had some basis in reality. However, such favoritism was more a

sation to engage in the transaction that no matter how perfect and corruption-proof the procedures laid down may appear on paper, some subtle devices are thought out to defeat their purposes. . . . [There is an] urgent need for a radical reform of the entire system and machinery for awarding contracts . . . contracts provide the most popular avenue for acquiring wealth by corrupt and fraudulent methods. . . ."[63]

The political corruption that occurred in contracting (and in other areas as well) took place through four main processes. First, the procedures or machinery for safeguarding against corruption were in some cases inadequate or defective. For example, in its report on the Nigerian Railway Corporation, a Tribunal of Inquiry found that "the tools which should have been fashioned and used all along to control operations . . . [were] either not available or wanting in material particular. The witnesses who testified on this subject . . . all agreed that the Corporation's systems of control were very deficient."[64] Deficient safeguarding procedures were most common in the case of small contracts. "Until March 1966, the system by which small contracts were awarded to contractors registered with the [Lagos City] Council was open to abuse, as officers in charge of sections of the City Engineer's Department were permitted to choose the contractors to be employed. . . ." While the favored contractors might have been selected for perfectly legitimate reasons, "the system could not preclude corruption."[65]

Inadequate safeguard machinery was not the most common problem. Even if the machinery was adequate, a second and more common problem was that the staff to carry out the safeguarding procedures was incapable of doing so effectively. Thus, in discussing contracts, the Working Party on Statutory Corporations indicated that it had no means of "ascertaining the exact extent to which incompetence affects the system of internal financial control . . . But if the widespread criticisms of the system of appointment, promotion and discipline in these institutions is well founded, there must be many persons holding positions involving financial and allied transactions for which they are not suitable either by qualification, training or experience."[66] Similarly, the Railway Tribunal

---

matter of unspoken and unrealized biases and preconceptions than of deliberate political manipulation.

[63]Nigeria, Federation, *Report of the Working Party on Statutory Corporations and State-Owned Corporations* (Lagos: Federal Ministry of Information, 1968), p. 22.

[64]Nigeria, Federation, *Report of the Nigerian Railway Corporation Tribunal of Enquiry Appointed Under the Tribunal of Enquiry Decree, 1966, to Enquire into the Affairs of the Nigerian Railway Corporation* (Lagos: Federal Ministry of Information, 1967), pp. 229-230. The specific problems are detailed in this report and are found in ordinary government departments as well as in statutory corporations.

[65]Nigeria, Federation, *Report of the Tribunal of Enquiry into the Affairs of the Lagos City Council for the Period Oct. 15, 1962 to April 18, 1966* (Lagos: Federal Ministry of Information, 1966), p. 237.

[66]Nigeria, Federation, *Report on Statutory Corporations*, p. 23.

castigated "the recklessness with which senior posts were filled with incompetent men" and stated that "the ills of the Corporation in the period of our Inquiry arose principally as a result of gross mishandling of staff matters and putting unqualified men in posts to which they were unsuited. Posts were 'Nigerianized' in the Corporation with reckless abandon. Well-qualified men were brushed aside and third-rate ones were put in positions in which they were complete failures."[67]

The third and most important process through which political corruption took place involved the power of high-level politicians to manipulate the safeguard procedures. When they wanted to favor particular contractors or groups of contractors, political leaders were able to exert virtually irresistible pressure on their subordinates to distort or simply ignore these procedures. Staff members usually had the alternatives only of acquiescing or of undergoing what they believed would be serious sanctions, including possible loss of their highly prized positions.[68] A number of Federal and Regional civil servants who have discussed this problem with the writer have expressed varying degrees of frustration, resignation, and anger. The inability of subordinates to resist political or other manipulation by the political figures who headed the Ministries or statutory corporations has been documented innumerable times in the post-coup Inquiries. Often, under pressure, "the . . . staff concerned willingly decide[d] to shut their eyes. . . ."[69]

Fourth, in a general atmosphere of high-level political corruption, venality tends to spread.[70] Government workers tended to become at least

[67]Nigeria, Federation, *Comments on the Report of the Tribunal of Enquiry*, p. 25, and *Report of the Railway Corporation Tribunal*, p. 219.

[68]See, e.g., Nigeria, Federation, *Report of the Railway Corporation Tribunal*, p. 277: "Dr. Ikejiani [illegitimately] took over the functions of the General Manager and Mr. Egbuna willingly surrendered. He told us that at 39 he did not want to lose his job."

[69]Federal Republic of Nigeria, *Comments of the Federal Military Government on the Report of Tribunal of Enquiry into the Affairs of the Nigerian Ports Authority* (Lagos: Federal Ministry of Information, 1968), p. 9; also pp. 6, 7. Federal Republic of Nigeria, *Report of the Tribunal of Enquiry into the Affairs of the Nigerian Ports Authority for the Period October 1, 1960 to December 31, 1965* (Lagos: Federal Ministry of Information, 1967), pp. 29, 30, 45, 72, 86; Federal Republic of Nigeria, *Comments of the Federal Military Government on the Report of the Tribunal of Enquiry into the Affairs of the Nigerian Railway Corporation for the Period October 1, 1960 to December 31, 1965* (Lagos: Federal Ministry of Information, 1968), pp. 3, 9, 11, 26, 35; Federal Republic of Nigeria, *The Policy of the Federal Military Government on Statutory Corporations and State-Owned Companies* (Lagos: Federal Ministry on Information, 1968), pp. 9, 16, 22.

[70]It is for this reason that "an atmosphere of corruption" is to be feared, according to Nehru: "People feel they live in a climate of corruption and they get corrupted themselves. The man in the street says to himself: 'well, if everybody seems corrupt, why shouldn't I be corrupt?' " R. K. Karanjia, *The Mind of Mr. Nehru* (London: Allen and Unwin, 1960), p. 61, quoted by Gunnar Myrdal, *Asian Drama* (New York: Twentieth Century Fund, 1968), p. 941. See also W. F. Wertheim, "Sociological Aspects of Corruption in Southeast Asia," *Sociologica Neerlandica* 1:2 (Autumn 1963): 143: ". . . corruption is furthered by a public opinion which takes it for granted that it is ubiquitous." Also David H. Bayley, "The Effect of Corruption in a Developing Nation," *Western Political Quarterly* XIX:4 (December 1966): 725.

apathetic, and some decided to partake of the potential gains. Petty corruption proliferated.[71]

The major purposes of the manipulation of contracting procedures were support of party operations and enhancement of personal income and wealth. Manipulation of government contracts for party financing and support is common in many countries. Faced with a paucity of funds from individual or large-company sources, Nigerian parties, like those in many other countries, relied heavily on their control of the public purse. The work of those who ran the political apparatus was often compensated by the award of government contracts or by other government patronage. Political supporters were also rewarded in the same manner.[72] Party funds were collected through kickbacks from such contracts (and from other government payments including the salaries of highly placed politicians). Kickbacks were often collected also on contracts awarded to other firms, including foreign firms, which then considered such outlays simply as a cost of doing business. Companies which refused to cooperate in this procedure, and there were some, tended to be frozen out except in undertakings in which their superiority was marked. Party financing through means such as these was common practice. As the Working Party on Statutory Corporations stated: "in the matter of contract award, a stage has been reached where something more than well worded procedures administered by spurious tender boards or greedy executives is required . . . We require a machinery which will ensure that government and [public] corporations' contracts will no longer be *the chief source from which political parties derive their revenues,* and that politicians appointed to public office will be free from certain party [financial] obligations fulfilment of which with the aid of their official positions can only earn them public contempt."[73]

Political and personal motives were intertwined in the manipulation of government contracting procedures. It could hardly have been otherwise. Many of the political leaders who channeled government expenditures into rewarding party supporters had been and continued to be businessmen themselves. Devoting themselves to political affairs and thus having less time for business activities, they certainly felt at least as deserving of

[71]For uncounted examples among public workers of grossly negligent or culpable acts of commission or omission regarding corruption see the various Inquiry Reports, passim.

[72]And political opponents were punished. See, e.g., the warning of the Eastern Region Premier to party rebels that "contractors will be blacklisted" by the Eastern Nigerian government unless they abandoned their opposition to his leadership. *West African Pilot,* July 14, 1958, quoted by Sklar, pp. 452-453.

[73]Nigeria, Federation, *Report on Statutory Corporations,* p. 22 (emphasis added). Although innumerable instances of contract manipulation for political purposes are described in the various post-coup Inquiries, there was a strong and probably justified belief that there had been even more corruption than the Inquiries revealed. See, e.g., the report on the Nigerian Ports Authority in the *Nigerian Tribune,* June 29, 1968, p. 1.

reward as businessmen who were less politically active. The colorful response of a Federal cabinet minister to strong press criticism of a land transaction which involved a clear abuse of his position for personal enrichment vigorously expressed this attitude. He pointed out that he "had been a company director and engaged in other business enterprises" before entering politics, and that from the criticized transaction he gained "a chicken feed rental in place of elephantine income" he would have made if he had devoted his time to private pursuits.[74] More important, for many political leaders personal enrichment was one of the main ends of political activity, and one common means of achieving this was by setting up politically favored economic ventures. The means used were essentially the same as those employed to secure party financing.

To illustrate the mishandling of government contracting for personal enrichment, let us consider one of the most flamboyant raiders of the public purse (although surely not the largest[75]), the Board Chairman of the Nigerian Railway Corporation. The Railway Tribunal found that "Dr. Ikejiani's behaviour was such that it completely destroyed the image of the Corporation in the eyes of the Corporation staff and the general public . . . he mismanaged the affairs of the Corporation in many respects." The Tribunal then listed a number of his self-enriching transgressions, including overpayment on Railway Corporation contracts in return for which he received free or nominally priced work on his personally owned houses and a private medical center, improprieties with respect to Corporation land, and abuses in the purchase of insurance for the Corporation, and concluded: "he claimed far more allowances than he was entitled to; he sold his own car to the Corporation for his own use; he built himself a chicken-run at a fantastic cost; he did far more than we can ever recount." As a result, "Dr. Ikejiani, within three years of becoming Chairman of the Corporation had acquired a fleet of cars, two pieces of land . . . shares . . . and had started to develop his property at Apapa Road . . . He had also built another house . . . The evidence that Dr.

[74]While he was a Federal cabinet minister, the Honorable Kingsley O. Mbadiwe received a 99-year lease on a valuable three-acre plot of government land ("a premier industrial site" in the minister's own words) in the Lagos metropolitan area. The annual rental was £ 1,170. The company in turn leased this land for 50 years at more than triple this rental to a government-sponsored firm in which government had a majority interest (Nigerpools). As a result of a rather unusual outburst of press criticism calling for his resignation, the minister returned the land to the Federal Government but stayed on in his cabinet post. (Lagos) *Daily Times,* February 25, 1965, pp. 1, 3, for the minister's statement quoted above; the continuing story ran for about two weeks.

[75]For example, a Western Nigerian Tribunal found that the former regional Minister of Finance "improperly enriched himself to the tune of over £ 924,000" while he was in public office. Nigeria, Western Region, *West Recovers Ill-Gotten Wealth From Five Public Men* Ibadan: Government Printer, 1968(?)), no page numbers. Some others probably made off with more.

Ikejiani had taken advantage of his position as Chairman of the Corporation to make personal gain for himself was overwhelming."[76]

Political exploitation took place at all levels and stages of the contracting process and in innumerable ways; "influence filter[ed] through the administrative pores."[77] Jobbery was easiest and most frequent in petty contracts, which were let by local governments, or, at the Federal and Regional levels, by procedures lacking the safeguards prescribed for major contracts. Ogunpola rightly said of the firms that got such contracts, "most . . . are very inefficient, having neither the experience nor the financial and equipment resources to carry out their assignments. They are in most cases a creation of excessive party political patronage and influence."[78] In a typical example, relating to Lagos City Council road works, ". . . little regard was paid to propriety in the selection of contractors to supply timber and road materials. Councillors . . . each put forward their own nominees for selection as the Council's suppliers and awards were made to all those chosen at the same unit prices without regard to their tenders. The City Engineer told the Committee in March 1966 that the Council was paying prices higher than those paid in the commercial sector, but his advice was unheeded."[79]

Political mishandling of the major contracts occurred in both the registration and the tendering procedures. In the registration procedure, "there has been a great deal of political interference with the work of officials who are supposed to ascertain the suitability of any applicant for registration in a particular category . . . [Registration] tests were in fact not strictly applied in many cases, especially in the lower categories."[80] Political influences also obtained in registration in the higher categories. One of the Northern Nigerian firms in the highest category, for example, was so registered for political reasons and was quite unable to carry out large contracts. When awarded such contracts, the contractor simply took a portion off the top and sublet it to a large foreign-owned firm.

In most discussions of the process by which contracts are awarded, there is a tendency to overemphasize the tendering procedure. In fact, contracts were not generally awarded by tendering. For example, of 166 building contracts let by the Northern Nigerian Ministry of Works during the three years 1960-1962, approximately 73 percent by number and 80

---

[76]Nigeria, Federation, *Report of the Nigerian Railway Corporation Tribunal of Enquiry,* pp. 267, 275, 276. For many other instances, see the various Enquiry Reports, passim.

[77]Sklar, p. 451.

[78]Ogunpola, p. 38. See also Nigeria, Eastern Region, *Perkins Report of the Enquiry into the Administration of the Affairs of the Enugu Municipal Council* (Enugu: Government Printer, 1960), particularly chapters 3 and 10, and p. 258, and Ronald Wraith and Edgar Simpkins, *Corruption in Developing Countries* (London: Allen and Unwin, 1963), p. 25.

[79]Nigeria, Federation, *Report of the Tribunal of Enquiry into the Affairs of the Lagos City Council,* p. 236.

[80]Ogunpola, p. 349.

percent by value were awarded by negotiation, i.e., without any bidding at all (see Table 21). The high proportion of contracts awarded by negotiation continued until the 1966 coup. Of the awards made through the bidding process, moreover, a continually decreasing share was made through open tendering.

In the bidding procedures, whether open or selective tendering, politics permeated the actual processes. We have previously seen that the tenders boards were dominated by political figures. These "spurious tender boards"[81] made use of ample opportunities for political manipulation. Normally, the Ministry of Works reported to the tenders board a fairly large number of bids within what was considered an acceptable range; the target number of acceptable-range bids was usually approximately six to ten, a number that would in all likelihood include some politically desirable firms. If selective tendering was being used, the list of firms invited to bid was ordinarily chosen not on any clearly economic basis—for there was "insufficient evidence" to make such judgments[82]—but on a political basis in the first place. The tenders board then had considerable leeway in selecting a firm from among those reported to it and was not bound to accept the bid that the Ministry of Works technical staff considered the best one. It was not even required to choose from among the bids falling within what the technical staff considered the acceptable range. Tenders boards sometimes called in the Ministry of Works engineer for direct questioning and on occasion induced him to alter his position in a way that would enable a particular, politically desirable, contract awardee to be selected. Such deviousness was made easier in many cases because insufficient detail and precision in Ministry of Works specifications (the use of "drawing and specification" rather than "Bills of Quantities") favored the use of "an insensitive estimating technique" and thus made it difficult for bidding firms to come up with carefully worked-out estimates.[83] In many cases, tenders boards simply ignored the recommendations of Ministry of Works officials. This was cautiously stated in a pre-coup report to the Northern Nigerian government by a team of foreign experts: "There have been cases where professional recommendations have been over-ruled and higher tenders accepted. In most cases reasons were given for setting these aside. We feel, however, that [this should be avoided]."[84] The implication of political corruption was confirmed to the writer before the 1966 coup by a number of thoroughly authoritative informants and has since been exhaustively documented in the post-coup Inquiries.

[81]Nigeria, Federation, *Report on Statutory Corporations*, p. 22.

[82]Northern Nigeria, *Report on Building Costs*, p. 58. The report continues cautiously: "It follows, therefore, that any selected list of contractors would be open to criticism and mistrust."

[83]Northern Nigeria, *Report on Building Costs*, p. 59.

[84]Northern Nigeria, *Report on Building Costs*, p. 60.

The award of contracts by negotiation, the most common practice, was even more susceptible to abuse. In the one-to-one negotiations there was no barrier to political chicanery, and political manipulation prevailed. As the report of the Northern Nigerian Government stated cautiously, contract award by negotiation was "in principle" not acceptable. It embodied most of the disadvantage of the tendering procedures used, "but with the further and finally condemning disadvantage caused by the removal of the competitive element . . . without having provided any safeguards or controls to ensure [an acceptable price]."[85] Here too the clear implication of political corruption has since been thoroughly documented in the post-coup Inquiries. Conscientious government officials proposed or supported measures that could have reduced the degree of political interference in the award of contracts,[86] but to little avail.

Political corruption was sometimes carried out by completely avoiding the stipulated selection procedure. The existing contract of a firm might be extended to cover additional projects without any semblance of a bidding process and without considering other possible contractors, as when a firm with a contract to build four warehouses for the Nigerian Ports Authority was given the assignment of building two more without submitting a bid.[87] Contractors that had already performed some work for an agency might thereafter be awarded future contracts without facing any competition. This "principle of retaining existing contractors presumably at any cost, and at the detriment of other outside contractors," even though the latter would have done the work more cheaply, was criticized by the Nigerian Ports Authority Tribunal.[88] It was common practice to divide up larger jobs so that the regular procedures did not apply, and to let out to favorites the subdivided petty contracts under the more relaxed procedures obtaining for such contracts.[89]

Then there was the practice of increasing the amount to be paid to the contractor beyond the agreed-upon price; "contractors' tenders rates were adjusted mostly upward after the contracts had been awarded."[90]

[85]Northern Nigeria, *Report on Building Costs*, pp. 59-60.

[86]See, e.g., the efforts of the Acting Permanent Secretary and the Chief Architect of the Ministry of Works of Northern Nigeria. Northern Nigeria, *Report on Building Costs*, p. 60.

[87]Federal Republic of Nigeria, *Report of the Tribunal of Enquiry into the Affairs of the Nigerian Ports Authority*, p. 30. The Tribunal stated: "It is our considered view that the Management in doing this acted most irregularly."

[88]Federal Republic of Nigeria, *Comments of the Federal Military Government on the Report of the Tribunal of Enquiry into the Affairs of the Nigerian Ports Authority*, p. 8.

[89]E.g.: "Officials divide large contracts into smaller sizes so as to come within category (b), *i.e.*, the fragments are made of £ 2,000 or less so that the District Engineer could award them." Nigeria, Federation, *Report of the Nigerian Railway Corporation Tribunal of Enquiry*, p. 101.

[90]Federal Republic of Nigeria, *Report of the Tribunal of Enquiry into the Affairs of the Nigerian Ports Authority*, p. 36. See also the unauthorized doubling of an upward contract adjustment by the assistant general manager of the Electricity Corporation of Nigeria, who received other benefits in return from the contractor. Nigeria, Federation, *Report of the*

Contracts awarded on a cost-plus basis worked out in a similar way.[91]

Often the politically selected contractor simply did not possess the required construction capability at all. It was common for such contractors to take a cut off the top (for themselves and/or party coffers) and then to sublet the job at a figure below the contract award to a contractor with the necessary competence. Thus, an indigenous contractor in the highest Northern Nigeria registration category stated candidly to the author in mid-1965 that his staff was not qualified to handle large jobs and that he had no large-scale modern equipment. When awarded a contract for a big undertaking, he did it "jointly" with a large expatriate firm. Government officials confirmed that this foreign firm in fact carried out all this Northern company's large jobs. Many of the small firms (quite a few of which, as already mentioned, existed in name only), and even the medium-size Nigerian companies, sublet all or most of the work.[92]

Verifiable figures on the amounts extracted from government are, of course, difficult or impossible to obtain in clandestine acts of political corruption. One politician put an estimate on the public record. Speaking of party financing, he said that "in the Federation, or some part of the Federation, it is now a common practice that five percent demands are being made for those awarded contracts."[93] The rake-off most commonly discussed by presumably knowledgeable people in the 1960s was 10 percent. Evidence from Northern Nigeria suggests at least 10 percent, probably 15 to 20 percent, and possibly even more. The always circumspect *Report on Building Costs* says: "What evidence is there for challenging the price that Government pays for its buildings? Firstly there is the example of the voluntary authorities [i.e. missionaries] who build considerably more cheaply—as a generalization . . . at about two thirds of the cost . . . [W]hen allowance has been made for . . . differential factors there remains a margin of between 15 and 20% apparently unaccounted for.[94] Perhaps it is more than coincidence that this margin tallies nearly enough with the figure obtained by evaluating the cost of building in England to the conditions in Northern Nigeria. Whereas by calculation it can be shown that similar buildings should be at least 20% cheaper in Northern Nigeria than in England, comparative estimates show them to

Electricity Corporation of Nigeria Tribunal of Enquiry (Lagos: Federal Ministry of Information, 1967), pp. 102-105.

[91]Federal Republic of Nigeria, *Comments of the Federal Military Government on the Report of the Tribunal of Enquiry into the Affairs of the Railway Corporation*, p. 9.

[92]Ogunpola, pp. 347, 352. Interviews indicate that this occurred in the Northern and Eastern regions as well.

[93]Nigeria, *Legislative Council Debates*, Session 1959-60, August 11, 1959, column 1765.

[94]Highly knowledgeable Northern government officials stated to the author in mid-1965 that the differential was much greater and that government paid contractors as much as two or three times the amount that missionary organizations paid for similar work.

be not more than 5% cheaper in the same relevant terms. . . ."[95] It seems
fairly certain then that if there is any significant contribution that can be
made to effect an immediate reduction in building costs, it lies in taking
positive action to ensure that future tenders do not carry this unexplained
margin."[96]

It seems most accurate to say that the levy on the government purse
varied. The amounts involved in the cases described in the post-coup
Inquiries differed greatly. The variousness of these cases suggests that
the magnitude of the rake-off depended on whether it was for political or
personal purposes or both, on the sense of security felt by the manipulating politicians, on the degree of control they exerted, and on many other
circumstances.

We have filled in at some length the point that political corruption in
contracting took place at many stages and in many ways. Almost always
government overpayments—often very large[97]—were involved. Let us
conclude our discussion of this point by dealing with political manipulation that involved not overpayment but tampering with allocation. Since
the early 1950s, governing parties have tended to allot roads, bridges,
water-supply improvements, and other desirable public works to areas in
which they have political support and to deprive opposition-supporting
areas. Sometimes there was an even more blatant kind of allocational
manipulation. For example, a prominent Nigerian economist has commented upon "the elaborate land and sea transport network of Finance
Minister Chief Okotie-Eboh's Omimi Shoe Factory," pointing out that
"a lesser entrepreneur with lesser connections, running a similar factory"
would be unlikely to get the same infrastructural assistance from government.[98] Another example is provided by the establishment of a poorly
located cement plant in Sokoto, Northern Nigeria, despite the realization

[95] A detailed set of comparative figures are presented in an appendix. Northern Nigeria,
Report on Building Costs, p. 149.

[96] Northern Nigeria, *Report on Building Costs,* p. 56 (paragraphs are run together).

[97] E.g., the overpayment by about £ 120,000 "as a result of a wrongful award" for a
Nigerian Ports Authority container berth: Federal Republic of Nigeria, *Comments of the
Federal Military Government on the Report of the Tribunal of Enquiry into the Affairs of
the Nigerian Ports Authority,* p. 16; or the unnecessary expenditure of "a very large part of
the £ 916,570 spent on . . . emergency maintenance dredging": *Report of the Tribunal of
Enquiry in the Affairs of the Nigerian Ports Authority,* p. 97.

[98] S. A. Aluko, "The Educated in Business: The Calabar Home Farm—A Case Study,"
Nigerian Journal of Economic and Social Studies VIII:2 (July 1966): 206. There were,
incidentally, other distortions in favor of big men. Thus, differential excise duties were
levied in Nigeria in mid-1965 on various types of domestically produced footwear. The ratio
of excise tax to pretax factory price was 20 percent for rubber and/or canvas footwear, 43
percent for low-quality leather footwear (a close competitor of rubber-canvas shoes), and 60
percent for plastic footwear (another competitor of rubber-canvas shoes). It is more than
coincidence that these levies were introduced by the Finance Minister mentioned in the text,
who was a major producer of the favored rubber-canvas footwear. E. Wayne Nafziger,
Nigerian Entrepreneurship: A Study of Indigenous Businessmen in the Footwear Industry,
University of Illinois Ph.D. dissertation, 1967, Urbana, Illinois, pp. 136-138.

that its uneconomic location would prevent it from being commercially viable. Beyond this, the heavy allocation of government resources to construction was probably affected by political considerations. There appears to have been a bias toward activities, like construction, which presented good opportunities for political and personal payoffs. These opportunities may explain why shortfalls in actual construction expenditures (below planned) were considerably less than shortfalls in any other kind of development expenditure.[99]

This chapter has discussed demand-channeling in government construction as a means of aiding indigenous enterprise. The final section has dealt with the permeation of government contracting operations by political corruption, discussing particularly the general processes through which corruption took place, its political and personal purposes, and the many stages and ways in which political manipulation was carried out.

This brings us to the end of the chapter, but further appraisal may be worthwhile. On the one hand, the prevalence of political considerations was not entirely inconsistent with the use of government purchasing power to promote indigenous economic development; the politically favored contractor did develop some competence. On the other hand, the development objective was distinctly subsidiary to the political objective. The effects of the latter's predominance will be discussed in Chapter 13. The non-political problems will also be further assessed in that chapter.

[99]See, e.g., Nigeria, Federation, *Federal Government Development Programme, 1962-68, First Progress Report,* Sessional Paper 3, 1964 (Lagos: Federal Ministry of Economic Development, 1964); Federal Ministry of Economic Development, *National Development Plan, Progress Report 1964* (Apapa, Nigeria: National Press, 1965).

Chapter 10

THE APPROVED
MANUFACTURERS SCHEME

The Approved Manufacturers Scheme was the most thoroughly worked-out demand-channeling program. The potential of such programs for stimulating domestic production was substantial. Government expenditures had grown between 1950 and 1962 at a rate more than five times the growth rate of gross domestic product and continued to expand more rapidly. In 1962-63 Federal and Regional government expenditures combined were 12.8 percent of gross domestic product.[1] While this percentage was low by international standards, it would have been much higher if the outlays of local governments, marketing boards, development corporations, and statutory corporations were added. Moreover, this figure understates the importance of government expenditures relative to the marketed portion of gross domestic product, for a substantial part of Nigeria's product was produced for subsistence. It understates even more sharply government's importance relative to modern-sector output.

The Program

The Approved Manufacturers Scheme was a further development and formalization of procedures that had already been employed by the Department (later the Ministry) of Commerce and Industries to stimulate domestic production. As one means of assisting domestic firms it was already aiding in other ways, the Department tried to promote government purchases from such firms. In the absence of a formal program, however, difficulties arose. The Department of Commerce and Industries had persuaded the Prisons Department in 1954 to order cloth for uniforms from the Kano Citizens Trading Company, a firm that was getting a great deal of all-around assistance. The price paid by the Prisons Department, incidentally, was below the normal import price (including import duty) that the Department would have paid if it had ordered through the Crown

---

[1]Charles R. Nixon, "An Analysis of Nigerian Government Expenditure Patterns, 1950-62," in Carl K. Eicher and Carl Liedholm (eds.), *Growth and Development of the Nigerian Economy* (East Lansing, Michigan: Michigan State University Press, 1970), p. 90.

Agents. The Financial Secretary's office remonstrated with the Prisons Department, however, and stated that it viewed such a purchase outside of normal channels "with grave concern." After further discussion, the Financial Secretary's office clarified its position: it was not opposed to local purchases in preference to imports, but such purchases should go through normal tendering procedures.

The Approved Manufactuers Scheme was worked out soon after this and was formally initiated in December 1955 by a circular from the Financial Secretary. It was established in response to the pressures discussed in the preceding chapter and also to those exerted by officials in the Department of Commerce and Industries and in other departments who were concerned with implementing the long-run strategy embraced in 1949 of development through indigenous private enterprise. Similar programs were established in most of Africa[2] and in many other countries.[3]

The Scheme required all departments of the Federal Government to purchase their supplies from domestic firms designated as Approved Manufacturers rather than from importers "in all cases where the Nigerian products are comparable in price and quality with imported products."[4] No distinction was made between indigenously owned and foreign-owned enterprises. It was hoped that the regional governments as well as the quasi-governmental corporations at the Federal and Regional levels would participate; they "were invited to adopt a similar plan,"[5] but as we will see they unfortunately did not do so.

The requirement of comparable price and quality was interpreted somewhat liberally; like government purchasing programs in most countries, the Scheme entailed preference for domestic concerns. The circular itself stated that local products should be bought when they are "reasonably competitive in price and quality" and reasonably expeditious delivery can be made.[6] In its implementation of the Scheme, the Federal Ministry of Works took this to mean that a 2½ percent price preference should be allowed to firms on the Approved Manufacturers list.[7] Moreover, even when a listed producer was unable to meet relaxed

[2]Theodore Geiger and Winifred Armstrong, *The Development of African Private Enterprise* (Planning Pamphlet 120) (Washington, D.C.: National Planning Association, 1964), p. 100.

[3]Kennard Weddell, *Aiding Small Industry Through Government Purchases* (Menlo Park, California: Stanford Research Institute, 1960).

[4]Nigeria, Federal Ministry of Commerce and Industry, *Approved Products: Federal Government of Nigeria Approved Manufacturers Scheme* (Lagos: Government Printer, 1961), p. 3.

[5]Nigeria, Federation, *Annual Report of the Federal Department of Commerce and Industries, 1956-57* (Lagos: Government Printer, 1958), p. 25.

[6]Nigeria, Federal Ministry of Commerce and Industry, *Approved Products*, p. 4.

[7]This was a small degree of preference compared to India's differential of up to 15 percent along with the reservation of some products entirely for small business. Weddell, pp. 20, 40, 49; M. C. Shetty, *Small-Scale and Household Industries in a Developing Economy* (London: Asia Publishing House, 1963), p. 211.

criteria of comparability with imports, the Federal Tenders Board was supposed to recommend that part of an order be placed with that firm and that the rest of the order could be imported. Only "in exceptional circumstances" was the government department to be authorized to import its entire requirement.[8]

Approved manufacturers also came to receive preference over unlisted domestic firms. The Federal Tenders Board often approved a listed firm for a contract even when an unlisted Nigerian firm had submitted a lower bid. Leaving aside possible political reasons, this practice was often followed because it was administratively easier. On a pending purchase, an early judgment had to be made about the reliability of the supplier and his product. However, Ministry of Commerce and Industries officials usually were too fully occupied to go right out and investigate the unlisted bidder, while they felt moderately confident of the reliability of a listed firm. Ministry officials indicated that firms that lost out in this way were subsequently investigated, and if their operations warranted they were placed on the Approved Manufacturers list so that they would not thereafter be at a disadvantage.

It was proposed that the Approved Manufacturers Scheme also embody a governmental imprimatur for capable producers comparable to the British designation of certain firms as suppliers to the royal household. Qualified enterprises would have been named as "Approved Suppliers to Government" and would have had the privilege of using on their labels and letterheads an appropriate symbol. This mark of prestige would have indicated that "a reasonable level of quality has been maintained by the company over a reasonable period."[9] This proposal was finally rejected, however, mainly because it implied a greater degree of Federal Government approval than was really involved in the Approved Manufacturers Scheme and would have been too subject to abuse.

There were other proposals for aiding the approved manufacturers. Suggestions were made for clustering aid, i.e., providing a cluster of many kinds of assistance to firms that had been selected for assistance under any program. Government officials had some inclination to work in this way but, given the limitations of personnel and other resources, no systematic approach of this nature was ever adopted.[10]

The Ministry of Commerce and Industries developed a roster of "Approved Products" and of "Approved Manufacturers" of those products,

[8]Nigeria, Federal Ministry of Commerce and Industry, *Approved Products*, p. 4.

[9]Ministry of Commerce and Industries internal memo dated 3rd January, 1961. A somewhat similar but more comprehensive governmental imprimatur, involving governmental inspection of accounts and business operations, was proposed by the Eastern Region government. Nigeria, Eastern Region, *Policies for Trade*, Sessional Paper 5 (1955), p. 2.

[10]The clustering of business-assistance measures to promising firms is favored by Weddell. This is the practice in India and also in the United States. Weddell, pp. 2-3, 11-13, 17-19, 29-31.

selecting from those firms which applied for approved status. Some firms applied on their own initiative, although many Nigerian businessmen did not even know of the existence of the Approved Manufacturers Scheme (or, for that matter, of the Ministry of Commerce and Industries). Many were encouraged to apply by the Ministry, particularly those being assisted in other ways, e.g., by Federal Loans Board loans. The applicants were investigated by the Ministry, which bestowed approved status only on those which were "reasonably capable and able to produce reasonably competitive products." The roster of approved products and manufacturers grew rapidly, particularly at first. Table 22 shows this growth from fiscal 1956-57 to fiscal 1961-62. Exact data are not available for subsequent years but the numbers kept increasing, though more slowly, year by year up to the Civil War. This growth was healthy. It is important in a program of this nature to keep the door open for new approvees.[11]

TABLE 22

Approved Manufacturers and Approved Products
for Fiscal Years 1956-57 to 1961-62

	Number of firms	Number of products[a]
1956-57	4	3
1957-58	45	25
1958-59	60	34
1959-60	n.a.	n.a.
1960-61	79	64
1961-62	92	79

SOURCES: Federal Ministry of Commerce and Industry; Nigeria, Federation, *Approved Products, Federal Ministry of Commerce and Industry—Approved Manufacturers Scheme* (Lagos: Federal Printing Division, 1961 and 1962)

[a]"Products" were actually groups of related products. Thus, while 79 products were specified in the published list for 1961-62, 117 items (many of which are groups of products) were named in the published list's alphabetical index of listed products.

The procedure to ensure preference to approved manufacturers depended on the size of the order. If the contemplated purchase of an approved product was below some cut-off level (£ 1,000 for most ministries, £ 2,000 for the Ministries of Works and Communications),[12] the ministry could handle its own order, perhaps going through its own ten-

[11]See, e.g., Weddell, p. 27.
[12]These were the cut-off levels in 1965; they had been lower in earlier years. Minor changes had also been made in procedures.

ders board. The ministry was ordinarily required to buy from an approved manufacturer. If, however, the product of such manufacturers was not "reasonably competitive" with imports, stipulated policy was somewhat ambiguous. The general-policy statement required purchases only of reasonably competitive approved products, but the implementation instructions in the Financial Secretary's circular (reflecting local pressures) called for purchase of the approved products rather than imports, save in "exceptional circumstances." This ambiguity contributed to problems, which will be discussed shortly, of nonenforcement and nonimplementation of the Scheme.

If the contemplated purchase exceeded the £ 1,000 or £ 2,000 maximum, the order was handled by the Ministry of Works and the Federal Tenders Board which operated under it. The Board comprised civil servants representing the Ministries of Works, Finance, and Commerce and Industries,[13] Regional Government representatives (who were sometimes political appointees), and a domestic businessman, and was chaired by the Parliamentary Secretary of the Federal Ministry of Works (a political figure). The Ministry of Works advertised for tenders for the forthcoming purchase and notified the appropriate approved manufacturers. The Federal Tenders Board compared the tenders received with the price of imports. Taking into account the 2½ percent price preference for approved manufacturers, the Federal Tenders Board then made a recommendation to the ministry purchasing the goods that all, part, or none of the required goods be purchased from the approved manufacturer.

According to stipulated procedures, approved products could normally be imported only with specific authorization following upon a recommendation by the Federal Tenders Board. Provision was also made for exceptional cases, "e.g., when stores are urgently required and no Nigerian manufacturer can supply from stock."[14] The Federal Ministry of Finance could authorize the department requiring the goods to bypass ordinary Scheme procedures. To eliminate the use of the exceptional procedure to circumvent the Scheme, the Crown Agents[15] were instructed in 1959 to fill such orders for approved products only if specific authorization from the Ministry of Finance were attached. When approved products were purchased through a middleman rather than directly from the producer, the head of the department making the purchase was "*required* to satisfy himself that he is in fact purchasing a product manufactured in Nigeria, and not an imported product."[16]

[13]The Ministry of Commerce and Industries was divided in 1965 into a Ministry of Industries (which was represented on the Tenders Board) and a Ministry of Trade.

[14]Nigeria, Federal Ministry of Commerce and Industry, *Approved Products*, p. 4.

[15]The Crown Agents, located in London, provided the major means by which the Nigerian Government purchased imported products, both before and after Independence.

[16]Nigeria, Federal Ministry of Commerce and Industry, *Approved Products*, p. 4 (emphasis in the original).

To a minor degree, the government preference extended to approved manufacturers was supplemented by large foreign-owned firms. A number of them had requested copies of the list of approved manufacturers and tried to buy from them, at least to some degree. Government was ambivalent about exerting pressure on private firms. For example, the secretary of the Nigerian Timber Association complained in November 1959 to the Ministry of Commerce and Industries that Leventis (which owned the Coca-Cola Bottling Company) had signed a contract with a South African firm for 80,000 wooden boxes, to be followed by continuing orders if the first one proved satisfactory. The Timber Association secretary asked that pressure to buy from Nigerian firms be applied to Leventis. The contacted official recommended to his superiors that an attempt be made to Nigerianize wooden-box manufacturing even though the Approved Manufacturers Scheme did not apply to private firms. He suggested dropping "an effective hint" to Leventis that the firm should buy locally produced boxes. Others in the ministry, however, took the position that Leventis probably had good reasons for its action, that the Nigerian Timber Association was big enough to get its own business, and that the fault probably lay with the Association and its members. No action was taken.[17] Still, foreign-owned firms were clearly aware of and not totally unresponsive to generalized national pressures for Nigerianization wherever possible.

Nevertheless, one of the very largest foreign-owned firms had retreated by 1965 from a policy of favoring Nigerian products. As a result of unfavorable experiences it had returned to its earlier policy of purchasing on the basis of purely economic considerations.

The Approved Manufacturers Scheme started impressively. It was directly responsible for a pronounced shift in the balance of textile purchases. In the fiscal year 1956-57 the Federal Government ordered 31,014 yards (15 percent of total orders) from domestic textile factories and 174,960 yards (85 percent) from overseas. In the following nine months of 1957 (April 1 to December 31) orders from local factories amounted to 199,592 yards (57 percent of the total) while orders of imports were 150,950 yards (43 percent).[18] Beyond this, appraisal of the impact of the Scheme suffers from lack of data. The Ministry of Commerce and Industries simply had no data in its files on government purchases from approved manufacturers. The civil servants who carried out the program were most qualified to make a judgment and they generally believed that the Scheme generated some limited reallocation of purchases to domestic producers. The Scheme seemed to have its greatest impact in increasing purchases from domestic producers of cloth and simple metal products.

---

[17]Similar ambivalence continued in the post-Independence years.

[18]Nigeria, *Legislative Council Debates, Session 1958-59* (Lagos: Government Printer, March 17, 1958), p. 911.

As a rough generalization, the simpler the product the more effective the Scheme tended to be.[19]

Problems

The Approved Manufacturers Scheme encountered a substantial number of difficulties which both reduced potential benefits and caused offsetting detrimental effects.

Economic and Administrative Shortcomings of Domestic Firms

The underlying economic and competitive weaknesses of Nigerian firms which gave rise to demand-channeling programs in the first place constituted a continuing problem in manufacturing as it did in contracting. Government departments were directed to purchase domestic goods that were reasonably comparable to imports in such matters as price, quality, reliability of product, and speed of delivery. Unfortunately many of the approved manufacturers produced inferior or variable quality products at higher prices and with slow and unreliable delivery schedules. On the one hand, from the earliest years of the Scheme these shortcomings engendered continuing pressures for heightened preferences, particularly for indigenous firms.[20] On the other hand, the disabilities of Nigerian firms made domestic purchasing expensive and troublesome for government agencies and gave rise to resistance to the Scheme. Friction between aspiring Nigerian businessmen and reluctant bureaucrats was a chronic characteristic of the Scheme.

Purchasing Procedures and Noncompliance   The shortcomings of Nigerian producers intensified and provided an excuse for an intransigent set of administrative problems.

The purchasing procedures required by the Scheme were cumbersome, inconvenient, and protracted. To place local orders for approved products, it was necessary to go through the slow-moving Federal Tenders Board. Local producers were informed of the government purchase intention through a notice in the Federal Government Gazette and given time to submit bids. After a month, the Board opened the bids, made a pre-

---

[19]The governments' small-business purchase programs in India and the United States were successful in Weddell's judgment. Weddell, pp. 16, 23.

[20]"It is practically impossible for these local industries to be able to compete with the foreign firms . . . Unless some special arrangement is made by the Government whereby these local industries can be helped, I do not think our local industries will be helped at all." (M. Maitama Sule, a prominent political leader, calling for greater preferences under the Approved Manufacturers Scheme for goods produced by indigenous firms.) Nigeria, *House of Representatives, Debates,* August 12, 1959, column 1802. See also the discussion of pressure for special favoritism for Nigerian producers at the beginning of Chapter 9 (Construction) and footnotes 2, 3, and 4 in that chapter.

liminary judgment, reported to the purchasing ministry, and asked that ministry for its own report at the next monthly meeting of the Board. When this report was received, often more than a month later, the Tenders Board made a decision. This decision then often required ministerial approval, particularly for large transactions. At its fastest the normal procedure required three months. Files of the Ministry of Commerce and Industries, however, show not infrequent lapses of more than six months between submission of bids and announcement of the Tenders Board decision. Only then could the purchase be contracted for, and further delay was then likely before the successful bidder could produce the specified goods. The delay seemed interminable to busy civil servants.

In contrast, orders for imported goods were simple and were usually consummated relatively quickly. The government department merely placed the order with the Crown Agents in London and then picked up the imports when they arrived.

Busy officials also found it particularly convenient to specify well-known brands in submitting an order rather than working out a detailed descriptive specification of the goods required. This, of course, almost always precluded local production. Nigerian businessmen periodically lodged vigorous complaints about this practice: "It was . . . surprising to find foreign branded products specified when the same product is manufactured in Nigeria. It was even more surprising when the Government specifying the foreign product was associated with the financing of the Nigerian producer."[21]

Given the difficulties entailed in the Scheme, it was not surprising that civil servants frequently circumvented or ignored the officially stipulated procedures. The Principal Industrial Officer (the official most directly concerned with the Scheme) felt that most departments abided by the strict letter of the regulations but violated the spirit. "I feel that the present attitude of mind of those responsible for ordering stores is at the moment 'am I forced to buy this thing locally or can I get away with indenting for it in the usual way through the Crown Agents.' " He concluded that the needed "change of heart can, I think, only be brought about by personal pressure from the top on all directly concerned . . ." (memo of January 7, 1959). The Lagos Chamber of Commerce correctly said: "Too often Governments pay lip service to this principle but, in fact, owing either to administrative difficulties or individual prejudices, their intentions are not implemented."[22] Enforcement procedures were lax.

Efforts to strengthen enforcement were made. For example, the Ministry of Finance sent a circular letter to all government departments on

---

[21]Lagos Chamber of Commerce, *Quarterly Review* IV:3 (September 1961): 3.
[22]Lagos Chamber of Commerce, *Quarterly Review* III:1 (January 1960): 6.

January 18, 1958, complaining about noncompliance, and the Department
of Commerce and Industries in December of that year chided the Federal
Public Works Department for its neglect of the Scheme. In 1959 tightened
procedures were introduced which, if they had been adhered to, would
have been adequate to do the job. However, follow-up remained deficient
throughout the entire pre-Civil War period and while evasion was curtailed somewhat it continued to be common. Assertion of a need for speed
provided the most common loophole. If a department stated that it required needed supplies right away, it could then bypass the Approved
Manufacturers procedures. Often in a case of noncompliance the only
response of the Ministry of Commerce and Industries was to send additional copies of the Approved Manufacturers list to the errant department
and to ask it to cooperate.

Staffing   Upper-level government officials felt that enforcement was not
the answer in any case. The problem was not seen as one of compelling
compliance but as one of staffing. What was needed, it was thought, was a
person of some seniority and weight to devote himself to "selling" the
scheme, to informing officials and securing their cooperation as well as
checking on them. This would have required all or a substantial part of his
time, and staff shortages did not permit this. Ghana had set up a Ghana
Supply Commission which, in carrying out its function of purchasing all
government supplies, was charged with the responsibility of encouraging
purchases of locally manufactured goods[23] and officials in Lagos regretted
that no similar step had been taken in Nigeria. (Nigeria's 1970-74 Plan
proposed the establishment of a new National Supply Organization responsible for all purchases for Federal Government and quasi-
Government departments of both imported and domestic goods. Such an
organization could increase the effectiveness of the Approved Manufacturers Scheme.[24]) Compliance problems were aggravated by personnel
policies which involved frequent shuffling of staff between ministries, so
that officials responsible for implementing the Approved Manufacturers
Scheme sometimes knew little about it.

Governmental Business Procedures   What might be called governmental
business procedures interfered in some ways with implementation of the
Approved Manufacturers Scheme. The Scheme was sometimes overrid-
den by an official inclination to support government-owned enterprises

[23]See *West Africa*, January 3, 1959, p. 14.
[24]Federal Republic of Nigeria, *Second National Development Plan 1970-74* (Lagos: Federal Ministry of Information, 1970), p. 232. A Nigerian National Supply Company was set
up concerned primarily "with maintaining reasonable price stability in the face of global
inflation," and the *Third Plan* proposed a reorganization and consolidation of the Company.
Federal Republic of Nigeria, *Third National Development Plan 1975-1980*, Vol. 1 (Lagos:
Federal Ministry of Economic Development, 1975), pp. 181, 186.

like Nigersol (construction) or the Nigerian National Press (printing) in preference to domestic private firms.[25] A firm that requested listing as an approved manufacturer of gum was told it could not be listed because the Federal Government Printer produced gum and was the supplier for all government departments. Moreover, government payment procedures were sometimes so protracted that Nigerian producers, who were frequently pinched for working capital, encountered severe financial pressures if they sold to government agencies.[26] A baker, for example, who had undertaken the interesting venture in protein-deficient Nigeria of baking bread containing peanut flour and who was selling the product to Federal Government hospitals and other institutions, had to wait so long for payment that he simply gave up the experiment.

Coverage Finally, a major administrative problem was inadequacy of coverage. A large portion of government and government-agency purchases did not come under the provisions of the Scheme. First, the Scheme covered only direct purchases but did not apply to goods supplied by contractors as part of a broader contract, e.g., fixtures supplied with a building. Government officials felt that regulations about such goods would, particularly given limitations on staff size, be thoroughly unenforceable. Second, the Scheme did not apply to the many statutory corporations and other quasi-governmental agencies like the Electricity Corporation of Nigeria and the Railway Corporation, which in the aggregate undertook expenditures of perhaps the same order of magnitude as the Federal Government.[27] Efforts to broaden the coverage of Scheme to include the statutory corporations had limited success. The Ministry of Commerce and Industries proposed to the statutory corporations on January 3, 1961, that they abide by the spirit of the Scheme and try to direct their purchases to approved manufacturers. Four [28] out of a relatively large number replied rather favorably but at the same time rather

[25]See, e.g., Peter Kilby, "Measures to Promote the Development of Indigenous Industries (A Report to the Federal Ministry and the Western Nigerian Ministry of Trade and Industry)," United States Agency for International Development, Lagos, 1962, pp. 7-8 (mimeographed); Geiger and Armstrong, p. 101.

[26]See, e.g., Geiger and Armstrong, p. 101.

[27]Total expenditures by Federal statutory corporations and other quasi-Federal Government organizations are not known, but in the aggregate their expenditures appeared to be on the same order of magnitude as those of the Federal Government itself. Rough estimates by Edwin Dean indicate that capital expenditures by seven major statutory corporations alone constituted approximately one-third of the combined 1962/63-1965/66 capital expenditures of the Federal Government and the Federal statutory corporations (Edwin R. Dean, *Plan Implementation in Nigeria*, 1962-66 [Ibadan: Oxford University Press, 1972] pp. 74-78, 280-283). The combined capital expenditures of *all* Federal statutory corporations *and* other governmental or quasi-governmental agencies not covered by the Approved Manufacturers Scheme (such as the Lagos Executive Development Board) were, of course, much larger than those of the seven major statutory corporations.

[28]The Nigerian Coal Corporation, the Nigerian Broadcasting Corporation, the Nigerian Ports Authority, and the Lagos Executive Development Board.

equivocally. For examply, the Lagos Executive Development Board said it would "welcome" a regulation requiring quasi-government organizations to comply but did not indicate that it would otherwise do so. Up to the Civil War it appears that little was actually accomplished in channeling statutory corporations' expenditures to approved manufacturers. Third, the Scheme was a Federal Government undertaking and did not apply at all to regional governments. This was another substantial omission, for expenditures by regional governments and quasi-government organizations during the 1960s were at approximately the same level as expenditures by the Federal Government.[29] Efforts made to enlist regional government support for the Scheme and the discouraging responses will be discussed shortly.

Political Manipulation

While administrative and other problems were substantial, the major shortcomings of the Approved Manufacturers Scheme were politically based. Government purchasing operations, like contracting, were much too substantial and accessible a source of funds for supporting party operations and for personal enrichment to be forgone by the political class.[30] The operation of the Scheme was characterized by the same general process of political corruption as in contracting, the same political and personal purposes, and a similarly wide variety of ways in which political manipulation was carried out.

The opportunities for chicanery were great. Orders of less than £ 1,000 (earlier £ 500) were easily mishandled because they could be placed directly with an approved manufacturer without going through the tendering procedure. In the public corporations too, few safeguard procedures obtained for small purchases. Thus, for such purchases, the Railway Tribunal found, inter alia, that "the local purchase order system was the most abused of the systems of purchase adopted by the corporation"; that "the Corporation paid enhanced prices for cheap articles which it did not order [i.e., which were passed off as more expensive items which *were* ordered] and lost very large sums of money through the negligence of its staff in failing to check goods delivered to them"; and that "there was no system of internal check and the absence of automatic check on goods received had led to a loss of over £ 11,000 in the case of the item electrodes alone."[31] The Electricity Corporation Tribunal found, for exam-

---

[29]Estimate derived from calculations by Dean, pp. 127-130, 165-169.

[30]This appears to be a universal pattern. It is generally assumed in South Asia, for example, that government purchasing agencies and public works departments are particularly corrupt. Gunnar Myrdal, *Asian Drama* (New York: Twentieth Century Fund, 1968), p. 944.

[31]Federal Republic of Nigeria, *Comments of the Federal Military Government on the Report of the Tribunal of Enquiry into the Affairs of the Nigerian Railway Corporation for the Period 1st October, 1960 to 31st December, 1965* (Lagos: Federal Ministry of Information, 1968), p. 14.

ple, that the "Chief Storekeeper is not fulfilling his functions properly . . . [and that] the practice whereby some purchases are authorised by the Chief Storekeeper should be discontinued forthwith as it leaves room for malpractices and fraud," and also that "the present procedure whereby area managers are authorised to sign official purchase orders in their own rights should be reviewed so as to close any opportunity for fraud."[32]

The larger orders were also subject to mishandling. Sometimes designated procedures were simply ignored. For example, the Public Works and Civil Aviation Departments refused to disclose the names of their tailoring contractors to the Department of Commerce and Industries. Another example: the Chief Personnel Officer of the Electricity Corporation "had acted contrary to the Corporation's tender procedure" in directly placing two orders for high-priced khaki drill for uniforms and an order for badges. He had "acted with complete disregard of the interest of the Corporation by ordering 30,000 badges when there are 2,000 officers requiring a badge each. The order for 40,000 yards of khaki was also excessive."[33] Sometimes the procedures were proper but the tenders board acted politically. As John Harris pointed out after a careful study of Nigerian sawmilling, "Some contracts [for lumber] go out on tender and *some* tenders are awarded on merit."[34] Political favoritism was facilitated by the fact that the Federal tenders board had some discretion (and properly so in view of the purpose of the Scheme) in placing at least partial orders with approved manufacturers even if the local product was far from competitive with imports.

Regionalism

A form of political interference with business-assistance programs manifested sharply in the Approved Manufacturers Scheme was regionalism. Regionalism of course occurred in construction; it was taken for granted that the regional governments would favor their own regionals in awarding construction contracts. What was different in the Approved Manufacturers Scheme was that the central government attempted to establish a truly *national* program and to enlist the cooperation of the regional governments, but regionalism prevented the realization of this aim.

Regional political leaders were wary of any restrictions on their control

[32]Nigeria, Federation, *Comments of the Federal Military Government on the Report of Tribunal of Enquiry into the Affairs of the Electricity Corporation of Nigeria* (Lagos: Federal Ministry of Information, 1968), pp. 12-13. Documentation of political corruption in purchasing is available for the statutory corporations and not for the Approved Manufacturers Scheme, but the practices were similar. However, my information indicates that the incidence was more limited in the Scheme.

[33]Nigeria, Federation, *Report of the Electricity Corporation of Nigeria Tribunal of Enquiry* (Lagos: Federal Ministry of Information, 1967), pp. 109-110.

[34]John R. Harris and Mary P. Rowe, "Entrepreneurial Patterns in the Nigerian Sawmilling Industry," *Nigerian Journal of Economic and Social Studies* VIII:1 (March 1966): 76 (my emphasis).

of governmental and quasi-governmental funds. To agree to a Scheme that would require them to purchase, say, the output of a firm located in another region or of a firm in their region that supported the political opposition would have been simply unthinkable. Aside from considerations of political advantage, ethnic chauvinism called for government purchasing to be carried out so that profits should go to regionals. Moreover, there was a "practical" emphasis on the here and now which manifested itself in regional parochialism and shortsightedness. Regional rather than national economic growth was sought; and concern was for immediate gains or short-run economic growth. Political leaders by and large were not impressed by the more uncertain and possibly only theoretical long-run regional benefits which would result from measures that promoted development in the country as a whole.

The reactions of the regional governments to a Federal Government letter of January 3, 1961, proposing a more comprehensive Approved Manufacturers Scheme reflected the determination of the regionally based leaders to retain control over regional government expenditures. The letter described the Scheme and proposed that it should be made national and should be supported by all governments. The Ministry of Commerce and Industries attempted to allay anticipated regional apprehension, stating: "it should be emphasized that the Approved Manufacturers' Scheme as at present drafted would not place any [regional] Government in the position of being required to purchase from a local manufacturer in another region where there was a manufacturer of the same product in the region concerned, but it would ensure that goods are purchased from within Nigeria, rather than being imported." The proposal, however, would have required that products of an extra-regional approved manufacturer be accorded preference over imports.

The results provided an amusing though discouraging case study of regional foot-dragging. After waiting for five weeks, the ministry sent reminders to the regions on February 10, 1961. Enugu (Eastern Nigeria) then replied that it supported the Scheme in principle but that Eastern Nigeria Financial Instructions required an Eastern Nigeria Approved Manufacturers List. The government therefore wanted more information before proceeding. Although further information was sent, nothing further developed. Kaduna (Northern Nigeria) replied to the second letter on February 21, 1961, stating that it would respond as soon as possible. A month later Kaduna wrote that it was still considering the proposal. No further correspondence took place. An official of the Northern Ministry of Trade and Industry subsequently recalled that some discussion of the proposal had occurred, but the Northern government had no inclination to buy the output of a factory located in another region and had simply let the proposal die. Ibadan (Western Nigeria) required two further reminders, by mail on March 2 and by telegram on March 22. Ibadan then replied stating that it had no record of the original detailed letter of January 3 and requested another copy of that letter. This was sent and finally, more than ten months after the Federal proposal was made, the Western Nigerian government accepted it with a proviso that was clearly unacceptable: that the Federal Government would put on the Approved Manufacturers list all firms nominated by the Western Nigerian government. This proposal was rejected and the idea of extending the Approved Manufacturers Scheme to the regions died. The Federal initiative had caused hardly a ripple. This writer found in interviews a few years later that many of the regional government officials who would be most concerned with implementing such a Scheme were largely or completely unaware even of its existence and that others were of the opinion, in the words of one official, that the Approved Manufacturers Scheme was "not functioning worth a ha'penny."

The regional governments did not have systematic analogues of the Approved Manufacturers Scheme. On smaller purchases, three sets of forces were operative: civil service standards, the desire for political or personal gain, and the desire to promote regional enterprises. Most government officials were genuinely motivated by civil service standards calling for purchasing operations to be carried on in the most economical manner. Some manifested considerable passion on this issue, as in the case of the regional civil servant who would not comment on large purchases but declared vigorously that he *knew* that the purchases of a particular product were based solely on economic criteria because he was personally responsible for making the decisions. Because of these civil service norms, the prevailing tendency was to buy from the most economical source, or at least the most economical convenient source, unless other forces deflected this tendency.

One set of deflecting forces arose from the quest for political or personal advantage at the lower levels of political power, involving an intermingling of small-scale personal corruption and local political favoritism. Such factors influenced the placing of local government orders for printing, the purchases of school books, and many other minor government expenditures.

Finally, although there were no formal programs, attempts to promote regional enterprise became increasingly legitimate. While these efforts were not very systematic and there was no enforcement, they were not entirely ineffective. Ibadan circulated to government departments and corporations a "Schedule of Industries Operating in Western Nigeria," a descriptive list with considerable information and comments about each firm listed; this list had some resemblance to and some of the functions of an Approved Manufacturers list. Ibadan also sent tender circulars to a list of Western producers and merchants in an effort to increase government patronage of local suppliers. Eastern Nigeria departments were also circularized and urged to buy listed products from Eastern firms. On occasion, the Organization and Methods Branch of the Premier's Office switched purchase orders from imports to products of regional firms; examples which came to my attention include galvanized buckets and shoes. Preference for regional firms was not an important consideration in Northern Nigeria because so few firms were owned by Northerners, but government memos advocating intraregional purchasing were circulated, and by the mid-1960s plans were being discussed to set up a regional counterpart to the Approved Manufacturers Scheme. These deliberate efforts to promote regional enterprise were effective "to some extent"; government agencies were "sometimes willing" to pay a higher price for regionally produced goods. Gradually there was a slight shift of regional government patronage toward regional firms. Motives were mixed, however, and it was not always clear, even to the decision-makers, to what degree purchases from regional firms were influenced by promotion-of-regional-enterprise considerations.

On larger expenditures, where the amounts were sufficient to attract the specific attention of upper-level leaders, purchasing decisions were more often influenced by considerations of political or personal gain. Sometimes the purchasing official turned to cooperative foreign sources which were willing to arrange a kickback.[35]

But where feasible an arrangement was usually made with a regional enterprise, and in such cases there was commonly an intertwining of the objectives of personal or political gain and the promotion of regional economic activity. Ordinarily such an enterprise agreed to a kickback and at the same time was also a leading indigenously owned firm of the kind that demand-channeling programs were meant to nurture.

[35]See, e.g., Sayre P. Schatz, "Crude Private Neo-Imperialism: A New Pattern in Africa," *Journal of Modern African Studies* 7:4 (December 1969).

Chapter 11

YABA INDUSTRIAL ESTATE

Another means of promoting economic development through assistance to indigenous business was through the device of an industrial estate. An industrial estate is "a tract of land which is subdivided and developed according to a comprehensive plan for the use of a community of industrial enterprises."[1] Industrial estates provide essential services such as roads, railroad sidings, water, electric power, telephone services, means of drainage of industrial effluents, etc. Continuing management, involving control of the sites and buildings of the occupants, is also generally provided for on an industrial estate. Provision may also be made for the construction of factory buildings to be made available to the occupants.

The most common type of industrial estate in Nigeria—sometimes called an "industrial tract"[2]—has been one which provides sites and essential public utility services but no buildings. This kind of industrial estate has been occupied almost solely by enterprises which have had substantial foreign interests.

The second kind of industrial estate found in Nigeria—sometimes called a "fully packaged estate"[3]—is one which also provides shell factory buildings and possibly some additional services. The Yaba Industrial Estate is of this type, and it is meant for indigenous Nigerian entrepreneurs.[4]

Description of the Estate

A venture like the Yaba Estate is expected to benefit industrialists primarily by reducing the capital required of them. Moreover, transportation,

[1]William Bredo, *Industrial Estates* (Glencoe, Illinois: The Free Press, 1960), pp. 1-2.
[2]Bredo, pp. 1-2.
[3]Bredo, pp. 1-2.
[4]See Sayre P. Schatz, "Aiding Nigerian Business: The Yaba Industrial Estate," *Nigerian Journal of Economic and Social Studies* VI:2 (July 1964): 199-218. See also "Industrial Estates," *Nigeria Trade Journal* 13:3 (July-September, 1965): 118-124, and Peter Kilby, *Industrialization in an Open Economy: Nigeria 1945-1966* (Cambridge: Cambridge University Press, 1969), pp. 316-320.

213

public utility, and other services can be provided to the clustered occupants of an industrial estate more cheaply and efficiently than they can be brought to scattered firms. Clustering also permits external economies, e.g., in providing watchmen, maintenance, and other caretaking services.

For these reasons, the establishment of an industrial estate had been favored by the Department of Commerce and Industries since at least 1951. In 1953 the International Bank Mission to Nigeria strongly favored the Department of Commerce and Industries proposals for the establishment of industrial estates. Further support for the industrial estate proposal was provided in 1955 by the West African Joint Overseas Group of the Institution of Civil, Mechanical and Electrical Engineers in a detailed commentary requested by the Government of Nigeria on the Report of the International Bank Mission.[5]

After some delay, an irregularly shaped 2¾ acre tract of Crown Land was secured, although the original plans had called for 5 acres. Construction started in February 1957, and the estate opened in November 1958. Construction costs were £.75,750, slightly higher than anticipated, and some additional capital costs were subsequently incurred for the construction of two additional single-unit buildings and for some other minor jobs.

Two explicit objectives were formulated. The most fundamental and ambitious may be called the nursery function. "The Industrial Estate might be described as a nursery for industrial enterprise. After a few years on the Estate tenants should have developed their industries to the stage where they can set up their own factories in one of the new industrial areas planned in the environs of Lagos. New tenants can then take their places, and in turn develop to the stage when they can launch out independently." It was hoped that no tenant would stay more than five years.[6] Thus, the Yaba Estate was meant to nurture a steady flow of successful, productive enterprises.[7]

Another purpose of the Yaba Industrial Estate was to serve as a pilot demonstration of the commercial viability of industrial estates for Nigerian businesses. It was hoped that the Estate could be run as a profitable venture and that its commercial success would lead to the private establishment of other industrial estates, as has occurred in some other countries. It was originally believed that the Yaba Industrial Estate would be self-supporting in its fourth year and profit-earning thereafter.

[5]*Commentary on the Report of the International Bank Mission by the West African Joint Overseas Group of the Institutions of Civil, Mechanical and Electrical Engineers*, p. 10.

[6]"Industrial Estate at Yaba," *Nigeria Trade Journal* 6:4 (October-December, 1958): 134.

[7]The nursery function has also been adopted in some industrial estates in the United States. Zenon S. Malinowski and William N. Kinnard, Jr., *The Place of Small Business in Planned Industrial Districts* (Storrs: Connecticut Institute of Urban Research, University of Connecticut, 1963).

One might say that there was also an implicit, and subsidiary, base-of-operations function. A partial aim of the Yaba Estate was to aid Nigerian manufacturing firms by providing them with a superior base of operations of a kind they could not have otherwise afforded.

Five one-story buildings were erected. There were the equivalent of thirty workshop units, measuring 30 by 40 feet, but many were subdivided so that thirty-nine units were available for tenants. Two additional one-unit buildings were subsequently constructed; thus, in the 1960s there were forty-one units. An office building was erected for the Ministry of Commerce and Industry personnel who administered the estate. A canteen and kitchen were established to serve meals to the workmen; these facilities were rented to a private operator in the same manner as the workshops. Showers and toilets were also put up, in compliance with the Labour Code.

A well-equipped engineering workshop was constructed on the estate. It contained "some of the finest modern machine tools in Nigeria,"[8] and offered a wide range of machine-shop services to the tenants, which, it was thought, would be of great value. "Hitherto when some non-stock part of a machine breaks, a replacement usually has to be obtained from overseas; in future it may be possible to construct the particular part locally and so get the machine back into service far quicker."[9] The services of the engineering workshop were also made available to businesses outside the Estate, but only when no Nigerian firm could perform the job that had to be done.

Although intended only for industrial firms, the Estate admitted nonindustrial businesses (e.g., sign-painting, typewriter repairs) because of a paucity of demand for space. Units were leased to the tenants, but the lease was terminable by the tenant at any time.

The rental charge was designed to cover what was called the "full economic cost" (explained below), but the rent collected during the first five years was reduced in accord with the nursery function of the Estate. A rent of about two-thirds the full economic cost was charged in the first two years and a slightly higher level was charged for the next three years. This increasing schedule of rent was intended to induce established firms to leave the Estate and make room for fledgling businesses that would be nursed to maturity there.

Rents were set to cover all the expenses charged to the Estate, including amortization of the investment over a thirty-year period, assuming all units were occupied and all rent due was collected. Hence the term, "full economic cost" rent. This term was misleading, however. Several costs properly chargeable to the Estate were not included in its bookkeeping

[8]"Industrial Estate at Yaba," p. 133.
[9]"Industrial Estate at Yaba," p. 133.

costs. Excluded were rent for the site, interest on the initial capital sunk into the Estate, the salaries of the Industrial Officer who supervised the Estate and of several other Ministry of Commerce and Industries employees, such as watchmen, who worked at the Estate, and costs of maintenance of roads and buildings by the Public Works Department (although an understated "notional charge" for the latter two types of costs was attributed to the Estate in calculating full economic cost rent). Government officials also believed that Estate buildings would actually last only twenty rather than thirty years, so that expected depreciation costs were understated. On the revenue side, anticipated receipts were overstated, for the original calculations did not make any allowance for uncollectable rent. Thus full economic cost rent fell far short of covering all of the costs of providing accommodation at the estate.

The number of firms occupying the Estate increased gradually, from 17 (employing 310 workers) in 1959, to 21 (employing 370) in 1961, to 25 (employing 431) in 1963, and 28 (employing 470 workers) in 1964. Firm size, in terms of number of employees, ranged in 1964 from 4 to 55. At that date, 5 of the firms were engaged in printing, 4 in garment production, 3 in furniture-making, 2 in commercial art, and others were engaged in tarpaulin-edging, tire-retreading, wood-carving, auto body repair and painting, shoe repair and manufacture, typewriter repairs, and electrical installation, and in the production of mattresses, sanitary napkins, lapel buttons, singlets, laboratory equipment for schools, and cosmetics.[10] It was the original intention to screen applicants fairly carefully and to admit only industrial producers, but pressure to keep the Estate fully occupied despite a disappointingly small number of applications resulted in the admission of clearly nonindustrial businesses like the sign-painting and typewriter-repair firms.

Industrial estates are used in many countries as a channel for rendering various kinds of aid to business, and this policy was followed at the Yaba Industrial Estate to the extent permitted by the availability of staff and other resources. It was believed that advice and assistance could be rendered more effectively and economically to firms concentrated on an industrial estate, where they are more easily observed and better known to officials, and that such firms, having undertaken to apply for and having been approved for industrial-estate accommodations, were likely to be a select group that could make relatively good use of advice and assistance.

The Industrial Officer who supervised the operation of the Estate tried to provide advice and assistance in the selection of equipment, in factory layout and installation of equipment, and in other matters. The services of the engineering workshop were meant primarily for occupants of the Estate. Commercial advice and assistance was also offered. Three firms on

[10]Kilby, p. 318.

the estate were listed by the Federal Government as approved manufac-turers.[11] The Ministry of Commerce and Industry also attempted to help Yaba Estate tenants by providing accounting assistance and in other minor ways. Other kinds of advice and assistance—industrial research services, favored treatment with respect to government loans, special assistance in determining credit sources and credit needs, warehousing facilities, help with recruitment and training of employees—are afforded by industrial estates in one country or another, although not at Yaba.

Another way industrial estates help tenants is by making it relatively easy and inexpensive for a thriving firm to acquire more space as its operations expand. At Yaba it was possible to expand simply by remov-ing the partitions that separate the units within one building.

Problems

A number of problems emerged in the operation of the Estate.

Rent Rental of land or buildings for manufacturing production was a difficult and intensifying problem in Lagos. Sites became increasingly difficult to secure. Some loan applicants, e.g., were rejected by the Fed-eral Loans Board simply because they had been unable to secure satisfac-tory sites after as much as two years of searching. Land rents were rising to a level that Nigerian businessmen found difficult to pay.[12] Rents at the Estate were a bargain, and foreign-owned firms would have been happy to lease any units that were available, primarily for warehouse space.

Nevertheless, the rent proved difficult or impossible for most of the tenants to pay. Even with the early-year reductions, rent charges for many firms were higher than they would have paid for the "bush" ac-commodations they would otherwise have secured outside.[13] A large proportion of the tenants were consistently behind in their payments. Rent arrears ranged up to periods of twelve months. About half of the firms that had ever been tenants up to 1962 had vacated because they could not pay the rent.

Tenants tended to consider rent payments one of their last obligations, because they found by experience that it was difficult for government to enforce prompt payment. The tenants interviewed by the writer stated

[11] It must be pointed out, however, that there was no indication this listing would not have been forthcoming for these firms even if they had not been tenants at the Estate.

[12] On the problems one firm encountered of high rents and difficulties in securing land, see Robert Waite, "Establishing an Electronics Industry in Nigeria," Unpublished MBA thesis, New York University, 1964, pp. 71-72, 95.

[13] Kilby has pointed out that workshop space about equivalent to that provided by a Yaba Estate unit rented for about one-fifth as much in Eastern Nigerian cities. Speaking of East-ern Nigeria, he stated that an "economic rent is far out of reach for 99 per cent of the Region's producers." Eastern Nigeria Ministry of Commerce, *The Development of Small Industry in Eastern Nigeria* (by Peter Kilby, United States Agency for International De-velopment) (no publisher indicated, 1962), p. 1.

that the "softness" of the government as a landlord was one of the major attractions of the Estate. The enforcement of rent commitments was difficult because the Ministry of Commerce and Industry, which administered the Estate, had no right to evict tenants. As the Estate is situated on Crown Land, it came under the jurisdiction of the Chief Federal Land Officer, and he was the sole arbiter of termination of tenancy. The Ministry of Commerce and Industry officials felt that the eviction process was uncertain and took inordinately long. There were delays in getting the Chief Federal Land Officer to bring a case to the courts. Once in the courts, further extended legalistic delays were encountered. Then the courts tended to be favorably disposed toward the tenants. Furthermore, strong political pressures were sometimes brought to bear by delinquent tenants with influence.

Location   A majority of the tenants complained that the location of the Industrial Estate was a handicap. They believed that they might have attracted customers from among the passersby if the Estate had been located on a principal thoroughfare. They wanted the government to counteract this handicap by giving much greater publicity to the firms on the Estate and by helping them sell their products.

While inconvenient location has sometimes been a problem for industrial estates, it cannot be considered a weighty problem at Yaba. Although the Estate is not on a commercial thoroughfare, it is certainly well within the densely populated Lagos metropolitan area. It is in a familiar section, adjacent to the well-known Sabo Market, and is easily accessible. Under these circumstances, it was hardly reasonable that government should single out the Estate occupants for extensive help in selling their output.

Engineering Workshop   The engineering workshop was greatly underutilised. Except for special circumstances the workshop tended to operate at much less than half and even less than a quarter of its one-shift capacity, and much of its work was on outside (non-Estate) orders. Therefore, the light engineering workshop did not function up to expectations, either in providing aid to the tenants or in terms of full utilization of Nigeria's scarce capital.

There were several reasons for this. First, the Ministry of Commerce and Industry had difficulty in securing a competent man to take charge of the workshop, causing, among other things, uncertain delivery dates. Second, many of the firms on the Estate, owing back rent, avoided using the engineering workshop. They felt that, if they should use (and pay for) the services of the workshop, they would be asked why they failed to pay their rent. Third, in setting charges that were estimated to cover fully the costs of workshop services, prices were made too high for most of the Estate tenants. Nevertheless, there was quite general agreement that reducing charges would not cause a substantial increase in tenant utilization of the workshop; and when the pricing policy *was* changed and charges were reduced for those tenants considered likely to pay for the services, there was little response. Fourth, because of estrangement between tenants and officials (to be discussed shortly), tenants exhibited a diffuse reluctance to approach the workshop. Fifth, and probably most important, most of the tenants on the Estate were not industrial enterprises of the kind originally envisaged. Tailors and other clothing producers, printers, commercial-art firms, typewriter repairers, shoe repairers, etc., did not have much need for the workshop services; they could generally get better servicing of their equipment from the original suppliers. Moreover, as has already been pointed out, outside orders for workshop services were limited as a matter of deliberate policy.

Aid to Tenants Despite Ministry of Commerce and Industry endeavors to aid tenants at the Yaba Industrial Estate, tenants complained about a lack of worthwhile advice or assistance. They maintained that the Industrial Officers at the Estate were not technically trained and were therefore unable to offer the kind of assistance needed, that a visit to the Industrial Officer resulted in "mere talking." The Ministry, on the other hand, charged that tenants did not make use of the assistance that was available. The Industrial Officer in charge during one of the writer's visits stated that he offered to assist the firms in any way he could, but that during his six months at the Estate not a single tenant had come to him. In response to tenants' complaints about lack of publicity, the Ministry had arranged free display space at a widely advertised International Trade Fair in Lagos, but once the space was made available few tenants bothered to prepare displays for themselves. Although they complained about lack of assistance, most of the tenants with whom this writer discussed this issue explained that, for one reason or another, they themselves had never, or practically never, sought the aid of the Industrial Officer.

There were several reasons for this apparently anomalous situation, in which the tenants complained about lack of aid but did not make use of what was available. First, the kind of aid offered to the tenants was not what they most needed. Their contention was correct that the Industrial Officer at the Estate during this writer's last visit and his predecessor were unable to provide technical aid. This is not a criticism of these officers, whose experience and abilities lay in other directions, but a reflection of staffing problems in Nigeria. Because of shortages of staff— and also funds—the amount and kinds of assistance available to the tenants fell short of what might reasonably be associated with an industrial estate for indigenous businessmen provided by a government with Nigeria's nurture-capitalism orientation. Even the plan for helping the more successful firms by enabling them to expand their workshop areas simply by removing partitions did not work as smoothly as hoped. It was only a fortunate coincidence if a firm that needed to expand was located next to a unit that was already or soon would be vacant. Consequently, expanding firms at Yaba sometimes had to split their premises into two separated units.

Second, the "our government" approach of many Nigerian businessmen, discussed in Chapter 5, entailed unrealistic expectations of direct and substantial help in their own day-to-day affairs. The conflict about assistance to Estate tenants was therefore intensified by sometimes rather extravagant expectations of aid. One tenant, for example, was indignant because his request for a chemical analysis of an imported component was turned down on the grounds that the government department approached was not capable of doing such complex work; on this basis, he maintained that the government offer of aid was valueless. Another maintained that government should assist him by finding buyers for all of his output. Many felt that they should get loans without security and without undergoing rigorous investigation of the viability of their project.

Third, some of the tenants' complaints had the look of outbreaks of annoyance and frustration caused by the formidable difficulties encountered in their business efforts. The complaint about lack of publicity for Estate firms represented this kind of situation (although other things were also involved), as is shown by the lack of interest in using display space at the Trade Fair once it was made available. A dispute about accounting assistance also seemed to reflect general annoyance and frustration. The dispute erupted over arrangements made by the Ministry for a retired civil servant to provide accounting services to the tenants on a fee basis two or three days a week. The tenants maintained that this person did not have enough time to serve all the firms and demanded more adequate accounting help. They also maintained that his fees were too high. It was the Estate supervisor's unequivocal opinion, however, and on the basis of his observations and interviews the writer concurs, that the complaint was a tactic in a campaign to reduce rents. The plan for providing accounting services fell through as a result of the dispute.

Finally, another reason for the conflict surrounding the issue of aid to tenants was the gulf between Nigerian businessmen and expatriate officials—the wide gap in communications, in feelings, in attitudes, in understanding of one another. In view of this gulf, better communication between officials and tenants was called for. Ministry officials felt quite strongly that they had informed the tenants clearly of the availability of advice. On the other hand, most tenants maintained that they had only recently been informed that assistance was available. Some of the proprietors were, as one tenant said, "too shy" to go for advice. Some expressed the feeling that expatriate officials were uninterested in helping and were really rather hostile. Some mutual antagonism undoubtedly existed between tenants and foreign officials; there had sometimes been bitter exchanges between them. Under these circumstances it would have been wise for the officials to have gone to greater lengths to assure the tenants of the Ministry's desire to supply whatever advice and assistance it could.

Demand for Units   There was an initial surge of demand for workshop units, and within a few weeks of the completion of the Estate all but eight had been let. However, demand soon slacked off, and the Estate was kept full only by relaxing the initial entrance requirements. The Ministry admitted many firms that originally would have been excluded as nonindustrial. It stimulated demand by giving concessions to potential new tenants, including a three-month rent-free period for moving in equipment and getting the unit ready for operations. The already mentioned fact that the government was a "soft-hearted landlord" helped to keep the Estate occupied. Some tenants entered the Estate on a "heads I win, tails you lose" basis: if their businesses turned out to be unprofitable they simply moved away, leaving their rent unpaid. (The government was singularly unsuccessful in collecting rental debts from such erstwhile tenants.) A foreign-owned firm which had been a month-to-month tenant almost since the inception of the Estate was still there six years later,[14] implying that no acceptable Nigerian firms had been awaiting entry into the Industrial Estate. Slack demand for units was also reflected in attempts by Industrial Officers to persuade businessmen to move to the Estate; many of the applicants to the Federal Loans Board, for example, were advised to do this.

Despite concessions to tenants and other efforts to keep the Estate full, there was a large turnover of tenants. During the Estate's first thirty-five months of operation, there had been approximately sixty tenants, two-thirds of whom had vacated.[15]

Appraisal

We turn now to an appraisal on the basis of the Yaba experience of fully packaged estates for Nigeria. For this purpose we ask first how well the Yaba Estate was run. If there were deficiencies in its establishment and administration, then a well-run industrial estate might make a better showing, and generalizations from the Yaba experience are suspect.

It was suggested by a former official that too much capital was sunk into the Estate, and that amortization charges and therefore rent could have been reduced by dispensing with the engineering workshop and by constructing simpler buildings. Problems of this nature have arisen in industrial estates elsewhere. "There is great danger of expensive overbuilding

---

[14]Kilby, *Industrialization*, p. 319.

[15]The writer found that similar difficulties in filling a fully packaged industrial estate were encountered in Nairobi, Kenya, in 1968, despite considerable subsidization to tenants in the form of below-cost rentals and other assistance.

of industrial estates in the general desire to improve factory space and working conditions. The designer of factory buildings in the less developed countries should constantly keep in mind the character of the alternative factory quarters available to industrialists off the estate, and the rather miserable premises from which they may have moved. While alternative premises off the estate may be inconvenient and undesirable in many respects, it must be remembered that they are cheap."[16] Thus, in Eastern Nigeria the kind of workshop typically employed for very small industry cost approximately £ 50,[17] no more than two or three months rent at the Yaba Estate. Even the workshops of cement construction employed by a minority of the very small-scale producers cost about £ 500, and therefore would have been completely paid for by a little more than seventeen months' "full economic cost" rent at Yaba. For many firms the greater cheapness of "bush" accommodations more than compensated for the disadvantages.[18]

The view that significant savings could have been made in the initial capital investment in the Yaba Estate was a solitary one, however. The International Bank recommendation for simpler structures than the Ministry of Commerce and Industry had originally envisaged had been adopted. The buildings are simple shedlike affairs constructed of cement blocks, and it is difficult to see how further substantial simplifications in design could have been achieved. Construction could have been less substantial, it is true. It is sometimes suggested that industrial estates in developing countries should use whatever cheap indigenous building materials are available, whether bricks, tiles, wood, bamboo, stabilized earth, or thatch.[19] Officials and tenants alike felt that such buildings would not have been suitable. Both groups believed that the cost of the buildings could not have been much reduced.

Some additional savings would have been possible if the Estate had disregarded the factory ordinances and similar regulations. This, however, would not have been politically feasible, nor, in the writer's opinion, would it have been wise. Real savings in capital costs could have been achieved if the engineering workshop had been excised from the project. However, it would have been difficult for the original planners of the project to have foreseen the gross underutilization of these facilities.

In any case, the saving that could have been realized from reduced initial capital costs was minor. If we make the rather strong assumption that the capital cost of the Estate could have been cut by one-fourth, this

[16]Bredo, p. 116.

[17]Eastern Nigeria Ministry of Commerce, *Development*, p. 32.

[18]See, e.g., Eastern Nigeria Ministry of Commerce, *Development*, p. 8.

[19]Bredo, p. 116.

[20]A one-fourth reduction of the initial capital cost of £ 76,000 would be £ 19,000. On the basis of the original thirty workshop units this amounts to £633 per unit. Amortized over thirty years, i.e., 360 months, this would be £1.15.-. a month.

would have yielded a saving when amortized over thirty years of about £ 1.15.–. a month per standard unit, not enough to ease significantly the tenants' rent problems. Moreover, we must set against the rent reduction the likelihood that there would have been some offsetting reduction in benefits from the simpler estate.

Turning from capital to current costs, it was the writer's impression that, except for the underutilized engineering workshop,[21] the Estate was run with reasonable efficiency. Government officials maintained that this was the case. More significant, the tenants, many of whom were quite antagonistic to the Ministry because of rent and other problems, also felt that the Estate was run reasonably well and were unable to suggest feasible ways in which costs could be reduced.

Leaving costs aside, we ask whether any other practices might have been adopted which would have made the Estate more helpful to the tenants. The suggestion most frequently and vigorously made by the tenants, aside from reduction of rent, was that the government should help the firms with the sale of their output. This could have been done, various tenants suggested, by publicizing the Estate more widely, by advertising the tenants' products, by government efforts to secure contracts for the firms, and by government patronage. Measures such as these, however, and practically all of the other measures suggested by the tenants—such as loans without security, special kinds of technical aid, etc.—would have involved the government in an expanded program of aid for the tenants. There appears to be no justification, however, for an expanded business-assistance program solely for the tenants and not essentially related to their tenancy.

We can now consider the implications of the Yaba performance for an expanded program of fully packaged industrial estates.

As a pilot project designed to demonstrate the profitability of operating similar estates on a private basis the Yaba Estate clearly failed. The Estate fell far short of covering its costs. We have already seen that the Estate was subsidized in various ways. Even with these subsidies, receipts barely covered current costs, leaving nothing to cover the depreciation of the capital investment.[22]

In its other major function, as a nursery for indigenous enterprises, the Yaba Industrial Estate was equally disappointing. Successful firms resisted moving from their subsidized haven. This was not an important problem, however, for this resistance was overcome. A much more fundamental failing lay in the limited number of tenants that grew beyond the nursery stage. By the outbreak of the Civil War in 1967 only two firms had

---

[21]It must be pointed out, however, that the workshop costs were a not insignificant portion of the Estate's running costs.

[22]Nigeria, Federation, *Reports of the Accountant-General* (for the years ending 31st March 1959, 1960, 1961) (Lagos: Government Printer, 1960, 1961, and 1962).

developed sufficiently so that they were able, with government assistance, to strike out on their own outside the Industrial Estate.

It was only in its subsidiary base-of-operations function that the Estate achieved a limited degree of success. The reluctance of the two most successful firms to leave the Estate indicated that the base-of-operations service of the Estate was beneficial to them, as it was to all firms that remained on the Estate. Evidently, for these firms tenancy on the Estate rather than elsewhere yielded a net advantage. It helped them to survive and perhaps to prosper. On the other hand, for the many firms that left the Estate, the net advantage of operating on the Estate was either nonexistent or too small to enable them to cope with the formidable problems that confront indigenous firms. Thus, for the minority of the tenants who remained on the Estate, the base-of-operations function was carried out successfully.

The conclusion is inescapable, however, that the Yaba Industrial Estate was unable to carry out its major functions. It gave evidence of the unprofitability rather than the profitability of industrial estates. It nurtured only two enterprises beyond the nursery stage. And in its base-of-operations function it was essentially a high-cost means of subsidizing a small number of indigenous businesses. In Nigeria, fully packaged industrial estates appear to be a rather expensive way of promoting limited benefits.

Chapter 12

LOANS PROGRAMS

The loans programs constituted the major means of promoting indigenous business.[1] They were intended to foster economic development by providing capital funds to promising Nigerian enterprises that would otherwise have been mired down by lack of finances. These programs—which were small-scale examples of development banks—were part of a worldwide pattern in the less-developed economies. There were well over three hundred development banks operating in developing economies in 1967, most of which, like the loans boards of Nigeria, had been established since World War II.[2]

The most important Nigerian loans programs for indigenous business were those of the regional loans boards and the Federal Loans Board. These succeeded the Nigeria Local Development Board, which was established in 1946 and terminated in 1949, and which was the first government agency whose duties included loan-making to Nigerian businessmen.[3]

Loans Board Operations

The formal loan-making procedures of the three regional loans boards and the Federal Loans Board (FLB) were, with numerous differences in detail, basically similar. (We will see later that actual procedures often deviated from the formal ones.) The procedure began with an approach to the loans board by a prospective borrower, although sometimes a gov-

---

[1]This chapter relies heavily on the author's two books on loans programs in Nigeria: *Development Bank Lending in Nigeria: The Federal Loans Board* (Ibadan and London: Oxford University Press, 1964) and *Economics, Politics and Administration in Government Lending: The Regional Loans Boards of Nigeria* (Ibadan and London: Oxford University Press, 1970).

[2]Joseph Kane, *Development Banking: An Economic Appraisal* (Lexington, Mass.: D. C. Heath, 1975), p. 3.

[3]The bodies called here the regional loans boards (a generic term, and not the official name of any agency) were established in 1949 as the Eastern, Northern, and Western Region Development Boards and were replaced as a result of the Nigerian constitutional changes of 1954 by the lending departments of the Eastern and Northern Region Development Corpo-

ernment agency might have made the initial suggestion to a prospective applicant. If the applicant had trouble in providing the kind of detailed project information required by the application, he often could get government assistance with the formulation of his proposal.

Once the application was submitted, it underwent a double appraisal, first for prospective commercial viability and then for collateral or security for the loan. The viability investigations were carried out by the appropriate technical departments of government, such as departments of trade, industries, fisheries, or agriculture. They investigated the market for the applicant's product, his proposed techniques, and his probable costs; they made some judgment about the ability of the applicant; and they appraised the sum requested by the applicant and often recommended a different amount, usually though not always smaller. The particular viability investigation procedures varied somewhat from time to time and board to board, but the formal procedures all had in common an assessment by civil service officials deemed capable of judging both the technology of the proposed project and its prospective commercial viability.

If the viability appraisal was positive, the loans board staff carried out an investigation of the security offered for the loan. For commercially promising projects, which were unfortunately rather infrequent, security requirements were sometimes relaxed. However, as problems of non-repayment and consequent financial stringency mounted, the loans boards tended to tighten up security requirements.

On the basis of the viability and security appraisals, the final decision on a loan application was made by the governing body of the loans board. Except for the earlier years of the regional loans boards, when they were appointed and controlled by the colonial government, the governing bodies were politically appointed. We will see that the regional boards, but not the FLB, acted in a highly partisan manner.

The boards had broad statutory powers to extend loans to virtually any kind of business venture, but in an effort to promote high-priority activities they all tended to restrict themselves. Loans were for indigenously owned and operated enterprises only. Beyond this, various types of activities deemed to be of low priority were excluded a priori. Loans were not extended for undertakings that could get financing through other channels, and partly for this reason retail and wholesale trading enterprises were barred. Other types of activities were excluded because they

---

rations and the Western Region Finance Corporation. They subsequently underwent a nomenclatural change involving the substitution of "Nigeria" for "Region," and the latter form of their names is used throughout this study. Eastern Nigeria also had an Eastern Region Finance Corporation from 1954 to 1956 and set up a Fund for Agricultural and Industrial Development in 1963; Western Nigeria had a network of Local Loans Boards from 1956 to 1964; Northern Nigeria established a Small Industries Credit Scheme in 1966.

were considered likely to fail in the Nigerian economic environment or because their contribution to Nigerian development was considered negligible, but these criteria were applied flexibly and rather inconsistently, and aside from the ban on trading enterprises, the basic economic criterion was probable commercial viability. For actual allocation of loans funds, the major category was small-scale manufacturing and related activities, particularly activities like sawmilling, furniture production, tailoring (i.e., clothes-making), baking, and rubber-processing. Services, e.g., hotels and dry-cleaning, and agriculture were also important recipients.

These loans were generally attractive. They were often extended for projects that could not get financing through normal commercial channels. Interest rates, generally in the 3-5 percent range but varying from 2 percent to 10 percent, were below normal commercial rates. The duration of loans was relatively liberal by commercial standards. Loan periods varied from one to ten years but were generally in the three-to-five year range. Since the loans were extended for durable fixed capital, however, even these relatively long terms sometimes created a pinch, particularly if the borrower experienced an initial period of losses. Borrowers often extended the de facto duration of loans, however, by the simple expedient of neglecting to make loan repayments on time.

The loans programs were of substantial magnitude in the Nigerian context, involving far larger sums than any other business-assistance programs.[4] In Western Nigeria, £ 1,700,000 was appropriated for loans to indigenous private enterprise.[5] In the Eastern Region the amount was £ 305,000.[6] In Northern Nigeria the sum was £ 1,425,000.[7] Thus, total funds appropriated for regional loans board loans to indigenous private enterprise were £ 3,430,000. The FLB received aggregate appropriations over its life-span of £ 564,000, making a grand total of approximately £ 4 million for these lending agencies.

The amounts actually loaned were considerably larger than the sums appropriated, for loan disbursements included the entire appropriations plus the relending of repayments received and interest receipts. While an accurate assessment of total loans is impossible,[8] it appears that total loans by the regional boards were somewhat less than double the amounts appropriated, i.e., between £ 6 and £ 6.5 million. The amount loaned by

[4]The figures presented in the text are very close approximations, but exact figures cannot be determined because of deficiencies (discussed in the next section of this chapter) in loans-board accounting procedures.

[5]This does not include approximately £ 1 million in tiny loans, averaging £ 16, made to peasant farmers between 1956-57 and 1961-62 by Western Nigeria's Local Loans Boards.

[6]This includes £ 183,000 loaned to private enterprise by the Eastern Regional Finance Corporation, a body which was absorbed by the Eastern Nigeria Development Corporation after two years. Not included, however, is a unique, politically motivated and arranged loan of £ 1 million to the Lagos-based African Real Estate and Investment Company, Ltd.

[7]This may include some money for small agricultural loans of the type made by the Local Loans Boards of Western Nigeria.

[8]See footnote 4.

the FLB was £ 445,000 until December 1962; additional loans were issued subsequently, and although exact amounts cannot be determined an estimate of £ 150,000 is reasonable, so that we may say that total FLB loans were approximately £ 600,000.[9]

The number of loans, although not large when judged by the development task confronting Nigeria, was more than large enough to enable a solidly based empirical judgment of the loans programs. For the Northern Nigeria Development Corporation and Western Nigeria Finance Corporation data can be pieced together on the number of operative loans (i.e., loans on the books at the beginning of the fiscal year plus loans made in the course of the year): 2,218 by the NNDC at the end of the 1963-64 fiscal year and 479 by the WNFC at the end of fiscal 1962-63.[10] This understates the number of loans actually issued in these two regions, for operative loans do not include those that had been fully repaid by the beginning of the fiscal year or those wiped off the books as bad debts or for other reasons.[11] The author's rough estimate is that loans actually made numbered 850 in Western Nigeria and 3,300 in Northern Nigeria. In the Eastern Region, 391 loans were issued up to fiscal 1961-62, so that the regional loans boards as a group issued approximately 4,550 loans. The FLB issued fewer but substantially larger loans. The number issued to the end of fiscal 1962-63 was 54.

All of the loans boards experienced a pattern of relatively rapid growth in lending activities followed by curtailment and standstill caused by financial stringency, which was occasioned mainly by loan-repayment difficulties. The funds shortage became crippling as early as 1956-57 in the Eastern Region, by 1961-62 in the Western Region, 1962-63 in the Northern Region, and for the FLB by 1963-64. In some cases the financial pinch was intensified by a few very large loans, especially the Eastern Region loan of £ 1,000,000 in 1959-60 to the African Real Estate and Investment Company, and Western Region loans of £ 120,000 to the Nigerian Fishing Company and £ 350,000 for rubber-raising and -processing to Joseph Asaboro Ltd.

The repayment records of all the loans boards were bad. Leaving a discussion of the reasons until later, let us examine these records. Table 23 shows for each of the RLBs the overdue ratio, i.e., principal overdue as a proportion of the total principal that had come due on all operative

[9]The disparity in magnitude between the FLB program and the regional programs is somewhat exaggerated by the fact that the FLB operated only from 1965 while the regional boards operated from 1949.

[10]Western Region figures exclude the approximately 65,000 Local Loans Board loans mentioned in footnote 5.

[11]The keeping of records on operative loans only is one of the major deficiencies in accounting procedures referred to in footnote 4, and is discussed in the next section of this chapter.

TABLE 23

Overdue Ratios of the Regional Loans Boards
(Percentages)

	WNFC[a]	ENDC[b]	NNDC
1954-55	31.6	n.a.	n.a.
1955-56	42.5	n.a.	1.5[c]
1956-57	53.4	n.a.	4.0
1956-57	53.4	n.a.	4.0
1957-58	52.7	n.a.	20.6
1958-59	57.2	68.4	23.4
1959-60	50.1	73.9	34.5
1960-61	55.2	77.7	28.1
1961-62	63.0	84.2	41.1
1962-63	73.7	87.3	47.9
1963-64	n.a.	n.a.	53.0

SOURCE: Sayre P. Schatz, *Economics, Politics and Administration in Government Lending: The Regional Loans Boards of Nigeria* (Ibadan and London: Oxford University Press, 1970), p. 101.

[a]For the Western Region, the extended overdue ratio is used (see footnote 12). For 1954-55 the data refer to the Western Region Development Board.

[b]It was possible to calculate the ENDC overdue ratios for 1958/59-1962/63 by combining materials from Tables 14 and 15 of the source.

[c]First three months of 1956.

loans.[12] The overdue ratios in all three regions increased dramatically, reaching levels of 87.3 percent in Eastern Nigeria, 53.0 percent in Northern Nigeria, and 73.7 percent in Western Nigeria. Thus, repayment records were bad and were getting steadily worse. This deterioration continued after 1962-63 in consequence of increasingly prevalent and unabashed political manipulation and diminishing economic buoyancy.

The overdue ratio might exaggerate the repayment problem because it encompasses only operative loans,[13] but it was possible to make a very

[12]For the Western Region an extended overdue ratio is used, in that the data include principal overdue of judgment debtors. These are delinquent borrowers against whom court judgments had been secured and who were then dropped from the regular accounts of the WNFC.

[13]Hence the denominator of the overdue ratio fails to include principal that had come due on fully repaid loans. There are, however, factors which tend to offset the exaggeration. Judgment debtors were excluded in the Eastern and Northern Region accounts. Accounts

close estimate of the repayment record on *all* regional loans board loans in
the Western Region, and this sustains the critical appraisal based on the
overdue ratios. Over the entire span of regional board operations in Western Nigeria up to the end of fiscal 1962-63, the ratio of all principal overdue to all principal that had come due on all loans was 55.4 percent. In
other words, borrowers had paid only 44.6 percent of all the principal that
had fallen due up to fiscal 1962-63. And, as already mentioned, the repayment records of the loans boards continued to deteriorate during the
1960s.

The FLB also experienced sizeable and growing repayment problems.
This was made quite clear in interviews with concerned officials, although
repayment accounts are not available. The FLB undertook to tighten up
its repayment collection procedures by instituting (much more readily
than the regional boards) court actions against delinquents and by auction-
ing off property pledged as security on delinquent loans. The FLB, unlike
the regional loans boards, seriously intended to collect repayments on all
its loans and made genuine and substantial efforts to do so.

Problems

The ability of the loans boards to make a significant contribution to
Nigerian economic development was crippled by three sets of problems:
political, administrative, and economic.

Political

The problem of political manipulation was of such overriding importance
in the case of the regional loans boards (but not the FLB) that all other
difficulties fade into relative insignificance. Basically the regional boards
were political instruments. They were used to sustain the party in power
and to reward party supporters. Original intentions of promoting economic development were soon relegated to the background.

Political factors loomed large in the loan-making decisions. The degree
to which they predominated varied, however. At some times and places
prospective viability of the proposed project also played a significant role.
At other times and places loans were made simply as political payoffs;
they were not intended for commercially viable ventures, and repayments
were not really expected. In the loan operations of the NNDC, political
influences originated at the local level. Applicants first had to pass a
preliminary screening by a Provincial Loans Board. This screening was
theoretically a viability and security investigation by local representatives

---

formally written off as bad debts (a rare occurrence) were excluded in all regions. Finally,
overdue interest is not included in the overdue ratios, and its inclusion would have raised the
ratios substantially.

of a technically appropriate ministry, but such representatives were usually incapable of appraising the proposed projects and were in fact seldom called upon. The judgments were generally made by the Native Authority (the local government unit) of the applicant, and political dissidents had little chance. Applications which passed the preliminary screening and reached the NNDC were also handled politically. Irresistible political pressures were brought to bear on civil servants charged with appraising commercial viability and security. Even then, economically based recommendations of civil servants were often disregarded for political reasons. Of the eight lean-period loans[14] made after 1962, six were issued before they were ratified by the proper body (the Loans Committee of the NNDC), and one of the other two was never ratified at all. An official investigation after the coup of January 1966 noted: "All these loans had been granted in an irregular manner, not following the channels laid down, and without proper security. None of the projects had been properly evaluated . . . [and all were] expedited by the Minister of Economic Planning."[15]

The influence of political factors in WNFC loan-making decisions is most clearly seen in the case of a £120,000 loan to the Nigerian Fishing Company. It was the largest approved to that date, and was issued in a period of severe financial stringency. The Nigerian Fishing Company was a partnership owned by two leading Western Nigerian political figures, one of whom was a member of the WNFC governing board and who participated in the meeting at which the loan was approved. It was approved before any real investigation of commercial viability had been carried out, and subsequent investigation was disregarded. The money was then disbursed, contrary to normal procedure, directly to the borrower and without any check or controls on how it was used. The company had been operating only four months when the loan was approved. The Western Region Premier took an active hand, and directed that the loan be made.[16]

Eastern Nigeria Development Corporation (ENDC) loans were also made politically. Ostensible investigations of the loanworthiness of projects were carried out *after* the loans were disbursed. The loan of £1 million to the African Real Estate and Investment Company was the most striking example of political manipulation. It was far and away the largest loan ever made by an Eastern Region loans board; it was three times the

---

[14]Lean period loans are those loans made by the NNDC during the period of financial stringency that began in 1962. They were all made on political grounds and were irregular in virtually every respect. Schatz, *Economics, Politics and Administration*, pp. 51-53; Northern Nigeria, *A White Paper on the Military Government Policy for the Reorganization of the Northern Nigeria Development Corporation* (hereinafter referred to as *NNDC White Paper*), pp. 27-40.

[15]*NNDC White Paper*, pp. 37-38, 40.

[16]Schatz, *Economics, Politics and Administration*, pp. 57-59.

aggregate of all other private loans outstanding at the time. It was made at a time when no funds at all were available to other borrowers, and to a company which operated primarily in Lagos, the Federal capital, rather than in the Eastern Region. The chairman of ENDC was also the chairman of the company which received the loan. The annual reports of the ENDC concealed the fact that the loan was ever made.[17]

Repayment enforcement was politically enfeebled. Government bodies had a generalized reluctance to take actions that antagonized the public, and businessmen in trouble felt bitterly antagonistic toward attempts to force repayments. They felt that it was government's obligation to provide additional assistance in such circumstances and to defer loan repayments or even waive them altogether. There was also selective leniency in dealing with politically influential debtors. They were often exempted from enforcement procedures by political intervention at the highest levels, as in the not unusual instance when the sale of the collateral of a delinquent Western Region stone-crushing firm that had borrowed £ 27,100 was canceled by the Premier himself after a discussion with several leading members of the governing party.[18]

Security procedures were also politically manipulated. Appraisals of property offered as collateral were conveniently flexible. When properties valued for security purposes at £ 1,400, £ 8,000, and £ 4,000 were sold because the debtors had defaulted, the loans board in Western Nigeria was able to realize only £ 230, £ 200, and £ 140 respectively. The lean-period loans of the NNDC, having been investigated after the coup of January 1966, provide the most completely documented examples of political manipulation of security requirements. As the White Paper stated: "Guarantors were accepted without question and few are in a position to honour their guarantees if called upon to do so." All of the lean-period loans were "without proper security" and some were "totally unsecured."[19]

Political factors influenced virtually all other facets of the regional loans programs. Government's limited capacity to provide business advice and assistance was generally made available to politically favored borrowers. For example, the Kano Citizens Trading Company, a small textile factory, received an unusually large loan (about the magnitude of the owners' equity) at a very low rate of interest (3 percent) and with minimal security requirements (only the assets of the firm), subsequently received another large loan, and got a great deal of assistance in setting up the factory, in operating it, in procuring supplies at favorable prices, and through government purchases of the largest part of its output.[20] Borrowers in politi-

---

[17]Schatz, *Economics, Politics and Administration*, pp. 60-61.
[18]Schatz, *Economics, Politics and Administration*, pp. 76-77.
[19]*NNDC White Paper*, pp. 38, 41.
[20]A major reason for favoring the company, however, was simply that it was the first indigenously owned manufacturing enterprise in Northern Nigeria.

cal favor were usually free of misapplication controls designed to prevent expenditure of loan funds for other than the approved purposes. In various minor ways also, the actions of the regional boards were politically slanted.

These political manipulations were facilitated by fortuitous and deliberate practices which concealed information from everyone. Concealment was to some degree an inadvertent byproduct of the loans-board accounting system, which recorded only new loans plus those still on the books at the beginning of the year (i.e., operative loans) and which included no record of loans fully repaid in preceding years, loans written off as bad debts, or delinquent loans on which court judgments had been secured. This system, even aside from numerous errors and omissions in the accounts, made it impossible for even a tenacious investigator to determine the number of loans made or the amounts authorized, disbursed, or repaid, and resulted in serious misconceptions by directly involved officials. Thus, in official testimony before the Coker Commission, the Premier of Western Nigeria (who had once been chairman of the WNFC) and the most recent chairman both overstated amounts overdue *tenfold* (and went uncorrected), and even an official Committee of Enquiry grossly underestimated the total magnitude of NNDC loans disbursed.[21]

A variety of deliberately obfuscatory practices kept outsiders much less informed than insiders. For example, sometimes very large loans, like the £ 1 million loan to the African Real Estate and Investment Company, went unreported. This loan was simply not mentioned in the texts of the ENDC annual reports, and in the 1959-1960 fiscal year, when most of the loan was issued, the report merely announced that no new loans had been approved during the year. The next annual report simply lumped this loan with others under the heading "Other Community Development" in an appendix. The loan could be found under its own name only in the 1962 and 1962-63 reports (not issued until 1965), and even then only in a forbidding appendix listing all ENDC's operative loans.[22]

In a revulsion against political domination and manipulation, the regions subsequently established loans boards that operated nonpolitically, like the Fund for Agricultural and Industrial Development in Eastern Nigeria and the Small Industries Credit Scheme of Northern Nigeria. These will be discussed briefly in the next chapter.

Administrative

An assortment of administrative problems afflicted all the loans boards, Federal as well as regional. The most basic of these was a chronic shortage of staff, particularly of personnel with the needed knowledge and experience. Staff shortages were prevalent not only in the loans boards themselves but also in the cooperating ministries which investigated pro-

[21]Schatz, *Economics, Politics and Administration*, pp. 28-29.
[22]Schatz, *Economics, Politics and Administration*, pp. 22-26.

ject viability and which were responsible for providing advice and assistance to borrowers.

The viability investigations of loan-seeking projects were undertaken by officials lacking the required technical expertise and commercial experience, a problem of which the loans boards were well aware. The verdict in the NNDC White Paper applied equally to all the loans boards: "When considering applications for loans, the Corporation depended too heavily on the advice of commercially unskilled persons and lacked competent staff to carry out investigations and appraisals."[23] Loans boards resorted to interdictive rules of thumb—such as minimal bookkeeping standards for applicants—which excluded some probably worthwhile projects. Personnel versed in property appraisal for security purposes were lacking. Loan-processing delays were sometimes substantial. A one-to-two-year lag between application and receipt of loan was common, and in some cases the delay was more than three years. And once loans were issued, the same personnel shortages that prevented adequate viability investigations also precluded the kind of business advice and assistance to borrowers that had originally been envisaged.

Administrative problems arose out of the difficulties most applicants encountered in meeting security requirements. Adequate collateral was uncommon. Titles to land and buildings offered as collateral were disputed, personal guarantors disavowed their obligations, bills of sale which assigned to the lender titles of specific identifiable items proved to have little value. If legal action was taken against a delinquent debtor, court proceedings were agonizingly slow and uncertain.

There were other administrative problems. The difficulties of administering security and other requirements were intensified by uncertainty and ambivalence in responding to the general national pressure for more rapid indigenous economic development. Despite security deficiencies the loans boards, rather reluctantly, relaxed their security standards. They were loath to exert the necessary effort and vigilance to prevent misapplication of funds[24] and were unable to muster up the combination of toughness and capability required to cope with clever and determined loan defaulters. It has already been pointed out that basic information about loans board activities was inadvertently concealed or obscured by the nature of the accounts, so that policy-makers did not have a clear picture of loans board operations. There were frictions between different parts of the lending apparatus, particularly between the governing boards and the civil service departments responsible for viability appraisal. The Nigerian-manned FLB, for example, felt a greater urgency about the need for rapid development of indigenous business than the foreign staff of the

---

[23]*NNDC White Paper,* p. 41.
[24]Except for the FLB, which compiled a good record in preventing loan misapplication after its first two years.

Industries Division of the Ministry of Commerce and Industries, which was very concerned with doing an expert job of viability appraisal. There were some angry disagreements when the Board approved a few applications which the Industries Division, despite some favorable comments, had adjudged not quite loanworthy. The Minister of Commerce and Industries upheld the Industries Division, and the Board declared that the Minister had been misled by a personally interested foreign official who later went into the same business for which the Nigerian applicant had been rejected.

Administrative problems, however, while far from inconsequential, were of considerably less importance than the political and economic difficulties. By themselves the administrative problems would not have prevented adequate accomplishment of the development objectives of the loans programs.

Economic

Political manipulation so dominated regional loans board activities that it tended to obscure all other problems. The FLB, however, managed to avoid political manipulation, and a study of FLB operations indicates that the fundamental problems confronting the loans boards were economic as well as political.

Nonpolitical behavior by a Nigerian agency having funds or favors to dispense was so unusual that it is necessary to demonstrate to the knowledgeable skeptic that such behavior occurred. The FLB was nonpolitical during the period under study for a unique combination of reasons. It was established during a period of national political coalition at the central government level and all three important parties were equally represented on the Board. Since none could manipulate the Board for its own political advantage, and since it was believed that a loans program for Nigerian businessmen could be an important instrument for promoting indigenous economic development, an agreement was reached to run the FLB nonpolitically. There were subsequent political pressures, but the FLB was able to fend these off because of the political balance of personnel on the Board, the firm insistence on economic criteria by the foreign-staffed Industries Division (which was in a strong position because it possessed very scarce technical skills), the momentum developed as a nonpolitical organization, and the satisfaction felt by the participants with such an operation.

The clearest evidence that loans were made nonpolitically is provided by the concurrence of the political Board with the nonpolitical, predominantly foreign-staffed Industries Division. Of 336 cases considered by the FLB,[25] the Board accepted the recommendations of the Industries

[25]This number represents all the applications considered by the Board from the establish-

Division on 96 percent of the applicants. There was thus little room for political manipulation.[26] Furthermore, in five of the nine cases approved by the Board despite Industries Division disapproval, the Minister of Commerce and Industries backed the Division and disapproved the loans. Thus, only four loans were issued despite Industries Division opposition. Three of these occurred in 1957, so that from 1957 to 1962 only one firm turned down by the Division received a loan. In each of these four cases, moreover, the Division appraisal, though on balance negative, had favorable things to say about the project. Finally, it is striking that there were five applications submitted by firms in which a minister or legislator had an interest, and all were turned down.

The paucity of viable projects has already been discussed in the chapter on Capital. Despite the availability of ample funds throughout most of the period studied, despite efforts to find loanworthy projects, despite efforts to help businessmen work up viable projects, despite the practice of revising applications to salvage any part of a submission that appeared promising, and despite considerable leniency on security requirements for promising projects, the FLB could find few ventures worth advancing funds to. Moreover, despite the fact that the firms which did receive loans constituted a highly select group of already established businesses, and despite the fact that borrowers received special attention and assistance from government, the loan recipients compiled a poor record of success.

A second economic problem was the high cost of the government effort to stimulate development through the loans programs (leaving aside all costs due to corruption and political manipulation or unusual administrative ineptness). This is discussed in the next chapter rather than here, but it must be considered a major economic problem.

Unfortunately, the loans programs, launched with such high hopes by Nigerians and foreign officials alike, were a failure. The political, administrative, and economic problems were overwhelming. The programs were responsible for relatively few successful ventures and large amounts of governmental development funds were drained away. Little was accomplished and at considerable cost.

---

ment of the FLB until August 1961, omitting a few applications which were acted upon at four early meetings for which the records were misplaced.

[26] All evidence indicates that the judgments of the foreign-staffed Industries Division were economically based. This emerges from the correspondence and files of the FLB, to which this writer had unimpeded access. Moreover, in extensive interviews with both Nigerians and foreigners who were involved with FLB operations, there was complete agreement that Industries Division personnel were nonpolitical. (It should be realized, incidentally, that in confidential personal interviews Nigerians were not at all loath to discuss political manipulation and were in fact vociferously and explicitly critical.) There was also agreement that Industries Division decisions were not influenced by simple bribery, and in Nigeria it was virtually impossible for foreign officials to have collected even a few bribes without this becoming widely known.

Chapter 13

ON THE EFFECTIVENESS
OF BUSINESS ASSISTANCE

In this chapter an attempt is made to distill some conclusions about business-assistance programs and about nurture-capitalism, as means of promoting economic development in Nigeria and perhaps in other developing economies as well.

First let us review the setting. We take as given here the economic situation delineated in Part II of the book: a paucity of investment opportunities that Nigerian businessmen could perceive as profitable and undertake successfully, caused partially by entrepreneurial shortcomings and partly by adversities in the economic environment; and an attempt by government to deal with this situation by means of business-assistance programs for private enterprise generally and particularly for indigenous private enterprise.

Even with the help of these programs, however, indigenous business did not fare well and contributed little to Nigeria's economic development. Separate statistics on Nigeria's indigenous private sector do not exist, so this judgment can only be impressionistic. A substantial piece of evidence lies in the paucity of viable projects discussed in Chapter 4, despite the existence of business-assistance programs. In any case, a similar judgment has been made implicitly by Nigeria's economic-policy makers. Disappointment with the performance of the indigenous private sector accounted for the divergence that developed beginning in the late 1950s between the stated and actual economic development orientations (between nationalistic and internationalist nurture-capitalism), involving increasing reliance upon foreign-owned enterprise for the development of the modern private economy. Similar disappointment accounted for the continued post-Civil War reliance on foreign enterprise as the main source of private investment despite the strong nationalistic desires for economic independence. Direct foreign investment comprised over half of all private fixed investment for 1970-74 according to Second Plan projections and a similar pattern was implicit in Third Plan projections for 1975-80.[1] If the Second Plan followed the usual definition,[2] so that in-

---

[1] See above, Chapter 3 under "Economic Development Orientation."
[2] The definition of direct foreign investment is nowhere made clear in the Plan.

vestment by domestically incorporated foreign-owned firms was not in-cluded in "direct foreign investment" then considerably more than half of the projected private fixed investment was by foreign-owned firms and thus the indigenous share was well below half. Moreover, part of indigen-ous investment is in simple agriculture and rural industries, so that the projected role of indigenous business in the modern sector of the economy was clearly a minor one. Disappointment with indigenous business per-formance was manifested in the Second Plan's discussion of "indigenisa-tion of ownership and control"; the Plan spoke not of the growth of Nigerian-owned modern enterprises but of government acquisition and control of foreign-owned enterprises on behalf of Nigerian society.[3] The indigenization of 1974 also reflected the belief that the indigenous business role was expanding inadequately.[4] Finally, the key entrepreneurial or developmental role was envisaged for the foreign entrepreneur. It was the foreign investor who was expected to perceive and, perhaps in partner-ship with Nigerian private investors or government agencies, to act upon new investment opportunities in the modern sector.

In view of the unsatisfactory indigenous business performance despite government help, this chapter inquires into the reasons for the ineffec-tiveness of the business-assistance measures and the nurture-capitalism orientation. There are, we suggest, three main sets of reasons, relating to government capability, the severity of the economic problem, and politi-cal corruption. The concluding section of the chapter deals with a mis-directed policy reaction to these problems.

Government Capability

Government ability to provide business-assistance was limited.

There were shortages of staff with the necessary skills, ability, and experience to carry out the business-assistance functions, for example, an official to supervise and "sell" the Approved Manufacturers Scheme within the government bureaucracy; an Industrial Officer for the Yaba Industrial Estate who could provide useful technical assistance for the tenants; investigators who could carry out competent security and viabil-ity appraisals of loans-board applications; personnel able to do prelimi-nary planning and costing of contracted-out public works to hold down costs and able to supervise subsequent construction to pressure contrac-tors into improving their efficiency and capability.

Problems relating to personnel were intensified by the gulf that often existed between those available for rendering technical and commercial advice and assistance (many of whom continued to be foreigners for a

---

[3]Federal Republic of Nigeria, *Second National Development Plan 1970-74* (Lagos: Fed-eral Ministry of Information, 1970), p. 289.

[4]See above, Chapter 3 under "Reliance on Indigenous Business."

number of years after independence) and the Nigerian businessmen. This gulf diminished with Nigerianization, although problems of communication remained between the relatively highly educated Nigerians in government and the little-educated Nigerians in business.

There were government structural problems. For example, the coverage of the Approved Manufacturers Scheme was inadequate, even at the Federal level alone, because the highly important quasi-governmental corporations were outside the scope of such an internally generated administrative program. Relations between government agencies carrying on allied activities were made difficult by lack of information about government operations. Even personnel *within* a government agency lacked basic data about that agency's operations (as, for example, the complete absence of data on purchases under the Approved Manufacturers Scheme or the tenfold overstatement by those responsible for loans-board operations of the amounts overdue), let alone personnel in agencies administering related programs.

Structural problems were increased exponentially by intense regional rivalries, such as that which prevented Federal-Regional government cooperation in a truly national Approved Manufacturers Scheme. Regionalism has been widely discussed in the literature on Nigeria and will not be examined further here. Suffice it to say that Nigerian regional rivalries impeded a unified attack on virtually any economic problem.[5]

[5]An interesting and never-reported example of regionalism emerged from a comparison of the unpublished and the official versions of a prestigious international consultant's large-scale study of Northern Nigeria's industrial potentialities. The study stated that expected increases in demand for fertilizer would require a fertilizer industry in Nigeria within a decade. In context, the consultant appeared to be recommending this for Northern Nigeria in the official report. This version, however, excised the two final sentences of the unpublished report's discussion of fertilizers: "It is possible that the consumption of nitrogen for tree crops in the Eastern and Western Regions would increase at a faster rate than in the North. If this were so, it would again appear to be more advantageous to locate a factory in the Eastern or Western Regions and utilise the available natural gas or the waste gas from the petroleum industry." Industrial and Process Engineering Consultants (Great Britain) and Sir Alexander Gibb and Partners, *Industrial and Economic Survey of Northern Nigeria* (London: 1963), p. 180. The official version was: Northern Nigeria, Ministry of Trade and Industry, *The Industrial Potentialities of Northern Nigeria* (no publication data, 1963 (?)) and the excised sentences would have appeared on p. 183.

On the oil-expelling industry, the following paragraph is omitted from the official report, where it would be on p. 90. This, plus the change of an unfavorable "will not" in the unpublished report (p. 79) to "may not" in the official report (p. 90), changes the tenor of the feasibility report from unfavorable to uncertain.

"There are thus many adverse factors which may affect the oil expelling industry and necessitate continued Government support in the form of duty remission to allow the millers a reasonable margin of profit. Rather than embark on an immediate programme expansion the Government should rather only allow increases in capacity once they have reviewed the crushing quota and ensured that the loss of export duties incurred is more than offset by the benefits derived from the local industry. However, we must point out that the installation of efficient up-to-date machinery and increased factory outputs should result in lower operating costs. The Government must therefore ensure that the local industry is given every incentive to operate at the maximum possible efficiency." *Survey*, p. 79.

The Economic Problem

Administrative capability was not the only or even the major problem. Even if government in Nigeria had been as competent as, say, a representative developed-economy government, the severity of the economic problem to be dealt with by the business-assistance programs was forbidding. The combination of entrepreneurial deficiencies and economic-environment adversities was so potent that an inordinate amount of business assistance would have been needed to generate substantial momentum in the indigenous private sphere. The entrepreneurial-environmental symphysis was rendered more unmanageable for government offices by related economic factors—like the poor quality of business accounts, records, and other sources of information which made it difficult for government agencies to make judgments about the firms and their prospects and to make wise selections of the firms best suited for government assistance, and the intense nationalistic pressures for unreasonable amounts and kinds of assistance for at least some firms regardless of their merits.

The intractability of the economic problem is best shown by a study the writer has made of business-assistance costs, specifically of the costs of loans board operations.[6] The estimate requires detailed explanation, even at the penalty of being tedious, for the data are far from exact and the final figures are startlingly high. We are interested in the costs that remain after eliminating those due to corruption and political manipulation, e.g., bad-debt losses on politically inspired loans.[7] To facilitate exposition, we call applications based on business rather than political considerations "legitimate applications," and loans made on the basis of a conscientious assessment of prospective commercial viability rather than on political grounds "legitimate loans." Costs after eliminating those due to political manipulation (and undue administrative ineptness) are called "legitimate costs." In these terms, the figure we seek is total legitimate costs per successful loan (i.e., per loan that resulted in a commercially successful operation).[8] The estimate is based on complementary data on Nigeria's

[6]See Sayre P. Schatz, *Economics, Politics and Administration in Government Lending: The Regional Loans Boards of Nigeria* (Ibadan and London: Oxford University Press, 1970), pp. 111-118. See also, Sayre P. Schatz, "The High Cost of Aiding Business in Developing Economies: Nigeria's Loans Programmes," *Oxford Economic Papers* 20:3 (November 1968): 428-432.

[7]The estimate is based on the level of administrative competence prevailing in the mid 1960s, so that it also eliminates costs due to the administrative ineptness of the early years or to gross administrative blunders. Moreover, we are excluding small loans for corn mills, rice mills, and other such simple ventures that process locally grown foodstuffs for consumption in the immediate vicinity. These relatively routine small loans constituted virtually a separate subprogram of the Loans Boards.

[8]Total legitimate costs per successful loan equal

$$\frac{LC_s + LC_u + LC_r}{SL}$$

Federal Loans Board and Regional Loans Boards. It was possible to develop certain basic cost data for the regional loans boards. Political, administrative, and economic effects are inextricably intertwined in these data, however, so the best way to make estimates regarding legitimate applications, loans, and costs was to combine regional data, in a manner that will be explained below, with data on the nonpolitical and reasonably competent operations of the Federal Loans Board.

First, we determined senior staff[9] time devoted to processing loan applications. We divided the lending process into its component tasks and discussed in detail the time required for each with the officials who were directly engaged in those operations. We were, almost without exception, able to check on the accuracy of the estimates by questioning more than one official in each region. We found that, from submission to verdict, an average of forty-seven senior staff working hours was required for processing legitimate applications that resulted in loans.

To find the total working time per loan, it was necessary to include time spent on applications that were finally rejected. First, we determined the proportion of legitimate applications that was rejected by turning to Federal Loans Board experience.[10] Approximately 80 percent of the bids that went through this Board's entire appraisal process were rejected, and we assume that the same ratio holds for legitimate applications to the regional loans boards.[11] Given this figure, it was necessary to estimate, second, the time spent per rejected request. These usually required less staff time than successful ones because the staff would often detect unworthy projects fairly quickly. This was partially offset by the fact that doubtful loan proposals were not infrequently returned by the board for modification, and many of these went through the appraisal process two or more times and were nevertheless finally rejected. More important, a great many bids were dropped by the applicants before they came to a final vote, when talks with officials made it clear that the projects had no chance for approval; these requests did not enter into the 80 percent rejection ratio although the staff time spent on them was sometimes substantial. Balanc-

---

where
LC_s = legitimate costs incurred on successful legitimate loans
LC_u = legitimate costs incurred on unsuccessful legitimate loans
LC_r = legitimate costs incurred on rejected legitimate applications
SL   = number of successful loans

[9]In accord with common usage in the Nigerian Civil Service, senior staff encompassed all civil servants earning a basic salary (in 1964-65) of at least £ 621.

[10]There was no direct way of determining this proportion for the regional loans boards. No figures existed on the number of applications rejected, nor was there any way of making a reasonable estimate of the proportion of applications that were legitimate.

[11]Federal Loans Board rejections actually amounted to 82 percent by one method of calculation and 89 percent by another. The 80 percent rejection figure adopted in the text therefore yields a conservative estimate of costs. Use of the 89 percent figure would have greatly increased the estimate of senior staff time spent on rejected applications.

ing these considerations, we estimated that time spent per rejected application was half that spent per approved request. Rejections outnumbered
approvals four to one, so that rejected applications required in the aggregate twice as many man-hours. Altogether, then, 141 processing hours
were devoted to legitimate applications for each loan made.

Moving on to the time spent per successful loan requires an estimate of
the proportion of loan-assisted projects that prospered. The Federal
Loans Board record[12] shows that, two to six years after receiving their
loans, 38 percent of the evaluated borrowers were functioning successfully, 41 percent had been unsuccessful, and 21 percent were in a shaky
state. The mortality rate of Nigerian enterprises suggests that most of the
shaky projects and a significant number of those operating successfully at
the time the study was done would fail in the course of a few more years.
A one-to-three success ratio on legitimate loans is therefore not an un-
generous estimate. On this basis, the processing cost per successful loan
was three times the cost per loan made, i.e., 423 hours. In money terms
this amounted to £ 404.[13]

Once a loan was approved, the loans boards incurred several other
administrative expenses, the largest of which was the cost of collecting
repayments. This was frequently a tortuous and protracted process, and
the loans boards devoted themselves largely to this task for substantial
periods of time. On the basis of fragmentary data[14] we estimated that
collection costs per legitimate loan were £ 124. Since only one-third of
the projects succeeded, the legitimate collection costs per successful loan
came to £ 372.

Administering the loans programs entailed other costs: procedures to
prevent borrowers from spending for purposes other than those authorized by the loan agreements, commercial and technical assistance to
borrowers, the large volume of work done by junior staff (typists, clerks,
messengers, etc.), and general overhead costs. A rough but conservative
estimate is that, for each loan made, these together amounted to one-half
of the senior staff costs of investigating the project, i.e., £ 22. This
amounts to £ 66 per successful project, so that total legitimate administrative costs per successful loan added up to £ 842.

Finally, the most substantial cost of all arose from bad debts. Since
such losses were heightened for the regional loans boards by political
manipulation and administrative ineptness, we turn again to the Federal
Loans Boards record to estimate the bad-debt costs of legitimate loans.

---

[12]The regional loans board record, greatly damaged by politically inspired loans, would
make for an unduly high cost estimate.
[13]Based on a study of the emoluments of Nigerian senior civil servants by S. O. Adamu of
the Nigerian Institute of Social and Economic Research.
[14]We could get partial data for Eastern Nigeria only and could make only a rough separa-
tion of legitimate collection costs from those incurred on politically inspired loans.

Debt collection has been notoriously poor for the unsuccessful two-thirds of the borrowers. We make the quite conservative estimate that one-third of the principal advanced to the unsuccessful legitimate borrowers will never be recovered (and that all of the money loaned to the successful borrowers will be repaid) so that altogether 22 percent of the money loaned will never be collected.[15] Since only one-third of the loans went to successful projects, the bad-debt cost per successful loan averages 66 percent of the magnitude of the loan.[16] For example, two of a typical trio of £ 1,000 loans would be unsuccessful, the principal lost would average £ 333 on each; thus the total bad-debt loss would be two-thirds of the £ 1,000 loan that was successful. In the aggregate, then, the net cost to government of each successful legitimate loan was £ 842 plus two-thirds of the value of the loan, i.e.,

$$\text{Cost} = £\ 842 + 2/3L,$$

where L represents the value of the loan.

These costs are extremely high. After all repayments, the average legitimate cost[17] per successful loan (i.e., per loan that financed a successful project) considerably exceeded the size of the loan.[18] The loans program therefore involved an enormous subsidy to indigenous business. These high costs, after eliminating the costs of political corruption and gross administrative ineptness, are an index of the severity of the economic problem caused by the entrepreneurial-environmental symphysis. This severity constitutes a major cause of the inability of indigenous business, even with assistance, to generate significant development momentum.

Political Corruption

This section deals with the impact of political corruption on indigenous private development. It makes the assessment that the effect was to heighten the difficulty of generating development momentum in the indig-

[15]This amounts to half of the money actually unrecovered by the regional loans boards during the years for which it was possible to calculate repayment ratios. Sayre P. Schatz, *Economics, Politics and Administration,* ch. 6.

[16]The assumption is implicitly made here that the size distributions of successful loans and of unsuccessful loans were approximately the same, i.e., that the proportion of success was not different for large or small loans. This accords with the Federal Loans Board experience; no relation was found between the size of the loans and their success. Sayre P. Schatz, *Development Bank Lending in Nigeria: The Federal Loans Board* (Ibadan and London: Oxford University Press, 1967), p. 94.

[17]Loans board interest receipts were not taken into account in this calculation of net cost. Such receipts were more than offset, however, by the implicit interest costs of the funds devoted to the loans program.

[18]The median Nigerian loans board loan was certainly below £ 2,000, even after excluding the small food-processing loans. Because of the exclusion, no more exact calculation of the median size of the loans we are dealing with is feasible.

enous private sector. Of course, the discussion must be less than conclusive, for we are dealing with matters that are impossible to measure, and one can only offer his best judgment.

Costs   One effect of political corruption in business-assistance programs (as well as in other government operations) was to increase the cost of carrying out these operations, thereby wasting scarce resources badly needed for many purposes. Costs tend to be increased in several ways.

We have seen that government revenues were transferred to party treasuries and to corrupt private pockets by excessive payments on construction and purchase contracts, by defaulted loans, and by other means. Such transactions, which we will call "illicit government transfer payments,"[19] clearly increased the costs of government operations.

These illicit transfers emerged not only in construction and purchase contracts and in loans, but in all kinds of government transactions. The government was bilked in tax assessments,[20] in the hiring of vehicles,[21] in the sale of taxi permits at unduly low prices,[22] in the allocation of government land,[23] in the allocation of market stalls at prices that made permits a source of windfall gain for the recipients,[24] in excessive hiring and overpayment of those hired as a form of political patronage,[25] in employment of unnecessary outside legal counsel,[26] and in many other ways.

[19]As distinguished from what may be called "illicit private transfer payments," i.e., illicit income extracted from the private sector, mainly in the form of bribes from businessmen trying to get government to take a particular action. Sayre P. Schatz, "Economic Effects of Corruption," Unpublished paper presented to African Studies Association, October 1969.

[20]"The City treasurer . . . devised a procedure for which there is no provision in the Assessment Act, whereby the annual value of properties might be reduced for rating [taxing] purposes whenever they are unoccupied, and that in his capacity as the appraiser, applied that procedure to reduce the annual rateable value of his house alone; . . . [he also] stretched the possible interpretation of the . . . [laws] beyond reasonable limits when he progressively reduced the annual rateable value of the Mainland Hotel and waived certain payments of rates and interests owed by its proprietors . . ." Nigeria, Federation, *Comments of the Federal Military Government on the Report of the Tribunal of Inquiry into the Affairs of the Lagos City Council, 1966* (Lagos: Federal Ministry of Information, 1966), p. 8.

[21]Nigeria, Federation, *Comments of the Military Government on Lagos, 1966*, p. 6.

[22]Rather than favoring owner-drivers, the City Treasurer "has made the operation of taxis the exclusive preserve of the already rich or otherwise gainfully employed. This has led to an unsavoury traffic in the sale of hackney permits or the hire of hackney permits for extravagant sums." Nigeria, Federation, *Comments of the Military Government on Lagos, 1966*, p. 16.

[23]Nigeria, Federation, *Comments of the Military Government on Lagos, 1966*, p. 18.

[24]Nigeria, Federation, *Comments of the Military Government on Lagos, 1966*, p. 18, and Nigeria, Eastern Region, *Perkins Report of the Inquiry into the Administration of the Affairs of the Enugu Municipal Council, 1960* (Enugu: Government Printer, 1960), ch. 3.

[25]Nigeria, Eastern Region, *Perkins Report*, ch. 3.

[26]"The Town Clerk was wasting public funds on the employment of outside solicitors when he could have made use of the Council's own not inconsiderable staff and was thereby helping his friend." Nigeria, Federation, *Comments of the Military Government on Lagos, 1966*, p. 11.

When government funds are clandestinely tapped, there are frequently substantial expenses of corruption. The concept's meaning can be elucidated by considering an example, say the purchase by government of unnecessary supplies (e.g., "the excessive purchase of mosaic tiles of which £ 1,448 worth are lying in the Corporation's stores"[27]) at a price that is inflated so as to provide a margin for illicit government transfer payments. We can break the government expenditure down into three components. First, the uninflated market value of the supplies needed by the government constitutes a necessary government expense. Second, the illicit income kicked back to the manipulating government official (for his own or party purposes) and possibly shared in also by the colluding seller constitutes an illicit government transfer payment. Beyond these, there is the cost of the redundant supplies. This cost does not become anyone's illicit income. It constitutes simply a waste incurred in the process of making illicit government transfers. Expenses of corruption are the socially wasteful costs of establishing and operating the instruments through which illicit government transfer payments are made—costs that would not otherwise have been incurred.

These expenses took many forms. Bad projects were started, such as the already mentioned Sokoto cement plant that was clearly commercially unviable. The establishment of notoriously bad "turnkey" projects[28] and other direct investments, carried out in collusion with dishonest equipment sellers, providers of suppliers' credits and contractor finance, and purveyors of phony feasibility studies, constitutes part of a widespread pattern which this writer has called "crude private neo-imperialism."[29] In many of these projects the illicit government transfer payments are dwarfed by the wasteful expenses of corruption. If, for example, a project is so bad that it terminates operations entirely, then all or virtually all of the costs of the equipment and structures and the other costs of establishing the enterprise, aside from the illicit government transfers, would be expenses of corruption. An expense of corruption also arose when governmental construction contracts were subdivided, so that the amounts fell into the more easily manipulated petty-contract category. Actual construction costs were increased because of this piecemeal way of carrying out the jobs. Similarly, political selection of incompetent contractors re-

[27]Federal Republic of Nigeria, *Comments of the Federal Military Government on the Report of the Tribunal of Inquiry into the Affairs of the Nigerian Railway Corporation for the Period 1st October, 1960 to 31st December, 1965* (Lagos: Federal Ministry of Information, 1968), p. 5.

[28]"A 'turnkey' project or factory is one in which the seller undertakes to have the factory built and provides management so that the factory is ready to come into operation at the turn of a key." Peter Kilby, *Industrialization in an Open Economy: Nigeria 1945-1966* (Cambridge: Cambridge University Press, 1969), p. 78.

[29]Sayre P. Schatz, "Crude Private Neo-Imperialism: A New Pattern in Africa," *Journal of Modern African Studies* 7:4 (December 1969).

sulted in "incompetence, waste and above all high building costs."[30] Another example of expenses of corruption: There were costly delays in authorizing essential work (e.g., port facilities at Port Harcourt[31]) because of considerations related to political manipulation. Finally, elaborate government apparatus was established and operated at considerable cost in order to "widen the scope for political patronage."[32] The main objective in setting up the regional marketing boards that replaced Nigeria's country-wide single-commodity boards in 1954 was to wrest control from British colonial officials who continued to dominate Nigeria's central but not its regional governments after 1954.[33] Control by Nigerian political leaders enabled them, inter alia, to make use of the vast marketing board funds for disbursement of illicit government transfer payments.

There were many other forms of expenses of corruption. Whenever they occurred, the sum transferred to the clandestine recipient as income was only part of the amount extracted *from* the government.

Costs were also increased by political abuse which resulted in shoddy work for the government and thereby reduced the value of the product that the government got for its money. For example, a confidential investigation of the Western Region Housing Corporation in 1962 found that a politically favored contractor had not carried out his building work adequately but was intransigent when the Housing Corporation staff made suggestions or complaints. Because of the contractor's high-level political connections, the staff was most reluctant to insist that the contractor fulfill his obligations.[34] As a result the houses constructed by this contractor were worth considerably less than the amounts paid for them.

Allocation of development expenditures   Political manipulation affects the composition as well as the costs of governmental development ac-

[30]G. Akin Ogunpola, "The Pattern of Organization in the Building Industry: A Western Nigeria Case Study," *Nigerian Journal of Economic and Social Studies* X:3 (November 1968): 349.

[31]Federal Republic of Nigeria, *Report of the Tribunal of Enquiry into the Affairs of the Nigerian Ports Authority for the Period October 1, 1960 to December 31, 1965* (Lagos: Federal Ministry of Information, 1967), pp. 63, 212; Federal Republic of Nigeria, *Comments of the Federal Military Government on the Report of the Tribunal of Enquiry into the Affairs of the Nigerian Ports Authority* (Lagos: Federal Ministry of Information, 1968), p. 14.

[32]A. L. Adu, *The Civil Service in the New African States* (London: Allen and Unwin, 1965), p. 213.

[33]H. A. Oluwasanmi, "Agriculture in a Developing Economy: A Study in Nigerian Economic Development," Prepublication manuscript, p. 338.

[34]See also Federal Republic of Nigeria, *Comments of the Federal Military Government on the Nigerian Ports Authority Inquiry,* p. 8: ". . . some contractors failed to observe certain aspects of the Contract agreements entered into with the Authority, yet there is no evidence to show that the Authority took any action against these defaulting contractors . . ." The point made here about lack of will to enforce contract provisions is distinct from the point in the preceding section about the limited supervisory capacity of the Ministries of Works.

tivities.[35] Projects are favored that entail good opportunities for payoffs. Projects are favored also which benefit powerful men (e.g., the already mentioned substantial transportation network serving the Finance Minister's shoe factory). Even attempts to *avoid* political corruption may affect the composition of expenditures by causing government to shun worthwhile programs that are prone to political abuse; many business-assistance programs are of this nature because they require discretion in the choice of worthy recipients. Furthermore, to the extent that corruption weakens government's administrative competence (see the next section), government leaders have reason to continue activities that are easy, familiar, and routine, even though they may be ineffective.[36]

Direct impact on program efficacy   Political corruption directly impaired the efficacy of programs to assist indigenous business in several ways:

First, by increasing costs in the ways just discussed and thereby reducing the effective amount available for business-assistance programs, political manipulation restricted their scope and vigor.

Second, the thrust of the business-assistance programs was deflected from the development objective toward political entrenchment and personal enrichment. Procedures for awarding loans, construction contracts, and government-purchase contracts were manipulated to favor political supporters or colluding businessmen, and these were not always the entrepreneurs most likely to further the country's economic development.

Third, government's "executive capacity," i.e., its ability to get things done, and particularly to carry out its business-assistance programs, was impaired. There appears to be general agreement, even among the more iconoclastic writers on the subject, that corruption weakens administrative competence. This may occur in a number of ways. Corruption may engender a leakage of administrative and political effort at all levels into self-seeking activities.[37] Widespread corruption may also induce some of the best civil servants to leave the country for assignments in international organizations.[38] Among the administrators who remain, corruption causes apathy. The incentive to administer business-assistance and other programs carefully is diminished when considerations relating to bribery, payoff, and political expediency override the painstaking work of the conscientious civil servants. "Where money or wirepulling decides promotion, and patient merit is denied advancement, trains really do not run to time, contracts do go to the wrong contractor, research produces

[35]See the latter part of the section titled "Political Problems" of Chapter 9 on Construction.

[36]J. S. Nye, "Corruption and Political Development: A Cost Benefit Analysis," *American Political Science Review* LXI:2 (June 1967): 423. See also the statement by M. McMullan, "A Theory of Corruption," *The Sociological Review* (July 1961): 183, that corrupt administration "restricts the range of policies available to a government."

[37]See, e.g., Nye's "waste of skills," p. 422.

[38]The writer has information that this was true of some Ghanaian and Nigerian civil servants in the 1960s. See also Nye, p. 423.

no discoveries, plans are not fulfilled. Teamwork, loyalty to the job disintegrate."[39] Feelings of accomplishment are vitiated and administrative proficiency declines.[40] Even insubordination is encouraged.[41] Honest officials sometimes shun personal responsibility because they fear that their decisions will be branded as corrupt. This gives rise to decision-making by a cumbersome, slow process of reference and conference, with everyone sharing the responsibility.[42] Government effectiveness may be further impaired because "authority cannot be efficiently delegated unless those in administrative positions are incorrupt."[43] Furthermore, careful scrutiny of programs that are not working well is inhibited. Aside from possible resistance by venal politicians, there is a strong tendency to attribute all shortcomings to corruption and it thereby becomes difficult to discern other problems. Thus, this writer found it almost impossible to convince Nigerians that the problems of the Federal Loans Board were not political. The glare of corruption was so bright that even sophisticated people were blinded to other problems.

The Exercise of Entrepreneurship   Political corruption in programs affecting business also affected the exercise of entrepreneurship. On the one hand, corruption may have had a stimulating effect by softening the restrictive impact of the nationalist and regionalist tendency to exclude foreign or minority groups that had been disproportionately successful in business. In Nigeria's footwear industry, for example, "a large percentage of minority-group manufacturing entrepreneurs encounter pressures to leave the area," partly because of "the power of economic restriction and discrimination by local authorities."[44] Bribery may have made it

---

[39]*The Economist* (London), June 15, 1957, p. 959. The article also makes the interesting point that "whatever appearances may suggest, graft beyond a certain point really does become incompatible with efficiency. . . . The thing that sometimes disguises this in some territories is that the new and restless desire of the middle classes for money-making, which is one of the main reasons for graft, is also often in itself the main motive force behind the sudden growth of economic enterprise."

[40]Schatz, *Economics, Politics and Administration,* pp. 123-126.

[41]For example, the Eastern Nigerian Minister of Commerce had a letter sent to the Chairman of the Tourist Corporation of the Region chastising him for drawing excessive personal allowances and for related abuses, and setting down guidelines that curtailed his opportunities to draw allowances in the future. The Chairman replied: ". . . please inform the hon. the Minister of Commerce that the content of the letter is ill-conceived and malicious. . . . The Chairman of the Corporation is a part-time Chairman, and the only one at that in the Eastern Region. His salary is £600 as against £1,500 and over of chairmen of other Corporations in the same Eastern Region. . . . I think you will cease to exhibit this rude example of official pettiness any more where I am concerned, otherwise I shall be forced to make very grave expositions of discrimination and nepotism in the Administration." Nigeria, Eastern Region, *Eastern House of Assembly Debates,* April 11, 1958, pp. 505-507.

[42]Gunnar Myrdal, *Asian Drama* (New York: Twentieth Century Fund, 1968), pp. 953-954.

[43]Myrdal, p. 954.

[44]E. Wayne Nafziger, *Nigerian Entrepreneurship: A Study of Indigenous Businessmen in*

possible for such minority groups to function despite the antagonistic atmosphere. It is not clear, however, to what degree bribes were actually effective in holding off minority-businessman restrictions (which are always somewhat restrained by basic economic considerations) and to what degree bribes were merely levies that some politicians could easily collect.

It is also possible that bribery may have been a lubricant that enabled some entrepreneurs to devote themselves more fully to running their business rather than contending with government bureaucracy. It may have induced officials to cut through red tape and expedite actions that would otherwise have been impeded or prevented by heavy-handed government procedures.[45]

On the other hand, the exercise of entrepreneurship may have been hindered. Some potential businessmen may have been discouraged by political favoritism or by a need for bribes. A survey of small Western Nigerian businessmen showed that almost half of those who knew enough about business-assistance programs to comment complained about favoritism or the need for bribery.[46] It may have been hyperbole, but Nigerian businessmen certainly insisted angrily that these problems drove or kept many people out of business.

Moreover, while bribery may expedite the individual case, other things being equal, the aggregate effect may be to *multiply* impediments to entrepreneurship through deliberate obstruction. Myrdal asserts that the expediting notion "is palpably wrong." He quotes an Indian Government report on corruption: "We have no doubt that quite often delay is deliberately contrived so as to obtain some kind of illicit gratification." The report states that the practice of paying "speed money" *induces* the delays that require the impatient businessmen to pay the expediting bribe: "this custom of speed money has become one of the most serious causes of delay and inefficiency."[47] Furthermore, the prevalence of bribery for

---

the Footwear Industry, University of Illinois Ph.D. dissertation, 1967, Urbana, Illinois, p. 144.

[45]This is the beneficial effect of corruption most frequently referred to in the literature. For example, Colin Leys, "What Is the Problem About Corruption?" *Journal of Modern African Studies* 3:3 (October 1965): 223: "Where bureaucracy is both elaborate and inefficient, the provision of strong personal incentives to bureaucrats to cut red tape may be the only way of speeding the establishment of the new firm."

[46]Sayre P. Schatz and S. I. Edokpayi, "Economic Attitudes of Nigerian Businessmen," *Nigerian Journal of Economic and Social Studies* IV:3 (November 1962): 4. See also Professor Aluko's description of the "almost unanimous resentment of government policy expressed by many Nigerian entrepreneurs" because "governments have not given enough technical assistance even when they could." S. A. Aluko, "The Educated in Business: The Calabar Home Farm—A Case Study," *Nigerian Journal of Economic and Social Studies* VIII:2 (July 1966): 201. The point in the text conflicts with one made by Joseph Nye about the effect of bribery in humanizing government for the small man: Nye, p. 420.

[47]Gunnar Myrdal, pp. 952-953, referring to Government of India, Ministry of Home Affairs, *Report of the Committee on Prevention of Corruption* (New Delhi: 1964). Margery

cutting red tape provides a strong incentive to politicians and officials to proliferate the discretionary controls that nurture deliberate, bribe-seeking delays.[48]

The prevalence of corruption may also divert entrepreneurial energies from assiduous pursuit of excellence in economic performance as the key to success into political performance and cultivation of the contacts required for surreptitious dealings. The effort required may be considerable: "the amount of human time and energy devoted to [cultivating special contacts and developing "pull"] is immense. . . . The loss in productive effort defies estimation."[49]

To recapitulate, we have said that political corruption tended to increase the costs of business-assistance programs, to alter the allocation of development expenditures in ways which are inimical to such programs, to impair directly the efficacy of these programs, and to weaken the exercise of entrepreneurship. It therefore undermined the effort to cope with the entrepreneurial-environmental symphysis by means of business-assistance programs.

Naive Policy Optimism

Limited government capability, the severity of the entrepreneurial-environmental symphysis, and the prevalence of political corruption were all weighty problems for an economic-development orientation relying heavily on government-assisted indigenous enterprise. Nevertheless, Nigerian policy-makers often tended to attack the task of developing indigenous business with what may be called naive policy optimism. This is the persistence of a bland optimism regarding the efficacy of a program without due regard for the problems and shortcomings revealed by experience or even for past failures.

Accepting the understandably strong desire for development as given, we can say that naive policy optimism arises from misapprehension. Its basis may be simple ignorance of past efforts.[50] A more important cause has been a tendency to attribute virtually all of the shortcomings of previous programs to political corruption or to relatively simple mistakes, and to believe therefore that the problems can be avoided by reform that ousts the rascals and/or by diligence and common sense. If this book so far has

---

Perham observes, "a little corruption may oil the joints of a stiff new machine but too much of it clogs the works": *The Colonial Reckoning* (London: Collins, 1963), p. 49.

[48]Myrdal, pp. 950-951.

[49]David H. Bayley, "The Effect of Corruption in a Developing Nation," *Western Political Quarterly* XIX:4 (December 1966): 726.

[50]See, for example, Gerald Faust's 1969 assertion, in proposing business-assistance programs, that there had been "A complete absence of government policies and incentives" for promoting small-scale industry in Nigeria.

shown anything, however, it is that there are intractable problems aside from those caused by political manipulation.

The phenomenon of naive policy optimism can best be elucidated by illustration. Consider the establishment of the Fund for Agricultural and Industrial Development (FAID) in Eastern Nigeria in 1963. It was set up in the optimistic belief that careful procedures and staffing and insulation from political pressures were all that were needed to make a small-business loans program a substantial contributor to economic development.[51] It represented a serious effort to operate a credit scheme effectively. It was run nonpolitically, as far as this writer could ascertain, and its organization and procedures were carefully thought out. Nevertheless, it seems clear that FAID was heading for serious trouble, although the Civil War disruption prevents any unequivocal appraisal.

The optimism that prompted FAID's establishment also caused approval of an overlarge proportion of the loan applicants. Approximately half of those who submitted the first detailed application form were approved despite the fact that, according to FAID officials, the applications (including those approved) were frequently vague and poorly thought out. This was an approval rate three times that of the Federal Loans Board, and it will be recalled that even with that greater selectivity and with government assistance only about one-third of the FLB borrowers functioned successfully. There is every reason to believe that FAID was disbursing a large proportion of its funds to projects that would not succeed and would not generate loan repayments and that the organization would soon have run out of money.

The establishment of the Small Industries Credit Scheme (SIC), which was a Northern Nigerian counterpart of FAID, was also a manifestation of naive policy optimism, but in this instance let us focus on the appraisal of that program by the foreign adviser rather than the operation itself.[52] It was Faust's thesis that "S.I.C. has proved that supervised credit can work. . . ." Stated more fully: "The experience of S.I.C. has shown that supervised credit for the small-scale entrepreneur can work but only with adequate technical and managerial assistance and favourable government policies and incentives."[53]

This was a clear case of naive policy optimism. For one thing, it was based on ignorance of past business-assistance efforts in Nigeria (see footnote 50 in this chapter). For another, the writer largely ignored the substantial costs of the comprehensive business-assistance programs

[51]FAID is described in detail in Schatz, *Economics, Politics and Administration,* pp. 131-141.

[52]See Gerald Faust, "Small Industries Credit Scheme in Northern Nigeria: An Analysis of Operational and Lending Patterns," *Nigerian Journal of Economic and Social Studies* XI:2 (July 1969), for a description of SIC.

[53]Faust, pp. 226, 205-206.

which he believed essential to the credit scheme[54] as well as the costs of the credit program itself.[55]

Finally, Faust's estimate of the success of SIC loans is highly dubious. Of 69 loan-supported ventures, Faust finds that 19 (28 percent) were unsuccessful and 13 (19 percent) were write-offs.[56] He considers the remaining 37 (53 percent) successful. However, loan repayments by 40 (60 percent) of the ventures were already delinquent at the time Faust wrote.[57] This means that a number of the firms that Faust considered successful were delinquent.[58] Furthermore, a number of other firms had not yet had a chance to become delinquent because no repayments had fallen due; grace periods before the initial loan repayment was required ranged from three months to two years.[59] Most important, some other firms judged successful at first would surely turn out to be unsuccessful. In all, Faust's sanguine appraisal appears to be based less on evidence than on optimism about the program to which he devoted himself.[60]

There were also many instances of naive policy optimism relating to other business-assistance measures in the pre-Civil War period. For example, despite the poor performance of the Yaba Industrial Estate, plans were going ahead for similar ventures elsewhere in Nigeria. Thus, Eastern Nigeria had an elaborate six-year plan (1965-1971) for the establishment of twenty-five industrial estates, many of them fully packaged.[61]

[54]He proposed government purchasing which favored small entrepreneurs, some unspecified means of control over the prices charged by foreign-owned suppliers, special income, customs, and excise tax privileges for small-scale industry, technical assistance, and managerial assistance, as well as financial assistance in the form of loans. Faust, pp. 205, 212-213.

[55]Moreover, loans programs are in themselves costly; see earlier in this chapter. In SIC costs were reduced by heavy reliance on Ford Foundation advisors and Peace Corps volunteers. Even so, SIC found "loan supervision difficult and extremely expensive." Moreover, increased salaries were needed to attract and retain well qualified Nigerians. Faust, pp. 207, 210.

[56]Unsuccessful projects are described as those "from which full repayment is expected although they have not performed as well as possible. They are not complete failures." Write-offs are described as "those loans from which losses are expected." Faust, p. 217.

[57]The article was apparently written in April 1969 and the formulation of the basic thesis undoubtedly occurred earlier. Most of the loans were probably less than two years old and many less than one year old when the thesis was developed.

[58]A minimum of eight. But if, on the basis of Faust's expectation of full repayment from the unsuccessful projects, we assume, say, one-third of the unsuccessful firms are not delinquent, the figure would be 16; that would be 23 percent of the ventures in addition to the 47 percent Faust labeled unsuccessful or write-offs. It should be pointed out, however, that Faust does not consider delinquency a serious matter. Faust, p. 218.

[59]Faust, p. 212.

[60]This interpretation is supported by formulations used throughout Faust's article, for example: ". . . it is very possible that S.I.C. would soon have become self-supporting; that is *assuming that mistakes would not have been repeated*" (p. 209; my emphasis); "As a result of experience gained . . . perhaps most failures would be successes" (p. 213); "A more rational approach" would have produced valuable results (p. 210); and "Considerably more capital could have been mobilized" if the right things had been done (p. 216).

[61]Those responsible for business-assistance policies in other African countries were quite

And naive policy optimism continued into the 1970s unabated. The Second and Third Plans optimistically embraced again a large constellation of credit schemes and many other previously tried business assistance programs without any discernible investigation of the unsatisfactory payoffs of these programs in the past.[62]

Our discussion of the problems and limitations of business-assistance programs has implications for development strategy. The concluding chapter considers potential development strategies for the future.

---

unaware of Nigerian (or other African) experience and were developing fully packaged industrial estates of their own; for example, Kenya, where one fully packaged estate was already in operation (and encountering severe problems) in 1968 and four others were planned; Uganda, where plans for such an estate were well along in 1968.

[62]See "Economic Development Orientation" in Chapter 3. On the establishment of a Western State government loans scheme for small-scale industry, see *West Africa*, January 5, 1976, p. 23.

PART IV

Conclusion

Chapter 14

CONCLUSION

We have discussed Nigerian economic problems and attempts that have been made to deal with them. In this concluding chapter we deal with long-run development strategy for Nigeria, specifically with policies for generating the successful modern-economy investment needed for accelerated development. We shall consider four possible sources of such investment: indigenous business, foreign business, profit-oriented public corporations, and social utility-oriented public corporations. Then on the basis of our judgment of the promise and problems of each of these sources, we shall present our tentative conclusions on the most promising economic development strategy for Nigeria.

Potential Sources of
Modern-Economy Investment

Indigenous Business

We have seen that the business-assistance approach in the period before the Civil War was, in the face of the entrepreneurial-environmental symphysis, unable to transform the indigenous private sector into a significant dynamic element in the modern economy. However, the prospects for this approach have been enhanced by the enlarged oil revenues and other developments in the Nigerian economy.

There have been a number of improvements in the economic environment, although changes have not all been for the better. For one thing, the new oil prosperity broadens the narrow domestic markets for Nigerian output and thus eases a major restrictive element in the economic environment. This effect can, of course, be exaggerated, for its magnitude is limited by the uses of the income from Nigerian oil. Some of it flows into the overseas accounts of the foreign oil firms and their foreign employees and suppliers. A substantial portion is spent abroad by government for equipment, materials, and services. Another large portion remains unspent, accumulating as government reserves. Of the income that reaches the local population, a highly disproportionate share goes to the strategically placed, interwoven political and economic elites and to the labor aristocracy.[1] These groups, interested in sophisticated products, in foreign travel, in foreign education for their children, in imports of all kinds, and also more inclined to save than their poorer compatriots, tend to spend relatively little on the simpler products produced by indigenous businessmen. Still, despite all these leakages, significant amounts of the oil income flow directly and indirectly to indigenous businessmen.

The indigenous entrepreneur's economic environment has improved in other ways. Infrastructural development is accelerated by expenditure of the oil revenues despite all the problems of allocation, coordination, waste, and corruption. The increased savings arising from larger incomes ease capital-availability constraints where they do exist. Government capability for implementing business-assistance and other programs has been enhanced by the virtual completion of the sometimes disruptive phase of Nigerianization of the public service, by the increasing number and turnout of educated Nigerians, and by the accumulation of experience by official personnel at all levels—although little of the government capability may be devoted to business-assistance measures, given the governmental preoccupation with implementation of Third Plan investment projects.

On the other hand, the economic environment was being subjected to heightened strain. Most indigenous businessmen felt that oil affluence was making environmental problems more rather than less severe. Port congestion, with more than four hundred ships awaiting berths at the end of 1975, many lying to for six months and longer, caused excruciating import delays and and enormous demurrage charges. Traffic congestion approaching a state of almost complete immobility in Lagos and growing severe elsewhere constituted a major and expensive obstacle to business activities. The telephone system, collapsing under the weight of increased demand and poor maintenance, was unreliable at best and often completely inoperative, so that communication often required traffic-intensifying, time-consuming personal visits. The railway, the airlines, and virtually all other facets of the infrastructure were more difficult to make use of satisfactorily. Crippling cement shortages, gasoline shortages, and shortages of other goods were endemic. Delays in getting capital goods and other supplies were prolonged. The difficulty of securing repair, consultative, specialist, and other services increased. The helpfulness and tempo of government services degenerated.

Thus, to the individual businessman, infrastructural and other economic environmental adversities appeared to be exacerbated. Indigenous entrepreneurs, struggling to make the leap to modern operations, were most intensely affected, for they were just beginning to rely more heavily

---

[1] By the labor aristocracy we mean the employees of government and of private firms in the relatively small modern sector of the economy. They constitute a small, affluent segment of the labor force.

on the interdependent network that constitutes the modern economy, but had not yet secured a firm foothold or established dependable relationships.

The aggravation of economic environmental difficulties should be seen in perspective, however. The new oil prosperity generated new demands upon the infrastructure and the entire economic network at a rate that outpaced the rate of improvement. There were many strains but, nevertheless, the economic environment was improving.

At the same time, indigenous entrepreneurial capacity continues to grow. The enhancement of entrepreneurship interacts in turn with the environmental gains in a mutually reinforcing manner. Progress in one reinforces and accelerates progress in the other.

As a result, indigenous enterprise should be able to play a stronger part in Nigerian economic development than it has in the past. While it is not plausible to expect more than a melioration of the entrepreneurial-environmental symphysis, Nigeria's economic-development orientation should retain a significant place for the indigenous business sector.

Foreign Investment

Foreign private enterprise has been much more effective than indigenous enterprise in generating modern-economy dynamism and there is every reason to expect this to continue. Foreign enterprise or investment is taken here to include privately initiated ventures in which government has an interest. The private investor has usually held a majority of the equity or voting shares in such partnerships, but this is not necessary. Voting stock might be divided equally with government or government might even have the majority holding. The critical attributes of private foreign investment are that the venture was adjudged prospectively profitable by a foreign firm and is run as a private enterprise.[2]

Certainly, foreign investors have provided the main propulsion so far in the directly productive sector of Nigeria's modern economy. We have seen that the Second National Development Plan counted upon a powerful investment thrust from the foreign sector—strong enough to allow government to direct the eager flow of foreign investment into socially desirable channels by differentially tightening or loosening controls and inducements without regard to possible inhibiting effects on the total in-

---

[2]Some projects cannot be unequivocally classified as either public or private. Government might have provided the main initiating impetus, might have sought an interested foreign partner, and might be the majority shareholder, but the foreign firm might have gone well beyond a management-agent role. It might have provided substantial equity funds, having adjudged the undertaking prospectively profitable given the conditions promised by the government, and it might have the authority to run the firm in a businesslike way, although government would inevitably have some say. Such an undertaking partakes of the critical attributes of private foreign investment and we would consider it essentially a private venture.

vestment stream. This intention was not realized, but the perspective was revived by the Third Plan.[3]

However, reliance upon foreign investment entails two formidable sets of problems. First, foreign capital formation may generate substantial dysbenefits, which seriously undermine and possibly negate its net value to the host country. The discussion of these dysbenefits, to follow, will constitute the major part of this section.

Second, even if foreign investment is on balance beneficial, there are substantial reasons for doubting that foreign enterprise can generate an adequate rate of directly productive investment. The adversity of the economic environment, while milder for externally owned business than for indigenous business, is severe enough to limit the emergence of profitable investment opportunities to a rate incommensurate with the needs and possibilities of oil-bolstered Nigeria. This problem of the grudgingness of the economic environment is intensified by the requirement by external investors of a high rate of profit to compensate for the possibilities of nationalization, expropriation, foreign-exchange restrictions, and associated risks and apprehensions.[4] Furthermore, even a rate of profit sufficient to compensate for these risks and anxieties might not be as attractive to particular investors as alternative opportunities elsewhere on the globe. These immediately operative factors restricting the flow of foreign investment are then reinforced by long-term restrictive considerations. Specifically, the dysbenefits already alluded to tend not only to reduce the utility of the investment but also over a period tend to limit the emergence of profitable opportunities, thereby reducing the long-term capital inflow.

Multifarious negative effects of foreign investment are alleged in the literature, particularly the writings on imperialism. Although some of the

[3]Federal Republic of Nigeria, *Third National Development Plan 1975-80* 1 (Lagos: Federal Ministry of Economic Development, 1975), p. 31.

[4]"Foreign firms are frequently reluctant to invest outside their own country because of fear of expropriation and because of uncertainty generated by unfamiliarity. For these reasons they tend to expect a rapid payoff on their investments." In Ghana, "the expectation of a high rate of return is an absolute necessity if foreign capital is to be attracted." Checchi and Company (an American consulting firm), *A Program to Accelerate Economic Growth in Ghana,* prepared for the Rockefeller Brothers Fund, Accra, Ghana, 1961, pp. 44, 48-49. This was pointed out to West Africans at an early stage of their approach to self-government by W. A. Lewis, *Report on Industrialization and the Gold Coast* (Accra, Gold Coast: Government Printing Department, 1953), p. 9.

In Nigeria, our highly tentative estimate is that pre-oil boom returns on foreign capital averaged about 30 to 35 percent, with rates somewhat lower in manufacturing than in distribution, services, and finance. This estimate is based on fragmentary data on yields on shares purchased on the Lagos Stock Exchange, in Asabia, "Share Valuation: The Nigerian Experience." Such yields were lower than returns on the amounts of capital actually invested in the firms, for "the exceptionally high rate of return which Nigerian businesses [i.e., businesses operating in Nigeria] have recorded in the past" (p. 12) caused stock-share prices to appreciate, thereby reducing the percentage return on the enhanced market value of stock.

charges are purely emotional invective, some of the critical comments are carefully considered, supported by an attempt to marshal evidence, plausible, and deserving of careful investigation. Such a study cannot be undertaken in the concluding chapter of a book on another topic. We shall, however, undertake to delineate some of the alleged dysbenefits of foreign investment that appear to have validity. While we make no attempt here to carry out a careful investigation of the reality or importance of these negative effects, we discuss only those allegations which in our judgment may actually have some basis in fact. The benefits of foreign investment are taken for granted in this context, so there is no attempt to balance the presentation by discussing these as well.

Another brief methodological point: Any discussion of the effects of foreign investment requires a point of reference. One can compare the consequences of outside investment with those of a complete absence of any investment in the projects in question, to the effects of investment by indigenous businessmen or by public corporations if they were capable of carrying out the same projects and doing so as well (or on the basis of one's surmise about how capable such investors would actually be), to some norm of ethical behavior on the part of the investor, etc. Any of these comparisons constitutes only a partial approach, shedding only an imperfect light on the value of external investment. In the following discussion, we will compare foreign capital formation to investment by a hypothetical public enterprise of the same capability. This is *not* to imply that public enterprises in developing economies are in fact as capable as foreign firms, for this is not the case, but this particular comparison will be useful in our subsequent discussion of the problems and potentialities of public-corporation investment.

Before considering the objective or "real" effects of foreign investment, we take note of a weighty subjective effect. Widespread feelings of dismay, self-criticism, anger, and even outrage are aroused by the dominant position of foreign firms in the modern economy and by the associated implicit but nonetheless powerful iteration and continuing reiteration of foreign superiority. The consequent anger and frustration, as expressed for example in the statement by the former Nigerian Minister of Economic Development that Nigerians unfortunately must realize "that we shall continue to be under the control of the imperialists and capitalists who have taken the lead in this world in economic development,"[5] constitute a cost of substantial magnitude.

We turn now to a series of *economic* effects of foreign investment.

1. Profits, of course, go to foreign enterprises rather than to our hypothetical public enterprise investing equally capably. This entails

---

[5]Nigeria, Federation, *Parliamentary Debates: House of Representatives, Second Session,* November 16, 1961.

some negative effects, which are heightened by the foreign investors' high-profit requirement. First, the net increment in *national* income or product (as distinguished from *domestic* income or product) generated by the investment is curtailed and might even be negative.[6] The net increase in output occasioned by the foreign investment may be small. The output of the foreign enterprise may be offset to a greater or lesser degree by reductions in production by indigenous firms which might lose customers or scarce productive resources to the alien investor. The foreign firm's profit must then be subtracted from this net increase in output (i.e., in value added) to find the contribution to national product, and if the profit flow is high it is possible that national product might even fall.[7] Second, any balance-of-payments benefits from the foreign investment may be curtailed and might be negative. They would be curtailed if profits were repatriated and if the outflow of repatriated profits exceeded the corresponding outflow of management fees, payments for foreign personnel, licensing or royalty payments, etc., that a public-corporation investor would engender. (It must be realized, of course, that the foreign enterprise generates an initial inflow of capital.) In the case of an alien firm producing an import substitute with a small domestic-value-added component, the positive balance-of-payments effect of the domestic value added might be outweighed by the repatriation of profits and other funds so that there would be a net outflow of foreign exchange. Third, funds available to the developing-economy government for reinvestment are reduced if profits accrue to an alien firm rather than a public enterprise. And if the public enterprise would reinvest domestically a larger portion of the profits than the foreign-owned company, the overall magnitude of domestic investment funds would be reduced.

2. The benefits of advanced-economy technology are enormous. Nevertheless, there are a number of drawbacks to the technology brought in by overseas investors. To the extent that these can be avoided, the benefits of the technology might be increased and/or the dysbenefits reduced.

For one thing, the foreign-investor technology is generally suited to the conditions of advanced rather than developing economies. It is usually inappropriately capital-intensive for countries characterized by relatively abundant labor and by large and growing problems of unemployment and underemployment. Tilting the technology toward greater labor intensity is difficult under any circumstances, but it is particularly unlikely that the

---

[6]National product is measured by income flows to nationals of a country, while domestic product is measured by incomes generated within the geographical boundaries of the country.

[7]See, e.g., J. Ilett, "Inducements for Industrial Development: When Are They Worthwhile?" *Yorkshire Bulletin of Economic and Social Research* 19:2 (November 1967): 105.

international corporation will do this because its techniques of management, organization, and control were developed for and are adapted to advanced-economy technology and conditions.

The use of capital-intensive techniques may then tend to prevent the development of a more appropriate technology. "The choice of capital-intensive techniques . . . favors the use of specialized machinery and consequently restrains the growth of demand for capital goods that could be produced in the periphery. The lack of investment in the capital-goods sector, in turn, prevents the development of capital goods embodying a *modern* labor-intensive technology. . . ."[8] The case for the use of a simpler technology can be seen as an infant-industry argument. "There is a short-term loss from failing to adopt the widely used technology [of the foreign investor]; there may be a long-term gain from adopting and ultimately disseminating a superior [domestically developed] technological standard. This is an infant industry argument."[9]

Finally, the technological expertise, which constitutes a strategic advantage of the foreign investor, is naturally regarded as a precious asset that should not be carelessly dissipated. Consequently, the foreign firm (unlike a public corporation) has a strong propensity to keep to itself, or to make available to other potential users only on stringent terms, not only the imported technology and expertise, but also the adaptative technology and expertise developed on the basis of the conditions in the less-developed economies.

3. Foreign investors may outmaneuver or simply swindle government representatives of the less-developed economy. The specific practices are highly variegated, and only a few examples are mentioned here.[10] Foreign firms may understate profits for tax and other reasons. This is not merely a matter of juggling the ostensible national source of profits to have them appear in a low-tax country, for this might just as well favor as disfavor a particular developing country. "Creative" accounting may well understate the overall magnitude of profits, particularly in countries lacking a high level of accounting sophistication. For example, foreign investors in

[8]Giovanni Arrighi, "International Corporations, Labor Aristocracies and Economic Development in Tropical Africa," in Robert I. Rhodes (ed.), *Imperialism and Underdevelopment: A Reader* (New York: Monthly Review Press, 1970), p. 229. Arrighi presents a thoughtful and complex analysis of the technology brought in by international investors and its ramifications in the developing economy.

[9]Charles P. Kindleberger, *American Business Abroad: Six Lectures on Direct Investment* (New Haven and London: Yale University Press, 1969), p. 84. Kindleberger was discussing foreign investment in advanced economies, but his point applies as well to less developed economies with the qualification that the technology that is superior for more-developed and for less-developed economies may differ.

[10]The practices are similar to those that have been encountered in setting up public enterprises in Africa. See Sayre P. Schatz, "Crude Private Neo-Imperialism: A New Pattern in Africa," *Journal of Modern African Studies* 7:4 (December 1969).

Nigeria set up their capital structures so that profits appeared in the form of (nontaxable) loan repayments.[11] Foreign investors have also set up capital structures in Nigeria that shift risk but not profit possibilities to government. Some companies were organized with unusually high debt-equity ratios, with the foreign interest investing its funds solely or primarily in equity capital while Nigerian government funds went primarily into debt capital. Consequently, the external investor stood to gain an extremely high percentage return on its investment if the venture proved successful, but if the venture proved unsuccessful, so that capital was eroded and perhaps the firm had to be liquidated, the equity margin was so narrow that the providers of loan capital stood to lose part of their investment; "debenture holders and other long-term creditors [were] in fact providing risk capital without any compensating claim on profits."[12] Phony feasibility studies were foisted on government. This practice was sometimes lubricated in Nigeria by illegitimate blandishments to ministers, inducing them to commit the government before civil servants had a chance to scrutinize the deals carefully. In some cases government agreed to highly and unnecessarily favorable terms for investors from abroad simply because it was unable to cope with the superior expertise, experience, and sophistication of the international enterprise.

4. Investment by a miltinational corporation may strengthen that firm's international monopolistic or monopsonistic power[13] (in contrast to public-corporation investment, which would weaken it). This bolstering of the international investor's market power is then likely to entail costs for the host country as well as for other countries dealing with that firm. Historically this kind of cost has been more important for Nigeria than for most African countries, for British West Africa had a stronger tendency toward monopolistic concentration than most parts of the continent.[14]

5. The international ties of investors from abroad entail various costs for the developing host countries. A local subsidiary of a multinational corporation may not act on the basis of domestic market conditions but may base its decisions on international considerations; the subsidiary may not attempt to maximize its own profits or optimize its own position, but may be directed by the firm's central office to act on the basis of the conditions and prospects facing the entire multinational enterprise.

[11]Peter Kilby, *Industrialization in an Open Economy: Nigeria 1945-1966* (Cambridge: Cambridge University Press, 1969), p. 122.

[12]Kilby, p. 122.

[13]"Monopoly . . . is one basis of direct investment and of international growth of the national corporation": Kindleberger, p. 187.

[14]W. Keith Hancock, *Survey of British Commonwealth Affairs, Vol. II. Problems of Economic Policy, 1918-1939, Part 2* (London: Oxford University Press, 1942; issued under the auspices of the Royal Institute of International Affairs), pp. 201-222.

Profitable operations in a developing country might be shifted elsewhere to a still more profitable site.[15] Firms, not being the single-minded profit maximizers depicted in theory, may deviate from profit maximization in ways that are harmful to the host country; for example, foreign-owned companies in Nigeria have tended to import machinery and supplies as well as expertise from customary trading partners in their home country rather than to seek the best international buy regardless of the nationality of the producers. Then, too, the kinds of products either for domestic sale or for export that the foreign investor will be interested in developing will be influenced by its particular character and relations, and the firm's criteria may not harmonize with the best interests of the developing economy.

6. A public enterprise can more easily take divergences or externalities into account in its reckoning than a private profit-oriented firm, i.e., can more easily act on the basis of the overall national importance of its economic activities. While government *can* to some degree induce private firms to act in accordance with shadow prices reflecting overall national criteria by appropriate tax, subsidization, and other policies, this is rarely done in fact. Moreover, such policies are limited; they are not capable of inducing comprehensive modifications of private-firm behavior in accord with any comprehensive conception of divergences.[16]

The broadly economic effects of foreign investment discussed in the preceding paragraphs are accompanied by effects which may be classified as broadly political. On the most global level, a country that relies upon foreign private investment must opt for a politico-economic system that accommodates capitalist enterprise. Spokesmen from both sides of the ideological fence tend to agree on this, differing primarily on what they consider desirable. Thus, a high-level economic adviser in Tanzania *warns* that cooperation with and reliance upon even selected foreign investors may lock even that socialist-oriented country into existing capitalist patterns. In contrast, the director of the United Africa Company expounds on the *desirability* of such a pattern. "The encouragement and protection of investment requires the adoption of an economic policy favourable to free enterprise. . . . I suggest that in Africa, under present conditions, the principal obstacle against investment is the encouragement of State control in activities where free enterprise would be effi-

[15]See, e.g., Jay R. Mandle, "Neo-Imperialism: A Comment," *Social and Economic Studies* XVI:3 (September 1967): 320-321; Michael Tanzer, *The Political Economy of the International Oil and the Underdeveloped Countries* (Boston: Beacon Press, 1969), p. 175.

[16]See, e.g., Reginald H. Green, "The Role of the State as an Agent of Economic and Social Development in the Least Developed Countries," *Journal of Development Planning* 6 (1974): 21.

cient . . . It is necessary that the host country should be convinced that private enterprise—national no less than expatriate—is the best way of creating wealth and developing a country's resources."[17]

Reliance upon international investment also entails pressures for particular orientations and policies within the capitalist framework. The country that needs foreign private capital feels impelled to create a climate attractive to those who provide it.[18] In accord with this imperative, Nigeria has emphasized a set of conservative fiscal, monetary, balance-of-payments, and other economic policies. As Nigeria's Prime Minister stated in 1958, the government "will not lend itself to any measures that would have the effect of lessening the confidence of overseas investors and of our own people in our financial and economic stability."[19] As for more unorthodox approaches, foreign officials and foreign investors "resolutely set their face against them."[20] Specific policies too are often influenced considerably by large foreign firms that would be affected. Large investors also may have a significant degree of freedom from control by host-country governments, as, for example, the refusal (according to Nigerian officials) of some foreign investors in partnership with Nigerian governments to provide anything more than vague overall figures to their governmental partners. Foreign-firm interests are still sometimes forcefully advocated by their home-country governments, as in the case of a stormy ambassadorial complaint to an African government which had repudiated a corruption-tainted and unfavorable contract. Other ways in which governmental suzerainty may be diminished by foreign investment have been discussed in many works.[21]

A country's ability to achieve broad national objectives that may conflict with relatively short-term interests of particular corporations may be diminished by reliance upon alien enterprise because in some cir-

---

[17]F. J. Pedler, "The Problem in East and West Africa," in *The Encouragement and Protection of Industries in Developing Countries,* Supplementary Publication No. 3, *International and Comparative Law Quarterly* (London: The British Institute of International Comparative Law, 1962), pp. 67-69.

[18]". . . this Government clearly recognises the necessity—indeed the urgent necessity—for inviting foreign capital and foreign technique into this Region to participate in the implementation of certain aspects of this Plan. . . . we must create in this Region and, in association with others in this country as a whole, an atmosphere sufficiently attractive and congenial to the immigration and habitation of foreign capital and techniques." Nigeria, Western Region, *General Information and Notes on Industrial Possibilities* (Ibadan: Government Printer, Western Region, 1954), p. 6.

[19]Federation of Nigeria, *Annual Report of the Federal Department of Commerce and Industries, 1957-58* (Lagos: Federal Government Printer, 1958), p. 3.

[20]Thomas Balogh, "Agricultural and Economic Development" in Rhodes (ed.), p. 215.

[21]See, e.g., Alice Hoffenberg Amsden, *International Firms and Labour in Kenya 1945-70* (London: Frank Cass, 1971), p. 131; Raymond Vernon, "The Multinational Enterprise and National Sovereignty," *Harvard Business Review* 45:2 (March-April 1967): 156-172; and Kindleberger, pp. 104-105.

cumstances it may be difficult to enlist the support of foreign-owned companies. The discussion of Canada by Aitken is illuminating in this regard. In the federal government's conception, the Canadian national interest has required "building and maintaining an integrated national economy." In pursuit of this conception, the federal government "has opposed corporate strategies that appeared likely to jeopardize the maintenance of national economic unity, and it has supported strategies that appeared likely to reinforce it." In Canadian political circumstances, where among other things the provincial governments pursue narrowly sectional interests, the support of large-scale private business for the broader politico-economic objective has been essential. "The feasibility of federal government policies . . . depends to a significant degree upon the extent to which they can attract the support of private business. This in turn depends upon the extent to which the corporate sector of the economy can be induced to link its fortunes to the federal government's conception of Canada's future."[22] To the degree that public (or indigenously owned private) enterprises are more likely than externally controlled corporations to link their fortunes with the national destiny, the presence of foreign-owned firms reduces government ability to pursue broad objectives.

The issue of the foreign investor's influence on the nature of the power structure constitutes the final political effect to be discussed here. Foreign investors, perhaps with the help of their home-country governments, may promote and bolster a group of leaders whom they deem "responsible" but whom critics regard as "compradores" or "imperalist lackeys." Fanon expresses the critical view mordantly. Of "the national middle class which takes over power at the end of the colonial regime" he says: "The national bourgeoisie of underdeveloped countries is not engaged in production, nor in invention, nor building, nor labor; it is completely canalized into activities of the intermediate type. Its innermost vocation seems to be to keep in the running and to be part of the racket." When in trouble, this class will "send out frenzied appeals for help to the former mother country."[23]

The political impact of foreign investment shades imperceptibly into the social, cultural, and other consequences. Fanon's attack on the bourgeoisie is clearly on cultural as well as political grounds. The bourgeoisie and other groups are said to become dependent. "The state bureaucracy and other sectors of the middle class—for example, the technical, managerial, professional, or intellectual elites—become clientele

---

[22]Hugh G. J. Aitken, "Government and Business in Canada: An Interpretation," *Business History Review* 38:1 (1964): 20-21.

[23]Frantz Fanon, "The Pitfalls of National Consciousness—Africa," in Robert I. Rhodes (ed.), p. 303.

when their interests, actions, and privileged positions are derived from their ties to foreign interests."[24] Exaggerated cleavages emerge between a relatively well-paid labor aristocracy and "the unskilled semi-proletarianized peasantry" and between the urban and rural populations.[25] In the shadow of the marked business and technological superiority of the foreign firms, the indigenous people deprecate their own culture and lose self-esteem.[26] A wide range of issues of this nature, only sampled here, have been discussed by critics of foreign investment.

To recapitulate, two broad problems are involved in relying on international investment. First, the rate of foreign investment is not likely to be adequate, particularly for a country that, like Nigeria, hopes to welcome such investment only selectively. This is partly because of the adversity of the economic environment coupled with the high profit requirement of foreign investors, and it is partly because of the long-run negative effects of the dysbenefits of foreign investment. Second, the substantial dysbenefits of foreign private capital inflow may make reliance upon public enterprise more desirable, depending upon the ability of public enterprise to carry out directly productive investments on a sufficiently large and effective scale.

Public Corporations

Modern-economy investment can also be carried out by public corporations. These might simply be profit-oriented or they might take divergences fully into account and thus be social utility-oriented. In the 1950s Nigeria turned to public corporations, primarily profit-oriented, to a significant extent. Experience with them was very disappointing, but let us consider public corporations more fully before drawing any conclusions from that experience.

One significant advantage of public corporations over private foreign investors for developing economies is that public enterprises are satisfied with a lower prospective rate of profit. This widens the range of investable projects in the modern economy. This additional-project margin is important because the rate of emergence of profitable investment opportunities, particularly of opportunities that are promising enough to attract foreign investors, is limited in most less-developed economies compared to the target rate of development in the modern economy.

[24]Susanne Bodenheimer, "Dependency and Imperialism: The Roots of Latin American Underdevelopment," in K. T. Fann and Donald C. Hodges (eds.), *Readings in U.S. Imperialism* (Boston: Porter Sargent, 1971), p. 163.

[25]Arrighi, in Rhodes (ed.), p. 239.

[26]See, e.g., the discussion of exaggerated notions of Nigerian business untrustworthiness held by Nigerian businessmen themselves, Sayre P. Schatz and S. I. Edokpayi, "Economic Attitudes of Nigerian Businessmen," *Nigerian Journal of Economic and Social Studies* IV:3 (November 1962): 264-265.

The additional-project margin is even greater if public corporations are social utility-oriented rather than profit-oriented. Still another band of directly productive investments is open to them—projects that would be insufficiently profitable for profit-oriented public corporations or even pecuniarily unprofitable, but which would be socially worthwhile because of their positive divergences.[27]

Countering the additional-project advantage of public enterprise are two sets of problems that afflict public corporations more severely than foreign investors: problems of managerial capability and of political corruption and interference. While supervisory or managerial shortcomings may not be inordinately severe for ordinary government affairs handled by the civil services, these shortcomings are acute in running large modern-business enterprises. This has been attested to by innumerable observers.[28] Modern-enterprise managerial deficiencies exist in virtually all underdeveloped economies and in fact are virtually a defining characteristic of underdevelopment.[29] The widespread nature of political corruption in Nigeria has already been discussed. It has flourished in the public corporations on a larger scale than in any other part of the Nigerian government structure.[30]

---

[27]This additional margin of directly productive investments might be offset to a greater or lesser degree by the rejection of profitable projects that do not have a net social utility because of negative divergences. If, however, the contention in Chapter 7 on divergences is correct, that positive divergences predominate in the less developed economies, then more projects would emerge as worthwhile than would be dropped.

[28]The literature on the poor performance of Nigeria's public corporations is vast. Summaries by leading Nigerian economists of widely accepted criticisms can be found in O. Aboyade, "Nigerian Public Enterprises as an Organizational Dilemma" (pp. 30-31, 36), A. E. Ekukinam, "Management Problems, Accountability and Government Control of Public Enterprises in Nigeria" (pp. 125-126), and P. N. C. Okigbo, "Government as a Surrogate Corporation" (pp. 111-113), all in *Public Enterprises in Nigeria: Proceedings of the 1973 Annual Conference of the Nigerian Economic Society* (Ibadan: Nigerian Economic Society, 1974). A listing of a large number of detailed, highly informative official reports can be found in Ekukinam's article. See also, Federal Republic of Nigeria, *Guidelines for the Third National Development Plan 1975-80* (Lagos: Federal Ministry of Economic Development and Reconstruction, 1973), p. 53.

Naturally, the poor performance affected government policy deliberations. For example, an internal government memorandum on the possibility of establishing a state trading agency to compete with or replace the large foreign-owned trading firms (by the late Professor Obasanmi Olakanpo) states that such an agency "would be most unlikely to secure the adaptability, elasticity, and enterprise that are necessary to progress. And it is putting it mildly to say that the experience of Government management of existing state enterprises does not at all encourage one to expect that our Government could deal with the tremendous task of managing a trading organisation." *Memo on Government Policy on Distributive Trade.*

[29]See, e.g., Hans W. Singer, *International Development: Growth and Change* (New York: McGraw-Hill, 1964), p. 154; W. Arthur Lewis, *Development Planning: The Essentials of Economic Policy* (New York: Harper and Row, 1966), p. 272.

[30]The investigations mounted after the coups of 1966 provided the best source of documentation. The Reports on these investigations are listed in the Ekukinam article mentioned in footnote 28.

Managerial deficiencies and political manipulation reinforced one another[31] and created a capability disadvantage for public corporations in comparison with foreign-controlled firms. This has had many manifestations. Ostensible pre-investment investigations have often been "inadequate (and sometimes patently defective)."[32] For example, in all but one of the Western Nigeria Development Corporation's plantation investments "detailed investigations of soil, climatic or marketing conditions, or prospects were never carried out prior to location; investment decisions were almost invariably strongly influenced by non-economic considerations. . . . Its decision to establish at least one major agricultural project in each of the political divisions of the region irrespective of variations in agricultural potentialities was but one in the long chain of politically-motivated investment decisions . . . [resulting in] the siting of several plantations in areas subsequently found to be highly unsuitable both in terms of rainfall and of other ecological conditions."[33] Similar viability-investigation deficiencies obtained for Western Region commercial and industrial ventures and for all types of ventures established by the other governments of the Federation.[34] Government enterprises and corporations "have all been found to carry on the payroll excessive numbers of employees."[35] "A very senior officer of one of the Corporations is recorded as stating before a Public Tribunal that the Corporation can operate efficiently as a commercial concern with its existing staff reduced by 25 percent. This statement confirms our discovery that one great source of waste in our Corporations lies in the creation of too many posts most of which do not require detailed scrutiny to be declared redundant."[36] The capability disadvantage has also manifested itself in many other ways: in "overcentralization of authority . . . inspired by . . . sheer love of power";[37] in unwise policy decisions; in day-to-day ineptness in running the enterprises; in illicit government transfer payments through excessive payments on construction and purchase contracts and through every other imaginable channel; in the use of contractor finance and supplier's credits to finance the venality; and in "overburdened and

[31]". . . the low quality of management has compounded the high incidence of direct ministerial intervention in routine operation of the public enterprises." Aboyade, p. 31.

[32]Aboyade, p. 31.

[33]O. Teriba, "Development Strategy, Investment Decisions and Expenditure Patterns," *Nigerian Journal of Economic and Social Studies* VIII:2 (July 1966): 245.

[34]Teriba, pp. 252-256; Arthur D. Little, Inc., *Industrial Finance Institutions and Policy: A Report to the Government of Western Nigeria* (1963); investigations after the 1966 coups.

[35]Okigbo, p. 111.

[36]Nigeria, Federation, *Report of the Working Party on Statutory Corporations and State-Owned Companies* (Lagos: Federal Ministry of Information, 1967), p. 15. See also *West Africa,* June 20, 1970, p. 662: "Although dealing with a static volume of activity, the [Mid-West] state development corporation doubled its overheads between 1963 and 1967, chiefly by acquiring redundant and unqualified staff."

[37]Ekukinam, p. 125.

unrealistic capital structures."[38] It is difficult to think of a problem that plausibly might have occurred that did not actually occur.[39]

Generally poor public-enterprise performance resulted. Costs were high; service was poor. The profit-oriented wholly or primarily publicly owned corporations were almost invariably unprofitable in marked contrast to the wholly or primarily foreign-owned firms.[40] It has generally been concluded that the resources devoted to directly productive public investments were badly allocated. The inference is usually also drawn that the poor record contraindicates reliance on directly productive publicly owned enterprises as a major means of carrying out *further* modern-economy investment. As W. Arthur Lewis has put it, the British model of the public corporation, manned by capable and conscientious personnel, free of the bureaucratic defects of the civil service and of the political and venal considerations often motivating politicians, and operated single-mindedly for the public good, is unrealistic for a country like Nigeria.[41] The pessimistic appraisal of the public-corporation role has been reinforced by findings like that of Professor (subsequently Commissioner of Economic Development and Reconstruction) Adedeji that the post-Civil War trend "has been towards increased centralization of control and deepening of the bureaucratisation processes in the management of public enterprises in Nigeria."[42]

Despite the unsatisfactory performance of public corporations in Nigeria so far, it might nevertheless be argued that an expansion of the role of public enterprise is necessary and that a historical perspective suggests that the negative conclusions just discussed are hasty. Alexander Gerschenkron's interesting thesis on the effects of relative backwardness

[38]Aboyade, p. 31.

[39]In a knowledgeable and insightful early discussion of Nigeria's public corporations, A. H. Hanson pointed out a number of problems in the 1950s. He discussed the following: a lack of flexibility in hiring, firing, promoting, and demoting; the political composition of the governing boards; the frequently amateurish functioning of the boards, which often constituted a nuisance or worse for the corporation managers; the gulf between Africans and Europeans on the boards and in the staffs of the corporations; uncertainty and conflict about the respective powers of the managers and the boards, and the possibility of abuse arising from the extensive power of the ministers if they chose to use them. A. H. Hanson, "Public Enterprise in Nigeria (I. Federal Public Utilities)," *Public Administration* (London) XXXVI (Winter 1958): 366-384.

[40]See, e.g., Gerald K. Helleiner, *Peasant Agriculture, Government and Economic Growth in Nigeria* (Homewood, Illinois: Richard D. Irwin, 1966), pp. 259-260; Kilby, pp. 24, 79; Teriba, passim; Arthur D. Little, Inc., *Industrial Finance Institutions;* O. Omorogiuwa, "Much Money Down the Drain," *West Africa,* July 4, 1970, p. 729; and Adebayo Adedeji, "The Men Who Keep Nigeria Going," *West Africa,* March 14, 1970, p. 281, and further instalments of that series in the April 4 and 11, 1970, issues. See also the references cited in footnote 28 of this chapter.

[41]W. Arthur Lewis, *Some Aspects of Economic Development* (London: Allen and Unwin, 1970), reviewed in *West Africa,* February 7, 1970, p. 161.

[42]Adebayo Adedeji, "The Men Who Keep Nigeria Going: 2," *West Africa,* April 4, 1970, p. 365.

at the onset of industrialization is pertinent. He maintains that the greater a country's relative economic backwardness at the initiation of industrialization (compared with contemporary advanced economies), the more centrally organized have its institutional instruments necessarily been for the increasingly strenuous task of catching up. Thus, the institutions for financing industrialization became progressively larger and more centralized in the successively industrializing European nations until, in late Czarist Russia (a late industrializer, characterized therefore by greater relative backwardness than France or Germany), the financing function was largely taken over by the government in the 1890s. Given Russian financial conditions and the magnitude of the finances needed for industrialization, "no banking system could conceivably succeed." Therefore, "Supply of capital for the needs of industrialization required the compulsory machinery of the government, which, through its taxation policies, succeeded in directing incomes from consumption to investment." The results were, in view of the incompetence and corruption characteristic of Nigerian public enterprises, of particular interest to us. Gerschenkron found: "There is no doubt that the government as an *agens movens* of industrialization discharged its role in a far less than perfectly efficient manner. Incompetence and corruption of bureaucracy were great. The amount of waste that accompanied the process was formidable. But when all is said and done, the great success of the policies pursued . . . is undeniable."[43] It is a cogent extension of the Gerschenkron thesis to argue that the magnitude of the effort required for modern industrialization in Nigeria is such that a further centralizing step is necessary. Government financing has not been adequate, as our discussion of the loans programs has shown, so government *execution* of industrialization may be required. One might argue further that, as in Russia, success is possible despite formidable incompetence, corruption, and waste.

Moreover, some of the deficiencies of Nigerian public enterprise arose out of circumstances that are not likely to continue. The early directly productive activities were undertaken under the aegis of economically unversed colonial officials and Nigerian political leaders at a time of general economic unsophistication, and these activities were uninformed by rational economic criteria—a pattern unlikely to recur in view of Nigeria's current level of economic sophistication. Investments in plantations and other large agricultural projects, for example, were carried out under "an agricultural development strategy that failed to fully take into account considerations of costs and benefits, and . . . of alternative approaches. . . ."[44] Most of the "industrial schemes" sprang from the

---

[43]Alexander Gerschenkron, *Economic Backwardness in Historical Perspective* (Cambridge, Mass.: Harvard University Press, 1962), pp. 19-20.
[44]Teriba, pp. 250-251.

oversimplified preconception that processing of local primary products was obviously the natural route toward industrial development,[45] and also from British focus on colonial primary products, processed or unprocessed, during the dollar-shortage period of the 1940s and 1950s. The public corporations were also "apt to be prodigal of funds," because money was lavishly provided in the early years through nonreturnable Marketing Board grants extended without regard to the corporations' capacity or the Regions' development possibilities and priorities.[46]

Furthermore, a strong case can be made that political manipulation rather than inability caused many of the major operational deficiencies of the public corporations, and that with realistically possible political changes the performance of public enterprise could be markedly better. "One of the factors most disastrous to management efficiency was political interference in the affairs of the corporations." With appropriate changes, a "repetition of the past political abuses in state enterprise might . . . be minimized if not completely eliminated."[47] Such an assessment gets support from an intra-African comparison. Charles Frank points out that during the same period there was a much higher degree of success of state enterprise in Uganda, "where the overall supply of people with the necessary abilities is certainly more limited than in Nigeria or Ghana. . . ." This indicates that "a crash [training and educational] program is neither necessary nor sufficient. The political milieu in which state enterprises operate is probably far more important."[48]

There are also grounds for hope in the accumulation of business and economic experience by Nigerian personnel and in the continuing and increasing outflow of Nigerian secondary school and university graduates. Moreover, Nigerian capabilities can be supplemented by the recruitment of foreign personnel or management teams. Although such recruitment is fraught with problems, on at least some occasions foreign

---

[45]Teriba, pp. 251-252.

[46]Teriba, p. 256.

[47]Ekukinam, pp. 127, 134. A somewhat stronger position was taken by Aboyade: ". . . the degree of poor performance by public enterprises in Nigeria was unnecessarily high, and could obviously have been reduced if not eliminated by a more honest political and bureaucratic leadership." Aboyade, p. 31. A still stronger earlier opinion was expressed in *Nigerian Opinion* I:8 (August 1965): 2: "To the extent that the public corporations have thus failed to achieve . . . efficient management, we suggest that this failure is not due particularly to the concept and structure of public corporations as such but to the lack of integrity on the part of the political class." Similar judgments have been made by many observers.

[48]Charles R. Frank, Jr., "Public and Private Enterprise in Africa," in Gustav Ranis (ed.), *Government and Economic Development* (New Haven: Yale University Press, 1971), pp. 116-117. Public enterprise was frequently more efficient and productive, in Holland at any rate, than parallel private undertakings, according to Jan Tinbergen, Conference on International Development, April 24-26, 1970, Capahosic, Virginia, cited in Denis Goulet and Michael Hudson, *The Myth of Aid* (Maryknoll, N.Y.: Orbis Books, 1971), pp. 68-69.

personnel have been used very successfully. In the case of the Kainji Dam, an undertaking backed by a genuine *political* commitment, much of the administrative capacity for the well-implemented project was recruited from abroad.[49] Equipment manufacturers, as distinguished from equipment salesmen, also tend to be helpful for they "have a vested interest in the success of the projects they equip—[as] an advertisement for their product. . . ."[50]

While one should not be naively sanguine about the emergence of the necessary political milieu and the heightening of staff-wide capability in Nigeria's public enterprises, neither should one simply dismiss the possibility. Certainly, many sophisticated and experienced Nigerian economists believe that Nigeria's future will hold greater reliance on public enterprises,[51] that this is desirable,[52] and that there are feasible ways of improving their performance.[53]

Let us recapitulate briefly. Public corporations, because they have a lower profit requirement and because they may be social utility-oriented rather than profit-oriented, have an additional-project advantage over foreign investors, i.e., directly productive investments are open to them that do not appeal to foreign investors. Conversely, in comparison to foreign-controlled firms, public corporations have had a capability *disadvantage* caused by deficiencies in managerial capability and by political manipulation. Although the capability disadvantage has been sizeable, it may be argued that a substantial expansion of the role of public enterprise may nevertheless be both necessary and salutary in the long term, and it may also be argued that the capability disadvantage can be considerably reduced. These considerations, while conflicting, nevertheless suggest that the public corporations can play a valuable role in carrying out directly productive investments in the modern economy.

Comparing public and foreign private enterprise, investment opportunities for public enterprise may arise from three possible sources. First, an additional margin of socially useful, directly productive investments may result from the lower profit-rate requirement of the profit-oriented public corporations. It will do so if and to the extent that the gap between the minimal acceptable profit rates of foreign and public investors exceeds the reduction in public-enterprise profitability caused by public-enterprise

[49]Edwin R. Dean, *Plan Implementation in Nigeria, 1962-66* (Ibadan: Oxford University Press, 1972), p. 168.

[50]Kilby, p. 78.

[51]E.g., Ekukinam, p. 129; Aboyade, pp. 37-43.

[52]E.g., Ekukinam, p. 130: "Government-in-business is becoming a way of life in Nigeria, and should. It does not depend, nor need it be defended, on ideological grounds. It is dictated by the economics of our time." Aboyade, pp. 37-41, presents an extensive set of arguments in favor of public enterprise in Nigeria.

[53]E.g., M. O. Kayode, "Management of Public Enterprises," in *Public Enterprises in Nigeria*, pp. 101-103; Okigbo, pp. 115-117; Ekukinam, pp. 131-134.

capability disadvantages. It is a reasonable supposition that the profit-rate gap exceeds the profitability reduction for some ventures, so that some public investment is warranted even if public corporations are profit-oriented.

Second, a further increment of worthwhile public-enterprise investment opportunities emerges if a social utility rather than a profitability calculus is used in making investment decisions. The shift from a profitability to a social utility criterion would both extend and curtail the list of investible projects for public enterprise. The addition to the list would consist of projects that fail to meet a pecuniary profit criterion but which, because of positive divergences, are considered desirable when net social utility is the determining criterion. The subtraction from the list would consist of projects that would be acceptable under a pecuniary profit criterion but that, because of negative divergences, are rejected under a net social utility criterion. If our hypothesis that positive divergences predominate in developing economies is correct,[54] the addition would substantially exceed the subtraction, so that a significant increment of directly productive investments would be warranted.

Third, public-corporation investment might be warranted in projects that appeal to private foreign investors because of their prospective profitability. Whether public enterprises should undertake such projects depends on the balance between two sets of factors. On the one hand, the capability disadvantage represents a negative factor. Any diminution of profit it causes, ceteris paribus, constitutes a net reduction of benefits to the country. On the other hand, a public enterprise will generate greater net benefits for the host country than a foreign enterprise of the same capability. The superior net benefits engendered by public enterprise represent for the most part the obverse of the dysbenefits of foreign private investment discussed earlier in this chapter. Net benefits of public enterprise, however, are reduced by any scare-off effect, i.e., by the degree to which the government's action of investing in spheres often considered the proper domain of the private investor scares off desirable foreign investment. Net benefits of public over foreign enterprise are also reduced by proper calculation of a shadow rate of interest on government funds used for the public enterprise; this rate would reflect the forgone alternative use of those funds. Such a cost is avoided in the case of a foreign investment to the degree that the foreign investor puts up money that would not otherwise be available in the host country.[55] It is our tentative judgment here too that for some projects the positive factors would exceed the negative, i.e., the greater net benefits of public enterprise would outweigh the capability disadvantages. In such cases, public

---

[54]See Chapter 7 and footnote 27 of this chapter.
[55]Host-country governments not infrequently provide the bulk of the necessary capital in the form of loans, infrastructure, and minority equity holdings.

investment in projects that are attractive to foreign private investors would be warranted.

In all, taking the three potential sources of public-enterprise investment opportunities together, a substantial rate of such investment appears to be desirable.

Economic Development Orientations

So far, this chapter has considered indigenous business, foreign investment, and public enterprise as possible sources of dynamism in Nigeria's modern economy. This section turns to the more comprehensive issue: a proposed economic development orientation for the country. Broad judgments of this kind must be tentative. Being keenly aware of the myriads of unknowns and uncertainties and of our own limitations, the development orientation we propose is open-ended in highly important respects. A partial orientation is discussed first, and then we turn to the more comprehensive development orientations into which this partial approach may fit.

A Pragmatic Approach

Indigenous, foreign, and public enterprise are each capable of mobilizing energies and contributing to development in their own ways. They each have a useful place in a Nigerian development strategy.

Even though indigenous private enterprise is unlikely to provide substantial dynamism in Nigeria's modern economy, it has an essential role. It carries out innumerable economic activities that are not performed by large (foreign) businesses and that neither governments nor any other collective or cooperative or public organizations are capable of undertaking or directing. Since these activities contribute to the well-being of society and in fact are essential, government policy should, first, generally *allow* such enterprise[56] to develop freely, unhindered by generalized governmental discouragement. Beyond that, the question arises whether government should continue its multifaceted efforts to assist and nurture indigenous business. We have seen that most business-assistance programs have had high cost-benefit ratios, and this is likely to continue. Thus, government should be predisposed against such programs unless there is a strong presumption, based on careful investigation, that a particular program will in fact yield a favorable ratio of benefits to costs. In general terms, the most promising kind of measure is one like a protective tariff or some form of subsidy, which does not entail substantial costs except to the degree that the aided enterprise actually produces the in-

[56]The discussion applies primarily to nonagricultural enterprise; the writer does not feel qualified to make proposals for agricultural policy.

tended output and does so at some stipulated minimum standard of efficiency. The magnitude of the tariff, subsidy, or other outlay should be related to the divergence between the imputed profitability of an unassisted efficient firm (i.e., probable profit or loss in the absence of government assistance and with production of stipulated minimum efficiency) and the (higher) net social utility of the firm's activities.

Foreign investment should be welcomed on a calculated discriminating basis. External enterprise has significant advantages over indigenous or public enterprise at Nigeria's stage of development. Already mentioned in the preceding section were the capability advantage of foreign corporations (based on greater managerial proficiency and greater freedom than public enterprise from the adverse effects of political manipulation) and the possibility that foreign enterprise may provide needed capital. Foreign investors also have greater ability to perceive relatively large-scale, modern investment opportunities. This arises partially from the foreign enterprise's wider international connections and more extensive knowledge of worldwide costs, supplies, demands, and other market conditions, and partially from its greater technological, scientific, and research knowledge and capabilities. With these advantages, foreign investment has a role to play in a pragmatic development orientation.

However, the counterbalancing disadvantages of foreign capital formation, already discussed, are not insubstantial. It would thus be wise to welcome potential investments only selectively. The best available information, intelligence, and expertise should be used to estimate host-country benefits and costs, keeping in mind the opportunity cost represented by the possibility of a public-enterprise alternative to foreign investment. The terms set for welcomed investments from abroad should be designed to maximize long-term host-country net benefits. This approach is generally similar to that proposed in Nigeria's *Second National Development Plan 1970-74*, except that we have placed considerable weight on the potential disadvantages of foreign investment and advantages of public enterprise.

Public corporations, as earlier discussion indicates, would carry out a substantial portion of the directly productive investment in the modern economy. These enterprises would be governed by shadow or accounting prices that reflect real costs and benefits, i.e., would be social utility-oriented rather than profit-oriented.

The partial development orientation proposed here involves also a number of other facets, relating to the use of underutilized resources, the rate of capital formation, and the level of taxation.

Nigeria needs to make better use of its potential productive capacity. The economy has been continually characterized by substantial underutilization of productive resources of all kinds. This has been most manifest in the case of labor. Open unemployment has been a significant problem at least since World War II,[57] and it has been growing ever more severe. Job applicants willingly pay 10 percent or more of a year's wages for a job, and a "con game" in the sale of nonexistent jobs was so widespread that governments publicly threatened stern action against the swindlers. Seasonal unemployment has also been widespread for decades.[58] Some farmers, who would otherwise have been seasonally idle after their harvest, have worked as migrant farm workers,[59] some few got seasonal factory jobs,[60] some got jobs in tin mines,[61] some engaged in barely remunerative trading activities,[62] many in equally unrewarding handicraft endeavors,[63] but most find no remunerative employment at all. Underemployment and minimal-productivity employment are pervasive. Large numbers loiter hopefully wherever occasional casual jobs might be secured, aspiring to earn small sums from time to time, and people spend long hours in the markets in an effort to earn or save minimal amounts.[64] Finally, the potential labor of women is even more underutilized than that of men.[65]

---

[57]In the late 1940s and early 1950s, for example, P. T. Bauer found that if employers wanted to expand their labor force at the going wage, the "only problem would be to control the mob of applicants." P. T. Bauer, *West African Trade* (Cambridge: Cambridge University Press, 1954), pp. 18-19.

[58]Discussing the 1950s, Stapleton spoke of the "months of almost complete idleness experienced by many farmers during the dry season." G. Brian Stapleton, *The Wealth of Nigeria* (London: Oxford University Press, 1958), p. 101.

[59]See, e.g., K. D. S. Baldwin, *The Niger Agricultural Project: An Experiment in African Development* (Oxford: Basil Blackwell, 1957), pp. 41-44.

[60]For example, most of the 140 workers in a Kano soap factory whose sales slacken during the rainy season. F. A. Wells and W. A. Warmington, *Studies in Industrialization: Nigeria and the Cameroons* (Ibadan and London: Oxford University Press, 1962), p. 102.

[61]Interviews with indigenous tin-mine operators.

[62]". . . it is suspected that a good deal of the produce appearing in the markets is either consumed by the seller whilst sitting in the markets or is taken back unsold to the farms." A. R. Prest and I. G. Stewart, *The National Income of Nigeria, 1950-51*, London, His Majesty's Stationery Office, 1953, Colonial Research Studies, No. 11, pp. 14-15.

[63]For example, insufficiently occupied farmers of Katsina Province turned to handicrafts of various kinds, but earned so little particularly in the face of competition from modern imports, that such activities were on the decline in the 1950s. Similarly an earlier survey of crafts in Abeokuta and Oyo Provinces found that incomes were very low, that the craftsmen were suffering from modern competition, and that even the more "modern" trades (e.g., motor mechanics, bicycle repairers, tailors) were hopelessly overcrowded. Kenneth C. Murray and A. Hunt-Cooke, *Native Minor Industries in Oyo and Abeokuta Provinces*, 1936, unpublished, cited in W. K. Hancock (1942), op. cit., pp. 293-94 and in Daryll Forde, "The Rural Economies" in Margery Perham, ed., *The Native Economies of Nigeria*, p.100. See also I. C. Jackson, *Advance in Africa: A Study of Community Development in Eastern Nigeria*, London, O.U.P., 1956, pp. 51-52, 61-69.

[64]"Nigeria . . . is characterized by under-utilization of human resources of varying forms. Under-employment and disguised unemployment are general, in rural agriculture as well as in traditional and modern small-scale crafts and trades." T. M. Yesufu, "Employment, Manpower and Economic Development in Nigeria: Some Issues of Moment," *Nigerian Journal of Economic and Social Studies*, March 1974, p. 51.

[65]For example, a Kano perfume firm employing three hundred women at peak periods always found that "vacancies could be filled several times over from those who applied." Wells and Warmington, p. 103. See also Bauer, p. 26.

There are also vast areas of idle arable land. The Food and Agricultural Organization estimated that less than 10 percent of Nigeria's land area is cultivated. The leading Nigerian agricultural economist estimated that more than half of the country's *cultivable* land is completely idle (*not* counting as idle the large areas in bush fallow, i.e., land that is part of the agricultural system but that is left temporarily unused to allow it to regain its fertility).[66]

Skilled, supervisory, and managerial labor, entrepreneurship, and capital have also been less than fully utilized. The already organized and ready-to-produce bundles of productive factors that constitute going concerns have been underutilized because most firms in Nigeria have produced substantially below capacity. The writer, in common with most other observers and with government officials and surveys, found this commonly the case in all kinds of firms—handicraft, small-scale industrial units, and relatively large and modern companies. Moreover, overtime or double- or triple-shift production would have been eagerly undertaken in most cases if the market warranted it.

Various methods for achieving the potential of underutilized resources have been employed or proposed, for example, community development, mobilization through a more or less coercive state apparatus, and somewhat vague proposals that a thoroughgoing socialist country can generate the necessary spirit and set up the necessary community organizations and procedures. Thoroughgoing socialist mobilization is, at this time, only an academic issue for Nigeria, so it will not be discussed in this context. (The final section of this chapter deals with thoroughgoing socialism.) As a means of economic mobilization, community development efforts have generally proven to have only short-lived efficaciousness. State coercion does not seem promising for Nigeria. Each method may have some effectiveness in some circumstances, but most promising in the writer's view would be some way of evoking voluntary effort in response to payment.

This requires a brief examination of the role of the market in the phenomenon of underutilization. A major cause of underutilization is the failure of the pricing system to transmit the socially appropriate impulses. For the reasons discussed in the chapter on divergences, money costs of employing underutilized resources frequently exceed real costs, while the consequent money receipts would often fall short of the real benefits that would be generated.[67] Thus, even though the real benefits of producing

---

[66]H. A. Oluwasanmi, *Agriculture and Nigerian Economic Development* (London: Oxford University Press, 1966), pp. 50, 193.

[67]This would appear to be the basis of Samir Amin's view that "the world-wide structures of relative prices" inappropriately "imposed upon the periphery" prevent the less developed economies from realizing possible production. Samir Amin, "Development and Structural Change: African Experience," in Barbara Ward, Lenore d'Anjoe, J. D. Runnalls (eds.), *The Widening Gap: Development in the 1970's* (New York: Columbia University Press, 1971), p. 324.

with underemployed resources might exceed the real costs, money receipts might fall short of money costs, so that such production would be rejected by a profit-seeking enterprise.[68]

One way of activating the immobilized resources would be through what the writer has called "directed demand." The government could provide a market for the socially beneficial but pecuniarily unprofitable potential output at profitable prices and then resell the goods at money-losing, market-clearing prices or distribute them in some other manner.[69] The underutilized resources would thereby be induced to produce additional socially useful output in response to monetary incentives. Such an approach would impose a financial burden on government, but the country would realize a *real* economic gain.[70] The financial burden could not only be easily borne by Nigeria's oil-rich government, but the approach would also provide an excellent means of distributing some of the oil revenues more widely and equitably than through the 1975 Udoji wage increases to the labor aristocracy.

Another high-priority development strategy would be a rate of capital formation as high as feasible. The Third Plan is disserviceable not because of its high-investment approach, but because of the euphoric and unrealistic application of such an approach. Our high-investment proposal arises from the assessment in Chapter 7 that modern-economy capital formation in countries like Nigeria tends to have substantial positive divergences, so that there exist a great many socially beneficial, though possibly pecuniarily unprofitable, investment opportunities. Many of the positive divergences or external social benefits of investments—such as the enhanced availability of labor acclimatized to modern production, of potential effective supervisors and middle-level managers, of the services of an increasingly capable network of supportive and specialized activities—are in a sense incipient or potential, and are actually realized only when they are embodied in projects undertaken by other investments. A high rate of investment in socially profitable projects will not require prolonged deprivation or austerity; to the contrary, if the investments are reasonably successful, they soon allow an increased level of both consumption and investment.

The proposals to increase the utilization of underutilized resources and to raise the rate of capital formation to the maximum feasible level, when

[68]In the public sector there would be a comparable situation if government rejected on budgetary grounds opportunities to provide public goods and services by means of underutilized resources that were more expensive in money terms though cheaper in real terms than the conventional methods.

[69]A comparable approach in the public sector would be for government to replace conventional methods by lower real-cost methods, employing underutilized resources (where such methods exist) even if higher money costs are involved.

[70]See the author's article, "Underutilized Resources, 'Directed Demand,' and Deficit Financing (Illustrated by Reference to Nigeria)," *Quarterly Journal of Economics* LXXIII:4 (November 1959), for a further discussion of this proposal, including criteria for allocation of government funds.

added to all the other growing demands upon government, call for a sizeable expansion of government expenditures. We deal with this issue first in rather general terms, abstracting from Nigeria's oil windfall. If our analyses of the utility of increasing resource utilization and of increasing the investment rate are correct, and given the general need for increasing government expenditures in developing economies, the limiting factor in defining the desirable level of government expenditures, assuming an effective government dedicated to development, would not be the social utility of such expenditures but the ability to raise revenues. The resistance to direct taxes, the lack of a taxpaying tradition, the ability of small indigenous companies to evade taxes by crude methods such as the failure to keep records, the probable ability of large foreign-owned companies to evade taxes by more sophisticated means, and other administrative and political difficulties all make it difficult to raise revenue for large government outlays. This brings the financing issue squarely before us.

The writer suggests a few guides. First, and very simply, taxation should be at the maximum feasible rate. Second, noninflationary funds can be secured through money creation. A growing economy needs an expanding money supply. Whatever institution creates that money in the first instance has control over newly created purchasing power (which is noninflationary if no more is created than the growing economy needs). If the government reserves for itself the right to create that money rather than delegating that power to the banking system, the government can spend it. Third, a moderate inflation is economically innocuous and perhaps even salutary, so some degree of inflationary deficit-financing is advisable.[71] In Nigeria, the pertinence of these precepts is lessened and may be obviated altogether by the magnitude of the oil revenues. For some years, at any rate, public revenues will exceed public capability of spending the money with any reasonable degree of efficacy.

We have delineated a partial development orientation in which the difficult job of development is pursued by making full use of the development strengths and potentials of indigenous private enterprise, foreign private enterprise, and public enterprise without doctrinaire commitment to or exclusion of possibilities. In this orientation, development policy takes full account of the divergences between the net social utility and the profitability of economic activity, i.e., the effects of investment and production that pecuniary profitability or market prices fail to reflect.

This orientation, which we will call "pragmatic developmentism," has been summarized in the preceding paragraph in its most general form. However, we have, in this section, specified the orientation more fully and concretely on the basis of the overall findings and judgments of this study. Given the predominance of benefits over dysbenefits among the profitability-social utility divergences, pragmatic developmentism stres-

---

[71]See, e.g., Schatz, "Underutilized Resources," pp. 642-644.

ses a high rate of capital formation and, concomitantly, the high rate of taxation ordinarily necessary to finance the investment. Within the context of a general expansion of investment, pragmatic developmentism suggests an enlargement of the public-enterprise role relative to that of foreign private enterprise in view of the dysbenefits of foreign investment and the better adaptability of public enterprise to the criterion of net social utility. Assistance for indigenous business is also part of such an orientation. However, given our findings on the limited effectiveness and high cost of business-assistance programs, we would drop the predisposition (or doctrinaire commitment) in favor of any and all plausible business-assistance programs, redirect resources toward those programs which incur substantial costs only to the degree that the aided enterprise actually produces the intended output at some stipulated minimum standard of efficiency, and probably reduce the total resources devoted to business assistance.

Pragmatic Capitalism and Pragmatic Socialism

Pragmatic developmentism could be part of or preliminary to any of the three more comprehensive development orientations to be discussed in this section and the next: pragmatic capitalism, pragmatic socialism, and thoroughgoing socialism.

Pragmatic capitalism and pragmatic socialism have important characteristics in common. The set of policies that comprise pragmatic developmentism constitutes a substantial part of either of these two broader orientations. These orientations also share a pragmatic approach to development, i.e., ideological commitment is secondary to judgments based on evidence and the lessons of experience. This does not mean that policy is determined in some crude, simple-minded way by the most recent failures or successes; it is recognized that ventures and policies that have worked poorly might be modified and made successful. Still, policy decisions are guided by facts, experience, and reason rather than by sheer commitment to an ideology.

Nevertheless, policy decisions are unavoidably influenced by ideology, more specifically by the prevailing policy predisposition and the desired politico-economic destination. Herein lies the difference between pragmatic capitalism and pragmatic socialism.

The important issues, particularly in less-developed countries, are usually surrounded by uncertainty. Even if the relevant theory is clear and universally accepted, a confident policy decision cannot be reached because the real-world situation is immersed in unknowns. There are uncertainties regarding the basic facts of the situation, uncertainties regarding the ability of the government machinery to implement a given measure, regarding the reactions of the population, the secondary repercussions of the policy, etc. In the prevailing uncertainty, decisions are inevitably influenced by the leadership's policy predispositions, based on a mélange of attitudes, emotions, and prior convictions. Decisions are also colored by the related matter of the desired politico-economic destination of those with power, i.e., the kind of political economy they want to establish.

One would expect differences on these matters between the pragmatic socialist and the pragmatic capitalist. There would be systematically different tendencies on issues which are historically, emotionally, and politically related to socialist-capitalist doctrinal battles, issues like income equalization vs. provision of material incentives, humanitarian concerns in production vs. maximization of efficiency and output, geographical dispersion of development vs. emphasis on poles of growth or growth centers, cooperative action vs. individualism and individual initiative, etc. There would also be differences on the efficacy of collective action or public ownership vs. private enterprise as means of promoting the nation's development. On a wide range of issues, even the most pragmatic leader has to make decisions that are not much more than expressions of faith in one's intuition and one's vision of a better society.

Thoroughgoing Socialism

Another development orientation is thoroughgoing socialism. There is no clear consensus regarding this approach, but its core is a sweeping reorganization of society: "the restructuring of the entire set of political-economic institutions shaped in the colonial past . . ."[72]

The proposed reorganization appears to have five major characteristics: (1) a bootstraps approach to production and its expansion; (2) the expansion of production is to be achieved through comprehensive involvement of the ordinary people; this involvement has two facets: a mobilization of the people's support, spirit, enthusiasm, and maximum effort, and popular participation in policy determination and planning at the local levels; (3) an inward-looking orientation; (4) government predominance in the economy; (5) a set of broad social goals. Let us consider each of these in turn.

First, there is to be a bootstraps reorientation of production. Production is not to be governed by pecuniary profitability or by the ordinary market signals, for these are considered thoroughly misleading. Instead it is to be shaped by efforts to utilize fully all available resources and by imaginative and innovative reconsideration of the nation's potentialities. On a national scale, labor and other local resources are to be utilized in a manner or spirit similar to that expressed in the disguised unemployment proposals of Nurkse and others,[73] or expressed in community development projects, the Chinese mobilizations, or the author's directed-

---

[72]Ann Seidman, "Alternative Development Strategies in Zambia," p. 1 (mimeographed).
[73]Ragnar Nurske, *Problems of Capital Formation in Underdeveloped Countries* (New York: Oxford University Press, 1967), ch. 2.

demand proposals.[74] The technology would generally have to be far simpler and cruder than prevailing advanced-economy techniques, but it would not remain stagnant. A substantial flow of innovations is expected to emerge from the experience, creativity, and initiative of the working population stimulated by official receptiveness and aided by expert advice provided by government.

The kinds of industries and of goods to be produced are indicated only in general terms. A more integrated national economy should be created, which can develop more broadly than an export-oriented economy. This requires industries such that "a wide range of products are produced and sold nationally from dominantly national inputs" and such that "most sectors of the economy sell a significant portion of their output to other national sectors for further processing, in other words, in which all sectors are integrated into an interlocking national production and consumption pattern."[75] Careful attention should be given to the possibility of developing linkages with the major export-producing activities. Manufacture should be geographically dispersed, and there should be considerable emphasis on rural industries. Enterprises should be labor-intensive, as befits the factor endowments of a less-developed economy, and should make productive use of the kinds of labor available. Agriculture would be reoriented toward domestic foodcrops and materials for domestic industry, while the latter would produce necessary farm implements and requisites for agriculture. A harmful overemphasis on export production, caused by the failure of the relative prices of domestic and export agricultural produce to reflect real values, would be corrected, although export production is not to be neglected.[76]

Second, a vital aspect of thoroughgoing socialism is the full participation of the ordinary people, rural and urban, in carrying out the bootstraps restructuring of production. For one thing, there must be a mobilization of the knowledge, imagination, enthusiasm, and effort of the population, all underutilized in the ordinary, primarily capitalist, production and development efforts of most underdeveloped economies. The ability to make use of these underutilized human attributes is the crucial advantage of the bootstraps reorientation of production.

In addition, the people must be genuinely involved in the formulation of plans and projects. They must have real input in the conception and choice of specific local projects and policies. This entails decentralization, as in Tanzania after 1972, with policy modifications and proposals regarding local implementation of national policies coming up from below. Many

[74]Described briefly earlier in this chapter.
[75]Green, p. 5. Green continues: "A fragmented economy is limited to primary production and total external trade dependence in a way that an integrated industrial economy is not, even if their overall foreign trade/domestic product ratios are similar. The degree of national linkage among productive sectors is a fairly good index of the true level of development."
[76]Amin, p. 324.

projects—like "cattle dips, three-mile roads, loading platforms for rural markets, small wayside storage bins, information links between villages where exchange is possible but not taking place, and cooperative bicycle shops"[77]—will grow out of popular needs, experience and initiative. Such participation by the people, whose "socialist consciousness" will have been raised, will also serve "as a force checking possible abuses of their position by the leaders."[78]

Third, the restructuring of the economy also requires an inward-looking reorientation. A reduction of ties with and dependence upon the capitalist world economy is essential; "it is integration into world markets that is the real obstacle to development."[79] Through such integration, the economy is penetrated by an inappropriate and harmful structure of relative prices which discourages otherwise feasible production that would make use of underutilized resources.[80] Competition with advanced-economy industries has the same effect. More generally, integration into the international capitalist economy is seen as causing (although the analysis is rather sketchy) the development and entrenchment of underdevelopment, i.e., the creation and strengthening of an economic structure, a technology, and an economic orientation which tend to perpetuate economic backwardness.

The turn inward does not entail an abrupt termination of foreign trade, a sudden expropriation of existing foreign investments, or even a complete cessation of all new foreign investments. The country is not faced simply with the unqualified alternatives that it either "must submit totally to imperialism or reject it in toto even in a transitional period . . . the Third World and the imperialist countries are reciprocally enmeshed. . . ."[81] Exports of the traditional primary products are to be continued and even increased. Some balance, not clearly spelled out, is to be achieved between maximizing foreign-exchange receipts from such sources, on the one hand, and vigorously shifting emphasis to development in other directions on the other hand. (Among the recommended shifts in emphasis are a redirection of trade from capitalist towards socialist countries and a reduction of dependence upon capitalist-country foreign aid.) Despite an ultimate aim of nationalizing all foreign investment, foreign investors in the meantime are to be welcomed on a selective calculating basis.

[77]Idrian Resnick, "Socialist Alternative for African Development: Decentralization in Tanzania," Paper presented to African Studies Association, Philadelphia, 1972, p. 17 (mimeographed).

[78]Giovanni Arrighi and John S. Saul, "Socialism and Economic Development in Tropical Africa," *Journal of Modern African Studies* 6:2 (July 1968): 163, 164, 166.

[79]Amin, p. 313.

[80]Amin, p. 324.

[81]Pierre Jalée, *The Pillage of the Third World* (New York: Monthly Review Press, 1968), p. 112. "Even the most vocal of socialists assume the necessity of dealing with 'the enemy' . . ." Arrighi and Saul, p. 158.

The fourth characteristic of thoroughgoing socialism is government predominance in the economy. The restructuring of the economy is to take place primarily "through a political-bureaucratic mechanism."[82] Thus, the application of conventional trade and exchange controls to private or to profit-maximizing public trading firms is not considered adequate to bring about the desired inward-looking reorientation. ". . . it is an illusion that control without substantial ownership is an effective way for a small and weak State to influence positively a broad range of decisions made by units of foreign-controlled firms."[83] Publicly controlled trading corporations need to exercise direct control, ordering imports and conducting the export trade in accord with national plans. In general, government should control the "commanding heights" of the economy, including all large productive enterprises and including also the nation's financial institutions to ensure that "all possible investible surpluses" are invested according to the plan.[84] Government also has to be intimately involved at the regional and local levels, as in Tanzania's 1972 policy of decentralization which shifted important government functions and high-level government personnel to the hinterlands.

The ultimate aim is complete public ownership, although petty capitalist enterprise might continue for a long time.

Finally, there is to be a socialist reorientation of the entire society. Thoroughgoing socialism is to entail not only public ownership of the means of production, but also the development of a more humanist, egalitarian, democratic community. Income differentials favoring the educated elite, the labor aristocracy employed by modern enterprises or by government, and the urban population are to be reduced. The academically oriented, elitist focus of the educational system is to be changed. The style of government is to be one of participatory democracy, with the people actually possessing real decision-making power. The vision is one of a good society.

The preceding discussion of the major features of thoroughgoing socialism has been characterized by substantial generality and even vagueness. This goes beyond the generality required by the highly variegated conditions found in the less-developed economies. An indefinite quality prevails even in thoroughgoing-socialist discussions of specific countries.[85] While largely sharing the ideals of the thoroughgoing

[82]Idrian N. Resnick, "Expunging Imperialism: An African Recipe," p. 6 (mimeographed).

[83]Green, p. 21.

[84]Seidman, pp. 34-35. See also Paul A. Baran, *The Political Economy of Growth* (New York: Monthly Review Press, 1957), which placed the issue of the utilization of the economic or investible surplus in the center of most subsequent Marxist analysis.

[85]See, e.g., Seidman's discussion of what we have called thoroughgoing socialism in Zambia. ". . . research is needed relating to the manifold complex aspects of particular features of the proposed strategy. Information is needed as to the potential resource base for

socialists, a pragmatic socialist like the author regards this indefinite quality with some apprehension. This leads us to a consideration of the relations between thoroughgoing socialism, pragmatic socialism, and pragmatic capitalism.

Common Ground in the Three Orientations

The discussion of thoroughgoing socialism makes it clear that such a
society is not expected to emerge in one sudden stroke as a result of a
sharp revolutionary change. There is to be a transitional period of indefinite duration during which the existing capitalist production and distribution processes and institutions are to be gradually modified and possibly
phased out.

The characteristics of this transitional phase, we see upon review, are
consistent with the partial orientation: pragmatic developmentism. Indigenous capitalists are to be relied upon for important economic activities.
For the critical task of raising agricultural productivity, agrarian capitalism is seen as essential.[86] In the nonagricultural sectors, indigenous
capitalists are to carry out a wide range of small-scale activities that are
likely to be beyond the capacity of either the overburdened state apparatus or the emergent local cooperative and collective units, at least for
a considerable period. A rational and diligent pursuit of foreign-exchange
earnings through traditional primary-product exports is to be continued.
Existing foreign investments are, if taken over, likely to be nationalized
with compensation rather than expropriated. Even new foreign investment is not to be ruled out.

Thus pragmatic developmentism is an essential aspect not only of
pragmatic capitalism and pragmatic socialism but also of thoroughgoing
socialism. Since all three orientations initially share a common ground,
although each would require successively greater socioeconomic and
political change, a grand battle does not have to be fought out in advance.
The supporters of each can move into pragmatic developmentism in alliance. Decisions affecting the subsequent course of the country can then
be made piecemeal as the issues arise. As evidence and experience ac-

---

rural pole-of-growth industries and their potential linkages; the kinds of industries to be
built; and alternative available technologies which might maximize employment and use of
local inputs. Research is required to determine what kinds of institutional changes are
essential to ensure that government control of the 'commanding heights' is effectively directed to implementing long term plans for resource allocation, as well as those needed to
encourage people to take initiative in building local industries and increasing agricultural
output of raw materials and foodstuffs for the growing industrial sector. . . . The people
themselves need to be involved in formulating all aspects of the long term plan, utilizing their
own local knowledge as well as appropriate inputs of technical information by experts":
Seidman, p. 38.

[86]At least by some. See, e.g., Amin, pp. 320-325. Arrighi and Saul (p. 152) are less certain,
believing that decisions on this issue "will involve some calculations" about alternatives.

cumulate, the operative room is narrowed for the predispositions and the judgments based more on intuition than on solid information which separate the pragmatic capitalist, the pragmatic socialist, and the thoroughgoing socialist. The differences between the three will not completely disappear—for example, although the pragmatic and the thoroughgoing socialist might share an ultimate vision, the former would be likely to give greater weight than the latter to definite short-term benefits as against probable or possible, less tangible, long-term benefits—but it may be of inestimable benefit to the country to postpone decisions until life brings them to the top of the agenda while information and experience accrue.

INDEX

Lightning Source UK Ltd.
Milton Keynes UK
UKHW010907071120
372987UK00003B/111